Government Procedures and Operations

snova
New York

Government Procedures and Operations

Maintaining an Independent and Ethical Supreme Court
Daniel L. Snyder (Editor)
2023. ISBN: 979-8-88697-885-8 (Hardcover)
2023. ISBN: 979-8-89113-054-8 (eBook)

Gun Control: Background Checks and Assault Weapons
Linda M. Sanders (Editor)
2023. ISBN: 979-8-88697-977-0 (Hardcover)
2023. ISBN: 979-8-89113-053-1 (eBook)

Infrastructure Cybersecurity: Protections, Threats, and Federal Programs
Michael V. Walls (Editor)
2023. ISBN: 979-8-89113-039-5 (Softcover)
2023. ISBN: 979-8-89113-052-4 (eBook)

COVID-19 in Nursing Homes: Impact, Transmission and Prevention
Fred C. Wallace (Editor)
2023. ISBN: 979-8-88697-673-1 (Hardcover)
2023. ISBN: 979-8-88697-683-0 (eBook)

The Significance of the COVID Pandemic in Nursing Homes
John S. Gill (Editor)
2023. ISBN: 979-8-88697-660-1 (Hardcover)
2023. ISBN: 979-8-88697-682-3 (eBook)

More information about this series can be found at
https://novapublishers.com/product-category/series/government-procedures-and-operations/

Sade W. Sato
Editor

The Legal Issues Surrounding Marijuana

snova
New York

NOTICE TO THE READER

Library of Congress Cataloging-in-Publication Data

ISBN: 979-8-89113-427-0

Published by Nova Science Publishers, Inc. † New York

Contents

Preface

The legal status of marijuana has been a topic of recurring interest in recent years. Marijuana was initially placed and today remains as a Schedule I controlled substance under the Controlled Substances Act (CSA). As a result, a person who grows, possesses, uses, sells, transports, or distributes marijuana, even if it is done in a way that is consistent with State law or authorized by a State license, is nonetheless in violation of the CSA and remains subject to Federal prosecution. This book outlines the laws that apply to controlled substances like marijuana, then analyzes several approaches that can be taken to change those laws.

Chapter 1 - Marijuana is a psychoactive drug that generally consists of leaves and flowers of the *Cannabis sativa* plant. Its history dates back thousands of years, but in the United States it became popular as a recreational drug in the early 20th century. Not long after its rise in popularity, the federal government began to exercise control over marijuana and other substances through its taxing authority, and it enacted criminal penalties for violations of drug laws. In 1970, the federal government enacted the Controlled Substances Act (CSA), which imposed a unified legal framework at the federal level to regulate certain drugs—whether medical or recreational, and legally or illicitly distributed. The CSA criminalized the manufacture, distribution, dispensation, and possession of marijuana, which included all of varieties of cannabis at the time (in 2018, the farm bill [P.L. 115-334] amended the CSA to exclude hemp—plant material that contains no more than 0.3% delta-9-tetrahydrocannabinol [delta-9-THC] on a dry weight basis).

Under the CSA, marijuana and its derivatives are classified as Schedule I controlled substances, which means the cultivation (or manufacture), possession, and distribution of marijuana are illegal except for the purposes of sanctioned research. While the CSA definition of marijuana changed in 2018, which resulted in the removal of hemp from the definition of marijuana, the status of marijuana as a Schedule I substance has remained unchanged for over 50 years. Many states, however, have established a range of laws and policies allowing for the medical and recreational use of marijuana over the last several decades. Most of these states have deviated from an across-the-board prohibition of marijuana, and it is now more the rule than the exception that states have laws and policies allowing for some cultivation, sale, distribution, and possession of marijuana or low-THC cannabis—many of which are contrary to the CSA. As of April 1, 2022, 37 states, as well as Puerto Rico, Guam, the U.S. Virgin Islands, and the District of Columbia, allow for the comprehensive medical use of marijuana, while 11 additional states allow for the medical use of low-THC cannabis. Also, 18 states, the District of Columbia, Guam, and the Northern Mariana Islands allow for recreational use of marijuana. These developments have spurred a number of questions regarding potential implications of the federal and state marijuana policy gap for federal law enforcement activities, for individuals who comply with state marijuana law but violate federal marijuana law, and for the nation's drug policies as a whole.

Under the principles of federalism, the federal government may preempt state marijuana laws and enforce the CSA. Thus far, the federal response to state actions to legalize marijuana has largely been to allow states to implement their own laws on the drug. The gap between federal marijuana law and federal enforcement policy and the issues it creates continue each year, although Congress has partly addressed this gap by restricting the Department of Justice's (DOJ's) ability to expend funds to enforce the CSA in states that allow medical marijuana. DOJ has nonetheless reaffirmed that marijuana growth, trafficking, and possession remain crimes under federal law irrespective of states' marijuana laws. To date, federal law enforcement has generally focused its efforts on criminal networks involved in the illicit marijuana trade.

Many observers voice apprehension over possible negative outcomes of marijuana legalization, including, but not limited to, (1) potential increases in marijuana use, particularly among youth; (2) potential increases in traffic accidents involving marijuana-impaired drivers; (3) marijuana trafficking from states that have legalized it into neighboring states that have not; and (4) U.S. compliance with international treaties. Proponents of legalization have pointed to possible positive outcomes that could result from marijuana legalization, including a new source of tax revenue for states and a decrease in marijuana related arrests that would free up resources for other law enforcement needs. Many states have yet to completely assess the full range of outcomes of their medical or recreational marijuana programs, particularly those that have only recently legalized the drug.

The marijuana policy gap creates unique consequences for individuals who act in compliance with state law but violate federal law. As organizations and individuals have pressed forward with the manufacturing, sale, and use of marijuana, consequences of the gap have arisen—two of the more publicized consequences for individuals are termination of employment due to marijuana use in states that have legalized medical or recreational marijuana, and a range of implications for researchers and postsecondary students on college campuses. Other consequences include, but are not limited to, an inability to obtain or dismissal from certain types of employment, the inability to purchase and possess a firearm, inadmissibility for federal housing, and ineligibility for certain visas.

The marijuana policy gap between the federal government and states has widened almost every year for over 25 years as more states legalize medical and/or recreational marijuana. It has only been a few years since states began to legalize recreational marijuana, but over 25 years since they began to legalize medical marijuana—no state has reversed its legalization, medical or recreational, since California first legalized medical marijuana in 1996. In addressing state-level legalization efforts and considering marijuana's current placement on Schedule I of the CSA, Congress could take one of several routes. It could elect to take no action, thereby maintaining the federal government's current marijuana policy and allowing the policy gap to expand if additional states legalize medical or recreational marijuana. Alternatively, it may decide that the CSA must be strictly enforced and not allow states to implement marijuana laws that conflict with the CSA. Or, it may take smaller steps to address the policy gap, such as continuing to include appropriations provisions that restrict DOJ's ability to expend funds to enforce federal law.

Congress could also choose to reevaluate marijuana's classification as a Schedule I controlled substance. If Congress were to alter the federal status of marijuana by lowering its schedule or even creating a new schedule, it may devote more resources to the Food and Drug Administration (FDA) to manage and assess the many medical marijuana products available across the country. If Congress alters marijuana's schedule, there are a number of issues that policymakers might address. These include, but are not limited to, issues surrounding availability of financial services for marijuana businesses, federal tax treatment, and the role of federal law enforcement in marijuana investigations. If Congress chooses to remove marijuana as a controlled substance under the CSA and remove criminal provisions, this would at least partly eliminate the policy gap with states that have authorized medical and recreational marijuana programs.

Whether Congress decides to address the gap with the states or not, federal control of cannabis has evolved from the strict laws and enforcement policies of the 20th century to allowing most states to implement laws authorizing the production and distribution of marijuana. Among other things, Congress may halt and reverse this evolution, continue to relinquish federal criminal control, or alter or eliminate federal criminal control of cannabis entirely.

Chapter 2 - This is an edited, reformatted and augmented version of Hearing before the Subcommittee on Crime, Terrorism, and Homeland Security, of the House of Representatives, Committee on the Judiciary, One Hundred Sixteenth Congress, First Session, Serial No. 116–33, dated July 10, 2019.

Chapter 3 - Federal law generally prohibits the production, distribution, and possession of marijuana for both medical and recreational purposes. Nonetheless, in recent years, many states have repealed state law criminal prohibitions on some marijuana-related activities, and medical and recreational cannabis businesses now operate openly in some parts of the United States.

In response to the growing disparity between state and federal law, Congress has enacted appropriations legislation prohibiting the Department of Justice (DOJ) from expending appropriated funds to prevent states from implementing their own medical marijuana laws. Federal courts have interpreted the appropriations rider to prohibit DOJ from bringing criminal drug prosecutions against certain private individuals and entities involved in the state-legal medical marijuana industry, but they have differed as to the scope of conduct the rider shields from prosecution.

This chapter first outlines the legal status of marijuana under federal and state law. It then discusses the medical marijuana appropriations rider and analyzes how federal courts have interpreted the provision. The chapter closes with key considerations for Congress related to the appropriations rider and the disparity between federal and state marijuana policy more generally.

Chapter 4 - The legal status of marijuana has been a topic of recurring interest in recent years, as states, federal legislators, and federal executive agencies consider how to regulate cannabis and its derivatives. What role can the President play in determining the legal status of a controlled substance such as marijuana?

That question came to the forefront during the 2020 Democratic presidential primary, with multiple candidates supporting legalization of marijuana and several pledging to legalize the substance nationwide if elected, either indirectly through administrative proceedings or directly by executive order. More recently, some commentators have called on President Biden to end criminal penalties for marijuana possession and use or grant clemency to federal marijuana offenders. Although the President cannot directly remove marijuana from control under federal controlled substances law, he might order executive agencies to consider either altering the scheduling of marijuana or changing their enforcement approach.

This chapter outlines the laws that apply to controlled substances like marijuana, then analyzes several approaches a president might take to change controlled substances law as written or as enforced. The chapter closes with a discussion of key considerations for Congress related to presidential power over controlled substances regulation.

Chapter 1

The Evolution of Marijuana as a Controlled Substance and the Federal-State Policy Gap*

Lisa N. Sacco

Abstract

Marijuana is a psychoactive drug that generally consists of leaves and flowers of the cannabis sativa plant. Its history dates back thousands of years, but in the United States it became popular as a recreational drug in the early 20th century. Not long after its rise in popularity, the federal government began to exercise control over marijuana and other substances through its taxing authority, and it enacted criminal penalties for violations of drug laws. In 1970, the federal government enacted the Controlled Substances Act (CSA), which imposed a unified legal framework at the federal level to regulate certain drugs—whether medical or recreational, and legally or illicitly distributed. The CSA criminalized the manufacture, distribution, dispensation, and possession of marijuana, which included all of varieties of cannabis at the time (in 2018, the farm bill [P.L. 115-334] amended the CSA to exclude hemp—plant material that contains no more than 0.3% delta-9-tetrahydrocannabinol [delta-9-THC] on a dry weight basis).

Under the CSA, marijuana and its derivatives are classified as Schedule I controlled substances, which means the cultivation (or manufacture), possession, and distribution of marijuana are illegal except for the purposes of sanctioned research. While the CSA definition of marijuana changed in 2018, which resulted in the removal of hemp from the definition of marijuana, the status of marijuana as a Schedule I

---

* This is an edited, reformatted and augmented version of Congressional Research Service, Publication No. R44782, dated April 7, 2022.

In: The Legal Issues Surrounding Marijuana
Editor: Sade W. Sato
ISBN: 979-8-89113-427-0

substance has remained unchanged for over 50 years. Many states, however, have established a range of laws and policies allowing for the medical and recreational use of marijuana over the last several decades. Most of these states have deviated from an across-the-board prohibition of marijuana, and it is now more the rule than the exception that states have laws and policies allowing for some cultivation, sale, distribution, and possession of marijuana or low-THC cannabis—many of which are contrary to the CSA. As of April 1, 2022, 37 states, as well as Puerto Rico, Guam, the U.S. Virgin Islands, and the District of Columbia, allow for the comprehensive medical use of marijuana, while 11 additional states allow for the medical use of low-THC cannabis. Also, 18 states, the District of Columbia, Guam, and the Northern Mariana Islands allow for recreational use of marijuana. These developments have spurred a number of questions regarding potential implications of the federal and state marijuana policy gap for federal law enforcement activities, for individuals who comply with state marijuana law but violate federal marijuana law, and for the nation's drug policies as a whole.

Under the principles of federalism, the federal government may preempt state marijuana laws and enforce the CSA. Thus far, the federal response to state actions to legalize marijuana has largely been to allow states to implement their own laws on the drug. The gap between federal marijuana law and federal enforcement policy and the issues it creates continue each year, although Congress has partly addressed this gap by restricting the Department of Justice's (DOJ's) ability to expend funds to enforce the CSA in states that allow medical marijuana. DOJ has nonetheless reaffirmed that marijuana growth, trafficking, and possession remain crimes under federal law irrespective of states' marijuana laws. To date, federal law enforcement has generally focused its efforts on criminal networks involved in the illicit marijuana trade.

Many observers voice apprehension over possible negative outcomes of marijuana legalization, including, but not limited to, (1) potential increases in marijuana use, particularly among youth; (2) potential increases in traffic accidents involving marijuana-impaired drivers; (3) marijuana trafficking from states that have legalized it into neighboring states that have not; and (4) U.S. compliance with international treaties. Proponents of legalization have pointed to possible positive outcomes that could result from marijuana legalization, including a new source of tax revenue for states and a decrease in marijuanarelated arrests that would free up resources for other law enforcement needs. Many states have yet to completely assess the full range of outcomes of their medical or recreational marijuana programs, particularly those that have only recently legalized the drug.

The marijuana policy gap creates unique consequences for individuals who act in compliance with state law but violate federal law. As organizations and individuals have pressed forward with the manufacturing, sale, and use of marijuana, consequences of the gap have arisen—two of the more publicized consequences for individuals are termination of employment due to marijuana use in states that have legalized medical or recreational marijuana, and a range of implications for researchers and postsecondary students on college campuses. Other consequences include, but are not limited to, an inability to obtain or dismissal from certain types of employment, the inability to purchase and possess a firearm, inadmissibility for federal housing, and ineligibility for certain visas.

The marijuana policy gap between the federal government and states has widened almost every year for over 25 years as more states legalize medical and/or recreational marijuana. It has only been a few years since states began to legalize recreational marijuana, but over 25 years since they began to legalize medical marijuana—no state has reversed its legalization, medical or recreational, since California first legalized medical marijuana in 1996. In addressing state-level legalization efforts and considering marijuana's current placement on Schedule I of the CSA, Congress could take one of several routes. It could elect to take no action, thereby maintaining the federal government's current marijuana policy and allowing the policy gap to expand if additional states legalize medical or recreational marijuana. Alternatively, it may decide that the CSA must be strictly enforced and not allow states to implement marijuana laws that conflict with the CSA. Or, it may take smaller steps to address the policy gap, such as continuing to include appropriations provisions that restrict DOJ's ability to expend funds to enforce federal law.

Congress could also choose to reevaluate marijuana's classification as a Schedule I controlled substance. If Congress were to alter the federal status of marijuana by lowering its schedule or even creating a new schedule, it may devote more resources to the Food and Drug Administration (FDA) to manage and assess the many medical marijuana products available across the country. If Congress alters marijuana's schedule, there are a number of issues that policymakers might address. These include, but are not limited to, issues surrounding availability of financial services for marijuana businesses, federal tax treatment, and the role of federal law enforcement in marijuana investigations. If Congress chooses to remove marijuana as a controlled substance under the CSA and remove criminal provisions, this would at least partly eliminate the policy gap with states that have authorized medical and recreational marijuana programs.

Whether Congress decides to address the gap with the states or not, federal control of cannabis has evolved from the strict laws and enforcement policies of the 20th century to allowing most states to implement laws authorizing the production and distribution of marijuana. Among other things, Congress may halt and reverse this evolution, continue to relinquish federal criminal control, or alter or eliminate federal criminal control of cannabis entirely.

Introduction

Marijuana is a psychoactive drug that generally consists of leaves and flowers of the cannabis sativa plant. Its history dates back thousands of years, but in the United States it became popular as a recreational drug in the early 20th century.[1] The delta-9-tetrahydrocannabinol (THC) content, which is the primary (but not the only) psychoactive chemical compound (cannabinoid) in cannabis,[2] is dependent on both the variety of the cannabis plant and the part used (see Appendix A for definitions of key terms used through this report).

Marijuana is the most commonly used illicit drug in the United States.[3] The percentage of the population 12 and older that reported using marijuana in the past month (i.e., current users) has generally increased over the last decade—from 6.9% in 2010 to 11.8% in 2020.[4] For youth (aged 12-17), the rate of past-month marijuana use over the same time period had some small year-to-year percentage changes, but the rate has remained relatively stable, especially when compared to adult use rates—the rate of past-month

---

[1] David F. Musto, *The American Disease: Origins of Narcotic Control*, 3rd ed. (New York: Oxford University Press, 1999), p. 219.

[2] Other psychoactive compounds, such as delta-8-THC, are also found in cannabis.

[3] In 2020, an estimated 32.8 million individuals in the United States aged 12 or older (11.8% of this population) were current users of marijuana. The Substance Abuse and Mental Health Services Administration (SAMHSA) defines *current use* as having used at least once in the past month. See Department of Health and Human Services (HHS), SAMHSA, *Results from the 2020 National Survey on Drug Use and Health: Detailed Tables*, October 2021, Tables 1.1A and 1.1B, https://www.samhsa.gov/data/report/2020-nsduh-detailed-tables (hereinafter, "*2020 NSDUH Tables*").

[4] For each year from 2010 to 2020, the estimated percentage of the population currently using marijuana was 6.9%, 7.0%, 7.3%, 7.5%, 8.4%, 8.3%, 8.9%, 9.6%, 10.1%, 11.5%, and 11.8% respectively. The difference between each year's estimate from 2010 to 2018 and the 2019 estimate (11.5%) is statistically significant at the .05 level. SAMHSA recommends using caution when comparing estimates between 2020 and prior years because of methodological changes for 2020. Due to these changes, SAMHSA did not conduct significance testing between 2020 and prior years. For 2002-2020 data, see *2020 NSDUH Tables*, Table 7.3B. Of note, some warn of potential bias in drug usage survey data because of misreporting by respondents. See Beau Kilmer, Jonathan P. Caulkins, and Gregory Midgette et al., *Before the Grand Opening: Measuring Washington State's Marijuana Market in the Last Year Before Legalized Commercial Sales*, RAND Drug Policy Research Center, 2013.

marijuana use among youth was 7.4% in 2010 and 6.7% in 2020.[5] During this time span, nearly half of the youth surveyed had a general perception that marijuana was relatively easy to acquire if desired.[6] Marijuana is readily available throughout most of the United States; in 2020, most Drug Enforcement Administration (DEA) field divisions reported that marijuana availability was high in their jurisdictions, and since that time more states have enacted laws authorizing medical and recreational marijuana programs.[7]

Under federal law, marijuana and its derivatives[8] are classified as Schedule I controlled substances under the Controlled Substances Act (CSA) unless specifically exempted or listed in another schedule (see the "Controlled Substances Act" section)—thus, their cultivation, distribution, or possession, except in the context of approved research studies, is prohibited at the federal level. In contrast, states have established a range of laws and policies allowing for the medical and recreational use of marijuana. Most states have deviated from an across-the-board prohibition of marijuana, and it is now more the rule than the exception that states have laws and policies allowing for some cultivation, distribution, and possession of marijuana or low-THC cannabis—many of which are contrary to the CSA. The gap between federal and state laws and policies on marijuana has expanded each year as states continue to enact laws that allow for the medical or recreational use of marijuana.

---

[5] For some years the difference from one year's estimate to the next were not statistically significant at the .05 level. SAMHSA recommends using caution when comparing estimates between 2020 and prior years because of methodological changes for 2020. Due to these changes, SAMHSA did not conduct significance testing between 2020 and prior years. See *2020 NSDUH Tables*, Table 7.6B.

[6] In 2010, nearly half (48.6%) of surveyed youth (ages 12-17) indicated that marijuana would be "fairly easy" or "very easy" to obtain. In 2020, this figure had decreased to 41.0%. See HHS, SAMHSA, *Results from the 2010 National Survey on Drug Use and Health: Summary of National* Findings, September 2011, p. 5; and 2020 *NSDUH Tables*, Table 3.1B.

[7] Just as the CSA does not distinguish between recreational and medical marijuana (it is all prohibited under the CSA), DEA does not distinguish between medical and recreational marijuana in discussing its availability, nor does it distinguish between state-authorized and non-state-authorized marijuana availability. U.S. Department of Justice (DOJ), Drug Enforcement Administration (DEA), *2020 National Drug Threat Assessment,* DEA-DCT-DIR-008-21, March 2021.

[8] The Agriculture Improvement Act of 2018 (2018 farm bill; P.L. 115-334) removed hemp and hemp derivatives from the CSA definition of marijuana. Industrial hemp is a variety of the cannabis plant that has low THC content and is cultivated for use in the production of a wide range of products. Hemp-derived cannabidiol (CBD) is promoted as treatment for a range of conditions, including epileptic seizures, post-traumatic stress disorder, anxiety, and inflammation—despite limited scientific evidence to substantiate many of these claims.

Cannabis Terms

The Cannabis sativa plant is often referred to as *cannabis*, an umbrella term that includes marijuana and hemp. Marijuana generally refers to the cultivated plant used as a psychotropic drug (whether for medicinal or recreational purposes). Hemp, which was removed from the CSA definition of marijuana in 2018, is cultivated for use in the production of a wide range of products, including foods and beverages, personal care products, dietary supplements, fabrics and textiles, paper, construction materials, and other manufactured and industrial goods. THC and cannabidiol (CBD) are thought to be the most abundant cannabinoids in the Cannabis sativa plant and are among the most researched cannabinoids for their potential medical value. While THC is the primary psychoactive compound found in marijuana, CBD is a nonpsychoactive compound found in both marijuana and hemp.

This report provides an historical background on federal marijuana policy; an overview of state trends with respect to marijuana decriminalization and legalization, for both medical and recreational uses; and an analysis of the gap between federal and state marijuana law and policy and certain implications and consequences of the gap. It reviews federalism and federal authority to preempt state marijuana laws and analyzes relevant issues for federal law enforcement and the consequences of state marijuana legalization. The report also outlines a number of related policy questions and options that Congress may consider, including federal tax treatment of marijuana, financial services for marijuana businesses, the medical nature of cannabis, oversight of federal law enforcement, evaluation of marijuana as a Schedule I controlled substance, and some options for addressing the gap.

Historical Background of Federal Marijuana Policy

To understand the evolution of U.S. marijuana control and the current marijuana policy gap between the states and the federal government, it is important to examine the history of marijuana as a controlled substance in the United States.

Early 20th Century

Early 20th Century Marijuana Control

In the early 20th century, enforcement of drug laws was primarily the responsibility of local police, and the Federal Bureau of Narcotics (FBN) occasionally assisted.[9] Due to reduced appropriations during the Great Depression, the FBN budget and the number of narcotic agents declined and remained low for years. Publicity and warnings of the dangers of narcotics, in particular marijuana, were primary methods of drug control for the FBN.[10] In seeking federal control of marijuana and uniform narcotic laws, Commissioner Anslinger and public officials from some states made personal appeals to civic groups and legislators and pushed for, and received, editorial support in newspapers; some newspapers maintained a steady stream of anti-marijuana messaging in the 1930s.[11]

Prior to 1937, growing and using marijuana was legal under federal law.[12] During the course of promoting federal legislation to control marijuana, Henry Anslinger, the first commissioner of the Federal Bureau of Narcotics (FBN),[13] and others submitted testimony to Congress regarding the immorality and harms of marijuana use, claiming that it incited violent and insane behavior.[14] Among other observations, Commissioner Anslinger noted that "the major criminal in the United States is the drug addict; that of all the offenses committed against the laws of this country, the narcotic addict is the most frequent offender."[15] States had already begun to ban the possession of marijuana during this time. The federal government created a de facto ban of

---

[9] David F. Musto, *The American Disease: Origins of Narcotic Control*, 3rd ed. (New York, NY: Oxford University Press, 1999), pp. 183-200, p. 228.

[10] Ibid., p. 214.

[11] Richard J. Bonnie and Charles H. Whitebread II, *The Marijuana Conviction: A History of Marijuana Conviction in the United States* (New York, NY: The Lindesmith Center, 1999), pp. 94-95; and Eric Schlosser, "Reefer Madness," *The Atlantic*, August 1994.

[12] States regulated marijuana, and some banned it prior to 1937.

[13] In 1930, the Federal Bureau of Narcotics (FBN) was established within the U.S. Treasury Department to handle narcotics enforcement.

[14] See statements by H. J. Anslinger, Commissioner of Narcotics, Federal Bureau of Narcotics, U.S. Department of the Treasury, and Dr. James C. Munch, before the U.S. Congress, House Committee on Ways and Means, *Taxation of Marihuana*, 75th Cong., 1st sess., April 27-30, May 4, 1937, HRG-1837-WAM-0002.

[15] U.S. Congress, House Committee on Ways and Means, *Taxation of Marihuana*, 75th Cong., 1st sess., April 27-30, May 4, 1937, HRG-1837-WAM-0002, p. 7.

marijuana under the Marihuana Tax Act of 1937 (MTA; P.L. 75-238).[16] The MTA imposed a high-cost transfer tax stamp on marijuana sales, but these stamps were rarely issued by the federal government.[17]

Mid-20th Century

In the decades that followed the enactment of the MTA, Congress continued to pass drug control legislation and further criminalized drug use. For example, the Boggs Act (P.L. 82-255), passed in 1951, established mandatory prison sentences for some drug offenses, while the Narcotic Control Act (P.L. 84-728) in 1956 further increased penalties for drug offenses, including marijuana offenses. In conjunction with growing support for a medical approach to addressing drug abuse, there was a strong emphasis on law enforcement control of drugs, including marijuana—which was gaining popularity as a recreational drug. Congress shifted the constitutional basis for drug control from its taxing authority to its power to regulate interstate commerce,[18] and in 1968 the FBN merged with the Bureau of Drug Abuse Control and was transferred from Treasury to the Department of Justice (DOJ).[19] Three years later, President Richard Nixon would declare a war on drugs.[20]

Congress and President Nixon enhanced federal control of drugs through the enactment of comprehensive federal drug laws—including the CSA, enacted as Title II of the Comprehensive Drug Abuse Prevention and Control

---

[16] Congressional testimony indicated that marijuana, while it was a problem in the Southwest United States starting in the mid-1920s, became a "national menace" in the mid-1930s (1935-1937). See statement by H. J. Anslinger, Commissioner of Narcotics, Federal Bureau of Narcotics, U.S. Department of the Treasury, before the U.S. Congress, House Committee on Ways and Means, *Taxation of Marihuana*, 75th Cong., 1st sess., April 27, 1937. In Leary v. United States (395 U.S. 6 (1968)), the MTA was overturned by the U.S. Supreme Court as a violation of the Fifth Amendment's privilege against compelled self-incrimination.

[17] Charles F. Levinthal, *Drugs, Society, and Criminal Justice*, 3rd ed. (New York, NY: Prentice Hall, 2012), p. 58.

[18] As stated in Article I, Section 8, clause 3 of the U.S. Constitution, "Congress shall have the Power ... To regulate Commerce with foreign Nations, and among the several States, and with the Indian Tribes." For more information about the commerce clause, see CRS Report R43023, *Congressional Authority to Enact Criminal Law: An Examination of Selected Recent Cases*.

[19] David F. Musto, *The American Disease: Origins of Narcotic Control*, 3rd ed. (New York, NY: Oxford University Press, 1999), p. 239. The shift in constitutional authority was part of the Drug Abuse Control Amendments of 1965 (P.L. 89-74).

[20] For a broader discussion of the federal government's drug enforcement history, see CRS Report R43749, *Drug Enforcement in the United States: History, Policy, and Trends*.

Act of 1970 (P.L. 91-513). The CSA placed the control of marijuana and other plant and chemical substances under federal jurisdiction regardless of state regulations and laws. In designating marijuana as a Schedule I controlled substance, this legislation officially prohibited the manufacture, distribution, dispensation, and possession of marijuana except for purposes of sanctioned research.[21]

Controlled Substances Act

Marijuana's listing as a Schedule I controlled substance under the CSA[22] indicates that the federal government has determined that

a) The drug or other substance has a high potential for abuse.
b) The drug or other substance has no currently accepted medical use in treatment in the United States.
c) There is a lack of accepted safety for use of the drug or other substance under medical supervision.[23]

The CSA places various substances in one of five schedules based on characteristics such as their medical use, potential for abuse, and safety or dependence liability.[24] The five schedules are progressively ordered, with substances regarded as the least dangerous and addictive classified as Schedule V and those considered the most dangerous and addictive classified as Schedule I.[25] As described in law, Schedule I substances have "a high potential for abuse" with "no currently accepted medical use in treatment in the United States" and cannot safely be dispensed under a prescription.[26] Schedule I substances may be lawfully used only for bona fide, federal government-approved research studies.[27]

---

[21] 21 U.S.C. §812 and §841. Of note, growing a marijuana plant is considered *manufacturing* marijuana. Marijuana (spelled as "marihuana") is defined under 21 U.S.C. §802(16).

[22] For more information on the CSA, see the text box, "Controlled Substances Act (CSA)," and U.S. DOJ, DEA, *The Controlled Substances Act*, https://www.dea.gov/controlled-substances-act.

[23] 21 U.S.C. §812(b)(1).

[24] 21 U.S.C. §812(b).

[25] When Congress enacted the CSA in 1970, it established "initial schedules" of controlled substances (21 U.S.C. §812(c), but specified that the schedules "shall be updated" periodically (21 U.S.C. §812(a)). The current list of controlled substances within their designated schedules may be found in 21 C.F.R. Sections 1308.11–15.

[26] 21 U.S.C. §812(b).

[27] 21 U.S.C. §823(f).

Controlled Substances Act (CSA)

The CSA was enacted as Title II of the Comprehensive Drug Abuse Prevention and Control Act of 1970.[28] It regulates the manufacture, possession, use, importation, and distribution of certain drugs, substances, and precursor chemicals. The CSA establishes how the federal government (1) regulates and facilitates the lawful production, possession, and distribution of controlled substances; (2) prevents diversion[29] of these substances for illegitimate purposes; and (3) penalizes unauthorized activities involving controlled substances.

Under the CSA, there are five schedules under which substances may be classified—Schedule I being the most restrictive. Substances placed onto one of the five schedules are evaluated on

- actual or relative potential for abuse;
- known scientific evidence of pharmacological effects;
- current scientific knowledge of the substance;
- history and current pattern of abuse;
- scope, duration, and significance of abuse;
- risk to public health;
- psychic or physiological dependence liability; and
- whether the substance is an immediate precursor of an already scheduled substance.

For an overview of the CSA and a discussion of select legal issues that have arisen under the act, see CRS Report R45948, *The Controlled Substances Act (CSA): A Legal Overview for the 117th Congress.*

The CSA has two overlapping legal schemes. Registration provisions require entities working with controlled substances, such as those who research marijuana,[30] to register with the government, take steps to prevent diversion and misuse of controlled substances, and report certain information

---

[28] P.L. 91-513; 21 U.S.C. §801 et. seq.

[29] DEA has explained that the term *diversion*, used in the context of the CSA, refers to "the redirection of controlled substances which may have lawful uses into illicit channels." Controlled Substances Quotas, 83 *Federal Register* 32784 (July 16, 2018).

[30] Every person or entity who manufactures or distributes any controlled substance, such as drug manufacturing companies, and every person who dispenses any controlled substance, such as doctors and pharmacists, must register with DEA.

to regulators.[31] Trafficking provisions establish penalties for the production, distribution, and possession of controlled substances outside the legitimate scope of the registration system.[32] DEA enforces both registration and trafficking provisions.

A violation of the CSA's registration requirements—including failure to maintain records or detect and report suspicious orders, noncompliance with security requirements, or dispensing controlled substances without the necessary prescriptions—generally does not constitute a criminal offense unless the violation is committed knowingly. However, in the event of a knowing violation, DEA may make an arrest and refer the case to the U.S. Attorney's Office, which may bring criminal charges against both individual and corporate registrants. A first criminal violation of the registration requirements by an individual is punishable by a fine and/or up to a year in prison.[33] For other violations of the CSA, potential penalties vary. Trafficking penalties vary based on the offense and the type and amount of the controlled substance in question, and certain sections of the CSA define more specific offenses, such as distributing controlled substances near schools or to individuals under age 21.[34] Unauthorized simple possession of a controlled substance may prompt a minimum fine of $1,000 and a term of up to a year in federal prison.[35] Trafficking of large quantities of Schedule I and Schedule II substances carries a prison sentence of 10 years to life and a fine of up to $10 million for an individual or a fine of up to $50 million for an organization.[36] Penalties increase for second or subsequent offenses, or if death or serious bodily injury results from the use of the controlled substance. Simple possession penalties are low compared to trafficking penalties, and DOJ has infrequently pursued simple possession charges against offenders compared to trafficking charges.[37]

---

[31] 21 U.S.C. §§821-832.

[32] 21 U.S.C. §§841-865.

[33] 21 U.S.C. §842(c)(2)(A).

[34] See 21 U.S.C. §859, §860.

[35] 21 U.S.C. §844(a).

[36] 21 U.S.C. §841(b)(1)(A). For example, trafficking of 1,000 kilograms or more of a mixture or substance containing a detectable amount of marijuana, or 1,000 or more marijuana plants regardless of weight, would carry this sentence.

[37] In FY2020, 98.4% (16,287) of 16,501 federal drug offenses involved drug trafficking. In FY2020, 19.9% (280) of 1,408 federal marijuana offenses involved marijuana possession and 80.1% (1,128) of federal marijuana offenses involved marijuana trafficking. See U.S. Sentencing Commission, *Quick Facts: Drug Trafficking Offenses*, June 2021, https://www.ussc.gov/; and *Interactive Data Analyzer*, Sentencing Outcomes for FY2020, https://ida.ussc.gov.

The Shafer Commission

As part of the CSA enacted in 1970, the National Commission on Marihuana and Drug Abuse, also known as the Shafer Commission, was established to study marijuana in the United States.[38] Specifically, the commission was charged with performing evaluations and examining issues including, but not limited to,

a) the extent of use of marihuana in the United States to include its various sources of users, number of arrests, number of convictions, amount of marihuana seized, type of user, nature of use;
b) an evaluation of the efficacy of existing marihuana laws;
c) a study of the pharmacology of marihuana and its immediate and long-term effects, both physiological and psychological;
d) the relationship of marihuana use to aggressive behavior and crime;
e) the relationship between marihuana and the use of other drugs; and
f) the international control of marihuana.[39]

The Shafer Commission, in concluding its review, produced two reports: (1) *Marihuana: A Signal of Misunderstanding*, and (2) *Drug Use in America: Problem in Perspective*.[40]

In its first report (published in 1972), the Shafer Commission discussed the perception of marijuana as a major social problem and how it came to be viewed as such.[41] It made a number of recommendations, including the development of a "social control policy seeking to discourage marihuana use, while concentrating primarily on the prevention of heavy and very heavy

---

[38] The commission was composed of two Members of the Senate, two Members of the House, and nine members appointed by the President of the United States. President Nixon appointed Raymond Shafer as the chairman.

[39] P.L. 91-513, §601(d).

[40] National Commission on Marihuana and Drug Abuse, *Marihuana: A Signal of Misunderstanding*, First Report of the National Commission on Marihuana and Drug Abuse, Washington, DC, March 1972 (hereinafter, "First Report of the Shafer Commission"); and National Commission on Marihuana and Drug Abuse, *Drug Use in America: Problem in Perspective*, Second Report of the National Commission on Marihuana and Drug Abuse, Washington, DC, March 1973 (hereinafter, "Second Report of the Shafer Commission").

[41] The commission stated that three factors contributed to the perception of marijuana as a major national problem, including "[1] the illegal behavior is highly visible to all segments of our society, [2] use of the drug is perceived to threaten the health and morality not only of the individual but of society itself, and [3] most important, the drug has evolved in the late sixties and early seventies as a symbol of wider social conflicts and public issues." First Report of the Shafer Commission, p. 6.

use."[42] In this first report, the commission also called the application of criminal law in cases of personal use of marijuana "constitutionally suspect" and declared that "total prohibition is functionally inappropriate."[43] Of note, none of the recommendations of this report were implemented, either administratively or legislatively.

In its second report (published in 1973), the Shafer Commission reviewed the use of all drugs in the United States, not solely marijuana. It examined the origins of the country's drug problem, including the social costs of drug use, and once again made specific recommendations regarding federal and state drug policy. Among its conclusions regarding marijuana, the commission indicated that aggressive behavior generally cannot be attributed to its use.[44] The commission also reaffirmed its previous findings and recommendations regarding marijuana and added the following statement:

> The risk potential of marihuana is quite low compared to the potent psychoactive substances, and even its widespread consumption does not involve social cost now associated with most of the stimulants and depressants (Jones, 1973; Tinklenberg, 1971). Nonetheless, the Commission remains persuaded that availability of this drug should not be institutionalized at this time.[45]

At the conclusion of the second report, the Shafer Commission recommended that Congress launch a subsequent commission to reexamine the broad issues surrounding drug use and societal response.[46] While a number of congressionally directed commissions regarding drugs have since been established,[47] no such commission has been directed to comprehensively review the issues of drug use, abuse, and response in the United States.

---

[42] First Report of the Shafer Commission, p. 134.

[43] Ibid., pp. 142-143.

[44] Second Report of the Shafer Commission, p. 158.

[45] Ibid., p. 224. In this statement, the Shafer Commission cites the following studies: R.T. Jones, *Mental Illness and Drugs: Pre-Existing Psychopathology and Response to Psychoactive Drugs*, Paper Prepared for the National Commission on Marihuana and Drug Abuse, 1973; and J.R. Tinklenberg, *Marihuana and Crime*, Paper Prepared for the National Commission on Marihuana and Drug Abuse, unpublished, October 1971.

[46] Second Report of the Shafer Commission, pp. 410-411.

[47] See, for example, the President's Media Commission on Alcohol and Drug Abuse Prevention and the National Commission on Drug-Free Schools.

Marijuana, Late 20th Century and Beyond

While heroin and cocaine were the primary drugs of concern for federal law enforcement during the 1970s and 80s (respectively), marijuana was also a target of the substantial investment in enforcement during the federal government's "war on drugs."[48] In the 1980s, marijuana arrests were a large part of federal drug enforcement, and there are some federal crime data available to illustrate this. The percentage of federal drug offenders charged with marijuana violations was 24% in 1980, increased to 40% in 1982, and decreased to 26% in 1986. Among federal drug offenders (12,285) charged with marijuana violations (3,221) in 1986, 70% were charged with distribution, manufacture, or importation, while the remaining 30% were charged with simple possession.[49] Today, the percentage of federal drug offenders charged with marijuana violations is much lower—in FY2020, 7% of federal drug offenders were marijuana offenders.[50]

Over the last several decades, federal law enforcement has generally focused its efforts on criminal networks rather than individual offenders; its current stance regarding drug (particularly marijuana) offenders appears consistent with this position.[51] DOJ has repeatedly emphasized that marijuana remains an illegal substance under the CSA, but it chooses to focus its enforcement efforts on the largest threats (e.g., transnational and domestic criminal organizations that traffic illicit drugs),[52] which generally has not included the state-authorized marijuana industries and individuals in possession of marijuana.

Since the 1990s, the federal government has shifted its stated drug control policy from one that is more focused on law enforcement to a comprehensive

---

[48] President Nixon's war on drugs involved greater emphasis on a law enforcement response to drug crimes.

[49] DOJ, Bureau of Justice Statistics, *Federal Offenses and Offenders: Drug Law Violators, 1980-86*, June 1988. Classifications were based on the most serious offense with which the individual was charged at case filing.

[50] U.S. Sentencing Commission, *2020 Annual Report and Sourcebook of Federal Sentencing Statistics*, Figure D-1. The U.S. Sentencing Commission derived information about the type of drug from the primary drug type (i.e., the type that produces the highest base offense level) in the case, and obtained the data from the presentence report, judgment and commitment order, or plea agreement. See Appendix A.

[51] See DOJ, DEA, *FY 2021 Performance Budget Congressional Budget Submission*; and U.S. Sentencing Commission, *Quick Facts: Drug Trafficking Offenses.*

[52] DOJ, DEA, *2020 National Drug Threat Assessment*, March 2021.

approach—one that focuses on prevention, treatment, and enforcement.[53] Further, sentencing for federal marijuana offenses has become less severe over the years. For various reasons, the mean prison sentence for federal marijuana offenses fell from 50 months in FY1992 to 24 months in FY2020.[54]

Evolution of Public Opinion

Changes in state and local marijuana laws over time have corresponded with a general shift in public attitudes toward the substance (see Figure 1). In 1969, 12% of the surveyed population supported legalizing marijuana; in 2021, that percentage had increased to 68% (+/- 3.0 percentage points).[55] Much of the shift in public opinion has occurred over the last 20 years. In addition, 59% (+/- 2.9 percentage points) of respondents indicated in 2015 that the federal government should not enforce federal marijuana prohibition laws in states that allow for its use.[56]

---

[53] See the annual *National Drug Control Strategy* and accompanying *National Drug Control Budget* issued by the Office of National Drug Control Policy.

[54] Some reasons for the decline are discussed in U.S. Sentencing Commission, *Mandatory Minimum Penalties for Drug Offenses in the Federal Criminal Justice System*, October 2017, https://www.ussc.gov/sites/default/files/pdf/research- and-publications/research-publications/2017/20171025_Drug-Mand-Min.pdf. One reason is that the number of offenders convicted of a drug crime carrying a mandatory minimum penalty had decreased by 44.7% from FY2010 through FY2016. See U.S. Sentencing Commission, *Interactive Data Analyzer*, Sentencing Outcomes for FY2020, https://ida.ussc.gov; and *1996 Sourcebook of Federal Sentencing Statistics*, Figures I and U.

[55] The specific question asked was "Do you think marijuana should be made legal or not?" See Gallup, *Support for Legal Marijuana Holds at Record High of 68%*, November 4, 2021 (based on poll data from October 2021). For purposes of this question, the poll does not distinguish between medical and recreational marijuana, nor does Gallup explain to respondents what "made legal" means. Of note, in September 2019 the Pew Research Center found similar (67%) levels of support for marijuana use to be legalized among American adults. For this poll, the specific question was "Do you think that the use of marijuana should be made legal, or not?"; see Andrew Daniller, *Two-thirds of Americans Support Marijuana Legalization*, Pew Research Center, November 14, 2019—data from Pew Research Center's online American Trends Panel conducted September 3-15, 2019. In a subsequent poll in 2021, Pew asked a different marijuana legalization question of survey respondents: "Which comes closer to your view about the use of marijuana by adults?" 60% of respondents chose "[i]t should be legal for medical AND recreational use"; 30% chose "[i]t should be legal for medical use ONLY"; and 8% chose "[i]t should NOT be legal." See Ted Van Green, *Americans Overwhelmingly Say Marijuana Should be Legal for Recreational or Medical Use*, Pew Research Center, April 16, 2021—data from a survey of U.S. adults conducted April 5-11, 2021.

[56] Pew Research Center for the People & the Press (Pew), *In Debate Over Legalizing Marijuana, Disagreement Over Drug's Dangers*, April 14, 2015 (based on poll data from March 2015). Of note, Pew has not asked about federal enforcement of marijuana prohibition laws since the 2015 poll.

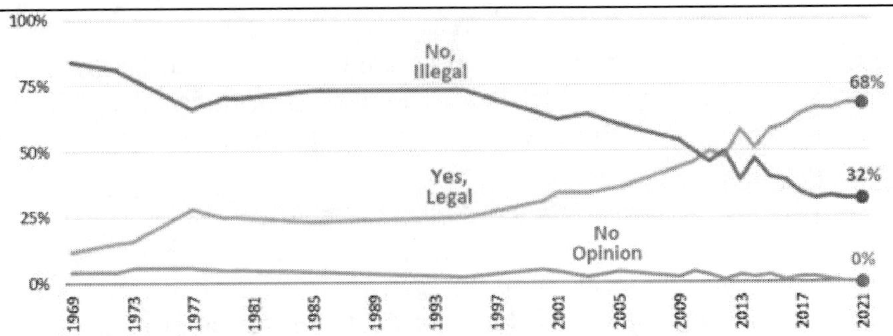

Notes: The question was "Do you think marijuana should be made legal or not?" Sample sizes and margins of error vary from year to year. Data from 2021 are based on landline and cellular telephone interviews conducted October 1-19, 2021, with a random sample of 823 adults aged 18 and older living in the United States.

Source: CRS presentation of data from Gallup News Service, *Gallup Poll Social Series: Crime*, http://www.gallup.com.

Figure 1. Public Opinion on Legalization of Marijuana, 1969-2021.

U.S. federal drug control policies—specifically those relating to marijuana—continue to generate debate among policymakers, law enforcement officials, scholars, and the public. Over the last 25 years since California legalized marijuana for medical purposes, the policy conversation for some has evolved from how strictly marijuana must be prohibited to how much should be allowed.[57]

[57] For example, see U.S. Congress, House Committee on Interstate and Foreign Commerce, Subcommittee on Public Health and Welfare, *Drug Abuse Control Amendments, 1970, Part 1*, 91st Cong., February 3-4, 1970; Robert S. Weppner and James A. Inciardi, "Decriminalizing Marijuana," *International Journal of Offender Therapy and Comparative Criminology*, vol. 22, no. 2 (June 1, 1978), pp. 115-126; U.S. Congress, House Committee on the Judiciary, *Full Committee Markup on H.R. 3884, the "Marijuana Opportunity Reinvestment and Expungement Act,"* 116th Cong., 2nd sess., November 21, 2019; and U.S. Congress, House Committee on the Judiciary, *Miscellaneous Measures*, Markup of the H.R. 3617, the Marijuana Opportunity Reinvestment and Expungement Act of 2021 or the MORE Act of 2021 (among other legislation), 117th Cong., 1st sess., September 29, 2021.

The Federal Status of Marijuana and the Expanding Policy Gap with States

In 1970, the CSA placed the control of marijuana under federal jurisdiction *regardless* of state regulations and laws, and while the definition of marijuana has recently been amended to exclude hemp and its derivatives, marijuana's Schedule I classification has remained unchanged for over 50 years. While the federal government maintains marijuana's current placement as a Schedule I controlled substance, states have established a range of laws and policies regarding its medical and recreational use.

To help illustrate the policy gap between the federal government and states, it is useful to compare the policies for the cultivation and distribution of marijuana. At the federal level, the cultivation and distribution of marijuana (regardless of whether it is for medical or recreational purposes) is considered drug trafficking, and the average prison sentence given to an individual convicted in federal court of marijuana trafficking was 29 months in FY2020.[58] In contrast, in many states the cultivation and distribution of marijuana is lawful and regulated (see Figure 2), and marijuana businesses that follow state law and regulation can earn profits from the cultivation and distribution of marijuana.

While the federal government maintains that marijuana has no medicinal value,[59] most states and territories allow for its use as medicine. While the federal government maintains a prohibition on marijuana because it is believed to have a high potential for abuse and to be a dangerous substance, 18 states, the District of Columbia (DC), and two territories allow for its recreational use. Since the federal government amended its definition of marijuana to exclude hemp, farmers in states have also forged ahead with hemp production, but they must be careful not to cultivate a product that has a THC value greater than 0.3% or they would instead be cultivating marijuana.

---

[58] U.S. Sentencing Commission, *Quick Facts: Marijuana Trafficking Offenses*, June 2021, https://www.ussc.gov/.

[59] See Appendix C for a discussion FDA and National Academies evaluations for the health effects of marijuana.

State Cannabis Law and Policy Trends

Over the past few decades, most states have deviated from an across-the-board prohibition of cannabis. It is now more the rule than the exception that states have laws and policies allowing for some manufacturing, sale, distribution, and possession of marijuana—all of which are contrary to the CSA, except for the purposes of sanctioned research.[60] Evolving state-level positions on marijuana include decriminalization measures as well (for definition of terms such as *decriminalization* and *legalization*, see Appendix A). See Figure 2 for a map of the various cannabis laws by state.

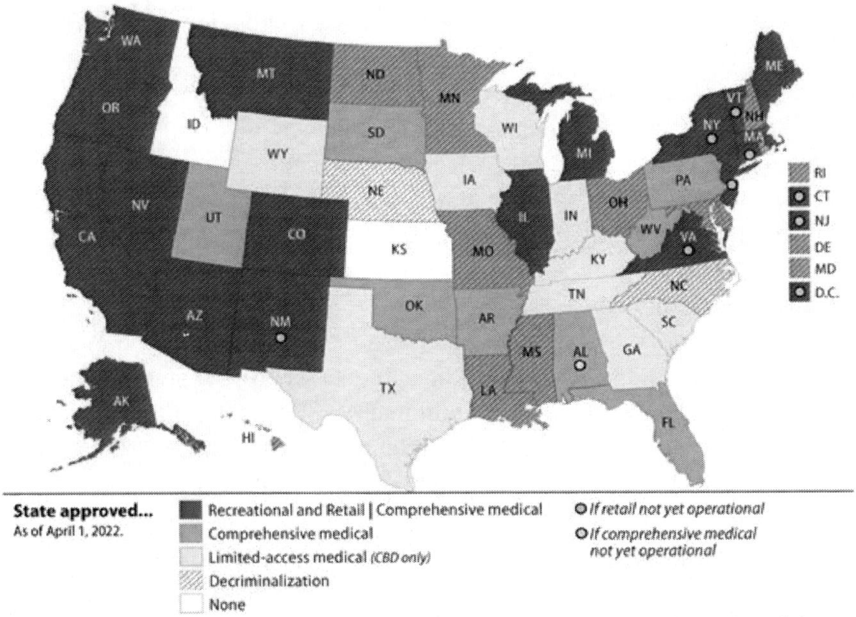

Source: CRS presentation of data from the National Conference of State Legislatures and CRS review of laws of the 50 states, territories, and District of Columbia (DC).

Notes: Limited-access medical refers to cannabis with low THC content or CBD oil used for a limited list of medical conditions. State-approved refers to state laws that either (1) allow for recreational and/or medical marijuana use and/or (2) decriminalize the possession of marijuana in small amounts. Decriminalization refers to a state's action to remove accompanying criminal penalties for possession of marijuana in small amounts; however, civil penalties

[60] With the change to the CSA definition of marijuana in the 2018 farm bill, the states that distribute CBD containing no more than 0.3% THC may not be in violation of the CSA.

remain. Of note, some states allow medical marijuana only for certain specified conditions. Further detail for the states with state-approved recreational use with no retail include the following: (1) While DC has approved recreational retail of marijuana, Congress has blocked DC from using funds to regulate and tax marijuana sales; (2) while Vermont has approved recreational use, it does not have a regulatory system for production or retail; and (3) the remaining states just recently approved recreational marijuana through a ballot measure and have not yet set up their retail systems. In 2020, South Dakota (SD) voters approved ballot measures to legalize recreational and medical marijuana, however, in 2021 a circuit court judge ruled the recreational measure to be unconstitutional. The SD Supreme Court upheld this ruling in 2021. The SD medical marijuana program is not yet operational. A 2018 Kansas (KS) law allowed for the sale of CBD products with 0% concentration of THC, but there is some confusion over the legality of CBD in KS because most CBD products have trace amounts of THC. Of the U.S. territories, Guam (GU) and the Northern Mariana Islands (MP) have approved recreational marijuana use and retail. GU, Puerto Rico, MP, and the U.S. Virgin Islands (USVI) have approved medical marijuana use. USVI has also approved decriminalization of marijuana. American Samoa has not taken any action to either decriminalize marijuana or approve recreational or medical marijuana.

Figure 2. State Cannabis Laws, April 2022.

Medical Marijuana

In 1996, California became the first state to amend its drug laws to allow for the medicinal use of marijuana. As of April 1, 2022, 37 states, the District of Columbia, Puerto Rico, Guam, and the U.S. Virgin Islands have comprehensive laws and policies allowing for the medicinal use of marijuana.[61] Eleven additional states allow for "limited-access medical cannabis," which refers to cannabis with low THC content or CBD oil used for a limited list of medical conditions.[62] Idaho, Kansas, Nebraska, and

---

[61] In November, 2020, Mississippi voters passed a ballot initiative to allow for medical marijuana, but it was overturned by the Supreme Court of Mississippi on May 14, 2021. On February 2, 2022, a new comprehensive medical marijuana law was enacted in Mississippi. See National Conference of State Legislatures, *State Medical Marijuana Laws*, February 3, 2022. "Comprehensive" medical programs describe those that allow adults to use a range of marijuana products (not only low-THC cannabis) to treat specified medical issues. Most states specify conditions for which medical marijuana may be used as treatment. Prior to enactment of the 2018 farm bill, CBD was considered to be marijuana under the CSA. See the "Change to CSA Definition of Marijuana" section of this report.

[62] As previously mentioned, CBD is a chemical compound in marijuana. Unlike THC, it does not have a psychoactive component.

American Samoa do not allow either comprehensive medical marijuana or low-THC cannabis. While the Northern Mariana Islands allow recreational marijuana, it has not authorized medical marijuana in any capacity.[63]

As noted, the CSA does not recognize the distinction states are making between the medical and recreational use of marijuana. Marijuana's classification as a Schedule I controlled substance reflects a finding that marijuana has "no currently accepted medical use in treatment in the United States."[64] Thus, states allowing its use for medical purposes are still at odds with the federal position. Federal law enforcement officers and attorneys may investigate, arrest, and prosecute individuals for medical marijuana-related offenses[65]; however, annual provisions in DOJ appropriations restrict DOJ's ability to expend funds to enforce the CSA in states that allow for *medical* use of marijuana (see the "Limiting Federal Enforcement in States: Directives through Federal Appropriations" section; the appropriations provision does not apply to state laws allowing recreational use of marijuana). Notwithstanding the appropriations rider, marijuana-related activity in states that allow for it may still result in serious legal consequences under federal law. DOJ-issued guidance in 2018 reaffirmed the authority of federal prosecutors to exercise prosecutorial discretion to target federal marijuana offenses "in accordance with all applicable laws, regulations, and appropriations."[66] DOJ emphasizes the investigation and prosecution of growers and dispensers who are violating state law and does not target those that are in compliance with state law and individual users of medical

---

[63] National Conference of State Legislatures, *State Medical Marijuana Laws*, February 3, 2022, and CRS review of laws of the 50 states, territories, and District of Columbia (DC).

[64] 21 U.S.C. §812(b)(1).

[65] Several courts have interpreted the appropriations rider to bar DOJ from expending any appropriated funds to prosecute activities involving marijuana that are conducted in "strict compliance" with state law. See United States v. McIntosh, 833 F.3d 1163, 1178 (9th Cir. 2016); Duval v. United States, 372 F. Supp. 3d 544, 555-56 (E.D. Mich. 2019); Sandusky v. Goetz, 2018 WL 6505803 at *4-5 (D. Colo. December 11, 2018); United States v. Jackson, 2019 WL 3239844 at *6-8 (E.D. Pa. June 5, 2019). However, activities that fall outside the scope of state medical marijuana laws remain subject to prosecution. For example, in United States v. Evans, the Ninth Circuit upheld the prosecution of medical marijuana growers who smoked some of the marijuana they grew because the defendants failed to show they were "qualifying patients" who acted in strict compliance with state medical marijuana law.

[66] Attorney General Jefferson B. Sessions, *Memorandum for All United States Attorneys*, U.S. Department of Justice, Marijuana Enforcement, Washington, DC, January 4, 2018.

marijuana.[67] (Federal enforcement priorities are discussed further in the "Federal Response to State Divergence" section.)

Recreational Marijuana

Recreational marijuana *legalization* measures remove all state-imposed penalties for specified activities involving marijuana. As of April 1, 2022, 18 states, DC, Guam, and the Northern Mariana Islands allow for the *recreational use* of marijuana. Until 2012, the recreational use of marijuana had not been legal in any U.S. state since prior to the passage of the CSA in 1970. In November 2012, citizens of Colorado and Washington voted to legalize, regulate, and tax marijuana for recreational use.[68] In November 2014, recreational marijuana legalization initiatives also passed in Alaska, Oregon, and DC. Two years later, in November 2016, recreational marijuana legalization initiatives passed in Massachusetts, California, Maine, and Nevada. In 2018, Michigan voters approved recreational marijuana use through a ballot initiative, and Vermont approved recreational marijuana use through the legislative process—the first state to approve recreational marijuana via legislation as opposed to a ballot initiative. In 2019, Illinois became the second state to enact legislation approving recreational marijuana use. In 2020, voters in Arizona, Montana, New Jersey, and South Dakota approved measures to allow recreational marijuana; however, in February 2021 a circuit judge ruled the South Dakota recreational marijuana measure to be unconstitutional.[69] In 2021, New York, Virginia, and Connecticut approved recreational marijuana through the legislative process.

These recreational marijuana initiatives legalized the possession of specific quantities of marijuana by individuals aged 21 and over, and (with the exception of DC and Vermont) set up state-administered regulatory schemes for the sale of marijuana[70]; however, there are variations among the initiatives. For example, Alaska, Arizona, California, Colorado, Connecticut,

---

[67] Communication between CRS and DEA on December 29, 2020. See also discussion in the "Enforcement Focused on Traffickers" section.

[68] For more detail regarding both Washington Initiative 502 and Colorado Amendment 64, see CRS Report R43034, *State Legalization of Recreational Marijuana: Selected Legal Issues*.

[69] On November 24, 2021, the South Dakota Supreme Court upheld this decision. See Teo Armus, "South Dakota voters said yes to legalizing marijuana. But a judge ruled it's unconstitutional," *The Washington Post*, February 9, 2021; and Jonathan Ellis and Joe Sneve, "South Dakota Supreme Court strikes down recreational marijuana amendment," *Argus Leader*, November 24, 2021.

[70] Regulatory schemes include restrictions and requirements for licensing the production, processing, and retail of marijuana, and procedures for the issuance of licenses.

Massachusetts, Maine, Michigan, Montana, Nevada, New Mexico, Oregon, Vermont, Virginia, and DC allow individuals to grow their own marijuana plants for recreational use,[71] while Illinois, New Jersey, and Washington do not. Currently, New York allows hemp farmers[72] to grow marijuana for recreational purposes, while all adults age 21 and older will be allowed to grow their own plants 18 months after retail sales begin in the state.[73] Recreational marijuana legalization initiatives also specify that many activities involving marijuana remain crimes. For example, in most states that have legalized recreational marijuana, it remains illegal to consume marijuana in a public place.

Decriminalization

Marijuana *decriminalization* differs markedly from *legalization*. A state decriminalizes conduct by lowering (e.g., making it a low-level misdemeanor with no possibility of jail time) or removing the accompanying criminal penalties; however, civil penalties may remain. If, for instance, a state decriminalizes the possession of marijuana in small amounts,[74] possession of it may still violate state law, but possession of quantities within the specified *small amount* may be considered a civil offense and subject to a civil penalty (e.g., a civil fine), not criminal prosecution. By decriminalizing possession of marijuana in small amounts, states are *not legalizing* its possession. *Legalizing* possession or other conduct involving marijuana would make that activity legal, or allowable under law, but that is not what decriminalization does. It may remain a low-level misdemeanor, or it may become a civil or local infraction.

Decriminalization initiatives by the states do not appear to be at odds with the CSA because both maintain that possessing marijuana is in violation of the

[71] South Dakota's Constitutional Amendment A would have allowed individuals to grow their own marijuana plants for recreational use, but a circuit court judge ruled the amendment to be unconstitutional. When New York enacts regulations for home grown marijuana plants, individuals in the state will be allowed to grow plants as well. Connecticut will allow for recreational home cultivation beginning July 1, 2023. See Teo Armus, "South Dakota voters said yes to legalizing marijuana. But a judge ruled it's unconstitutional," *The Washington Post*, February 9, 2021; Don Cazentre, *NewYorkUpstate.com*, "Legal marijuana in NY: What you need to know about possession, growing, business opportunities," April 6, 2021; and State of Connecticut, Governor Ned Lamont, *Governor Lamont Signs Bill Legalizing and Safely Regulating Adult-Use Cannabis*, press releases, June 22, 2021.

[72] In order to meet state licensing requirements, farmers must have been growing hemp for at least two of the previous four years. See NY S.B. 8084.

[73] See Marijuana regulation and taxation act, 2021, NY S.B. 854.

[74] Typically one ounce or less, but the amount varies from state to state.

law. For example, individuals in possession of one ounce or less of marijuana in Nebraska are in violation of both the CSA and Nebraska state law. The difference lies in the associated penalties for these federal and state violations. Under the CSA, a person convicted of simple possession (first offense) of marijuana may be punished with up to one year imprisonment and/or fined not more than $1,000.[75] Under Nebraska state law, a person in possession (first offense) of an ounce or less of marijuana is subject to a civil penalty of not more than $300.[76]

Decriminalization in Cities

Just as there are disparities between state and federal marijuana laws and policies, some cities' decriminalization initiatives run contrary to the laws and policies of their states. Several cities have by law or policy decriminalized marijuana possession independent of what has occurred at the state level. For example, in November 2014, prior to New York State's decriminalization of marijuana possession in 2019, former New York City (NYC) Mayor de Blasio and former-NYC Police Commissioner Bratton announced a change in marijuana enforcement policy; individuals found to be in possession of 25 grams or less of marijuana[77] may have been eligible to receive a summons instead of being arrested.[78]

In Pennsylvania, the state government has not decriminalized marijuana possession,[79] but Pittsburgh, Philadelphia, State College, Harrisburg and other cities in Pennsylvania have all decriminalized possession in some form. For example, in 2016 Harrisburg's city council unanimously voted to make possession of 30 grams or less of marijuana punishable by a $75 fine and public use punishable by a $150 fine.[80]

---

[75] 21 U.S.C. §844.

[76] Also, the judge may order the offender to attend a drug use and abuse education course. See Section 28-416 of the Nebraska Revised Statutes.

[77] Under NY Pen. Law Section 221.10 in 2014, a person was guilty of criminal possession of marijuana in the fifth degree when he knowingly and unlawfully possessed "1. marihuana in a public place ... and such marihuana is burning or open to public view; or 2. one or more preparations, compounds, mixtures or substances containing marihuana and... are of an aggregate weight of more than twenty-five grams."

[78] City of New York, *Transcript: Mayor de Blasio, Police Commissioner Bratton Announce Change in Marijuana Policy*, November 10, 2014.

[79] Under Pennsylvania state law, the possession of 30 grams or less of marijuana is a misdemeanor offense punishable by 30 days in jail and/or a $500 fine.

[80] Christine Vendel, "It's official: Harrisburg council reduces penalties for pot possession," *Penn Live*, July 5, 2016; and City of Harrisburg, City Council.

Marijuana as Medicine and Federal Involvement

During the past 25 years, there have been significant policy shifts at the state level to allow certain patients to obtain marijuana for medicinal purposes. However, the federal government does not recognize marijuana as having any currently accepted medical use, and it continues to be listed on Schedule I under the CSA. Under federal law, a drug must be approved by the Food and Drug Administration (FDA) before it may be marketed in the United States. To date, FDA has not approved a marketing application for marijuana for the treatment of any condition. However, FDA has approved one marijuana-derived drug and three marijuana-related drugs that are available by prescription. Epidiolex, which contains CBD as its active ingredient, is approved for the treatment of seizures associated with two rare and severe forms of epilepsy. It is the first (and only) FDA-approved drug containing a purified drug substance derived from marijuana.[81] Following its approval, DEA issued an order placing FDA-approved drugs that contain cannabis-derived CBD with no more than 0.1% THC on Schedule V of the CSA, and in April 2020 DEA notified GW Pharmaceuticals that Epidiolex is no longer subject to the CSA.[82] FDA has also approved two drugs containing synthetic THC (i.e., Marinol [and its generic versions] and Syndros) and one drug containing a synthetic substance that is structurally similar to THC but not present in marijuana (i.e., Cesamet). These products are used to treat nausea and vomiting caused by chemotherapy as well as loss of appetite for individuals with human immunodeficiency virus (HIV). Additional drugs containing marijuana-derived THC and CBD are reportedly being developed (see Appendix B for further discussion).[83]

---

[81] The U.S. Food and Drug Administration (FDA), "FDA approves first drug comprised of an active ingredient derived from marijuana to treat rare, severe forms of epilepsy," June 25, 2018, https://www.fda.gov/newsevents/newsroom/ pressannouncements/ucm611046.htm.

[82] DOJ, DEA, "Schedules of Controlled Substances: Placement in Schedule V of Certain FDA-Approved Drugs Containing Cannabidiol; Corresponding Change to Permit Requirements," 83 *Federal Register* 48950, September 28, 2018; GW Pharmaceuticals, *GW Pharmaceuticals plc and Its U.S. Subsidiary Greenwich Biosciences, Inc. Announce That EPIDIOLEX® (cannabidiol) Oral Solution Has Been Descheduled And Is No Longer A Controlled Substance*, press release, April 6, 2020, https://ir.gwpharm.com/news-releases/news-release-details/gw-pharmaceuticals-plc-and- its-us-subsidiary-greenwich-1.

[83] National Institutes of Health (NIH), National Library of Medicine, Clinicaltrials.gov, accessed January 13, 2022, https://clinicaltrials.gov/ct2/results?cond=&term=Cannabidiol &cntry=&state=&city=&dist=.

Although FDA has approved only one marijuana-derived drug and three marijuana-related drugs for specific purposes, some states allow for dispensing of marijuana for a wide range of medical conditions. To date, there is insufficient scientific evidence to support claims of the effectiveness of marijuana for treating many of these conditions. In 2017, the National Academies of Sciences, Engineering, and Medicine (NASEM) issued a report evaluating the use of cannabis and its constituent substances for various diseases and conditions (for more information about the report, see Appendix C). In general, the NASEM found conclusive or substantial evidence that cannabis or cannabinoids (but not necessarily marijuana or marijuana-derived cannabinoids) are an effective treatment for chronic pain, chemotherapy-induced nausea and vomiting, and self-reported symptoms of spasticity (i.e., intermittent or constant involuntary muscle movement) among patients with multiple sclerosis. However, for the remaining conditions examined, the NASEM found insufficient or no evidence of potential therapeutic effects of cannabis or cannabinoids.

Randomized controlled trials (RCTs) are considered the gold standard of clinical and epidemiologic research to determine if a proposed treatment (e.g., marijuana) is more effective than an existing treatment or no treatment (i.e., placebo). As of January 2022, a database maintained by the National Library of Medicine (NLM) at the National Institutes of Health (NIH) lists numerous domestic and international RCTs involving cannabinoids—including THC and CBD—derived from marijuana as treatment for a variety of conditions, including Amyotrophic Lateral Sclerosis (ALS), pain, and schizophrenia.[84] However, much of this research is in its nascent stages; therefore, conclusive evidence on the use of marijuana to treat various health conditions will likely not be available for some time. There are also still many unknowns regarding *how* marijuana would be used as a medical treatment if approved, including the individual and combined clinical benefits of THC, CBD, and other cannabinoids; proper dosage; and effects of different routes of administration, among others.[85] In addition, the short- and long-term health effects of marijuana use are also largely unknown, in part due to the challenges of researching marijuana in the United States.[86]

---

[84] See NIH's database at https://clinicaltrials.gov/ct2/home (accessed January 13, 2022).

[85] National Academies of Sciences, Engineering, and Medicine (NASEM), *The Health Effects of Cannabis and Cannabinoids: The Current State of Evidence and Recommendations for Research*, Washington, DC, 2017, doi: 10.17226/24625, p. 396.

[86] The Schedule I status of marijuana has reportedly created difficulty for researchers who seek to study marijuana but are potentially unable to meet the strict requirements of the CSA or

Federal Regulation of Marijuana Research

Conducting research with marijuana involves several federal agencies: DEA, FDA, and the National Institute on Drug Abuse (NIDA), which is housed within NIH. Before conducting research with marijuana, an investigator must obtain a DEA registration,[87] an FDA review of an investigational new drug application (IND) or research protocol, and marijuana from NIDA or another DEA-registered source.[88] The U.S. Department of Health and Human Services (HHS) has issued guidance to aid researchers in conducting medical research on marijuana in compliance with DEA, FDA, and NIDA requirements if the researcher chooses to obtain their marijuana through NIDA's Drug Supply Program (DSP).[89] For all controlled substances, researchers must obtain a registration issued by the Attorney General (DEA, by delegation of authority),[90] in accordance with relevant federal law and regulations.[91] Among other requirements, DEA and FDA regulations require registrants to comply with strict storage requirements for controlled substances.[92] CSA

seek a different strain, potency, or quality of marijuana for their research than what is lawfully available. See Heike Newman, "Cannabis Clinical Investigations in Colorado 2019," *Food and Drug Law Institute*, July/August 2019; L. Sanders, "The CBD Boom is Way Ahead of the Science," *Science News*, March 27, 2019; and NASEM, *The Health Effects of Cannabis and Cannabinoids: The Current State of Evidence and Recommendations for Research*, Washington, DC, 2017, doi: 10.17226/24625, p. 396.

[87] A separate, additional registration is needed for Schedule I substances.

[88] As of April 1, 2022, there are five federally registered manufacturers of marijuana.

[89] DEA has registered additional marijuana growers outside of NIDA's DSP, and researchers will have options beyond what is available through the DSP. See DOJ, DEA, "Controls To Enhance the Cultivation of Marihuana for Research in the United States," 85 *Federal Register* 82333-82355, December 18, 2020; and NIH, "Announcement for the Department of Health and Human Services' Guidance on Procedures for the Provision of Marijuana for Medical Research," May 1999, https://grants.nih.gov/grants/guide/notice-files/not99-091.html. For regulatory requirements under the CSA, see CRS Report R45948, *The Controlled Substances Act (CSA): A Legal Overview for the 117th Congress*.

[90] As authorized under 21 U.S.C. Section 871, the Attorney General may delegate any of his/her control and enforcement functions under the CSA to any DOJ officer or employee—many of these functions are performed by DEA.

[91] See 21 U.S.C. §822. This requirement is also described under 21 C.F.R. Section 1301.11(a): "Every person who manufactures, distributes, dispenses, imports, or exports any controlled substance or who proposes to engage in the manufacture, distribution, dispensing, importation or exportation of any controlled substance shall obtain a registration unless exempted by law or pursuant to §§1301.22 through 1301.26."

[92] For the purposes of ensuring the secure storage and distribution of *all* controlled substances, all applicants and registrants must generally "provide effective controls and procedures to guard against theft and diversion of controlled substances." See 21 C.F.R. §1301.71. FDA's investigational new drug regulations provide that if the investigational drug is a controlled substance, the investigator must take adequate precautions, including proper storage of the drug "to prevent theft or diversion of the substance into illegal channels of distribution." See 21 C.F.R. §312.69.

requirements are most stringent for Schedule I substances (these requirements are discussed further in Appendix B). In addition to federal requirements, some states require researchers to comply with state-specific medical or government requirements to conduct clinical trials or other activities involving Schedule I substances.[93]

To obtain a DEA registration for purposes of conducting research with a Schedule I controlled substance (e.g., marijuana), the applicant must submit to DEA a protocol containing specified information, including a description of the planned research and information about the quantity of the substance to be used for it.[94] DEA must process the registration application and research protocol and forward a copy of each to the HHS Secretary (FDA, by delegation of authority) within seven days of receipt. If the Schedule I controlled substance is intended to be studied in human clinical trials, the researcher must obtain a pre-IND number from FDA, submit the IND to FDA, and certify to DEA that the IND has been submitted to FDA.[95] An IND must include information about the proposed clinical study design, completed animal test data, and the lead investigator's qualifications, among other things.[96] For INDs concerning Schedule I controlled substances, FDA is required, within 30 days of receipt, to review and comment on the scientific merit of the studies and qualifications of the investigators conducting the research and to report this information to DEA.[97] For a research protocol, FDA must provide this information to DEA within 21 days of receipt of the protocol.[98]

If FDA determines that the applicant is qualified and competent and the research protocol is meritorious, it notifies DEA of such determination. If FDA determines that the protocol is not meritorious and/or the applicant is not qualified or competent, it must notify DEA of this determination and provide the reasons for it.[99] DEA is required to issue a certificate of registration within 10 days of receiving FDA's notice, unless DEA determines that the certificate

---

[93] NASEM, *The Health Effects of Cannabis and Cannabinoids: The Current State of Evidence and Recommendations for Research*, Washington, DC, 2017, doi: 10.17226/24625, p. 380.

[94] 21 C.F.R. §1301.18.

[95] NIH, "Announcement for the Department of Health and Human Services' Guidance on Procedures for the Provision of Marijuana for Medical Research," May 1999, https://grants.nih.gov/grants/guide/notice-files/not99-091.html.

[96] 21 C.F.R. Part 312.

[97] 21 C.F.R. §1301.32(a).

[98] Ibid.

[99] 21 C.F.R. §1301.32(c).

should be denied.[100] DEA makes the final determination on approving research using Schedule I substances and drugs.[101]

Researchers should soon be able to acquire marijuana for research through DEA and its registered marijuana growers. Currently, researchers may only gain access to marijuana through NIDA. If researchers continue to access marijuana through NIDA, they must comply with NIH requirements. NIDA supplies researchers with marijuana from the National Center for Natural Products Research at the University of Mississippi, which has a contract with NIDA. This was the only official source in the United States through which researchers could obtain marijuana for research purposes for over 50 years.[102] Researchers who seek to use this source need to make an inquiry to NIDA to determine availability and associated costs. If NIDA determines that marijuana is available for the researcher's study, it will provide the researcher with a letter of authorization (LOA) to reference NIDA's marijuana Drug Master File (DMF) on file with FDA.[103] As of April 1, 2022, DEA has five registered manufacturers of marijuana. According to DEA, researchers will be able to obtain marijuana from these growers with minimal DEA involvement.[104]

Some researchers have argued that the federal regulations that guide marijuana research unnecessarily impede its advancement.[105] DOJ and HHS have taken some steps to make marijuana research easier, including the following:

- In June 2015, HHS eliminated one step in obtaining research-grade marijuana for research that is not funded by NIH. HHS eliminated the Public Health Service review of non-federally funded research

---

[100] 21 C.F.R. §1301.32(b).

[101] 21 C.F.R. §1301.32; and FDA Manual of Policies and Procedures MAPP 4200.1, "Consulting the Controlled Substance Staff on INDs and Protocols That Use Schedule I Controlled Substances and Drugs," https://www.fda.gov/media/71646/download.

[102] NIDA, "NIDA's Role in Providing Marijuana for Research," https://www.drugabuse.gov/drugs-abuse/marijuana/ nidas-role-in-providing-marijuana-research.

[103] A DMF is a submission to FDA "that may be used to provide confidential detailed information about facilities, processes, or articles used in the manufacturing, processing, packaging, and storing of one or more human drugs." See FDA, "Drug Master Files (DMFs)," https://www.fda.gov/drugs/forms-submission-requirements/drug-master-files- dmfs.

[104] See DOJ, DEA, "Controls To Enhance the Cultivation of Marihuana for Research in the United States," 85 *Federal Register* 82340, December 18, 2020.

[105] See NASEM, *The Health Effects of Cannabis and Cannabinoids: The Current State of Evidence and Recommendations for Research*, Washington, DC, 2017, doi: 10.17226/24625, p. 382; and Pet. for Writ of Mandamus at 13, In re Scottsdale Research Inst., No. 19-1120 (D.C. Cir. June 6, 2019).

protocols involving marijuana and the utilization of the existing FDA IND process for drug development.[106]

- In December 2015, DEA announced a waiver to make it easier for researchers conducting clinical trials with CBD to modify their research protocols and obtain more CBD than was initially approved.[107]
- In August 2016, DEA announced a new policy intended to increase the number of approved sources of research-grade marijuana.[108]
- In August 2019, former Attorney General Barr announced that DEA is "moving forward with its review of applications for those who seek to grow marijuana legally to support research."[109]
- In December 2020, DEA published a final rule that, among other things, requires all registered manufacturers who cultivate marijuana (for research purposes only) "to deliver"[110] their total crops to DEA with limited exception; however, the crops may remain at the manufacturers' registered locations. DEA is to purchase and take possession of such crops (not later than four months after harvest ends) by designating a secure storage mechanism at the registered location and controlling access to the marijuana.[111]

Some have contended that marijuana provided to researchers is "both qualitatively and quantitatively inadequate."[112] DEA's addition of new manufacturers of marijuana may lead to better quality and a sufficient quantity

---

[106] HHS, "Announcement of Revision to the Department of Health and Human Services Guidance on Procedures for the Provision of Marijuana for Medical Research as Published on May 21, 1999," 80 *Federal Register* 35960-35961, June 23, 2015.

[107] DOJ, DEA, "DEA Eases Requirements for FDA-Approved Clinical Trials on Cannabidiol," press release, December 23, 2015.

[108] DOJ, DEA, "Applications to Become Registered under the Controlled Substances Act to Manufacture Marijuana to Supply Researchers in the U.S.," 81 *Federal Register* 53846-53848, August 12, 2016.

[109] DOJ, DEA, *DEA announces steps necessary to improve access to marijuana research*, press release, August 25, 2019, https://www.dea.gov/press-releases.

[110] The marijuana is not technically delivered to DEA but rather DEA travels to the manufacturer and accepts delivery at the manufacturer's registered location, where DEA will maintain possession or designate a different location if adequate storage does not exist at the manufacturer's registered location.

[111] DOJ, DEA, "Controls To Enhance the Cultivation of Marihuana for Research in the United States," 85 *Federal Register* 82333-82355, December 18, 2020.

[112] Marc Kaufman, "Federal Marijuana Monopoly Challenged," *Washington Post*, December 12, 2005; and DOJ, DEA, "Lyle E. Craker; Denial of Application," 74 *Federal Register* 2101, January 14, 2009.

of marijuana for research purposes. As of April 1, 2022, DEA has five registered marijuana growers listed on their website.[113] (For further discussion of the marijuana supply policy issue, see Appendix B.)

Exemption of Hemp from the CSA and Implications for Hemp and CBD Oil

From 1970 until 2018, the federal government's definition of marijuana included hemp and its derivatives, and widespread hemp production was generally prohibited. In 2018, Congress amended the definition to reflect the differences in the chemical and psychoactive properties between hemp and marijuana.

Distinguishing between Hemp and Marijuana Plants for Law Enforcement Purposes

It is difficult for law enforcement to distinguish between hemp and marijuana plants—both are cannabis plants, but hemp is defined in statute as containing no more than 0.3% delta-9-THC. These plants look, smell, and feel the same. Drug-sniffing dogs are unable to distinguish between them.[114]

While a binary roadside test is available to U.S. law enforcement[115] to help determine the nature of a product (i.e., whether it is hemp or marijuana), a roadside test that gives the exact percentage of THC is not yet available.[116] These precision tests must currently be conducted in a laboratory.

---

113 DOJ, DEA, Diversion Control Division, *Marihuana Growers Information*, https://www.deadiversion.usdoj.gov/ drugreg/marihuana.htm.

114 Debra Cassens Weiss, "New Hemp Laws Leave Police and Prosecutors Dazed and Confused," *ABA Journal*, August 9, 2019.

115 The test turns one color when detecting products with a higher concentration of THC and another color if the product has low THC. Jodie Fleischer, Katie Leslie, and Steve Jones et al., "New Police Drug Test Aims to Tell Pot From CBD," *NBC Washington*, July 18, 2019; and CRS correspondence with DEA, July 9, 2019.

116 New field tests with more precision are in development. See, for example, Olga Kuchment, "Is it hemp or marijuana? Scanning technology may provide an instant answer," *AgriLife Today*, February 10, 2020.

Change to CSA Definition of Marijuana

The 2018 farm bill (P.L. 115-334) amended the CSA to exclude hemp—plant material that contains no more than 0.3% delta-9 THC on a dry weight basis[117]—from the statutory definition of marijuana.[118] This provision allows for the cultivation of hemp and hemp-derived products at or below the 0.3% delta-9 THC threshold,[119] as defined in statute, from being regulated as a Schedule I controlled substance. A DEA registration is no longer required to cultivate or research hemp and hemp-derived products; however, hemp remains subject to U.S. Department of Agriculture (USDA) regulation. Further, it remains subject to DEA scrutiny due to the nature of cannabis and methods of production.[120] Changes enacted in the 2018 farm bill now allow for the cultivation, processing, marketing, and sale of hemp and hemp-derived products that meet the statutory definition of hemp—if it is produced by an authorized grower in accordance with the 2018 farm bill, associated federal USDA regulations, and applicable state regulations.[121] (See Appendix D for further information regarding federal regulation of hemp production).

---

[117] *Dry weight basis* means the weight of the material after it has been dried at high temperature (generally until reaching a constant mass).

[118] For the CSA definition of *marijuana*, see 21 U.S.C. §802(16).

[119] While Epidiolex—a marijuana-derived drug—contains less than 0.3% delta-9 THC, it was approved and placed in Schedule V prior to the enactment of the 2018 farm bill (i.e., prior to the change in the statutory definition of marijuana). As such, despite meeting the current statutory definition of *hemp* in 7 U.S.C. Section 1639o, it remains in Schedule V. 83 *Federal Register* 48950, September 28, 2018.

[120] Remaining concerns for farmers and manufacturers of hemp and CBD products are accidental growth of marijuana plants instead of hemp plants and the THC level changes (sometimes over the 0.3% threshold) during the manufacturing process. In August 2020, DEA issued an interim final rule to formally provide in their regulations the scope of DEA regulatory controls over marijuana, THC, and other marijuana-related constituents and acknowledge the change to the CSA definition of marijuana to exclude hemp and its constituents. See DOJ, DEA, "Implementation of the Agriculture Improvement Act of 2018," 85 *Federal Register* 51639-51645, August 21, 2020.

[121] Regulatory plans involving hemp under the oversight of states and tribes will need to include the following requirements: maintenance of relevant production information; THC testing; procedures for disposal of plants (and products from those plants) that exceed hemp THC levels; procedures to comply with USDA's enforcement provisions; procedures for conducting random, annual inspections of hemp producers; procedures for submitting hemp production information to USDA; and certification by state and tribal regulators that they have adequate resources and personnel to implement required procedures.

Marijuana's Status Moving Forward

Over the years, several entities have submitted petitions to DEA to reschedule marijuana.[122] In August 2016, after a five-year evaluation process done in conjunction with FDA, DEA rejected two petitions, one submitted by two state governors and a second submitted by a New Mexico health provider, to move marijuana to a less-restrictive schedule under the CSA.[123] Consistent with past practice,[124] the rejections were based on a conclusion by both FDA and DEA that marijuana continues to meet the criteria for inclusion on Schedule I—namely that it has a high potential for abuse, has no currently accepted medical use, and lacks an accepted level of safety for use, even under medical supervision.[125]

Congress (through legislation and hearings) has also demonstrated interest in altering the schedule status of marijuana. In recent years, Members of Congress have introduced various bills that would change the Schedule I status of marijuana. In the 116th and 117th Congress, for instance, the House passed the Marijuana Opportunity Reinvestment and Expungement Act of 2019 (MORE Act; H.R. 3884) and the MORE Act of 2021 (H.R. 3617), respectively. The MORE Act (both H.R. 3884 from the 116th Congress and H.R. 3617 from the 117th Congress) would remove marijuana from CSA control entirely, among other things. The Senate did not vote on the MORE Act in the 116th Congress, and as of April 1, 2022, it has not taken up H.R. 3617. Several other bills that would deschedule or alter the Schedule I status of marijuana have been introduced in the 117th Congress.

122 Any interested party may petition the Administrator of DEA to initiate rulemaking proceedings to reschedule a controlled substance. See 21 U.S.C. Section 811(a) and 21 C.F.R. Section 1308.43(a) for relevant rules and regulations.

123 In 2011, the governors of Rhode Island and Washington jointly petitioned DEA to have marijuana and "related items" removed from Schedule I of the CSA and rescheduled as medical cannabis in Schedule II. In 2009, Bryan Krumm, a health provider in New Mexico, petitioned DEA to have marijuana removed from Schedule I of the CSA and rescheduled in any schedule other than Schedule I.

124 DEA has previously denied petitions to reschedule marijuana. For example, in 2002 a petition was filed to have marijuana removed from Schedule I and rescheduled as cannabis in Schedule III, IV, or V. In 2011, DEA rejected the petition. See DOJ, DEA, "Denial of Petition to Initiate Proceedings to Reschedule Marijuana," 76 *Federal Register* 40552-40589, July 8, 2011.

125 See DOJ, DEA, "Denial of Petition to Initiate Proceedings to Reschedule Marijuana," 81 *Federal Register* 53767- 53845, August 12, 2016; and DOJ, DEA, "Denial of Petition to Initiate Proceedings to Reschedule Marijuana," 81 *Federal Register* 53687-53766, August 12, 2016.

Federal Response to State Divergence

Although state laws do not affect the status of marijuana under federal law or the ability of federal law enforcement to enforce it, state legalization initiatives have spurred a number of questions regarding potential implications for federal laws and policies, including federal drug regulation and enforcement, and banking for marijuana businesses. Thus far, the federal response to states' decriminalizing or legalizing marijuana largely has been to allow states to implement their own laws on the drug. DOJ has nonetheless reaffirmed that marijuana growth, possession, and trafficking remain crimes under federal law irrespective of states' marijuana laws. Federal law enforcement has generally focused its efforts on criminal networks involved in the illicit marijuana trade. Federal banking regulators have yet to issue any formal guidance in response to state and local marijuana legalization efforts; however, in February 2014 the Treasury Department's Financial Crimes Enforcement Network (FinCEN) issued guidance on financial institutions' suspicious activity report requirements when serving marijuana businesses.

Federalism: Federal Preemption and the Anti-Commandeering Doctrine[126]

The gap between the federal CSA,[127] which criminalizes the cultivation, distribution, and possession of marijuana, and certain state marijuana laws, which authorize some of those same activities, raises questions regarding "the proper division of authority between the Federal Government and the States"[128] under both the preemption and anti-commandeering doctrines. The Supremacy Clause of the U.S. Constitution generally establishes that federal law is supreme to, and may preempt, conflicting state laws.[129] However, the federal government's preemptive authority is subject to certain limitations, including the anti-commandeering doctrine, which generally prohibits the federal government from forcing states to perform regulatory activities on the

---

[126] This section was authored by David H. Carpenter, Legislative Attorney in CRS's American Law Division (ALD). It uses citation and other editorial styles consistent with ALD's reports.

[127] Comprehensive Drug Abuse Prevention and Control Act of 1970, Pub. L. No. 91-513, Title II, 84 Stat. 1236, 1242 (codified as amended at 21 U.S.C. §§ 801–904).

[128] New York v. United States, 505 U.S. 144, 149 (1992).

[129] U.S. CONST. art. VI, cl. 2.

federal government's behalf.[130] See Appendix E for a comprehensive legal discussion of the federal preemption and anti-commandeering doctrines, and how the courts have handled the conflict between federal CSA and state marijuana laws.

Enforcement Focused on Traffickers

Federal law enforcement generally focuses its counterdrug efforts on criminal networks involved in the illicit drug trade. Federal marijuana enforcement efforts, largely focused on *traffickers and distributors* of marijuana rather than users, appear to be consistent with this position.[131] Arrests for marijuana possession offenses are largely made by state and local police.[132] President Barack Obama once noted that "[it] would not make sense from a prioritization point of view for us to focus on recreational drug users in a state that has already said that under state law that's legal."[133] Officials in the Trump Administration also indicated that prosecuting traffickers over users was a priority; and while there was some uncertainty about the future of marijuana policy under the Trump Administration, then-Attorney General Sessions noted that federal law enforcement would continue to focus their marijuana-related enforcement efforts on criminal organizations over "routine cases."[134]

---

[130] Murphy v. NCAA, 138 S. Ct. 1461, 1476 (2019) ("The legislative powers granted to Congress are sizable, but they are not unlimited. The Constitution confers on Congress not plenary legislative power but only certain enumerated powers. Therefore, all other legislative power is reserved for the States, as the Tenth Amendment confirms. And conspicuously absent from the list of powers given to Congress is the power to issue direct orders to the governments of the States. The anticommandeering doctrine simply represents the recognition of this limit on congressional authority.").

[131] DEA's mission "is to enforce the controlled substances laws and regulations of the United States and bring to the criminal and civil justice system of the United States, or any other competent jurisdiction, those organizations and principal members of organizations, involved in the growing, manufacture, or distribution of controlled substances appearing in or destined for illicit traffic in the United States; and to recommend and support non-enforcement programs aimed at reducing the availability of illicit controlled substances on the domestic and international markets." See https://www.dea.gov/mission.

[132] In 2015, the Government Accountability Office concluded that DOJ has not historically targeted possession of small amounts of marijuana for personal use on private property, and has left lower-level marijuana activity to state and local law enforcement authorities through enforcement of their own drug laws. See U.S. Government Accountability Office (GAO), *State Marijuana Legalization: DOJ Should Document Its Approach to Monitoring the Effects of Legalization*, GAO-16-1, December 2015, p. 9.

[133] "Marijuana Not High Obama Priority," *ABC Nightline*, December 14, 2012.

[134] Remarks by Attorney General Jeff Sessions at a Georgetown Law student symposium hosted by the Federalist Society, March 10, 2018, https://www.c-span.org/video/?442403-

Similarly, then-Attorney General Barr noted he would continue to "prioritize the prosecution of significant drug traffickers, rather than drug users or low-level drug offenders."[135] During his 2021 Senate confirmation hearing, Attorney General Garland indicated that the Biden Administration will maintain this position.[136]

Department of Justice Guidance Memos for U.S. Attorneys

DOJ has articulated federal marijuana enforcement policy through several memoranda providing direction for U.S. Attorneys in states that have medical use of marijuana programs. After states began to legalize the medical use of marijuana, DOJ reaffirmed that marijuana growth, possession, and trafficking remain crimes under federal law irrespective of state law.[137] In 2009, former Deputy Attorney General David Ogden authored a memo for selected U.S. Attorneys that reiterated that combating major drug traffickers remains a central priority and stated

> [t]he prosecution of significant traffickers of illegal drugs, including marijuana, and the disruption of illegal drug manufacturing and trafficking networks continues to be a core priority in the [Justice] Department's efforts against narcotics and dangerous drugs, and the Department's investigative and prosecutorial resources should be directed towards these objectives. As a general matter, pursuit of these priorities should not focus federal resources in your States on individuals whose actions are in clear and unambiguous compliance with existing state laws providing for the medical use of marijuana.[138]

In a follow-up memorandum to U.S. Attorneys in 2011, former Deputy Attorney General James Cole restated that enforcing the CSA remained a core

---

1/attorney-general-jeff-sessions-judicial-authority. He stated that federal law enforcement would not be able to, even if it wished to, take over "state enforcement of routine [marijuana] cases."

[135] William P. Barr, "Questions for the Record, William P. Barr, Nominee to be United States Attorney General," January 27, 2019.

[136] U.S. Congress, Senate Committee on the Judiciary, *The Nomination of the Honorable Merrick Brian Garland to be Attorney General of the United States: Responses to Questions for the Record to Judge Merrick Garland, Nominee to be United States Attorney General*, 117th Cong., 1st sess., February 2021, pp. 23-25.

[137] United States Attorney's Office, "Statement From U.S. Attorney's Office on Initiative 502," press release, December 5, 2012.

[138] Deputy Attorney General David W. Ogden, *Memorandum for Selected United States Attorneys*, U.S. Department of Justice, Investigations and Prosecutions in States Authorizing the Medical Use of Marijuana, Washington, DC, October 19, 2009, pp. 1-2.

priority of DOJ, even in states that had legalized medical marijuana. He clarified that "[t]he Ogden Memorandum was never intended to shield such activities from federal enforcement action and prosecution, even where those activities purport to comply with state law."[139] Deputy Attorney General Cole warned those who might assist medical marijuana dispensaries in any way that "[p]ersons who are in the business of cultivating, selling or distributing marijuana, *and those who knowingly facilitate such activities* [emphasis added], are in violation of the Controlled Substances Act, regardless of state law."[140] This has been interpreted by some to mean, for example, that building owners and managers are in violation of the CSA if they allow medical marijuana dispensaries to operate in their buildings.[141] Deputy Attorney General Cole further warned that "[t]hose who engage in transactions involving the proceeds of such activity [cultivating, selling, or distributing of marijuana] may be in violation of federal money laundering statutes and other federal financial laws."[142]

In an August 2013 memorandum (the Cole memorandum), Deputy Attorney General Cole stated that while marijuana remains an illegal substance under the CSA, DOJ would focus its resources on the "most significant threats in the most effective, consistent, and rational way," and outlined eight marijuana enforcement priorities for DOJ:[143]

- preventing the distribution of marijuana to minors;
- preventing revenue from the sale of marijuana from going to criminal enterprises, gangs, and cartels;
- preventing the diversion of marijuana from states where it is legal under state law in some form to other states;
- preventing state-authorized marijuana activity from being used as a cover or pretext for the trafficking of other illegal drugs or other illegal activity;

---

139 Deputy Attorney General James M. Cole, *Memorandum for United States Attorneys*, U.S. Department of Justice, Guidance Regarding the Ogden Memo in Jurisdictions Seeking to Authorize Marijuana for Medical Use, Washington, DC, June 29, 2011, p. 2.

140 Ibid.

141 Jennifer Medina, "U.S. Attorneys in California Set Crackdown on Marijuana," *New York Times*, October 8, 2011, p. 10.

142 Deputy Attorney General James M. Cole, *Memorandum for United States Attorneys*, U.S. Department of Justice, Guidance Regarding the Ogden Memo in Jurisdictions Seeking to Authorize Marijuana for Medical Use, Washington, DC, June 29, 2011, p. 2.

143 Deputy Attorney General James M. Cole, *Memorandum for all United States Attorneys*, U.S. Department of Justice, Guidance Regarding Marijuana Enforcement, Washington, DC, August 29, 2013, p. 1.

- preventing violence and the use of firearms in the cultivation and distribution of marijuana;
- preventing drugged driving and the exacerbation of other adverse public health consequences associated with marijuana use;
- preventing the growing of marijuana on public lands and the attendant public safety and environmental dangers posed by marijuana production on public lands; and
- preventing marijuana possession or use on federal property.[144]

In a February 2014 memorandum, Deputy Attorney General Cole further reinforced these enforcement priorities, specifically as they related to the prosecution of marijuana-related financial crimes. This memorandum directed the U.S. Attorneys that "in determining whether to charge individuals or institutions with ... [certain financial] offenses based on marijuana-related violations of the CSA, prosecutors should apply the eight enforcement priorities described in the August 29 guidance."[145]

In October 2014, DOJ released another memorandum to the U.S. Attorneys that asserted the applicability of the eight enforcement priorities in Indian Country.[146] It responded to the tribes' requests for guidance on CSA enforcement on tribal lands. DOJ reiterated that the 2013 Cole memorandum did not prohibit the federal government from enforcing federal law in Indian Country, and added the following:

> The eight priorities in the Cole Memorandum will guide United States Attorneys' marijuana enforcement efforts in Indian Country, including in the event that sovereign Indian Nations seek to legalize the *cultivation or use* of marijuana in Indian Country [emphasis added].[147]

Unlike the Cole memorandum, DOJ did not specifically refer to *distribution* and regulation of marijuana. It was unclear whether distribution of marijuana would be tolerated on tribal lands should tribal governments seek

---

[144] Ibid., pp. 1-2.

[145] Deputy Attorney General James M. Cole, *Memorandum for All United States Attorneys*, U.S. Department of Justice, Guidance Regarding Marijuana Related Financial Crimes, Washington, DC, February 14, 2014, p. 2.

[146] Executive Office for United States Attorneys, *Policy Statement Regarding Marijuana Issues in Indian Country*, October 28, 2014.

[147] Monty Wilkinson, *Memorandum,* U.S. Department of Justice, Policy Statement Regarding Marijuana Issues in Indian Country, Washington, DC, October 28, 2014.

to legalize and distribute marijuana. Despite the lack of clarity, some tribes moved forward with plans to grow and sell marijuana at tribe-owned stores on tribal lands.[148] Since the memo was released, DEA has led some marijuana enforcement actions on tribal lands involving tribe-authorized marijuana activity.[149]

In January 2018, DOJ issued another memorandum (Sessions memorandum) to the U.S. Attorneys on marijuana enforcement. In it, then-Attorney General Sessions emphasized the CSA prohibition of marijuana cultivation, distribution, and possession and its associated penalties. He also pointed out that these marijuana activities may "serve as the basis for the prosecution of other crimes, such as those prohibited by the money laundering statutes, the unlicensed money transmitter statute, and the Bank Secrecy Act.... [T]hese statutes reflect Congress's determination that marijuana is a dangerous drug and that marijuana activity is a serious crime."[150] Sessions also noted in the memorandum that DOJ had "well-established principles" dating back to 1980 to decide which marijuana activities to prosecute, and because these principles exist, the previous DOJ memoranda were unnecessary and rescinded.[151]

While DOJ has not released additional memoranda on marijuana enforcement since the Sessions memorandum, then-Attorney General Barr indicated his discomfort with "ignoring the enforcement of federal law."[152] On the other hand, Barr also stated during his nomination hearing that he did not

---

[148] "Native American Tribes Approve Plan to Grow and Sell Marijuana in Oregon," *The New York Times*, December 19, 2015; Jackie Valley, "Las Vegas Paiutes' Newest Venture: Medical Marijuana," *Las Vegas Sun*, March 1, 2016; Noelle Crombie, "Warm Springs Tribes Launch Ambitious Pot Venture, Hope for Economic Windfall," *The Oregonian - Oregon Live*, April 29, 2016; John Gillie, "Two Marijuana Retailers Opening Soon in City that Still Bans Cannabis Sales," *The News Tribune*, January 28, 2017; Saint Regis Mohawk Tribal Council, *Tribal Election Board Certifies Medical Marijuana Ordinance and Adult Use (Recreational) Marijuana Referendum Results*, December 23, 2019, https://www.srmt-nsn.gov/; and Dalton Walker, "Red Lake Nation approves medical cannabis," *Red Lake Nation News*, May 29, 2020.

[149] Steven Nelson, "DEA Raid on Tribe's Cannabis Crop Infuriates and Confuses Reformers," *U.S. News & World Report*, October 26, 2015; and Cary Spivak, "Milwaukee Journal Sentinel," November 18, 2015.

[150] Attorney General Jefferson B. Sessions, *Memorandum for All United States Attorneys*, U.S. Department of Justice, Marijuana Enforcement, Washington, DC, January 4, 2018.

[151] Ibid.

[152] See comments made by former Attorney General Barr in response to questioning from Senator Murkowski, U.S. Congress, Senate Committee on Appropriations, Subcommittee on Commerce, Justice, Science, and Related Agencies, *Hearing to review the Fiscal Year 2020 funding request and budget justification for the U.S. Department of Justice*, 116th Cong., 2nd sess., April 10, 2019.

intend to target marijuana businesses that had relied on the Cole memorandum for guidance.[153] Attorney General Garland stated the following in his official responses to questions from his Senate confirmation hearing: "I do not think it the best use of the Department's [DOJ's] limited resources to pursue prosecutions of those who are complying with the laws in states that have legalized and are effectively regulating marijuana."[154]

Monitoring Enforcement Priorities

In a 2015 review of the DOJ memoranda and evaluation of DOJ efforts to monitor effects of state legalization relative to DOJ guidance (which predated the Sessions memorandum), the Government Accountability Office (GAO) concluded that "DOJ has not historically devoted resources to prosecuting individuals whose conduct is limited to possession of small amounts of marijuana for personal use on private property. Rather, DOJ has left such lower-level or localized marijuana activity to state and local law enforcement authorities through enforcement of their own drug laws."[155] GAO recommended that DOJ monitor the effects of state-level marijuana legalization initiatives relative to the eight DOJ enforcement priorities outlined in the Cole memorandum. GAO's evaluation noted that DOJ was already taking a number of steps to help assess these effects. For instance, DOJ indicated that U.S. Attorneys were in contact with officials in states that had legalized marijuana, and through these interactions could communicate federal enforcement priorities, assess the implications of legalization relative to the priorities, and identify specific areas of federal concern. In addition, DOJ reported that it relies upon information from sources such as "federal surveys on drug use; state and local research; and feedback from federal, state, and local law enforcement" to assess the effects of state-level legalization initiatives.[156] GAO concluded that DOJ had not documented its specific monitoring process, and recommended that DOJ develop a "clear plan" for

---

[153] See comments made by former Attorney General Barr in response to questioning from Senator Booker, U.S. Congress, Senate Committee on the Judiciary, *Nomination of the Honorable William Pelham Barr to be Attorney General of the United States*, 116th Cong., 1st sess., January 15, 2019.

[154] U.S. Congress, Senate Committee on the Judiciary, *The Nomination of the Honorable Merrick Brian Garland to be Attorney General of the United States: Responses to Questions for the Record to Judge Merrick Garland, Nominee to be United States Attorney General*, 117th Cong., 1st sess., February 2021, pp. 23-25.

[155] U.S. Government Accountability Office, *State Marijuana Legalization: DOJ Should Document Its Approach to Monitoring the Effects of Legalization*, GAO-16-1, December 2015, p. 9.

[156] Ibid., p. 27.

how it will monitor and document the effects of state marijuana legalization on federal enforcement priorities.[157] Since the Sessions memorandum rescinded the previous DOJ guidance memos (which included the enforcement priorities GAO focused on), DOJ has not indicated whether it monitors and documents the effects of state marijuana legalization on federal enforcement priorities.

Limiting Federal Enforcement in States: Directives through Federal Appropriations[158]

In each fiscal year since FY2015, Congress has included provisions in appropriations acts that prohibit DOJ from using appropriated funds to prevent certain states and territories and the District of Columbia from "implementing their own laws that authorize the use, distribution, possession, or cultivation of medical marijuana."[159]

On its face, the appropriations rider bars DOJ from taking legal action against the states directly in order to prevent them from promulgating or enforcing medical marijuana laws.[160] In addition, federal courts have interpreted the rider to prohibit certain federal prosecutions of private individuals or organizations that produce, distribute, or possess marijuana in accordance with state medical marijuana laws. In the 2016 case *United States v. McIntosh*, the U.S. Court of Appeals for the Ninth Circuit held that the rider

---

[157] Ibid.

[158] This section was authored by Joanna Lampe, Legislative Attorney in CRS's American Law Division (ALD). It uses citation and other editorial styles consistent with ALD's reports.

[159] *See* Consolidated and Further Continuing Appropriations Act, 2015, P.L. 113-235 (113th Cong. 2014); Consolidated Appropriations Act, 2016, P.L. 114-113 (114th Cong. 2015); Consolidated Appropriations Act, 2017, P.L. 115-31 (115th Cong. 2017); Consolidated Appropriations Act, 2018, P.L. 115-141 (115th Cong. 2018); Consolidated Appropriations Act, 2019, P.L. 116-6 (116th Cong. 2019); Consolidated Appropriations Act, 2020, P.L. 116-93 (116th Cong. 2019); Consolidated Appropriations Act, 2021, P.L. 116-260 (116th Cong. 2020); and Consolidated Appropriations Act, 2022, P.L. 117-103 (117th Cong. 2022) . The FY2022 provision lists 52 jurisdictions, including most of the states, the District of Columbia, the Commonwealth of the Northern Mariana Islands, Guam, Puerto Rico, and the U.S. Virgin Islands. Continuing resolutions used to cover gaps in enacted funding for DOJ have extended the provision. *See, e.g.*, Continuing Appropriations Act, 2021 and Other Extensions Act, P.L. 116-159 (116th Cong. 2020).

[160] *Cf.* United States v. Marin All. for Med. Marijuana, 139 F. Supp. 3d 1039, 1044 (E.D. Cal. 2015) (citing DOJ's interpretation that the appropriations rider prohibits "federal actions that interfere with a state's promulgation of regulations implementing its statutory provisions, or with its establishment of a state licensing scheme").

> prohibits the federal government only from preventing the implementation of those specific rules of state law that authorize the use, distribution, possession, or cultivation of medical marijuana. DOJ does not prevent the implementation of [such rules] when it prosecutes individuals who engage in conduct unauthorized under state medical marijuana laws. Individuals who do not strictly comply with all state-law conditions regarding the use, distribution, possession, and cultivation of medical marijuana have engaged in conduct that is unauthorized, and prosecuting such individuals does not violate [the rider].[161]

The Ninth Circuit has issued several decisions allowing federal prosecution of individuals who did not strictly comply with state medical marijuana laws, notwithstanding the appropriations rider, and several district courts have followed that holding.[162]

In the 2022 case *United States v. Bilodeau*, the U.S. Court of Appeals for the First Circuit agreed with the Ninth Circuit that the rider means "DOJ may not spend funds to bring prosecutions if doing so prevents a state from giving practical effect to its medical marijuana laws."[163] However, the First Circuit declined to adopt the Ninth Circuit's holding that a defendant must demonstrate *strict compliance* with state law before the rider bars prosecution.[164] The First Circuit noted that the text of the rider does not explicitly require strict compliance with state law, and that, given the complexity of state marijuana regulations, "the potential for technical noncompliance [with state law] is real enough that no person through any reasonable effort could always assure strict compliance."[165] Thus, the court concluded that requiring strict compliance with state law would likely chill state-legal medical marijuana activities and prevent the states from giving effect to their medical marijuana laws.[166] The court further held, however, that it would not have any effect on Maine's medical marijuana laws to prosecute "the defendants' cultivation, possession, and distribution of marijuana aimed

---

[161] United States v. McIntosh, 833 F.3d 1163, 1178 (9th Cir. 2016).

[162] United States v. Evans, 929 F.3d 1073, 1078-79 (9th Cir. 2019); United States v. Kleinman, 880 F.3d 1020, 1027-30 (9th Cir. 2017); Duval v. United States, 372 F. Supp. 3d 544, 555-56 (E.D. Mich. 2019); United Sates v. Bloomquist, 361 F. Supp. 3d 744, 749-51 (W.D. Mich. 2019); United States v. Jackson, 2019 WL 3239844 at *6-8 (E.D. Pa. June 5, 2019).

[163] 2022 WL 225333 at *5 (1st Cir. Jan. 26, 2022).

[164] *Id.*

[165] *Id.*

[166] *Id.* While the court held that something less than strict compliance was required to avoid prosecution under the rider, it declined to "fully define [the] precise boundaries" of its alternative standard. *Id.* at *6.

at supplying persons whom no defendant ever thought were qualifying patients under Maine law."[167]

It remains to be seen whether and how the difference in reasoning between the Ninth Circuit and the First Circuit will make a practical difference in federal marijuana prosecutions. In theory, the First Circuit's analysis could make it easier for defendants to invoke the appropriations rider to bar prosecutions. In practice, however, resource limitations and enforcement priorities have historically meant that federal marijuana prosecutions target individuals and organizations that clearly have not complied with state law.[168] Thus, one of the judges in *Bilodeau* agreed with the panel's interpretation of the rider but wrote a concurrence noting that, in practice, the First Circuit's standard might not be "materially different from the one that the Ninth Circuit applied."[169]

Marijuana-related activities that fall outside the scope of the appropriations rider remain subject to prosecution under the CSA.[170] By its terms, the rider applies only to state laws related to *medical* marijuana; it does not bar prosecution of any activities related to recreational marijuana, even if those activities are permitted under state law.[171] In addition, although the appropriations rider restricts DOJ's ability to expend funds to enforce federal law for as long as it remains in effect, the rider "does not provide immunity from prosecution for federal marijuana offenses."[172] Congress could repeal the

---

[167] *Id.* at *6.

[168] *See, e.g.*, *id.* at *9 (Barron, J., concurring).

[169] *Id.*

[170] *Cf.* United States v. Nixon, 839 F.3d 885, 886 (9th Cir. 2016) (per curiam) (holding that the appropriations rider does not "impact[ ] the ability of a federal district court to restrict the use of a medical marijuana as a condition of probation"); Sandusky v. Herrera, 2020 WL 2129212 at *4 (D. Colo. May 5, 2020) (dismissing as moot a habeas claim from an individual subject to supervised release following conviction for a marijuana offense because the U.S. Probation Office is not part of DOJ and "[t]he appropriations rider, by its plain language, does not apply to the federal courts").

[171] In practice, DOJ typically has not prosecuted individuals who possess marijuana for personal use on private property, but instead has "left such lower-level or localized marijuana activity to state and local authorities through enforcement of their own drug laws." U.S. Government Accountability Office, *State Marijuana Legalization: DOJ Should Document Its Approach to Monitoring the Effects of Legalization*, GAO-16-1, 9 (Dec. 2015); *but cf.* Memorandum from Jefferson B. Sessions, Attorney Gen., U.S. Dep't of Justice, on Marijuana Enforcement to all United States Attorneys (Jan. 4, 2018), https://www.justice.gov/opa/press-release/file/1022196/download (reaffirming the authority of federal prosecutors to exercise prosecutorial discretion to target federal marijuana offenses "in accordance with all applicable laws, regulations, and appropriations").

[172] United States v. McIntosh, 833 F.3d 1163, 1179 n.5 (9th Cir. 2016).

rider at any time or could decline to include it in future appropriations laws. If Congress were to repeal the rider or allow it to lapse, DOJ would be able to prosecute future CSA violations as well as violations that occurred while the rider was in effect, subject to the applicable statute of limitations.[173] In the alternative, Congress could expand the scope of the rider to include recreational marijuana or other controlled substances. Regardless of whether they are subject to criminal prosecution, participants in the cannabis industry may face numerous collateral consequences arising from the federal prohibition of marijuana.[174]

Federal Financial Laws and Financial Services for Marijuana Businesses[175]

Because marijuana is a Schedule I controlled substance under the CSA,[176] financial institutions and their directors, officers, employees, and owners might be subject to criminal and administrative sanctions[177] for providing financial services to marijuana businesses, even if those marijuana businesses operate in states that have legalized certain marijuana-related activities.[178]

---

[173] *Id.*

[174] For additional information about the collateral consequences of marijuana-related activities, see the "Marijuana Policy Gap" section of CRS Report R45948, *The Controlled Substances Act (CSA): A Legal Overview for the 117th Congress*, by Joanna R. Lampe.

[175] This section was authored by David H. Carpenter, Legislative Attorney in CRS's American Law Division (ALD). It uses citation and other editorial styles consistent with ALD's reports.

[176] For legal discussion of the CSA, see CRS Report R45948, *The Controlled Substances Act (CSA): A Legal Overview for the 117th Congress*.

[177] *See, e.g.*, United States v. HSBC Bank USA, N.A., No. 12-CR-763, 2013 U.S. Dist. LEXIS 92438, 31–38 (E.D. N.Y. July 1, 2013) (approving a deferred prosecution agreement with a financial institution for, among other things, "fail[ing] to implement an effective [anti-money laundering] program to monitor suspicious transactions ... [which] permitted Mexican and Colombian drug traffickers to launder at least $881 million in drug trafficking proceeds through HSBC Bank USA undetected"; the agreement "imposes upon HSBC significant, and in some respect extraordinary, measures," including forfeiture of $1.256 billion, remedial measures, and the admission of criminal violations).

[178] United States v. McIntosh, 833 F.3d 1163, 1179 n.5 (9th. Cir 2016) ("The prior observation should also serve as a warning. To be clear, § 542 [of the Consolidated Appropriations Act, 2016, Pub. L. No. 114–113, 129 Stat. 2242, 2332–33 (2015)] does not provide immunity from prosecution for federal marijuana offenses. The CSA prohibits the manufacture, distribution, and possession of marijuana. Anyone in any state who possesses, distributes, or manufactures marijuana for medical or recreational purposes (or attempts or conspires to do so) is committing a federal crime. The federal government can prosecute such offenses for up to five years after they occur. *See* 18 U.S.C. § 3282. Congress currently restricts the

Although DOJ and FinCEN have issued guidance on the interplay of federal marijuana laws and discordant state legalization efforts, many financial institutions have been unwilling to provide financial services to state-authorized marijuana businesses because of the legal risks under federal law.[179]

Bank Secrecy Act[180] and Federal Anti-Money Laundering Laws

Financial institutions generally do not sell, possess, or distribute the products or assets of their financial services customers.[181] Consequently, auxiliary liability (e.g., aiding and abetting, conspiracy)[182] aside, financial services institutions generally would not engage directly in actions barred by the CSA. However, financial institutions commonly acquire proceeds generated by their customers' product sales. As described below, financial institutions that acquire proceeds generated by marijuana businesses could be subject to civil and criminal asset forfeiture, prosecution under the Bank Secrecy Act and criminal anti-money laundering laws, and administrative enforcement actions.[183]

---

government from spending certain funds to prosecute certain individuals. But Congress could restore funding tomorrow, a year from now, or four years from now, and the government could then prosecute individuals who committed offenses while the government lacked funding. Moreover, ... a new administration could shift enforcement priorities to place greater emphasis on prosecuting marijuana offenses.").

[179] *See, e.g., Guidance on Provision of Financial Services to Medical Marijuana & Industrial Hemp-Related Businesses in New York State*, N.Y. DEP'T OF FIN. SERVS., 2 (Jul. 3, 2018), https://www.dfs.ny.gov/docs/legal/industry/ il180703.pdf ("Because marijuana currently is still listed on Schedule I under the Federal Controlled Substances Act, medical marijuana ... businesses operating in accordance with New York State laws and regulations continue to have difficulty establishing banking relationships at regulated financial institutions. The ability to establish a banking relationship is an urgent issue today for the legal cannabis industry. So long as it remains difficult to open and maintain bank accounts, the industry will largely rely on cash to conduct business and operate.").

[180] The "Bank Secrecy Act" is commonly used to refer to Titles I and II of Pub. L. No. 91-508 and includes the Currency and Foreign Transactions Reporting Act, Pub. L. No. 91-508, Title II, 84 Stat. 1114, 1118–24 (1970) (as amended and codified at 12 U.S.C. §§ 1829b, 1951–59; 31 U.S.C. §§ 5311–32). The Bank Secrecy Act requires reports and records of transactions involving cash, negotiable instruments, or foreign currency and authorizes the Secretary of the Treasury to prescribe regulations to insure that adequate records are maintained of transactions that have a "high degree of usefulness in criminal, tax, or regulatory investigations or proceedings." *Id.*

[181] Financial institutions do, at times, take legal possession of their clients' assets, such as after a customer defaults on a loan secured by real property or business inventory.

[182] 18 U.S.C. § 2 (aiding and abetting); 21 U.S.C. § 846 (conspiracy under the CSA).

[183] *See, e.g.,* 12 U.S.C. § 1818; 18 U.S.C. § 981(a)(1), 1956, 1957.

Federal law authorizes the seizure of property connected to unlawful marijuana activity through civil and criminal asset forfeiture proceedings. Consequently, federal authorities could potentially confiscate funds a bank acquires from marijuana businesses that are derived from the proceeds of marijuana sales,[184] even if state law permits those sales.[185] For example, if a bank lends to a state-authorized medical marijuana dispensary, federal authorities might be able to require the bank to forfeit loan payments the dispensary makes to the bank on the grounds that such payments can be traced to federally prohibited marijuana sales.[186]

In addition to the risk of asset forfeiture, federal anti-money laundering (AML) laws (i.e., Sections 1956 and 1957 of the criminal code) criminalize the handling of financial proceeds that are known to be derived from certain unlawful activities,[187] including selling and distributing marijuana.[188] Violators of anti-money laundering laws may be subject to fines and imprisonment,[189] and any real or personal property involved in or traceable to prohibited transactions is potentially subject to civil or criminal forfeiture.[190] For example, a bank employee could be subject to a twenty-year prison sentence and criminal fines under Section 1956 for knowingly engaging in a financial transaction involving marijuana-related proceeds with the intent to promote a further offense, such as withdrawing funds generated from marijuana sales from a business checking account to pay the salaries of

---

[184] 18 U.S.C. § 981(a)(1) ("The following property is subject to forfeiture to the United States ... (C) Any property, real or personal, which constitutes or is derived from proceeds traceable to ... any offense constituting 'specified unlawful activity' (as defined in section 1956(c)(7) of this title) [i.e., the list of predicate offenses for money laundering (18 U.S.C. § 1956)], or a conspiracy to commit such offense.").

[185] United States v. McIntosh, 833 F.3d 1163, 1179 n.5 (9th Cir. 2016).

[186] 21 U.S.C. §§ 853, 881.

[187] 18 U.S.C. §§ 1956(c)(7), 1957(f)(3). See "Specified Unlawful Activities" in CRS Report RL33315, *Money Laundering: An Overview of 18 U.S.C. § 1956 and Related Federal Criminal Law* (providing a full list of predicate offenses).

[188] 18 U.S.C. §§ 1956, 1957. See CRS Report RL33315, *Money Laundering: An Overview of 18 U.S.C. § 1956 and Related Federal Criminal Law* (providing a detailed analysis of federal anti-money laundering laws).

[189] Section 1956 violations are punishable by imprisonment for not more than twenty years and fines of up to $500,000 or twice the value of the property involved, whichever is greater. 18 U.S.C. § 1956(a)(1). Section 1957 violations are punishable by imprisonment for not more than ten years and fines of up $250,000 (or $500,000 for organizations) or twice the value of the property involved in the transaction, whichever is greater. *Id.* §§ 1957(b), 3571, 3559. Conspiracy to violate either section carries the same maximum penalties, as does aiding and abetting the commission of either offense. *Id.* §§ 2, 1956(h). *See, e.g.*, United States v. Lyons, 740 F.3d 702, 715 (1st Cir. 2014).

[190] 18 U.S.C. §§ 981(a)(1)(A), 982(a)(1).

medical marijuana dispensary employees.[191] Similarly, a bank officer could face a ten-year prison term and criminal fines under Section 1957 for knowingly receiving deposits or allowing withdrawals of $10,000 or more in cash that is derived from distributing and selling marijuana.[192]

Moreover, federal law requires financial institutions[193] to aid law enforcement in investigating and prosecuting those who violate federal laws, including the CSA.[194] For example, the Secretary of the Treasury has exercised authority to require financial institutions to file suspicious activity reports (SARs)[195] with FinCEN regarding financial transactions[196] suspected to be derived from illegal activities,[197] including marijuana sales.[198] Depository institutions and certain other financial institutions[199] also must establish and maintain AML programs. AML programs are designed to prevent financial institutions from facilitating money laundering and financing terrorist activity, as well as to ensure that the institutions' officers and employees have sufficient knowledge of their customers and their customers' businesses to identify when filing SARs is appropriate.[200] Additionally,

---

[191] *Id.* § 1956(a)(1)(A)(i).

[192] *Id.* § 1957(a), (d).

[193] For the purposes of the Bank Secrecy Act and anti-money laundering laws, the term "financial institution" is defined broadly to include banks, savings associations, credit unions, broker dealers, insurance companies, pawnbrokers, automobile dealers, casinos, cash checkers, travel agencies, and precious metal dealers, among others. 31 U.S.C. § 5312(a)(2).

[194] 12 U.S.C. §§ 1951–59; 31 U.S.C. §§ 5311–32.

[195] 31 U.S.C. § 5318(g). Filing suspicious activity reports (SARs) are mandatory under certain circumstances, but financial institutions may file SARs even when not mandated by law. *See, e.g.,* 12 C.F.R. §§ 1020.320(a) (banks); 31 CFR § 1022.320(a) (money services businesses).

[196] "Transaction" is defined as:

> means a purchase, sale, loan, pledge, gift, transfer, delivery, or other disposition, and with respect to a financial institution includes a deposit, withdrawal, transfer between accounts, exchange of currency, loan, extension of credit, purchase or sale of any stock, bond, certificate of deposit, or other monetary instrument, security, contract of sale of a commodity for future delivery, option on any contract of sale of a commodity for future delivery, option on a commodity, purchase or redemption of any money order, payment or order for any money remittance or transfer, purchase or redemption of casino chips or tokens, or other gaming instruments or any other payment, transfer, or delivery by, through, or to a financial institution, by whatever means effected.

Id. § 1010.100(bbb).

[197] 18 U.S.C. §§ 1956(c)(7), 1957(f)(3). *See* "Specified Unlawful Activities" in CRS Report RL33315, *Money Laundering: An Overview of 18 U.S.C. § 1956 and Related Federal Criminal Law* (providing a full list of predicate offenses).

[198] 21 U.S.C. §§ 841–90; 31 U.S.C. § 5318(g); 31 C.F.R. § 1020.320.

[199] There are several different types of depository institutions, including state- and federally chartered banks, savings associations, and credit unions.

[200] *See generally id.* §§ 5318(h)(1), 1020.200–20. *See also* 12 U.S.C. § 1786(q)(1) (credit unions); *id.* § 1818(s) (banks and savings associations). Even in the absence of suspicion,

federal regulators can subject financial institutions, their employees, and certain affiliated parties[201] to administrative enforcement actions for violating the Bank Secrecy Act or AML laws.[202] For example, federal banking regulators[203] implement comprehensive supervisory regimes that are designed to ensure that depository institutions are managed and operated safely and soundly to maintain financial stability and comply with applicable state and federal law. To this end, banking regulators have strong, flexible administrative enforcement powers, which they may use against depository institutions and their directors, officers, controlling shareholders, employees, agents, and affiliates that act unlawfully, including by engaging in marijuana-related activities that violate the CSA or anti-money laundering laws.[204]

---

financial institutions must file currency transaction reports (CTRs) with FinCEN relating to transactions involving $10,000 or more in cash or other "currency." 31 U.S.C. § 5313; 31 C.F.R. §§ 1020.300–20, 1010.300–70. "Currency" is defined as:

The coin and paper money of the United States or of any other country that is designated as legal tender and that circulates and is customarily used and accepted as a medium of exchange in the country of issuance. Currency includes U.S. silver certificates, U.S. notes and Federal Reserve notes. Currency also includes official foreign bank notes that are customarily used and accepted as a medium of exchange in a foreign country.

Id. at § 1010.100(m).

The willful failure to file SARs and CTRs is punishable by imprisonment for not more than five years or not more than ten years in cases of a substantial pattern of violations or transactions involving other illegal activity. 31 U.S.C. § 5322. Structuring a transaction to avoid the reporting requirement exposes the offender to the same maximum terms of imprisonment. *Id.* § 5324(d). *See* CRS Report RL33315, *Money Laundering: An Overview of 18 U.S.C. § 1956 and Related Federal Criminal Law* (providing a detailed description of penalties for violations of Bank Secrecy Act reporting and monitoring requirements).

201 *See, e.g.,* 12 U.S.C. §§ 1813(u) (defining "institution-affiliated party" to include, among others, "any director, officer, employee, or controlling stockholder ... of, or agent for, an insured depository institution," as well as any independent contractor ... who knowingly or recklessly participates in any violation of any law or regulation; any breach of fiduciary duty; or any unsafe or unsound practice which caused or is likely to cause more than a minimal financial loss to, or a significant adverse effect on, the insured depository institution.").

202 *See, e.g.,* 12 U.S.C. §§ 1786, 1818, 1831o.

203 For these purposes, the federal banking regulators are the Office of the Comptroller of the Currency (OCC) for national banks and federal savings associations; the Board of Governors of the Federal Reserve System for domestic operations of foreign banks and state-chartered banks that are members of the Federal Reserve System; the Federal Deposit Insurance Corporation (FDIC) for state savings associations and state-chartered banks that are not members of the Federal Reserve System; and the National Credit Union Administration (NCUA) for federally insured credit unions. *Id.* §§ 1766, 1813(q). The Bureau of Consumer Financial Protection (CFPB) also has certain consumer compliance regulatory authority over depository institutions. *Id.* §§ 5481–5603.

204 *See, e.g., id.* § 1786 (credit unions); *id.* §§ 1818, 1831o (banks and savings associations). *See also* Press Release, Off. of the Comptroller of the Currency, OCC Assesses $2.5 Million Civil Money Penalty Against Gibraltar Private Bank and Trust Company for Bank Secrecy

Banking regulators may, for instance, issue cease-and-desist orders, impose civil money penalties, and issue removal and prohibition orders that temporarily or permanently ban individuals from working for depository institutions.[205] Banking regulators also have authority, under certain circumstances, to revoke an institution's federal deposit insurance and to take control of and liquidate a depository institution.[206] For example, a criminal conviction for violating the Bank Secrecy Act or AML laws is an explicit ground for appointing the Federal Deposit Insurance Corporation "as receiver [to] place the insured depository institution in liquidation."[207]

Because of these legal risks, many financial institutions are unwilling to provide financial services to the marijuana industry, often leaving marijuana businesses unable to accept debit or credit card payments, use electronic payroll services, maintain checking accounts, or use other common banking services.[208] Consequently, many marijuana businesses reportedly operate exclusively in cash,[209] raising concerns about, among other things, tax collection compliance and public safety.[210]

FinCEN Guidance to Financial Institutions

In response to state and local marijuana legalization efforts, FinCEN issued guidance on marijuana-related financial crimes to advise financial institutions on SAR reporting requirements when serving marijuana businesses operating

---

Act Violations (Feb. 25, 2016), https://www.occ.gov/news-issuances/news-releases/2016/nr-occ-2016-20.html (ordering the payment of a civil money penalty and remedial actions for allegedly "fail[ing] to maintain an effective Bank Secrecy Act/Anti-Money Laundering (BSA/AML) compliance program.").

205 *See, e.g.,* 12 U.S.C. § 1786 (credit unions); *id.* §§ 1818, 1831o (banks and savings associations).

206 *See, e.g., id.* §§ 1786–87 (credit unions); *id.* §§ 1818, 1821, 1831o (banks and savings associations).

207 *Id.* § 1821(c)(5)(M), (d)(2)(E).

208 *See, e.g., Guidance on Provision of Financial Services to Medical Marijuana & Industrial Hemp-Related Businesses in New York State*, N.Y. DEP'T OF FIN. SERVS., 2 (Jul. 3, 2018), https://www.dfs.ny.gov/legal/industry/ il180703.pdf ("Because marijuana currently is still listed on Schedule I under the Federal Controlled Substances Act, medical marijuana ... businesses operating in accordance with New York State laws and regulations continue to have difficulty establishing banking relationships at regulated financial institutions. The ability to establish a banking relationship is an urgent issue today for the legal cannabis industry. So long as it remains difficult to open and maintain bank accounts, the industry will largely rely on cash to conduct business and operate.").

209 *Id.*

210 *See* Tom Angell, *Trump Treasury Secretary Wants Marijuana Money in Banks*, FORBES (Feb. 6, 2018), https://www.forbes.com/sites/tomangell/2018/02/06/trump-treasury-secretary-wants-marijuana-money-in-banks/ #3c9bc4ed3a53.

in compliance with state or local laws.[211] The guidance identified transactions that might trigger federal enforcement priorities,[212] noting

> Because federal law prohibits the distribution and sale of marijuana, financial transactions involving a marijuana-related business would generally involve funds derived from illegal activity. Therefore, a financial institution is required to file a SAR on activity involving a marijuana-related business (including those duly licensed under state law), in accordance with this guidance and [FinCEN regulations].[213]

FinCEN also advised financial institutions serving marijuana businesses to file SARs under the following conditions:

- A marijuana limited SAR should be filed when a financial institution determines, after exercising due diligence, that a marijuana-related business for which the institution is providing financial services is not engaged in any activities that violate state law or implicate the investigation and prosecution priorities outlined in the guidance, including distributing to minors and supporting drug cartels or similar criminal enterprises;[214]
- A marijuana priority SAR should be filed when a financial institution believes a marijuana-related business for which the institution is providing financial services is engaged in activities that implicate prosecution priorities;[215] and
- A marijuana termination SAR should be filed when a financial institution finds it must sever its relationship with a marijuana-related business to maintain an effective AML program.[216]

---

[211] FinCEN Marijuana Guidance 2014, *supra* note 182. Although DOJ rescinded several marijuana-related guidance documents, FinCEN's guidance remains in effect. The Administration could reverse or otherwise make significant changes to its enforcement priorities and policies. *See generally* CRS Report R43708, *The Take Care Clause and Executive Discretion in the Enforcement of Law.*

[212] FinCEN Marijuana Guidance 2014, *supra* note 182.

[213] *Id.* at 3.

[214] *Id.* at 3–4.

[215] *Id.* at 4. These enforcement priorities were originally outlined in the 2013 Cole Memorandum. 2013 Cole Memorandum, *supra* note 182.

[216] FinCEN Marijuana Guidance 2014, *supra* note 182, at 4–5.

The FinCEN guidance also lists examples of red flags that may indicate that a marijuana priority SAR is appropriate.[217]

As of September 30, 2021, FinCEN reported that it has received 219,097 marijuana-related SARs and that 755 depository institutions reported providing some form of financial services to marijuana-related businesses.[218] However, the depth and breadth of financial services that depository institutions are providing marijuana businesses is unclear.[219] Moreover, whether these depository institutions are serving businesses that are directly involved in cultivating and selling marijuana, or are only serving entities that are indirectly involved in the marijuana business (e.g., landlords renting office space to marijuana businesses) is uncertain.[220]

Select Outcomes of State Marijuana Legalization

States' actions to legalize marijuana for medical and recreational purposes changed the landscape for the drug's availability to the states' adult populations. In 1996, California became the first state to legalize marijuana for medical purposes, and since then, 36 states have followed suit.[221] In 2012, Washington and Colorado became the first two states to expand access to marijuana to all adults by legalizing its use for recreational purposes. Since then, 16 states[222] and the District of Columbia have followed suit. Even as

---

[217] *Id.* at 5–7. Some examples of red flags noted in the guidance are, "[t]he business is unable to produce satisfactory documentation or evidence to demonstrate that it is duly licensed and operating consistently with state law"; and "[a] customer seeks to conceal or disguise involvement in marijuana-related business activity." *Id.* at 6.

[218] *Marijuana Banking Update*, DEP'T OF TREASURY, FINCEN, https://www.fincen.gov/sites/default/files/shared/305326_MJ%20Banking%20Update%204th%20QTR%20FY2021_Public_Final.pdf (last visited March 25, 2022).

[219] Robert Rowe, *Compliance and the Cannabis Conundrum*, ABA BANKING J. (Sept. 11, 2018), https://bankingjournal.aba.com/2018/09/compliance-and-the-cannabis-conundrum/ ("According to FinCEN, by the end of the third quarter 2017, it had received nearly 40,000 SARs reporting activity associated with a marijuana-related business. The great majority of those were marijuana limited SARs, indicating that the industry continues to offer some level of services to the cannabis industry. No one knows, though, how extensive those offerings are or what kinds of banking relationships do exist. Anecdotal reporting suggests it is very limited").

[220] *Id.*

[221] See Figure 2 for all states that have adopted a comprehensive medical marijuana program.

[222] The other 16 states that have legalized recreational marijuana are Alaska, Arizona, California, Connecticut, Illinois, Maine, Massachusetts, Michigan, Montana, New Jersey, New Mexico, New York, Nevada, Oregon, Vermont, and Virginia. In 2020, South Dakota

more jurisdictions legalize marijuana, some observers continue to voice concerns over the possible negative outcomes of legalization. Some of these concerns were outlined as enforcement priorities by DOJ in monitoring state legalization.[223] These include, but are not limited to, the potential impact of legalization on (1) marijuana use, particularly among youth; (2) traffic-related incidents involving marijuana-impaired drivers; and (3) trafficking of marijuana from states that have legalized it into states that have not. On the other hand, some observers have pointed to the potential positive outcomes from marijuana legalization, including new tax revenue for states and a potential decrease in marijuana-related arrests, which may free up resources for law enforcement to address other needs.

While state legalization of medical marijuana began over 25 years ago, state legalization of recreational marijuana is relatively recent and, as a result, not all outcomes are known. Further, while some states have taken measures to evaluate the impact of their recreational legalization programs, the same evaluation measures generally were not taken by states following medical marijuana legalization. This section of the report focuses on select issues associated with legalization of medical and recreational marijuana publicly identified by Congress and DOJ in their enforcement priorities (see the "Department of Justice Guidance Memos for U.S. Attorneys" section).[224] Of note, the data included in this section of the report on the effects of marijuana legalization should be interpreted with caution, as they are fairly limited. Conclusions made at this time about the comprehensive impact of marijuana legalization, specifically the impact of more recent legalization efforts, may be premature without broader inclusion of both historical data and additional years of post-legalization data, as well as consideration of other factors aside from legalization.[225] Finally, much of what is known about the implementation

---

legalized recreational marijuana, but in 2021 a circuit judge ruled the South Dakota recreational marijuana measure to be unconstitutional.

[223] See James M. Cole, *Memorandum for all United States Attorneys*, U.S. Department of Justice, Guidance Regarding Marijuana Enforcement, Washington, DC, August 29, 2013, pp. 1-2.

[224] See statements from U.S. Congress, House Committee on the Judiciary, *Full Committee Markup of …H.R. 3884, the "Marijuana Opportunity Reinvestment and Expungement Act of 2019" or the "MORE Act of 2019"*, 116th Cong., 1st sess., November 20, 2019; and U.S. Congress, Senate Committee on the Judiciary, *Is the Department of Justice Adequately Protecting the Public from the Impact of State Recreational Marijuana Legalization*, 114th Cong., 2nd sess., April 5, 2016.

[225] For example, in this section the decline in the number of marijuana arrests over time is discussed in the context of marijuana legalization, but other factors such as how the overall crime rate might have changed during the same time is not discussed. Also, drug use may be influenced by many factors including availability of the drug, family and peer influence, level of education, economic status, and community-level variables.

of recreational marijuana comes from the early adopters[226]—Washington and Colorado—and their experiences do not necessarily mean that other states share or will share the same experiences if they choose to legalize recreational marijuana.

Marijuana Use in the United States

Marijuana is the most commonly used illicit drug in the United States. In 2020, an estimated 32.8 million individuals aged 12 or older used marijuana in the past month.[227] The percentage of past-month users has gradually increased over the last 12 years (a time frame during which a majority of states legalized marijuana in some form)—from 6.1% in 2008 to 11.8% in 2020.[228] The rate of past-month marijuana use among youth (ages 12-17) during this time period declined—from 7.0% in 2008 to 6.5% in 2017 and 2018—before rising to 7.4% in 2019 and then dropping to 5.9% in 2020,[229] while adult (age 18 and older) use steadily increased—from 6.3% in 2008 to 12.4% in 2020.[230]

---

[226] Washington and Colorado both have produced several reports discussing the impact of marijuana legalization following recreational legalization in their respective states. Both states had previously legalized marijuana for medical purposes but did not produce such reports until recreational marijuana was legalized.

[227] Referring to the month prior to an individual's response to the survey question about drug use.

[228] *2020 NSDUH Tables*, Tables 1.1A and 1.1B. For each year from 2008 to 2020, the estimated percentage of the 12 and older population currently using marijuana was 6.1%, 6.7%, 6.9%, 7.0%, 7.3%, 7.5%, 8.4%, 8.3%, 8.9%, 9.6%, 10.1%, 11.5%, and 11.8% respectively. The difference between each year's estimate from 2008 to 2018 and the 2019 estimate (11.5%) is statistically significant at the .05 level. SAMHSA recommends using caution when comparing estimates between 2020 and prior years because of methodological changes for 2020. Due to these changes, SAMHSA did not conduct significance testing between 2020 and prior years.

[229] For some years from 2008-2019, including the difference between the 2018 and 2019 estimate, the difference from one year's estimate to the next were not statistically significant at the .05 level. Further, SAMHSA recommends using caution when comparing estimates between 2020 and prior years because of methodological changes for 2020. Due to these changes, SAMHSA did not conduct significance testing between 2020 and prior years. See *2020 NSDUH Tables*, Table 7.6B.

[230] For each year from 2008 to 2020, the estimated percentage of the adult (18 and older) population currently using marijuana was 6.0%, 6.6%, 6.8%, 6.9%, 7.3%, 7.6%, 8.5%, 8.4%, 9.1%, 9.9%, 10.5%, 11.9%, and 12.4% respectively. The difference between each year's estimate from 2008 to 2018 and the 2019 estimate (11.9%) is statistically significant at the .05 level. SAMHSA recommends using caution when comparing estimates between 2020 and prior years because of methodological changes for 2020. Due to these changes, SAMHSA did not conduct significance testing between 2020 and prior years. See *2020 NSDUH Tables*, Table 7.9B.

An increase in adult use was expected by some experts[231] given that legal medical and recreational marijuana programs increase legal access for adults but not juveniles, except under limited circumstances. A 2019 review of existing research on the impact of marijuana legalization that revealed medical marijuana laws increase adult but not adolescent use is consistent with this view.[232] Further, several studies have either concluded that state medical and recreational marijuana laws have had no effect on youth use or have shown an association between the enactment of these laws and a subsequent decline in youth use.[233] Two studies have indicated that adolescent use may decline after state recreational legalization.[234] Other studies have shown youth and/or adolescent use did not increase in states following recreational and medical marijuana legalization and that youth and/or adolescent marijuana use were already elevated in these states prior to legalization.[235]

---

[231] Cari Nierenberg, "Marijuana's Popularity Among US Adults Continues to Grow. Here's Why," *Live Science*, August 10, 2017.

[232] Rosanna Smart and Rosalie Liccardo Pacula, "Early Evidence of the Impact of Cannabis Legalization on Cannabis Use, Cannabis Use Disorder, and the Use of Other Substances: Findings from State Policy Evaluations," *The American Journal of Drug and Alcohol Abuse*, October 11, 2019.

[233] Julie K. Johnson et al., "Medical marijuana laws (MMLs) and dispensary provisions not associated with higher odds of adolescent marijuana or heavy marijuana use: A 46 State Analysis, 1991-2015," *Substance Abuse* (March 2021); Aaron Sarvet et al., "Medical marijuana laws and adolescent marijuana use in the United States: a systematic review and meta-analysis," *Addiction*, vol. 113, issue 6 (June 2018), pp. 1003-1016; Carol J. Boyd, Phillip T. Veliz, and Sean Esteban McCabe, "Adolescents' Use of Medical Marijuana: A Secondary Analysis of Monitoring the Future Data," *Journal of Adolescent Health*, vol. 57, issue 2 (August 2015), pp. 241-244; Esther Choo et al., "The impact of state medical marijuana legislation on adolescent marijuana use," *Journal of Adolescent Health*, vol. 55, issue 2 (August 2014), pp. 160-166; Sarah D. Lynne-Landsman, Melvin D. Livingston, and Alexander C. Wagenaar, "Effects of State Medical Marijuana Laws on Adolescent Marijuana Use," *American Journal of Public Health*, vol. 103 (August 2013), pp.1500-1506; D. Mark Anderson, Benjamin Hansen, and Daniel I. Rees, "Medical Marijuana Laws and Teen Marijuana Use," IZA Discussion Paper Series (No. 6592), May 2012; Sam Harper, Erin C. Strumpf, and Jay S. Kaufman, "Do Medical Marijuana Laws Increase Marijuana Use? Replication Study and Extension," *Annals of Epidemiology*, vol. 22, issue 3 (March 2012), pp. 207-212; and D. Mark Anderson and Daniel I. Rees, "Medical Marijuana Laws, Traffic Fatalities, and Alcohol Consumption," IZA Discussion Paper Series (No. 6112), November 2011.

[234] D. Mark Anderson, Benjamin Hansen, and Daniel Rees, "Association of Marijuana Laws With Teen Marijuana Use: New Estimates From the Youth Risk Behavior Surveys," *Journal of the American Medical Association Pediatrics*, vol. 173, no. 9 (July 2019); and Magdalena Cerda et al., "Medical marijuana laws and adolescent use of marijuana and other substances: Alcohol, cigarettes, prescription drugs, and other illicit drugs," *Drug and Alcohol Dependence*, vol. 183, issue 1 (February 2018), pp. 62-68.

[235] Kristie Ladegard, Christian Thurstone and Melanie Rylander, "Marijuana Legalization and Youth," *Pediatrics*, vol. 145 (May 2020), p.165-174; and Aaron Sarvet et al., "Medical

Monitoring Use and Health Effects

Some states that have legalized marijuana are monitoring changes in drug use patterns in their states as well as changes in the emerging research on the health effects of marijuana. For example, new studies of marijuana's effect on brain functioning and development are often published in medical journals. Some have pointed to a negative effect on brain development while others point to an effect that is not necessarily positive or negative.[236] For more information on the health effects of marijuana use, see Appendix B and Appendix C.

A concern of policymakers is that youth perception of the harmfulness of marijuana may be lower in states that allow for either or both medical and recreational marijuana. Perceived harmfulness of marijuana use appears to be decreasing generally among adolescents in the United States; however, the enactment of state laws legalizing medical marijuana is associated with *increases* in perceived harmfulness among young adolescents (8th graders).[237] Researchers explained that young, impressionable adolescents may decide that marijuana is something for use by individuals who are sick, which may cause marijuana use to be less appealing as a recreational activity. Further, within-state media coverage of potential harms associated with marijuana use may increase around the time that medical marijuana laws are passed, which could potentially influence their opinions as well.

---

marijuana laws and adolescent marijuana use in the United States: a systematic review and meta-analysis," *Addiction*, vol. 113, issue 6 (June 2018), p. 1003-1016.

[236] National Institute on Drug Abuse, *What are marijuana's long-term effects on the brain?*, July 2020, https://www.drugabuse.gov/publications/research-reports/marijuana/what-are-marijuanas-long-term-effects-brain; Catherine Orr, Philip Spechler, and Zhipeng Cao, "Grey Matter Volume Differences Associated with Extremely Low Levels of Cannabis Use in Adolescence," *The Journal of Neuroscience*, vol. 39, no. 10 (March 2019), pp. 1817-1827.

[237] Katherine M. Keyes, Melanie Wall, and Magdalena Cerdá et al., "How does state marijuana policy affect US youth? Medical marijuana laws, marijuana use and perceived harmfulness: 1991–2014," *Addiction*, vol. 111, no. 12 (July 9, 2016).

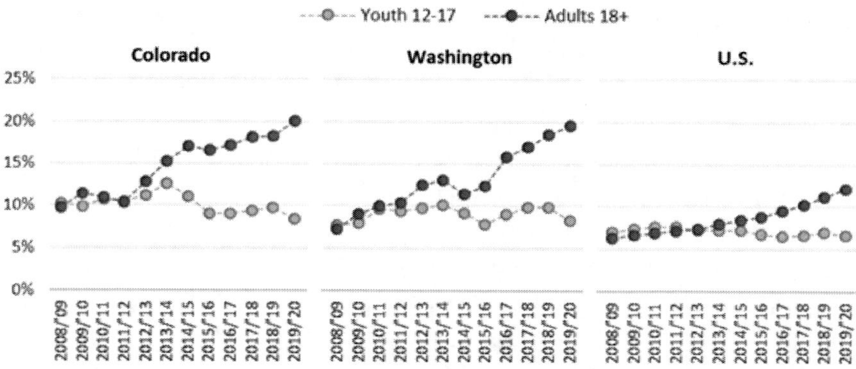

Source: Created by the Congressional Research Service (CRS) based on available population data from the Substance Abuse and Mental Health Services Administration (SAMHSA), *National Survey on Drug Use and Health (NSDUH)*, State Data, 2008/2009, 2010/2011, 2011/2012, 2012/2013, 2013/2014, 2014/2015, 2015/2016, 2016/2017, 2017/2018, 2018/2019, and 2019/2020, http://www.samhsa.gov/data/.

Notes: This figure presents yearly estimates of current marijuana use in Colorado, Washington, and the United States. SAMHSA defines *current use* as having used at least once in the past month. To review year-to-year, statistically significant changes, if any, see the NSDUH state data reports. Annual state-level estimates are based on two calendar years of pooled NSDUH data, so two consecutive sets of estimates have a one-year overlap. For more information on the NSDUH methodology, see *2019-2020 National Survey on Drug Use and Health: Guide to State Tables and Summary of Small Area Estimation Methodology*.

Figure 3. Estimates of Current Marijuana Use in Colorado, Washington, and the United States Overall, 2008-2020; Percentages Among Youth (ages 12-17) and Adults (ages 18 and older).

State data for 2019/2020 from the National Survey on Drug Use and Health show that the 10 states (including the District of Columbia) with the highest percentages of current marijuana use among individuals 12 and older (16.80–21.85%) are all states that have legalized recreational and medical marijuana use, except for Rhode Island, which has only legalized medical marijuana).[238] However, causal inferences between the implementation of

[238] Using 2019/2020 survey data, the 10 states (including the District of Columbia) with the highest prevalence estimates (by percentage of the state's population aged 12 and older) for current marijuana use are: Alaska, 17.09%; Colorado, 18.94%; the District of Columbia, 18.24%; Maine, 17.10%; Massachusetts, 16.80%; Montana, 16.98%; Oregon, 19.26%; Rhode Island, 17.69%; Vermont, 21.85%; and Washington, 18.66%. See SAMHSA, *2019-2020 National Surveys on Drug Use and Health: Model-Based Prevalence Estimates (50*

both medical and recreational marijuana programs and increased marijuana use among individuals 12 and older cannot be made for several reasons, particularly since three of the states (not including Rhode Island, which did not legalize recreational marijuana) included in this top-tier marijuana use category had either not yet legalized recreational marijuana in 2019 or 2020, or did not yet have the ability to sell recreational marijuana when the survey data were collected.

Marijuana Use in Washington and Colorado

In the first two states that legalized recreational marijuana (Washington and Colorado, in November 2012), the percentages of adults (ages 18 and older) and youth (ages 12-17) who reported use in the past month changed from 2010/2011 to 2019/2020 according to survey data. For adults, the *national* data show a consistent increase (see Figure 3), while the Washington and Colorado data show generally larger but less consistent increases. The *national* youth use data show a slight but consistent decline from 2010/2011 to 2016/2017, then a slight increase over several years, and then a decline again in 2019/2020. Washington and Colorado youth use data have varied more over the years, but 2018/2019 levels are generally similar to or slightly below those of 2010/2011. Washington and Colorado had higher percentages of adult and youth marijuana use each year compared to national estimates—both before and after recreational legalization began—and the difference has increased after recreational legalization.[239]

The Colorado Department of Public Health and Environment (CDPHE) was given the responsibility to "monitor changes in drug use patterns, broken down by county and race and ethnicity, and the emerging science and medical

States and the District of Columbia), Table 3. Of note, the 10 states (including the District of Columbia) with the highest prevalence estimates were nearly the same in the previous set of data (2018/2019), with one difference: Nevada (a state that authorizes recreational marijuana use) was included in the top 10, and Massachusetts was not. See *2018-2019 National Survey on Drug Use and Health National Maps of Prevalence Estimates, by State*, Table 3a.

239 SAMHSA, *National Survey on Drug Use and Health (NSDUH)*, State Data, 2010/2011, 2011/2012, 2012/2013, 2013/2014, 2014/2015, 2015/2016, 2016/2017, 2017/2018, 2018/2019, and 2019/2020, http://www.samhsa.gov/data/. The observed differences between estimates were not evaluated in terms of statistical significance—the probability that an observed difference in the population estimates would occur due to random variability if there were no difference in the estimates being compared. To review year-to-year, statistically significant changes, see the NSDUH state data reports.

information relevant to the health effects associated with marijuana use."[240] In the most recent report, the CDPHE notes a number of different trends related to marijuana exposure and hospitalizations in Colorado. For example, the number of marijuana exposures reported to Rocky Mountain Poison and Drug Safety (the poison center in Colorado) increased from 222 in 2017 to 276 in 2019, with increases mostly attributed to unintentional, marijuana-only exposures among children 0 to 5 years old. However, the number of exposure reports among adults 30 years and older have decreased over this time period. Of note, edible marijuana products continue to account for the highest proportion of marijuana product exposures reported to the poison control center in Colorado.[241] CDPHE labeled some trends in marijuana use as "encouraging" and others as "trends to continue monitoring" (see Appendix F).

Marijuana-Related Traffic Incidents

Marijuana has been shown to impair driving ability if the driver has recently used the drug.[242] According to the National Highway Traffic Safety Administration (NHTSA), "[l]ow doses of THC moderately impair cognitive and psychomotor tasks associated with driving, while severe driving impairment is observed with high doses, chronic use and in combination with low doses of alcohol."[243] However, the connection between marijuana usage and an increase in a driver's risk of crashing is not clearly established.[244] Some may be concerned that recreational or medical marijuana legalization could be associated with an increase in marijuana-related traffic incidents. In Colorado, despite limited traffic data, there are some indicators of marijuana's impact on

---

[240] Colorado Revised Statutes, Title 25, §1.5-110. The most recent report is CDPHE, Retail Marijuana Public Health Advisory Committee, *Monitoring Health Concerns Related to Marijuana in Colorado: 2020*, January 2021.

[241] Ibid., pp. 60-64.

[242] See Rebecca L. Hartman and Marilyn A. Huestis, "Cannabis effects on driving skills," *Clinical Chemistry*, vol. 59, no. 3 (March 2013), pp. 478-492; and Rebecca L. Hartman, Timothy L. Brown, and Gary Milavetz et al., "Cannabis effects on driving lateral control with and without alcohol," *Drug and Alcohol Dependence*, vol. 154 (September 1, 2015), pp. 25-37.

[243] National Highway Traffic Safety Administration (NHTSA), *Drug and Human Performance Fact Sheets: Cannabis/Marijuana (Δ 9 -Tetrahydrocannabinol, THC)*, https://one.nhtsa.gov/people/injury/research/job185drugs/ cannabis.htm.

[244] For a broader discussion of this issue and marijuana and traffic safety overall, see CRS Report R45719, *Marijuana Use and Highway Safety*.

traffic safety in Colorado. For example, from 2008 to 2019, the percentage of individuals participating in treatment for driving under the influence (DUI) and reporting marijuana as their primary drug increased from 4% to 12%.[245]

In monitoring the effects of recreational marijuana legalization in Washington State,[246] government researchers with the state's Office of Financial Management, Forecasting and Research Division report that the percentage of drivers involved in traffic fatalities testing positive for THC (either THC only or THC in combination with other drugs/alcohol) gradually declined from 2013 to 2017, while the percentage of alleged impaired drivers testing positive for THC-only gradually increased over the same time period.[247] A recent study of traffic fatalities in both Colorado and Washington shows evidence of an increase in traffic fatalities after Colorado implemented its recreational marijuana laws, but no increase in Washington. The authors pointed to differences in how the state laws were implemented (e.g., density of recreational retail sites), out-of-state marijuana tourism, and other local factors to possibly explain the different results.[248]

In several studies of the effects of medical marijuana legalization, researchers found that the enactment of medical marijuana laws were generally associated with a reduction in traffic fatalities. Some point to the hypothesis that marijuana and alcohol are substitutes for each other and reduced alcohol consumption as a possible reason for the reduction in fatalities.[249]

---

[245] Jack K. Reed, *Impacts of Marijuana Legalization in Colorado: A Report Pursuant to Senate Bill 13-283*, July 2021, p. 42 (hereinafter, "*Impacts of Marijuana Legalization in Colorado*").

[246] While medical marijuana has been legal in Washington since 1998, it may have been viewed as an individual doctor/patient decision outside the scope of public health policy. The legalization of recreational marijuana and the potential for greater availability of the drug in the state likely prompted a closer look at potential health effects on the state's population.

[247] Washington State Office of Financial Management, Forecasting and Research Division, *Monitoring Impacts of Recreational Marijuana Legalization*, 2019 Update Report, June 2019, p. 9 (hereinafter, "*Monitoring Impacts of Recreational Marijuana Legalization*").

[248] Julian Santaella-Tenorio, Katherine Wheeler-Martin, and Charles J. DiMaggio et al., "Association of Recreational Cannabis Laws in Colorado and Washington State With Changes in Traffic Fatalities, 2005-2017," *Journal of the American Medical Association Internal Medicine*, June 22, 2020.

[249] Julian Santaella-Tenorio et. al., "US Traffic Fatalities, 1985–2014, and Their Relationship to Medical Marijuana Laws," *American Journal of Public Health,* vol. 107 (January 2017); D. Mark Anderson, Benjamin Hansen, and Daniel I. Rees, "Medical Marijuana Laws, Traffic Fatalities, and Alcohol Consumption," *The Journal of Law & Economics*, vol. 56, no. 2 (May 2013), p. 333-369; and D. Mark Anderson and Daniel I. Rees, "Medical Marijuana Laws, Traffic Fatalities, and Alcohol Consumption," IZA Discussion Paper Series (No. 6112), November 2011.

NHTSA has noted that there is no national marijuana impairment standard for drivers.[250] There are several reasons for this, but a primary one is that measuring marijuana impairment is not very straightforward—THC alone is not a strong indicator of impairment.[251] NHTSA is conducting research to help develop a psychomotor, behavioral, and cognitive test that would indicate the degree of driving impairment and elevated risk of crash involvement due to marijuana use.[252] In the meantime, states have developed their own legal thresholds for marijuana impairment. Colorado law states that drivers with 5.0 ng/mL of active THC in their blood can be prosecuted for DUI. In addition, law enforcement officers may base arrests on observed impairment (for alcohol or drug-related impairment).[253]

In 2021, Congress and President Biden enacted several marijuana impairment-related provisions in the Invest in America Act (P.L. 117-58). It requires the Secretary of Transportation to submit a report and recommendations on: (1) increasing and improving access for researchers studying marijuana impairment to marijuana available at dispensaries; (2) establishing a national clearinghouse to collect and distribute marijuana for scientific research that includes marijuana available at dispensaries; (3) facilitating access for researchers located in states that have not legalized marijuana, to marijuana from such clearinghouse for purposes of research on marijuana-impaired driving; and (4) identifying "federal statutory and regulatory barriers" to marijuana research and the establishment of a national clearinghouse. Notably, this provision relies on the marijuana definition in Section 4008 of the FAST Act (P.L. 114-94) which defines marijuana as "all substances containing tetrahydrocannabinol," and presumes CSA and regulatory changes that would be necessary for researchers to be able to access marijuana from dispensaries and not from a DEA-registered source. The Invest in America Act also directs the Secretary of Transportation to establish a new competitive grant program for states and tribes to educate the public on the dangers of drug-impaired driving.

---

[250] Richard P. Compton, *Marijuana-Impaired Driving - A Report to Congress*, NHTSA, DOT HS 812 440, July 2017.

[251] Ibid., p. 13.

[252] Ibid. NHTSA indicates that others are working on this kind of test as well.

[253] Colorado Department of Transportation, *FAQs: Cannabis and Driving*, https://www.codot.gov/safety/alcohol-and-impaired-driving/druggeddriving/marijuana-and-driving.

Marijuana Arrests

The number of marijuana-related arrests[254] is expected to go down in jurisdictions that have legalized marijuana for medical and recreational use, but especially in recreational marijuana states where adult use is not restricted to those with a medical card. Washington and Colorado are the focus of this section, given that they provide the most years of data. Washington reports that "between 2012 and 2015 the number of incidents including [p]ossessing or [c]onsuming [m]arijuana decreased by 65 percent [from 5,786 to 1,999]."[255] Since that time, the number of incidents involving marijuana increased in 2016 and 2017, before decreasing in 2018 to 2,397.[256]

In Colorado, since the legalization of recreational marijuana, the number of marijuana arrests has decreased by 68%, from 13,225 in 2012 to 4,290 in 2019.[257] Since 2015, the most common marijuana charge in Colorado has been possession under age 21. In FY2019, there were 3,071 recorded offenses for marijuana possession under age 21 in Colorado.[258]

Marijuana Trafficking

Marijuana trafficking remains a major policy issue in the United States. Officials in states that have legalized marijuana use have pointed to expectations that illicit marijuana trafficking would decline after legalization. However, officials in states that have not legalized marijuana have cited the trafficking of other-states'-authorized marijuana into their states.[259] Further, state legalization has changed the landscape of the domestic black market for marijuana and U.S. supply and demand.

---

[254] For offenses such as marijuana sales, possession, and production.

[255] *Monitoring Impacts of Recreational Marijuana Legalization*, p. 12. "As defined by the FBI, an 'incident' occurs when any law enforcement officer investigates a scene or situation, whether that investigation results in an arrest or not. Incidents involving multiple illicit drugs or other criminal activities are only counted once, and are included in whichever category is listed first by the local law enforcement agency. The order used by those agencies is not hierarchical."

[256] *Monitoring Impacts of Recreational Marijuana Legalization*, p. 15.

[257] Marijuana arrests include those for sales, smuggling, possession, production, and "unspecified."

[258] *Impacts of Marijuana Legalization in Colorado*, p. 29.

[259] See Josh Ingold and Ricardo Baca, "Supreme Court denies Oklahoma and Nebraska challenge to Colorado pot," *The Denver Post*, March 21, 2016, Updated on October 2, 2016.

Transnational Trafficking

Mexican transnational criminal organizations have historically been the primary foreign suppliers of marijuana to the United States, with smaller amounts also coming from Canada and the Caribbean.[260] While there are anecdotal reports about the effects of state legalization initiatives on the domestic marijuana black market, officials have cited an intelligence gap with respect to understanding how domestic legalization has affected the amount of Mexican-produced marijuana entering the United States.[261] For instance, estimates of domestic marijuana consumption do not speak to the source of the marijuana, and drug seizure data from federal, state, and local law enforcement agencies do not include the marijuana's origin. This is because there is no marijuana signature or profiling program like there is for cocaine, methamphetamine, heroin, and fentanyl[262] that can help determine the geographic origin of seized marijuana.

Marijuana cultivation in Mexico has declined, along with trafficking into the United States, and some have linked this to changes to state-level marijuana policies in the United States and decreased U.S. demand for lower-quality Mexican marijuana.[263] Decreased marijuana production has also been linked to an increase in Mexican production of other drugs. Reportedly, the trafficking organizations have shifted production to more profitable drugs such as heroin and methamphetamine.[264] Nonetheless, DEA's outlook on marijuana trafficking is that "Mexico-produced marijuana will continue to be trafficked into the United States in bulk quantities and may increase in quality to compete with domestic-produced marijuana."[265]

Since the first states began legalizing marijuana for recreational use in 2012,[266] there has been a decline in seizures of the drug by U.S. Customs and

---

[260] DEA, *2020 National Drug Threat Assessment*, March 2021, p. 57.

[261] DEA, *2015 National Drug Threat Assessment*, October 2015, p. 71.

[262] For more information on these programs, see CRS Report R45812, *Illicit Drug Flows and Seizures in the United States: What Do We [Not] Know?*.

[263] See, for example, Brianna Lee, Danielle Renwick, and Rocio Cara Labrador, *Mexico's Drug War*, Council on Foreign Relations, January 24, 2019; Seth Robins, *Marijuana Seizures Plummet in U.S. and Mexico. Will Illegal Profits Follow?,* InSight Crime, November 9, 2018; and Kate Linthicum, "With U.S. Competition Hurting Its Marijuana Business, Mexico Warms a Little to Legalization," *Los Angeles Times*, January 27, 2018.

[264] See, for example, Kate Linthicum, "With U.S. Competition Hurting Its Marijuana Business, Mexico Warms a Little to Legalization," *Los Angeles Times*, January 27, 2018; and Nick Miroff, "Losing Marijuana Business, Mexican Cartels Push Heroin and Meth," *The Washington Post*, January 11, 2015.

[265] DEA, *2020 National Drug Threat Assessment*, March 2021, p. 58.

[266] Older data were not available, and therefore trends following medical marijuana legalization are not discussed.

Border Protection (CBP). CBP seized 582,413 pounds of marijuana nationwide at and between ports of entry in FY2020, which is down more than 80% from 2,822,478 pounds in FY2012.[267] There was also a "sharp decline," beginning in FY2013 and continuing through FY2020, in the number of individuals sentenced for federal marijuana trafficking offenses.[268] Experts have noted that this decline in sentencing could be driven by a number, or a combination, of factors such as a reduction in federal law enforcement actions against marijuana-related drug offenders, more successful efforts by drug traffickers to conceal their illicit contraband entering the United States, and reductions in the amount of illicit marijuana being shipped into the United States.[269]

Further, according to the United Nations Office on Drugs and Crime (UNODC), the COVID-19 global pandemic and related restrictions implemented by governments around the world has "inevitably affected all aspects of the illegal drug markets, from the production and trafficking of drugs to their consumption."[270] The impact varies based on geographic area, type of substance, and type of restrictions. For cannabis, UNODC explains that there is less of an impact on trafficking of cannabis due to the local nature of cannabis: production often takes place near consumer markets, and traffickers are less reliant on long trans-regional routes for distribution as compared to other illicit drugs.[271]

Trafficking from States That Have Legalized into Other States

The trafficking of marijuana from where it was produced in accordance with state laws and regulations into another state where it remains illegal is one area of concern for federal law enforcement. Some officials have alleged that there has been increased marijuana trafficking from states that have legalized marijuana possession or sale for medical or recreational purposes to nearby states. This is an especially acute concern for states that have legalized

---

[267] U.S. Customs and Border Protection (CBP), *CBP Enforcement Statistics*, https://www.cbp.gov/newsroom/stats/drug-seizure-statistics. FY2012 and FY2013 data retrieved in February 2019.

[268] U.S. Sentencing Commission, *Quick Facts: Drug Trafficking Offenses*, FY2017. Data from FY2016 – FY2020 are from U.S. Sentencing Commission, *Quick Facts: Marijuana Trafficking Offenses*, FY2017, June 2021.

[269] Christopher Ingraham, "Federal Marijuana Smuggling is Declining in the Era of Legal Weed," *The Washington Post*, May 26, 2016, referencing statements by Beau Kilmer, a drug policy researcher at RAND Corp.

[270] United Nations, Office on Drugs and Crime, *COVID-19 and the drug supply chain: from production and trafficking to use*, 2020, p. 1.

[271] Ibid., p. 5.

recreational marijuana that allows individuals from out of state to purchase marijuana from dispensaries. For instance, the Rocky Mountain High Intensity Drug Trafficking Area (HIDTA) reported that its task force investigations in Colorado identified marijuana produced in the state that was destined for at least 21 different states in 2020.[272] In addition, the Northwest HIDTA notes that between 2012, when recreational marijuana was legalized in Washington, and August 2017, Washington-produced marijuana was destined for at least 38 states.[273] Similarly, the Oregon-Idaho HIDTA indicated that Oregon-produced marijuana was interdicted en route to 37 states between July 2015 and January 2018.[274] These HIDTA reports note that the means by which marijuana and its derivatives are transported out of state include vehicles, airplanes, and mail, sometimes facilitated by both the open web and the dark web.[275] Notably, of the marijuana produced in states that have legalized and diverted to other states, it is unclear what proportion was produced legally in compliance with state laws and regulations and what proportion was produced illegally.

In December 2014, Nebraska and Oklahoma filed a lawsuit in the U.S. Supreme Court[276] against Colorado claiming that the plaintiff states' law enforcement and criminal justice systems had been adversely affected by Colorado's laws legalizing marijuana.[277] The complaint included claims that Colorado's "statutes and regulations are devoid of safeguards to ensure

---

[272] Rocky Mountain High Intensity Drug Trafficking Area, *The Legalization of Marijuana in Colorado: The Impact Volume 8*, updated September 2021. For more information on the HIDTA program, see CRS Report R45188, *High Intensity Drug Trafficking Areas (HIDTA) Program*.

[273] Northwest High Intensity Drug Trafficking Area, *Washington State Marijuana Impact Report, Volume 2*, August 2017.

[274] Oregon-Idaho High Intensity Drug Trafficking Area, *An Initial Assessment of Cannabis Production, Distribution, and Consumption in Oregon 2018—An Insight Report, First Edition—Updated Version*, August 6, 2018.

[275] Rocky Mountain High Intensity Drug Trafficking Area, *The Legalization of Marijuana in Colorado: The Impact Volume 5*, updated September 2018; and Oregon-Idaho High Intensity Drug Trafficking Area, *An Initial Assessment of Cannabis Production, Distribution, and Consumption in Oregon 2018—An Insight Report, First Edition—Updated Version*, August 6, 2018. For more information on the dark web, see CRS Report R44101, *Dark Web*.

[276] The Constitution provides the Supreme Court with original jurisdiction over "Controversies between two or more States," meaning such claims can be filed directly with the Supreme Court without first being litigated in the lower federal courts. U.S. CONST., art. III, §2. cl. 1.

[277] Jack Healy, "Nebraska and Oklahoma Sue Colorado Over Marijuana Law," *The New York Times*, December 18, 2014.

marijuana cultivated and sold in Colorado is not trafficked to other states."[278] In March 2016, however, the Supreme Court declined to hear the case.[279]

The Changing Domestic Black Market

Changes in the domestic black market for marijuana have been reported as states have moved to legalize it for medical and recreational purposes. DEA notes that there are various sources of marijuana that may contribute to the black market in the United States: illicit marijuana (both foreign- and domestic-produced) and state-approved marijuana (for medical or recreational use) that is diverted to the black market.[280]

Demand for higher-quality marijuana has generally increased in the United States. Notably, marijuana produced in Mexico is generally considered to be a low-grade or commercial-grade product and of lower quality compared to the marijuana produced in the United States and Canada.[281] Further, it is not just U.S. consumers who demand higher-quality marijuana; for example, there have been anecdotal reports of traffickers moving high-quality marijuana produced in the United States across the Southwest border for sale and distribution in Mexico.[282] U.S. officials have not publicly reported data on the quantity or frequency of this outbound smuggling, and it is unclear what proportion of the marijuana smuggled out of the United States is being grown in accordance with state medical and/or recreational marijuana laws and subsequently diverted out of the country.

Illicit domestic marijuana cultivation is carried out by U.S. residents as well as by foreign criminal networks, and it may be grown at both indoor and outdoor grow sites—including on public lands.[283] DEA has noted that cultivation on public lands is "undiminished despite state legalization."[284]

---

[278] States of Nebraska and Oklahoma v. State of Colorado, S. Ct., Complaint, p. 3.

[279] Nebraska and Oklahoma v. Colorado: Motion for Leave to File a Bill of Complaint Denied on March 21, 2016, SCOTUSblog, https://www.scotusblog.com/case-files/cases/nebraska-and-oklahoma-v-colorado/; see also David G. Savage, "Supreme Court Rejects Challenge to Colorado Marijuana Law From Other States," *The Los Angeles Times,* March 21, 2016.

[280] DOJ, DEA, *2020 National Drug Threat Assessment*, March 2021, p. 50.

[281] DOJ, DEA, *2020 National Drug Threat Assessment*, March 2021, p. 57.

[282] See, for example, Marissa J. Lang, "Mexico is Poised to Legalize Marijuana, but Advocates Don't Like the Details," *The Washington Post*, November 8, 2020; Jean Guerrero, "Mexico's Demand for Potent California Marijuana Creates Southbound Smuggling," *KPBS*, October 21, 2016; and John Burnett, "Legal Pot In the U.S. May Be Undercutting Mexican Marijuana," NPR All Things Considered, December 1, 2014.

[283] See, for example, NPR Morning Edition, "Illegal Pot Operations in Public Forests are Poisoning Wildlife and Water," November 12, 2019.

[284] DEA, *2020 National Drug Threat Assessment*, March 2021, p. 53.

DEA further notes that indoor cultivation has certain advantages over outdoor grow sites such as privacy, security, and climate control providing the potential for year-round harvests. In addition, DEA has indicated that marijuana concentrates such as hash, hash oil, and kief remain a concern for federal law enforcement, in part because they have much higher percentages of THC.[285] DEA has also stated that one effect of state marijuana legalization initiatives has been an increase in seizures of marijuana concentrates and an increase in the number of THC extraction laboratories in the United States.[286]

In addition to black market marijuana that is grown illegally, there is a gray market in which marijuana is being *grown legally* in accordance with state laws and regulations but then *sold illegally.* For instance, in some jurisdictions it may be legal to grow and possess small quantities of marijuana, but there may be no regulatory structure for, or even a prohibition on, selling it. In some instances, marijuana may be provided as a *gift* to individuals who purchase other, non-marijuana goods.[287] Another gray market example involves entities that are operating as legal marijuana businesses but are not licensed as such. For instance, there are reports of marijuana businesses in California that have not acquired the necessary licenses but are nonetheless operating. Some claim that gray market businesses may be able to undercut legitimate businesses because they not only save money by not acquiring licenses, but they also save money by not following regulations on security and testing, and might even sell counterfeit goods.[288]

Notably, public discourse around the potential effects of legalization on the black and gray markets often involves discussions of *recreational* legalization even though medical marijuana is not immune from being diverted to the black or gray markets. Many question whether or how a regulated and taxed recreational marijuana framework would affect the black market. However, policymakers may similarly question how a medical marijuana framework might also or alternatively affect the black and gray markets. For instance, some jurisdictions—such as in Colorado—have reported black and gray market activity associated with early medical use initiatives in addition to later recreational legalization.[289]

---

[285] Ibid., p. 55.

[286] Ibid.

[287] See, for example, discussions of Michigan and District of Columbia laws by Mike Adams, "Cannabis Businesses in Michigan Gift Marijuana to Bypass Law," *Forbes*, December 15, 2018.

[288] See, for example, Alex Halperin, "Can Legal Weed Ever Beat the Black Market?," *The Guardian*, March 18, 2019.

[289] Colorado Office of the Governor, *Marijuana Grey Market*, August 16, 2016.

Legalization Impact on Criminal Proceeds

Various organizations have assessed the potential profits generated from illicit drug sales, both worldwide and in the United States, but estimates of illicit sales of marijuana are uncertain. For example, the former National Drug Intelligence Center (NDIC) estimated that the sale of illicit drugs in the United States generates between $18 billion and $39 billion in wholesale drug proceeds for Colombian and Mexican drug trafficking organizations annually.[290] The proportion of this estimate that is attributable to marijuana sales, however, is unknown.[291] Without a clear understanding of (1) actual proceeds generated by the sale of illicit drugs in various markets across the United States, (2) the proportion of total proceeds attributable to the sale of marijuana, and (3) the proportion of marijuana sales controlled by criminal organizations and affiliated gangs, any estimates of how state marijuana legalization, for medical and recreational purposes, has affected, or may in the future affect, drug trafficking organizations are likely to be speculative or anecdotal.

Illicit marijuana proceeds are generated at many points along the supply chain, including production, transportation, and distribution. Experts have debated which aspects of this chain— and the related proceeds—would be most heavily affected by marijuana legalization. In addition, the potential effect of marijuana legalization in some subset of the states (complicated by varying legal frameworks and regulatory regimes) may be more difficult to model precisely than the effect of federal marijuana legalization. For instance, in evaluating the potential fiscal effect from the 2012 Washington and Colorado legalization initiatives on the profits of Mexican drug trafficking organizations, the Organization of American States (OAS) hypothesized that

---

[290] DOJ, National Drug Intelligence Center, *National Drug Threat Assessment 2009,* December 2008, p. 49.

[291] A 2006 Office of National Drug Control Policy figure estimated that over 60% of Mexican drug trafficking organizations' revenue could be attributed to marijuana sales. However, this estimate is over a decade old, and a number of researchers and experts have questioned the accuracy of the number and provided other estimates of marijuana proceeds. See, for example, Beau Kilmer, *Debunking the Mythical Numbers about Marijuana Production in Mexico and the United States*, RAND Drug Policy Research Center. See also U.S. Government Accountability Office (GAO), *Drug Control: U.S. Assistance has Helped Mexican Counternarcotics Efforts, but Tons of Illicit Drugs Continue to Flow into the United States*, GAO-07-1018, August 2007. Another estimate has placed the proportion of Mexican DTO export revenues attributable to marijuana at between 15% and 26% of total drug revenues. See Beau Kilmer, Jonathan P. Caulkins, and Brittany M. Bond et al., *Reducing Drug Trafficking Revenues and Violence in Mexico: Would Legalizing Marijuana in California Help?*, RAND International Programs and Drug Policy Research Center, 2010.

"at the extreme, Mexican drug trafficking organizations could lose some 20 to 25 percent of their drug export income, and a smaller, though difficult to estimate, percentage of their total revenues."[292]

Other scholars have based their estimates of the potential financial effects of marijuana legalization on drug trafficking organizations on a hypothetical federal legalization of marijuana. Large transnational drug trafficking organizations have historically generated a majority of their marijuana-related income from exporting the drug to the United States and selling it to wholesalers on the U.S. side of the border.[293] This revenue could be jeopardized if the United States were to legalize the production and consumption of recreational marijuana. Of note, the Tax Foundation has estimated that the annual U.S. marijuana market is $45 billion.[294] Another organization, the ArcView group, estimated that marijuana sales across the United States and Canada generated a combined $53.3 billion in 2016—of which $46.4 billion was attributed to the black market.[295] Under a legalization regime, some portion of the revenue that might otherwise be generated by traffickers could be lost to authorized sellers (in the form of profits) and governments (in the form of taxes).

Even if legalization of marijuana in the United States undercuts drug trafficking organizations' marijuana profits, it is important to consider the shifting landscape of how these traffickers generate proceeds, which may include other illicit drugs, commodities, or activities. For instance, researchers and officials have noted declines in marijuana seizures by border officials coinciding with increasing state-level marijuana legalization initiatives and production of domestic marijuana in the United States.[296] At the same time, there have been increases in seizures of other illicit drugs;[297] increased seizures could reflect, among other things, greater smuggling activity

---

292 Organization of American States, *The Drug Problem in the Americas: Studies: The Economics of Drug Trafficking*, p. 41.

293 Beau Kilmer, Jonathan P. Caulkins, and Brittany M. Bond et al., *Reducing Drug Trafficking Revenues and Violence in Mexico: Would Legalizing Marijuana in California Help?*, RAND International Programs and Drug Policy Research Center, 2010.

294 Gavin Ekins and Joseph Henchman, *Marijuana Legalization and Taxes: Federal Revenue Impact*, Tax Foundation, May 12, 2016.

295 Will Yakowicz, "Illegal Pot Sales Topped $46.4 Billion in 2016, and That's Good News for Marijuana Entrepreneurs," *Inc.*, January 17, 2017. Of note, ArcView is a cannabis investment and market research firm.

296 See, for example, David Agren, "Mexican Cartels Pushing More Heroin after U.S. States Relax Marijuana Laws," *USA Today*, February 20, 2018.

297 See CBP enforcement statistics at https://www.cbp.gov/newsroom/stats/cbp-enforcement-statistics.

associated with increased production and demand for other illicit drugs, as well as profits from their sale. As such, even if domestic legalization initiatives are associated with declining foreign marijuana production and smuggling by transnational criminal networks, these criminals may be generating increased proceeds from a shift to other illicit drugs and related activities. In addition, they could generate proceeds from black or gray market operations within the United States.

Tax Revenue

Proponents of marijuana legalization often point to new tax revenue as a positive outcome of state legalization of retail sale. All of the states that have legalized marijuana for recreational purposes levy some combination of specific taxes (or excise taxes) and business licensing fees at the marijuana cultivation and/or retail sales levels, in addition to general state sales taxes.[298] Excise tax rates on the cultivation and retail sales of marijuana are more commonly levied on an ad valorem basis, or as a percentage of retail price.[299] According to calculations of state data by the Institute on Taxation and Economic Policy (ITEP), annual excise tax revenue collected by states with legalized recreational sales surpassed $1 billion in 2018.[300]

The tax treatment of medical marijuana varies by state. In some states, medical marijuana is indirectly taxed further back on the distribution chain at the cultivator level. In Pennsylvania, for example, state law requires growers/processors to pay a 5% excise tax on the "gross receipts from the sale of medical marijuana to the dispensary."[301]

---

[298] For a summary of these rapidly changing state law developments, see resources such as Federation of Tax Administrators, "Status of State Taxation/Sales of Marijuana," at http://m.taxadmin.org/marijuana/#; Carl Davis et al., "Taxing Cannabis," Institute on Taxation and Economic Policy (ITEP), January 23, 2019, at https://itep.org/taxing-cannabis/; and Janelle Cammenga, "How High Are Taxes on Recreational Marijuana in Your State?" Tax Foundation, April 24, 2019, at https://taxfoundation.org/2019-recreational-marijuana-taxes/. As mentioned in the "Recreational Marijuana" section of this report, Washington, DC, has not legalized the commercial sale of recreational marijuana.

[299] This is in contrast to federal and state conventions to tax products like cigarettes and tobacco on a per unit basis.

[300] See Figure 5 in Carl Davis et al., "Taxing Cannabis," Institute on Taxation and Economic Policy (ITEP), January 23, 2019, at https://itep.org/taxing-cannabis/.

[301] Pennsylvania Department of Revenue, *Medical Marijuana Gross Receipts Tax*, https://www.revenue.pa.gov/ GeneralTaxInformation/.

While some states utilize marijuana-related revenue streams for general spending purposes, others have approved measures to dedicate a portion of this revenue for spending on a wide range of programs, such as education, economic development, public safety and criminal justice, and public health and substance abuse.[302]

Overall, these tax and spending regimes have been subject to change, as government officials and voters respond to changes in revenue collections and budget priorities.

Employment and Educational Consequences of the Marijuana Policy Gap for Individuals

The marijuana policy gap between the federal government and states has widened nearly every year for over 25 years. Consequences of the gap are discussed throughout this report, and this section examines a selection of consequences for individuals who act in compliance with state law but violate federal law. As individuals have pressed forward with manufacturing, sale, and use of marijuana, consequences of the gap have arisen—two of the more publicized consequences for individuals in states that legalized marijuana, as discussed in this section of the report, are termination of employment due to marijuana use and implications for postsecondary students.

Employment and Legal Marijuana Use[303]

Although 18 states and the District of Columbia now permit the recreational use of marijuana, these developments have not restricted the ability of employers to terminate employees for such use. The laws of most of the states that have legalized recreational marijuana use indicate that employers may continue to maintain policies that prohibit employees' use of the drug.[304] For

---

[302] See Appendix A in Carl Davis et al., "Taxing Cannabis," Institute on Taxation and Economic Policy (ITEP), January 23, 2019, at https://itep.org/taxing-cannabis/.

[303] This section was authored by Jon Shimabukuro, Legislative Attorney in CRS's American Law Division (ALD). It uses citation and other editorial styles consistent with ALD's reports.

[304] *See, e.g.*, Alaska Stat. § 17.38.220(a); Cal. Health & Safety Code § 11362.45(f); Colo. Const. Art. 18, § 16(6)(a); 410 Ill. Comp. Stat. 705/10-50(a); Mass. Gen. Laws ch.94G, § 2(e); Nev. Rev. Stat. § 595.180.1(a); Vt. Stat. Ann. tit. 18, § 4230a(e)(3).

example, California law provides that nothing in the statute legalizing recreational marijuana use "affect[s] the ability of employers to have policies prohibiting the use of cannabis by employees and prospective employees, or prevent[s] employers from complying with state or federal law."[305] It is the case, however, that the laws of some states that have legalized medical marijuana specifically aim to protect medical marijuana users from discrimination in the workplace.[306]

In two jurisdictions that permit both medical and recreational marijuana use but do not explicitly address in law an employer's ability to prohibit or discourage such use by employees, courts have declined to recognize wrongful termination claims involving the medical use of the drug.[307] A claim of wrongful termination in violation of public policy is permitted in many jurisdictions as an exception to the common law employment-at-will doctrine, which allows an employer to terminate an employee for any reason other than what is prohibited by law.[308] A wrongful termination claim is premised on the belief that the law should not permit an employee to be discharged for engaging in an activity that is beneficial to the public welfare.[309] In general, a wrongful termination claim encompasses four broad categories of conduct: (1) refusing to commit an unlawful act; (2) exercising a legal right; (3) fulfilling a public obligation, such as military service; and (4) whistleblowing.[310]

An employee asserting a wrongful termination claim must often establish a clear public policy that would be undermined if the individual's dismissal were sustained.[311] This public policy may be located in a state's statutes or regulations.[312] After reviewing medical marijuana laws in Washington and the

---

[305] Cal. Health & Safety Code § 11362.45(f).

[306] Iris Hentze, *Cannabis and Employment: Medical and Recreational Policies in the States*, National Conference of State Legislatures, November 1, 2021.

[307] Roe v. TeleTech Customer Care Management (Colorado) LLC, 257 P.3d 586 (Wash. 2011); Coles v. Harris Teeter, LLC, 217 F.Supp.3d 185 (D.D.C. 2016).

[308] *See* John F. Buckley IV and Ronald M. Green, 2018 State by State Guide to Human Resources Law § 5.04 (2018).

[309] *Id.*

[310] *Id.*

[311] *See, e.g., Coles*, 217 F.Supp.3d at 188 ("[A] plaintiff pleading a wrongful-termination claim based on the public- policy exception must identify a policy source that provides a 'clear mandate' in support of his claim").

[312] *TeleTech Customer Care Mgmt.*, 257 P.3d at 595 ("A statute may provide a public policy mandate for purposes of a wrongful termination claim even where the employer's conduct is beyond the reach of the statute's remedies."); *Coles*, 217 F.Supp.3d at 188 ("District of Columbia courts ... recognize a very narrow public-policy exception for cases in which the employee's termination offends some mandate of public policy that is firmly anchored in either the Constitution or in a statute or regulation which clearly reflects the particular public policy being relied upon.") (internal quotation marks omitted).

District of Columbia, courts in these jurisdictions rejected wrongful termination claims on the grounds that these laws did not establish a clear public policy that would require an employer to accept its employee's medical marijuana use.[313]

In *Roe v. TeleTech Customer Care Management (Colorado) LLC*, a newly hired employee who was authorized to use marijuana to treat her migraine headaches was terminated after she tested positive for marijuana in a drug test.[314] The employee maintained that her termination was in violation of a clear public policy allowing medical marijuana use in compliance with the Washington State Medical Use of Marijuana Act (MUMA), which provides a defense against the prosecution of physicians who authorize the use of the drug and patients who are engaged in its medical use.[315] The Washington Supreme Court concluded, however, that MUMA's provisions could not support a "broad public policy that would remove all impediments to authorized medical marijuana use or forbid an employer from discharging an employee because she uses medical marijuana."[316] The Court explained that the statute made little reference to medical marijuana use and employment, and that no other Washington court had found an unimpeded right to use the drug for medical purposes.[317]

Similarly, in *Coles v. Harris Teeter*, a District of Columbia federal district court rejected an employee's wrongful termination claim on the grounds that the District's Legalization of Marijuana for Medical Treatment Amendment Act did not provide a clear public policy mandate for an employer to accept an employee's medical marijuana use.[318] Rather, the court maintained that the act appeared to "leave room for employers to remove workers who fail a drug test for marijuana use or violate workplace drug-prevention policies."[319] In addition, the court observed that the District's decision to permit medical marijuana use should not be construed to establish a clear public policy against an employer's ability to terminate an employee for such use. The court observed

> [T]he District here can at most be said to maintain a public policy that decriminalizes and allows the consumption of marijuana for private medical

---

313 *TeleTech Customer Care Mgmt.*, 257 P.3d at 596; *Coles*, 217 F.Supp.3d at 188.
314 *TeleTech Customer Care Mgmt.*, 257 P.3d at 589.
315 *Id.*
316 *Id.* at 596.
317 *Id.*
318 *Coles*, 217 F.Supp.3d at 188.
319 *Id.*

reasons. That is a far cry from prohibiting employers from terminating such users.[320]

Although *TeleTech Customer Care Management* and *Coles* involved medical rather than recreational marijuana use, they arguably suggest that a wrongful termination claim based on recreational use may not be successful if a state's laws do not clearly address whether an employer must accommodate an employee's recreational marijuana use.

Issues for Students at Postsecondary Institutions

Differing state and federal laws regarding the treatment of marijuana have brought to light a range of implications for postsecondary students at institutions of higher education (IHEs), as discussed below.

Federally Required Institutional Drug Abuse Prevention Policies

Section 120 of the Higher Education Act (HEA; P.L. 89-329), as amended, specifies that to be eligible to receive funds or other forms of financial assistance under any federal program, an IHE must certify to the Department of Education (ED) that it has adopted and implemented a program to prevent the use of illicit drugs and alcohol by students and employees.[321] IHEs must, among other requirements, annually distribute to students and employees standards of conduct that "clearly prohibit, at a minimum, the unlawful possession, use, or distribution of illicit drugs and alcohol by students and employees on the institution's property or as part of any of the institution's activities" and that describe applicable local, state, or federal legal sanctions.[322] Thus, because marijuana is designated as a Schedule I drug under federal law, many IHEs, including those located in states or localities that have legalized or decriminalized marijuana, prohibit the possession, use, or distribution of it on campus.[323]

An IHE's prohibition of marijuana on campus may have varying implications. For example, it may affect students with medical marijuana

---

[320] *Id.*

[321] This requirement was first enacted under the Drug-Free Schools and Communities Act Amendments of 1989 (P.L. 101-226).

[322] HEA §120(a)(1); 20 U.S.C. §1011i(a)(1).

[323] See, for example, University of Colorado, Boulder, "CU Boulder Alcohol & Other Drugs Policy," https://www.colorado.edu/aod/penalties, accessed March 23, 2022.

prescriptions. In these instances, students may be required to store and use medical marijuana off campus. This issue may be particularly acute for students who live in on-campus residences and may have limited access to off-campus locations at which they could use their medical marijuana without risking sanctions by their IHE.[324] In addition, due to an IHE's prohibition of marijuana on campus, some IHEs may choose not to conduct research on marijuana, as they may be at risk of losing federal funds should they do so.[325]

Student Eligibility for Federal Student Aid

Title IV of the HEA authorizes the primary federal programs that provide financial assistance for postsecondary education. These programs include the Pell Grant program[326] and the Direct Loan program.[327] For over 20 years, HEA Section 484(r) specified that individuals convicted of specified drug-related offenses were ineligible for HEA Title IV student federal student aid.[328] Individuals who were convicted of the possession or sale of controlled substances under federal or state (but not local or municipal) law during a period of enrollment for which they are receiving HEA Title IV federal student aid were subject to having that aid eligibility temporarily or indefinitely suspended.[329] An individual's period of ineligibility depended on whether the conviction was for the sale or possession of drugs and whether he or she had previous offenses. An individual who lost eligibility temporarily could regain it the day after the period of ineligibility ended, or when he or she successfully completed a qualified drug rehabilitation program that included passing two unannounced drug tests. An individual who lost eligibility for an indefinite period could regain eligibility after successfully completing a qualified drug rehabilitation program that includes passing two unannounced drug tests (the individual was not required to complete the rest of the program after passing

---

[324] Eric S. Davidson, "Marijuana and the Drug Free Schools and Campuses Act," November 2015, https://www.eiu.edu/ihec/Marijuana%20and%20DFSCA.pdf.

[325] Owen Daugherty, "Risk of losing federal funding reason why medical marijuana research won't happen," *The Lantern*, August 23, 2017, https://www.thelantern.com/2017/08/risk-of-losing-federal-funding-reason-why-medical- marijuana-research-wont-happen/. See also Marijuana Moment, "Lawmakers want legal protections for universities that research marijuana," *Boston Globe*, April 26, 2019.

[326] For additional information, see CRS Report R45418, *Federal Pell Grant Program of the Higher Education Act: Primer*.

[327] For additional information, see CRS Report R45931, *Federal Student Loans Made Through the William D. Ford Federal Direct Loan Program: Terms and Conditions for Borrowers*.

[328] The provision was first enacted under the Higher Education Amendments of 1998 (P.L. 105-244).

[329] HEA §484(r); 20 U.S.C. §1091(r).

the two tests), or having the conviction reversed, set aside, or removed from his or her record and meeting additional criteria.[330] In December 2020, the FAFSA Simplification Act (Division FF, Title VII of the Consolidated Appropriations Act of 2021; P.L. 116-260) repealed the HEA Section 484(r) provisions relating to ineligibility for HEA Title IV aid due to drug-related convictions. Beginning with the 2021-2022 award year (July 1, 2021-June 30, 2022), the HEA Section 484(r) restrictions on HEA Title IV aid eligibility due to drug-related convictions no longer impact a student's eligibility for such aid.[331]

Separately, the Anti-Drug Abuse Act of 1988 (P.L. 100-690) authorizes federal and state judges to deny certain federal benefits, including HEA Title IV student aid, to individuals convicted of drug trafficking or possession under federal or state law. The suspension of benefits is at the discretion of the court and may range from up to one year for a first drug possession conviction to permanent ineligibility for a third drug trafficking conviction.[332]

Other Consequences of Marijuana Use under Federal Law

Aside from the consequences already discussed in this section, marijuana use may subject an individual to a number of other consequences under federal law regardless of whether that individual has been convicted of a marijuana-related offense. Other consequences include, but are not limited to, the inability to purchase and possess a firearm, inadmissibility for federal housing, and ineligibility for certain visas.

Firearms: Marijuana users may lose their ability to purchase and possess a firearm. Under the Gun Control Act of 1968 (18 U.S.C. Chapter 44), as amended, it is unlawful to possess, ship, transport, receive, or dispose of any firearm or ammunition to any person "who is an unlawful user of or addicted to any controlled substance" as defined by the CSA.[333]

---

[330] For additional information, see U.S. Department of Education, Office of Federal Student Aid, *2019-2020 Federal Student Aid Handbook*, vol. 1, pp. 20-21.

[331] Institutions of higher education were authorized to implement these changes as early as June 17, 2021, but were required to implement them no longer than 60 days thereafter. U.S. Department of Education, Early Implementation of the FAFSA Simplification Act's Removal of Requirements for Title IV Eligibility Related to Selective Service Registration and Drug-Related Convictions, 86 *Federal Register*, 32252-32253, June 17, 2021.

[332] 21 U.S.C. §862.

[333] 18 U.S.C. §§922(g)(3), 924(a)(2) and 27 C.F.R. §478.11.

Federally Assisted Housing: Federal law establishes that "illegal drug users" are ineligible for federally assisted housing.[334] The law requires public housing agencies and owners of federally assisted housing to establish standards that would allow the agencies or owners to prohibit admission to, or terminate the tenancy or assistance of, any such applicant or tenant.[335]

Immigration: Under the Immigration and Nationality Act (8 U.S.C. Chapter 12), individuals may be deemed ineligible for immigrant and nonimmigrant visas if they are violators of any (federal, state, and foreign) laws or regulations involving controlled substances.[336]

International Policy Context and Response

As states have continued to legalize recreational and medical marijuana and widened the policy gap between the states and federal government, some observers have expressed concern regarding the United States' compliance with international treaties.

International drug control is based on three foundational U.N. treaties: the (1) 1961 Single Convention on Narcotic Drugs as amended by the 1972 Protocol, (2) 1971 Convention on Psychotropic Substances, and (3) 1988 Convention against Illicit Traffic in Narcotic Drugs and Psychotropic Substances.[337] These treaties generally seek to curb the recreational use of dangerous and addictive narcotics and psychoactive substances while ensuring their availability for legitimate medicinal and scientific uses.

With respect to marijuana, state parties to the U.N. drug control treaties have committed to strict controls on the nonmedical, nonscientific cultivation, production, and use of cannabis, cannabis resin, extracts and tinctures of cannabis, as well as organic and synthetic cannabinoids, including THC and dronabinol.[338]

Despite international commitments to limit the global marijuana market, the drug remains among the most widely used in the world—leading multiple

---

334 42 U.S.C. §§13661-13662.

335 For a broader discussion of legal consequences of marijuana use, see CRS Report R43435, *Marijuana: Medical and Retail—Selected Legal Issues*.

336 8 U.S.C. §1182(a)(2)(A).

337 The texts of the three drug control treaties and the updated schedules of narcotic drugs and psychotropic substances under international control are available at https://www.unodc.org/unodc/en/commissions/CND/conventions.html.

338 Dronabinol is a cannabinoid and is the active ingredient in Marinol. See Appendix A.

countries to call for changes in the international community's approach to its control. According to the United Nations, some 200 million people aged 15 to 64 years reported in 2019 using cannabis at least once in the past year (4.0% of the world's population).[339] Cannabis plant cultivation is also nearly ubiquitous around the world. According to the United Nations, cannabis plants were cultivated in at least 151 countries between 2010 and 2019.[340] According to the International Narcotics Control Board (INCB), established by the 1961 Single Convention on Narcotic Drugs as an independent body to monitor country compliance with their treaty commitments, global licit production of cannabis grew from 1.4 tons in 2000 to 650.8 tons in 2020.[341]

In certain countries, national-level policy approaches to marijuana are changing. Some are considering the option to legalize and regulate marijuana, including for recreational use. The first country to legalize recreational use of marijuana was Uruguay in 2013, followed by Canada in 2018. In 2019, the Australian Capital Territory (the federal territory including Australia's capital Canberra) legalized cannabis possession and use. Several countries have decriminalized marijuana by eliminating or reducing the criminal penalties associated with some or all aspects of its cultivation, sale, and consumption.

Potentially reflecting international appetite for a change in how the international community approaches marijuana control, the Expert Committee on Drug Dependence (ECDD) of the World Health Organization (WHO) formally recommended in January 2019 to revise the scheduling of cannabis and several of its derivatives under the U.N. drug control treaties.[342] The U.N. policy-making body on drug matters, the Commission on Narcotic Drugs (CND), considered the WHO's proposals during its 63rd reconvened session, in December 2020.[343] At the meeting, States Parties voted to remove cannabis and cannabis resin from Schedule IV (most restrictive) of the 1961 Single Convention on Narcotic Drugs as amended by the 1972 Protocol, while

---

339 United Nations Office on Drugs and Crime (UNODC), *World Drug Report 2021*, Booklet 2, June 2021, p. 21.

340 UNODC, *World Drug Report 2021*, Booklet 3, June 2021, p. 11.

341 International Narcotics Control Board (INCB), *Report of the INCB for 2019*, February 27, 2020, p. 29; and *Report of the INCB for 2021*, March 10, 2022, p. 28.

342 World Health Organization (WHO), letter to the Secretary-General of the United Nations, January 24, 2019.

343 UNODC, *WHO Scheduling Recommendations on Cannabis and Cannabis-Related Substances*, March 2020, https://www.unodc.org/unodc/en/commissions/CND/Mandate_Functions/current-scheduling-recommendations.html.

continuing to list both on Schedule I.[344] The United States voted in favor of this proposal, explaining

> The vote of the United States to remove cannabis and cannabis resin from Schedule IV of the Single Convention while retaining them in Schedule I is consistent with the science demonstrating that while a safe and effective cannabis-derived therapeutic has been developed, cannabis itself continues to pose significant risks to public health and should continue to be controlled under the international drug control conventions.
>
> Further, this action has the potential to stimulate global research into the therapeutic potential and public health effects of cannabis, and to attract additional investigators to the field, including those who may have been deterred by the Schedule IV status of cannabis.[345]

Developments in U.S. marijuana laws and policies at the state level, particularly those that relate to recreational marijuana initiatives, have raised some concerns about the United States' compliance with international treaty obligations. The INCB has long been critical of jurisdictions that legalize recreational use of marijuana, including state-level U.S. policies. In its 2020 annual report, the INCB warned that

> legalization measures or regulations that permit the use of any controlled substance, including cannabis, for non-medical purposes are inconsistent with the obligations of States parties, in particular those included in article 4, paragraph (c), of the 1961 Convention
>
> [Single Convention on Narcotic Drugs of 1961] as amended. The Board calls upon all States to respect their Convention obligations in the development of their national drug control policies.[346]

---

[344] Schedule I includes substances that are liable to abuse and to produce ill effects, but may have potential therapeutic uses. Schedule IV includes substances listed under Schedule I, but whose liability risks are not offset by substantial therapeutic opportunities. Other substances listed on both Schedules I and IV include heroin and carfentanil. See United Nations, The International Drug Control Conventions, Schedules of the Single Convention on Narcotics Drugs of 1961 as amended by the 1972 Protocol, as at 7 May 2020, ST/CND/1/Add.1/Rev.6.

[345] U.S. Department of State, *U.S. Explanation of Vote on Changes in the Scope of Control of Cannabis and Cannabis-Related Substances*, December 2, 2020, https://vienna.usmission.gov/cnd-explanation-of-vote-on-changes-in-the-scope-of-control-of-cannabis-and-cannabis-related-substances/.

[346] INCB, *Report of the INCB for 2020*, March 25, 2021, p. 66. With regard to U.S. programs, the INCB further reported in its 2018 annual report that "most medical cannabis programmes in the United States do not comply with requirements of the international drug

Select Issues for Congress—The Path Forward

Given the current marijuana policy gap between the federal government and most states, there are a number of issues that Congress may address. These include, but are not limited to, marijuana's designation as a Schedule I controlled substance, financial services for marijuana businesses, federal tax issues for these businesses, oversight of federal law enforcement and its role in enforcing federal marijuana laws, and states' implementation of medical marijuana laws and the involvement of federal health care workers. Congress has raised these issues in hearings, through appropriations, and in bills introduced over the last several years.

Consideration of Marijuana as a Schedule I Drug: Expand, Minimize, or Eliminate the Policy Gap

As the gap between federal and state laws and policies on marijuana widens each year, policymakers might decide to reevaluate federal marijuana law and policy. In addressing state-level legalization efforts, Congress could take one of several routes. It could elect to take no action, thereby upholding the federal government's current marijuana policy and enforcement priorities and allowing states to carry on with implementation of recreational and medical marijuana laws. Alternatively, it may decide that the CSA must be enforced and direct federal law enforcement to dismantle state medical and recreational marijuana programs. Or, it could continue to take smaller steps to alleviate some of the problems associated with the policy gap, such as enacting appropriations provisions that temporarily restrict DOJ's ability to expend funds to enforce federal marijuana laws in states with medical marijuana programs, or altering the CSA definition of marijuana as it did with the 2018 farm bill. Congress may also decide to eliminate the gap altogether.

Take No Action Regarding the Gap

If Congress elects to take no action and uphold the federal government's current marijuana policy and enforcement priorities, the gap between the states' policies and those of the federal government likely will continue to

---

control treaties or United States national law" due to lax regulatory controls. See INCB, *Report of the INCB for 2018*, March 5, 2019, p. 9.

expand if recent trends continue. Each year, more states legalize recreational and medical marijuana further expanding the policy gap and its consequences.

Bolster the Federal Position or Expand the Gap

Another option would be for Congress to bolster the federal position on marijuana or take action to directly expand the gap with states (presuming that states continue to take actions to legalize and continue to not reverse such actions) such as reaffirming the dangers of marijuana, allowing for increased action against or within the states that have legalized (such as removing the appropriations riders and/or directing DOJ to take action), or increasing penalties for federal marijuana offenses.

Reaffirm the Dangers of Marijuana

Congress may choose to reaffirm that marijuana is a dangerous substance that is likely to be abused and has no recognized medical use. In report language and directives to agencies, Congress could authorize education initiatives and point to conclusions drawn by DEA and HHS in the 2016 decision to keep marijuana on Schedule I of the CSA—a decision based on the FDA's scientific evaluation and the legal standards of the CSA—that reaffirms the agencies' views that marijuana "does not have a currently accepted medical use in treatment in the United States, there is a lack of accepted safety for its use under medical supervision, and it has a high potential for abuse."[347] Further, Congress may choose to appoint a commission to review the comprehensive issue of marijuana use, abuse, enforcement, and treatment responses in the United States.

Increased Enforcement Action Against or Within States

Congress may decide that the CSA must be enforced and press for increased action against or within states to attempt to stop state-sanctioned, recreational or medical marijuana programs. Congress could stop utilizing the medical marijuana appropriations rider that prohibits DOJ from using appropriated funds to prevent states from implementing medical marijuana laws. This likely would create an even wider policy gap between the states and the federal government as most states have either comprehensive medical marijuana programs or allow recreational marijuana and developed retail systems, and

[347] DOJ, DEA, *Acting Administrator Rosenberg Response to request for Marijuana Rescheduling*, August 11, 2016.

some have both.[348] Nevertheless, as discussed in this report, federal law supersedes state law, and it is within the federal government's power to enforce all of the CSA, including marijuana law, in states and territories. It may decide to preempt all state laws authorizing recreational and medicinal use of marijuana. Arguably, this may close the gap as it would force states to realign their marijuana laws and policies with those of the federal government.

Increase Penalties for Marijuana Offenses

Congress may elect to increase penalties for federal marijuana offenses. Currently, illicit acts involving large quantities of marijuana carries a federal prison sentence of 10 years to life and a fine of up to $10 million for an individual or a fine of up to $50 million for an organization.[349] Penalties increase for subsequent offenses or if use of the substance causes death or serious bodily injury. Congress may increase the criminal fines and number of years for these offenses to reaffirm and strengthen the current federal prohibition on marijuana.

Minimize the Gap

Congress could choose to minimize the gap between the states and federal government, and begin to alleviate the consequences of the gap on individuals, state governments, and federal agencies.

Smaller Steps

In taking smaller steps to minimize the gap, Congress could adopt measures similar to the DOJ appropriations rider to minimize enforcement of federal law in states with medical marijuana programs, and alleviate the impact of the Schedule I status of marijuana on institutions, businesses, and individuals. For example, it could eliminate the education funding provision that an IHE must certify to ED that it has adopted and implemented a program to prevent the use of illicit drugs and alcohol by students and employees in order to receive federal funding.[350] It could also pass measures to prevent DOJ from using

---

[348] Of note, federal law enforcement arguably lacks the manpower and resources to tackle the issue. DEA confronts a variety of drug threats in the United States and abroad. It would have to considerably realign resources to target the marijuana industry in the United States. See DOJ, DEA, *FY2022 Performance Budget Congressional Budget Submission.*

[349] 21 U.S.C. §841.

[350] This requirement was first enacted under the Drug-Free Schools and Communities Act Amendments of 1989 (P.L. 101-226). See "Issues for Students at Postsecondary Institutions."

funds to prevent states from implementing *recreational* marijuana laws[351] or pass measures to increase researchers' access to a wider variety of marijuana for scientific research purposes or streamline Schedule I requirements for researchers.[352]

Reevaluate Marijuana

Similar to what was done with the Shafer Commission and the study of marijuana (see "The Shafer Commission"), Congress may consider establishing a commission of experts[353] to evaluate the efficacy of marijuana laws in the United States and address other issues such as the medicinal value and harm of marijuana use.[354] If a commission were to determine that marijuana no longer should be a Schedule I substance, Congress could decide to take legislative action to remove it from Schedule I. In doing so, Congress might (1) place marijuana on one of the other schedules (II, III, IV, or V) of controlled substances; (2) create another schedule or separate classification for marijuana under the CSA; or (3) remove marijuana as a controlled substance altogether.[355]

If marijuana remains a controlled substance under the CSA under any existing schedule, the existing conflict with states that have legalized recreational marijuana would remain, but if Congress chooses to reschedule,

---

[351] For example, in the 117th Congress, an amendment was offered (to amend H.R. 4505) that, if it had been enacted, would have prohibited DOJ from interfering with *any* state marijuana laws in FY2022 regardless if the laws allow medical or recreational.

[352] For example, the Medical Marijuana Research Act (H.R. 5657; as passed by the House on April 4, 2022) would amend Schedule I registration requirements to ease the process for those who wish to register to research marijuana. It would also direct DEA to register (1) practitioners to conduct medical marijuana research, and (2) manufacturers and distributors to supply marijuana for such research. Further, it would direct HHS (jointly with DOJ) to implement a specialized process for supplying marijuana products available through state-authorized marijuana programs to researchers until manufacturers and distributors can provide a sufficient supply of marijuana for medical research. Alternatively, the Cannabidiol and Marihuana Research Expansion Act (S. 253; as passed by the Senate on March 24, 2022) would establish new CSA research protocols specifically for marijuana and direct DEA to accelerate the process for the agency to respond to applicants that seek to manufacture marijuana for research, among other things. Unlike H.R. 5657, it would not direct HHS/DOJ to implement a process for researchers to use products from state-authorized marijuana programs.

[353] Experts may include law enforcement, medical doctors, drug policy researchers, and drug treatment experts, among others.

[354] This would be similar to the efforts of the National Commission on Marihuana and Drug Abuse, also known as the Shafer Commission, which was established under the CSA to study marijuana in the United States. See "The Shafer Commission" for further discussion.

[355] Congress has introduced a number of bills that would, among other things, either move marijuana to another schedule or remove it from the CSA altogether.

that may help resolve conflicts with comprehensive state medical marijuana laws. A Schedule II-V classification under the CSA would allow for lawful prescriptions for marijuana. Alternatively, the creation of a new schedule solely for marijuana would give Congress an opportunity, aside from rescheduling to Schedules II-V or removing it from the CSA, to modify the legal status of marijuana under the CSA. For example, it could design a new schedule that allows for medical and recreational distribution while maintaining some control over the amount and quality of the substance.

Eliminate the Gap

As previously noted, Congress may decide to preempt all state laws authorizing recreational and medicinal use of marijuana, and arguably, this may close the gap as it would force states to realign their marijuana laws and policies with those of the federal government. Pursuant to the Supremacy Clause, Congress can preempt state law through federal statutes like the CSA; however, the CSA provides that it does not preempt state laws "unless there is a positive conflict between [the CSA] and that State law so that the two cannot consistently stand together" (see Appendix E for further discussion of the Supremacy Clause and preemption).

If Congress chooses to remove marijuana as a controlled substance under the CSA and its criminal provisions, this would largely eliminate the policy gap with states that have authorized recreational and comprehensive medical marijuana. In eliminating criminal control over marijuana and all cannabis, Congress may still take actions that allows for regulatory control. These are a few examples:

- it could devote additional resources to the FDA and USDA to ensure the safety and quality of the many different available cannabis products,
- it could seek to regulate and tax commercial marijuana activities, and
- it could enable and promote the trade of cannabis products made in the United States.

Whether Congress decides to address the gap with the states or not, the states have continued to act on marijuana legalization, further expanding the policy gap, and no state has reversed its legalization of either medical or recreational marijuana.[356]

---

[356] Several initiatives have been overturned in court or halted by Congress.

Provision of Financial Services to the Marijuana Industry

Given the limited guidance issued by FinCEN and DOJ, many financial institutions remain reluctant to enter openly into relationships with state-authorized marijuana businesses.[357] Some marijuana businesses and marijuana industry proponents have raised concerns that even when marijuana businesses are able to open bank accounts or secure other financial services, those customer relationships are frequently terminated in relatively short order, especially when the existence of such relationships with the financial institutions becomes public.[358]

Over the years, legislative proposals have been introduced that are designed to jump start financial relationships with state-authorized marijuana businesses.[359] Of particular note, the Secure And Fair Enforcement Banking Act of 2021 (SAFE Banking Act; H.R. 1996; S. 910),[360] would, among other things, attempt to

- constrain federal banking regulator authority to penalize depository institutions for providing financial services to marijuana businesses operating in compliance with state laws; and
- protect depository institutions and their personnel from some legal liability under the anti-money laundering laws and asset forfeiture laws when providing financial services to, or investing proceeds derived from serving, marijuana businesses operating in compliance with state laws.

Of note, the SAFE Banking Act was added as an amendment to the National Defense Authorization Act (NDAA) for Fiscal Year 2022 (H.R. 4350) which passed the House in September 2021, but it was *not* included in the Senate version of the NDAA for FY2022 (S. 1605) which was ultimately enacted into law (P.L. 117-81). SAFE Banking Act provisions were again

357 Sophie Quinton, *Why Marijuana Businesses Still Can't Get Bank Accounts*, The PEW Charitable Trusts, March 22, 2016.

358 Ibid. See also David Migoya, "Oregon bank opens doors to Colorado marijuana businesses," *The Denver Post*, January 20, 2015.

359 See, for example, S. 683, 114th Congress (2015); S. 1726, 114th Congress (2015); H.R. 1538, 114th Congress (2015); H.R. 2076, 114th Congress (2015); S. 1152, 115th Congress (2017); H.R. 2215, 115th Congress (2017); H.R. 1595, 116th Congress (2019); S. 1200, 116th Congress (2019); H.R. 1996, 117th Congress (2021); and S. 910, 117th Congress (2021).

360 See also S. 1200, 116th Congress (2019).

included in the House-passed America COMPETES Act of 2022 (H.R. 4521), but as of April 1, 2022, this bill has not been considered by the Senate.

While such measures, if enacted, might encourage some new entrants into the industry, many financial institutions and their federal regulators may remain apprehensive about ties to marijuana businesses while the drug is listed as a Schedule I controlled substance under the CSA. In the absence of legislative change to the CSA, federal marijuana enforcement priorities and policies could quickly be reversed or otherwise be significantly altered so as to greatly increase the risk of legal liability.[361]

Federal Tax Treatment

Marijuana producers and retailers may not deduct the costs of selling their product (e.g., payroll, rent, advertising) for the purposes of federal income tax filings.[362] The Internal Revenue Code (IRC) Section 280E states that

> No deduction or credit shall be allowed for any amount paid or incurred during the taxable year in carrying on any trade or business if such trade or business (or the activities which comprise such trade or business) consists of trafficking in controlled substances (within the meaning of schedule I and II of the Controlled Substances Act) which is prohibited by Federal law or the law of any State in which such trade or business is conducted.

Media reports indicate that the Internal Revenue Service (IRS) has enforced Section 280E in audits of marijuana-related businesses by refusing to accept these businesses' deductions.[363] IRC Section 280E does not prohibit a marijuana business from deducting the costs of cultivating or acquiring marijuana as a "cost of goods sold," though.[364] Effectively, the disqualification of deductions constitutes an implicit tax on marijuana-related businesses equal to the value of the tax benefit of such deductions if these

---

361 See, generally, CRS Report R43708, *The Take Care Clause and Executive Discretion in the Enforcement of Law*.

362 For more legal analysis, see CRS Report R44056, *Marijuana and Federal Tax Law: In Brief*.

363 See, for example, Jeff Daniels, "IRS Said to be Auditing Colorado Marijuana Businesses," *CNBC*, July 12, 2016, http://www.cnbc.com/2016/07/12/irs-said-to-be-auditing-colorado-marijuana-businesses.html; and Will Yankowicz, "Marijuana Companies' Biggest Battle Might Be Against the IRS," *Slate*, July 1, 2016, http://www.slate.com/blogs/moneybox/2016/07/01/legal_cannabis_businesses_pay_taxes_under_a_code_reserved_for_illegal_drug.html.

364 See CRS Report R44056, *Marijuana and Federal Tax Law: In Brief*.

firms had engaged in an industry that was legal under federal law. One such public case involves the Sacramento-based Canna Care marijuana dispensary. The IRS disallowed $2.6 million in deductions for employee salaries, rent, and other costs over a three-year period, which resulted in the business owing $875,000 in additional taxes. Canna Care challenged the IRS in U.S. Tax Court, but ultimately the court upheld the IRS ruling.[365] The IRS has also successfully challenged marijuana-related businesses attempting to structure business entities, in part, to work around Section 280E.[366]

The discrepancies between federal, state, and local tax treatments of marijuana-related businesses create economic incentives to engage in the underground economy, all else being equal. In addition to the uncertainty of federal tax enforcement procedures (and costs of any related legal assistance), the inability of marijuana businesses to deduct their business expenses is effectively an implicit tax up to 37% (if organized as sole-proprietor or partnership) or 21% (if organized as a C corporation) on these expenses.[367] These implicit taxes are paid in addition to state and local sales and special excise taxes. The status quo administration of federal tax laws creates an economic advantage for illicit marijuana sellers, who are not subject to direct taxation of their sales.

Marijuana-related tax bills in the 116th and 117th Congress have varied in scope. One bill would have exempted a business that conducts marijuana sales in compliance with state law from the Section 280E prohibition against allowing business-related tax credits or deductions for expenditures in connection with trafficking in controlled substances.[368] A second bill would

---

[365] See Canna Care, Inc. v. Commissioner, T.C. Memo 2015-206, October 22, 2015, at https://www.ustaxcourt.gov/ UstcInOp/OpinionViewer.aspx?ID=10586. The Ninth Circuit Court of Appeals upheld the tax court's decision. For more details, see Canna Law Blog, "Cannabis Taxes and Section 280E: Canna Care v. The IRS," August 13, 2017, at https://www.cannalawblog.com/cannabis-taxes-and-section-280e-canna-care-v-the-irs/.

[366] See, for example, see Robert McVay, "Tax Court Deals Another Blow to Cannabis Management Company Model," Canna Law Blog, December 28, 2018, at https://www.cannalawblog.com/tax-court-deals-another-blow-to-cannabis- management-company-model/.

[367] With 21% being the top marginal tax bracket for corporations and 37% being the top marginal tax bracket for individuals under the federal income tax code. The 37% rate is temporary through 2025, and is before the potential application of the temporary Section 199A 20% deduction for passthrough business income. For more information on Section 199A, see CRS In Focus IF11122, *Section 199A Deduction for Pass-through Business Income: An Overview*. It is unclear whether businesses selling marijuana in states that legalized recreational sales will be able to claim Section 199A because of the prohibitions in Section 280E.

[368] The Small Business Tax Equity Act of 2019 (H.R. 1118; S. 422), 116th Congress.

have removed marijuana from the schedule of controlled substances (and, indirectly, IRC Section 280E restrictions on marijuana),[369] while a third would have imposed a federal excise tax on domestic recreational marijuana retail sales that would begin at 10% of the price and escalate to 25% over four years.[370] After this phase-in period, the 25% tax rate would apply to a "prevailing sales price" of marijuana products sold in the United States in the past year, as determined by the Secretary of the Treasury. Products containing a marijuana derivative would also be taxed, in part, based on THC content. Another bill would remove marijuana's federal designation as a controlled substance and impose a federal excise tax on manufacturers' sales of marijuana and marijuana products, which would fund various business programs and create a grant program to fund services for those "most adversely affected by the War on Drugs."[371]

Like many of the state excise tax regimes, the federal proposals that would levy a tax based on a percentage of the price of marijuana, also known as an ad valorem tax, could introduce questions that may complicate tax compliance and administration. For example, when a product containing marijuana is bundled with non-marijuana components (e.g., edible ingredients, oils, or consumption devices), does the tax apply to the final product or just the value of the marijuana-derived component? When a marijuana producer sells input products (e.g., dried leaves, marijuana extracts) to a related, downstream producer, would the IRS have difficulties in enforcing that the two businesses applied the tax rate to an arm's length transfer price similar to two unrelated parties?

In contrast, a per unit tax typically is less likely to introduce such administrative complications.[372] It would also decouple the projected revenues from the tax from the pre-tax price of marijuana, which would be expected to decline as production increases. The tax rate could also be indexed for inflation to maintain the purchasing power of the tax rate imposed. A per unit tax regime, though, would require specifying the types of products subject to tax and unit of tax (e.g., dried marijuana leaf weight versus freshly picked, or wet, weight; THC content).[373] Such a tax, if imposed at the manufacturer and

---

369 The Regulate Marijuana Like Alcohol Act (H.R. 420), 116th Congress.

370 The Marijuana Revenue and Regulation Act (H.R. 1120; S. 420), 116th Congress.

371 The Marijuana Opportunity Reinvestment and Expungement Act of 2021 (H.R. 3617), 117th Congress.

372 At the federal and state levels, per unit taxes are commonly administered on items such as cigarettes (per pack), alcoholic beverages (volume), and gasoline (volume).

373 For a more general analysis of federal proposals to tax marijuana, see CRS Report R43785, *Federal Proposals to Tax Marijuana: An Economic Analysis*.

importer level, would also simplify and focus administration on a smaller number of collection points (compared to the retail excise tax).[374]

Oversight of Federal Law Enforcement in States That Have Legalized Marijuana

Given the issues that have arisen from the marijuana policy gap, Congress may conduct oversight of federal law enforcement and its role in enforcing federal marijuana laws. There are a number of issues Congress may review including how state marijuana legalization has affected agency missions, joint operations between state and local law enforcement, and federal law enforcement policy and priorities.

Review of Agency Missions

In exercising its oversight authorities, Congress may choose to examine the extent to which (if at all) federal law enforcement missions—in particular, DEA's mission—are affected by state legalization of marijuana. For instance, policymakers may elect to review the mission of each federal law enforcement agency involved in enforcing the CSA and examine how its drug-related investigations may be influenced by the varying state-level policies regarding marijuana. As noted, federal law enforcement has generally prioritized investigations of drug traffickers and dealers over that of low-level drug users. Policymakers may question whether these policies and priorities are implemented consistently across states with different drug policies regarding marijuana.

Cooperation with State and Local Law Enforcement

One issue policymakers may debate is how to conduct oversight of multi-jurisdictional drug task forces, fusion centers, and other coordinating bodies charged with combating marijuana-related crimes and other threats to public safety. Policymakers may consider whether federal, state, and local law enforcement agencies are able to achieve task force goals related to marijuana control when there is a gap between state and federal marijuana policy, and between neighboring states that have conflicting policies. Policymakers may choose to evaluate whether certain drug task force strategies and operations

---

[374] This is similar to federal excise taxation of cigarettes and alcoholic beverages, where the tax is imposed at the manufacturer or producer level, or at the importer level.

should be modified in states that have established laws and policies that are either inconsistent—such as in states that have *decriminalized* small amounts of marijuana possession—or are in direct conflict—including states that have *legalized* either medical or recreational marijuana—with federal drug policy. For instance, might there be any internal conflicts that prevent task force partners from collaborating effectively to carry out their marijuana-related investigations? Does it create conflict between state and federal parties when local law enforcement officers are required to return seized marijuana?

Of note, the Arizona Court of Appeals ruled that patients who possess marijuana in compliance with the Arizona Medical Marijuana Act are entitled to the return of their marijuana that law enforcement may have seized during a traffic stop.[375] In states such as Colorado, media reports indicated that some local law enforcement officers avoided seizing marijuana in certain cases because they do not want to have to return the marijuana to its owner—an act that is tantamount to distribution of a Schedule I controlled substance, a violation of federal law.[376] In 2017, the Colorado Supreme Court ruled that police officers cannot be forced to return marijuana to defendants even if they are acquitted of marijuana crimes.[377]

Evaluating Federal Enforcement Priorities and Monitoring the Effects of State Legalization of Marijuana

When states began to legalize medical and recreational marijuana, DOJ issued a series of memos describing federal enforcement priorities for states with legal marijuana programs. Additionally, according to DOJ, it monitors the effects of state legalization by

- collaborating among its own components and with other federal agencies in assessing marijuana enforcement-related data;
- prosecuting cases that threaten federal enforcement priorities; and
- consulting with state officials about areas of federal concern.[378]

---

[375] State v. Okun, 231 Ariz. 462 (Ariz. Ct. App. 2013). The U.S. Supreme Court denied certiorari in 2014. Arizona v. Okun, 572 U.S.___, 134 S. Ct. 1759 (2014).

[376] Jessica Maher, "Law enforcement conflicts still exist with legal pot," *Reporter-Herald*, January 2, 2014.

[377] People v. Crouse, 2017 CO 5, 388 P.3d 39 (2017 Colo).

[378] U.S. Government Accountability Office (GAO), *DOJ Should Document Its Approach to Monitoring the Effects of Legalization*, GAO-16-1, December 30, 2015. GAO has not reassessed DOJ's efforts to monitor state legalization since release of the 2015 report.

As of December 2015, however, DOJ had not documented its efforts to monitor the effects of state legalization and ensure that its enforcement priorities are being emphasized. It is unclear if and how metrics[379] were being used to determine the impact of state marijuana laws and policy, and whether federal intervention is needed in states that have legalized.[380] For example, one of the eight enforcement priorities listed in the Cole memo was to prevent the diversion of marijuana to other states, such as from Colorado to neighboring Kansas, a state that has not legalized marijuana. While it seems Colorado marijuana is the prevalent illicit marijuana available in Kansas,[381] DOJ did not take action against Colorado's medical or recreational marijuana programs. It is unclear what level of trafficking would be necessary to trigger action by the federal government against state marijuana laws.

Congress may choose to exercise oversight over DOJ's enforcement priorities and methods for tracking illicit marijuana-related activity in the states. DOJ may alter or reverse its enforcement priorities at any time. In May 2021, Attorney General Garland indicated that DOJ would not be using its resources to interfere with state marijuana laws.[382]

Medical Marijuana

Congress may consider a number of issues related to its authority over medical marijuana. Two of the more prominent issues for Congress has been its direction to DOJ to not interfere with states' implementation of medical marijuana laws and veterans' access to medical marijuana.

State Medical Marijuana Laws and Federal Law Enforcement

State medical marijuana laws have raised questions for federal policymakers about enforcing federal law related to marijuana when individuals or

---

[379] It is unclear if DOJ used metrics, and if it did, it is also unclear what metrics were used.

[380] U.S. Government Accountability Office (GAO), *DOJ Should Document Its Approach to Monitoring the Effects of Legalization*, GAO-16-1, December 30, 2015, pp. 30-31.

[381] According to a report from the Kansas Attorney General, "the major effect of Colorado marijuana 'legalization' appears to be that high grade marijuana from Colorado has to a large extent replaced lower grade marijuana from Mexico and home grown marijuana." See Attorney General, State of Kansas, *"Legalization" of Marijuana in Colorado: The Impact on Kansas*, Compiled by Assistant Solicitor General Dwight Carswell, October 10, 2016, p. 1.

[382] U.S. Congress, House Committee on Appropriations, Subcommittee on Commerce, Justice, Science, and Related Agencies, *Fiscal Year 2022 Budget Request for The Department of Justice*, 117th Cong., 1st sess., May 4, 2021.

organizations are acting in compliance with state law. Since 2015 Congress has included policy riders in appropriations acts each year to prohibit DOJ from using funds to prevent states from implementing their medical marijuana laws.[383] Congress may decide to alter, maintain, or reverse this provision.[384] Notably, in a March 2021 White House press briefing, the Biden Administration signaled its support for federal decriminalization of marijuana and indirectly voiced its support for medical marijuana in referring to campaign statements made in 2020: "He [President Biden] spoke about this on the campaign. He believes in decriminalizing the use of marijuana, but his position has not changed."[385]

In the 116th Congress, legislation was introduced that would have amended the CSA such that provisions relating to marijuana would not apply to a person who is acting in compliance with relevant state law.[386] Policymakers may alternatively choose to more closely examine the finer points in state medical marijuana laws, and direct federal agencies such as DEA to intercede, as laws are not uniform across the country and law enforcement has voiced concern over some details of state medical marijuana programs. For example, according to an investigation by Rocky Mountain Public Broadcasting Service (RMPBS), federal law enforcement believes that home cultivation contributed to the growth of the black market in Colorado. While Colorado has since reduced the number of medical marijuana plants allowed to be grown, it previously allowed individuals to grow up to 99 plants

---

383 See the Consolidated and Further Continuing Appropriations Act, 2015 (P.L. 113-235), §538; the Consolidated Appropriations Act, 2016 (P.L. 114-113), §542; the Consolidated Appropriations Act, 2017 (P.L. 115-31), §537; the Consolidated Appropriations Act, 2018 (P.L. 115-141), §538; and the Consolidated Appropriations Act, 2019 (P.L. 116-6), §537. The medical marijuana provision remained in effect during the FY2020 continuing resolution (the Continuing Appropriations Act, 2020, and Health Extenders Act of 2019; P.L. 116-59) that continued appropriations for the bureaus and agencies funded through the annual Commerce, Justice, Science, and Related Agencies appropriations until November 21, 2019.

384 The medical marijuana policy rider would cease to be in effect if Congress does not either continue to put it in the appropriations act, or add futurity language (thereby making it permanent).

385 The White House, Office of the Press Secretary, "Press Briefing by Press Secretary Jen Psaki, March 30, 2021," March 30, 2021, https://www.whitehouse.gov/briefing-room/press-briefings/2021/03/30/press-briefing-by-press- secretary-jen-psaki-march-30-2021/; and Bob Woods, "The cannabis industry could be a big winner on Election Day," *CNBC*, October 18, 2020.

386 See, for example, the Responsibly Addressing the Marijuana Policy Gap Act of 2019 (S. 421/H.R. 1119) and the Compassionate Access, Research Expansion, and Respect States Act of 2019 (CARERS Act of 2019, H.R. 127).

(with a doctor recommendation).[387] Congress, among other options, could choose to refine its annual appropriations rider[388] to disallow laws that permit a large number of homegrown marijuana plants for personal medical use.

State Medical Marijuana Laws and the Department of Veterans Affairs

A topic of particular interest to federal policymakers has been how federal health care providers—especially those in the Department of Veterans Affairs (VA)—may have changed how they conduct their work in states with medical marijuana laws. VA policy allows for Veterans Health Administration (VHA) providers to discuss marijuana use with patients and does not deny health care services to veterans who participate in state marijuana programs. However, VHA providers are prohibited from completing the forms that are necessary for patients to access medical marijuana.[389] In recent years, Members in both chambers have introduced legislation that would allow VHA providers to complete such forms.[390] The VA is against allowing its providers to complete these forms at this time for several reasons: (1) the uncertainty about the clinical benefits of marijuana, (2) the often unknown potency in marijuana products available in state marijuana programs, and (3) based on guidance from DEA, VHA providers would not be exempt from criminal sanctions per enforcement of the CSA.[391]

---

[387] Colorado residents may now grow up to six plants per resident over age 21. See State of Colorado, *Home Grow Laws*, https://www.colorado.gov/pacific/marijuana/home-grow-laws; and Lori Jane Gliha, John Ferrugia, and Brittany Freeman, "Cultivating Crime: How Colorado Became a Major Exporter of Illegal Marijuana," *Rocky Mountain PBS News*, December 12, 2018, p. http://www.rmpbs.org.

[388] This is the annual appropriations rider that prohibits DOJ from using funds to prevent states from implementing their medical marijuana laws, which is discussed in other sections of this report.

[389] Department of Veterans Affairs, Veterans Health Administration (VHA), *Access to VHA Clinical Programs for Veterans Participating In State- Approved Marijuana Programs*, VHA Directive 1315, Washington, DC, December 8, 2017, https://www.publichealth.va.gov/marijuana.asp. This directive will expire on December 31, 2022.

[390] See the Veterans Equal Access Act (H.R. 1647 in the 116th Congress); the Medical Cannabis Research Act of 2019 (H.R. 601 in the 116th Congress); and the Veterans Cannabis Use for Safe Healing Act (H.R. 2191 in the 116th Congress). Other bills have also attempted to address veterans' access to cannabis including the Veterans Cannabis Use for Safe Healing Act (H.R. 430 in the 117th Congress); the Veterans Medical Marijuana Safe Harbor Act (H.R. 2588; S. 1183); the VA Medicinal Cannabis Research Act of 2021 (H.R. 2916; S. 1467 in the 117th Congress); the Veterans CARE Act (H.R. 2932 in the 117th Congress); the Common Sense Cannabis Reform for Veterans, Small Businesses, and Medical Professionals Act (H.R. 3105 in the 117th Congress); and the Fully Informed Veteran Act of 2021 (H.R. 3601).

[391] U.S. Congress, House Committee on Veterans' Affairs, Subcommittee on Health, *Statement of Dr. Keita Franklin, National Director for Suicide Prevention, Office of Mental Health*

Conclusion

The discrepancies between federal and state marijuana laws result in businesses and individuals operating in a lawful manner in their respective states, but in an unlawful manner under federal law. The federal government holds that a product containing 0.3% THC or more is a dangerous substance, and federal law largely prohibits its cultivation, use, and sale; however, an adult may enter a marijuana dispensary in certain states and purchase a product with up to 90% THC content. Congress may address the gap between the states and the federal government in any number of ways to learn more about marijuana use. It may commission additional studies on: the medicinal benefits and the health risks of cannabis use, cannabis as a source of tax revenue, implications of legalization on criminal justice system resources, the impact of marijuana prohibition on individuals convicted of marijuana offenses, implications of marijuana legalization on the FDA and USDA, and other related issues of congressional concern.

Federal control of cannabis has evolved from the universal strict laws and policies of the 20th century to today where medical marijuana production and distribution is allowed in 37 states and 18 states allow access to marijuana for all adults. Congress may halt and reverse this evolution, take no action on the issue, continue to relinquish federal criminal control, or it may eliminate federal criminal control of cannabis altogether. Congress may consider the implications that any change to cannabis control would have for criminal drug control in the United States and around the world.

Appendix A. Key Terms Used in the Report

The following are key terms used through this report:

Cannabinoid: A naturally occurring chemical compound found in cannabis is referred to as a cannabinoid.

> *Cannabidiol (CBD):* CBD is a nonpsychoactive compound found in both marijuana and hemp. It is heavily researched for its potential medicinal value.

---

and Suicide Prevention, Veterans Health Administration (VHA), Department of Veterans Affairs, 116th Cong., 1st sess., April 30, 2019, pp. 8-11.

Delta-8-tetrahydrocannabinol (THC): Delta-8-THC is a psychoactive compound found in the Cannabis sativa plant, but not in significant amounts.

Delta-9-THC: Delta-9-THC is an abundant cannabinoid found in the Cannabis sativa plant, and is the primary psychoactive compound found in marijuana. Like CBD, it is heavily researched for its potential medicinal value. Generally in this report, delta-9-THC is referred to as "THC."

Cannabis: The Cannabis sativa plant is often referred to as cannabis, an umbrella term that includes marijuana and hemp. Delta-9-THC and CBD are thought to be the most abundant cannabinoids in the Cannabis sativa plant.

Criminalization: This term refers to the act of making an activity a criminal offense. Committing such an offense subjects an individual to criminal penalties.

Decriminalization: This term can be defined in different ways, but with drug offenses, generally it refers to the removal of criminal penalties for the offense (e.g., for small, personal-consumption amounts of a controlled substance), and instead, makes the offense a civil or local infraction. It may also refer to a jurisdiction making the possession of a controlled substance a very low misdemeanor with no possibility of jail time.

Hemp: Hemp is a variety of the Cannabis sativa plant that is grown specifically for industrial use. It was removed from the CSA definition of marijuana in 2018 and is cultivated for use in the production of a wide range of products, including foods and beverages, personal care products, dietary supplements, fabrics and textiles, paper, construction materials, and other manufactured and industrial goods.

Section 1639o of Title 7 of the *U.S. Code* defines hemp as follows:

> the plant Cannabis sativa L. and any part of that plant, including the seeds thereof and all derivatives, extracts, cannabinoids, isomers, acids, salts, and salts of isomers, whether growing or not, with a delta-9 tetrahydrocannabinol concentration of not more than 0.3 percent on a dry weight basis.

Legalization: This term refers to the act of making an activity legal, or allowable under law, which was previously illegal.

Marijuana (or "marihuana" as it is spelled in the CSA): Marijuana generally refers to the cultivated plant used as a psychotropic drug (whether used for medicinal or recreational purposes). Delta-9-THC is its primary psychoactive compound.

Section 802 (16) of the CSA defines marijuana as follows:

(A) Subject to subparagraph (B), the term "marihuana" means all parts of the plant Cannabis sativa L., whether growing or not; the seeds thereof; the resin extracted from any part of such plant; and every compound, manufacture, salt, derivative, mixture, or preparation of such plant, its seeds or resin.

(B) The term "marihuana" does not include—(i) hemp, as defined in section 1639o of title 7; or (ii) the mature stalks of such plant, fiber produced from such stalks, oil or cake made from the seeds of such plant, any other compound, manufacture, salt, derivative, mixture, or preparation of such mature stalks (except the resin extracted therefrom), fiber, oil, or cake, or the sterilized seed of such plant which is incapable of germination.

Appendix B. Approved Cannabis-Related Drugs and Research

To date, FDA has not approved a marketing application for marijuana. FDA has approved Epidiolex, a prescription drug containing CBD (the primary nonpsychoactive compound in cannabis). Epidiolex—approved to treat seizures associated with two rare and severe forms of epilepsy—contains CBD extracted from the cannabis plant and is the first (and only) FDA-approved drug containing a purified drug substance derived from marijuana.[392]

FDA also has approved three marijuana-related products. Marinol and Syndros, which contain the active ingredient dronabinol (a synthetic THC), are approved as anti-emetics (to reduce nausea or prevent vomiting) for patients on chemotherapy and as appetite stimulants for patients with AIDS-related weight loss.[393] Generic versions of Marinol have been approved as well. While Marinol (capsules) and Syndros (an oral solution) have the same pharmacology, the two formulations differ in their physical and chemical properties and are in different schedules of the CSA. Marinol (and generic

---

[392] FDA, "FDA approves first drug comprised of an active ingredient derived from marijuana to treat rare, severe forms of epilepsy," June 25, 2018, https://www.fda.gov/newsevents/newsroom/pressannouncements/ucm611046.htm. *Epidiolex* is the proprietary or brand name of the drug, while *cannabidiol* is the nonproprietary or generic name, which is the same as the drug's active ingredient.

[393] FDA first approved dronabinol in 1985 under the trade name Marinol, which is registered to AbbVie Inc. See http://www.accessdata.fda.gov/scripts/cder/ob/results_product.cfm?Appl_Type=N&Appl_No=018651.

versions) are in Schedule III, while Syndros is in Schedule II.[394] Cesamet, which contains the active ingredient nabilone (whose chemical structure is similar to THC and is synthetically derived), is FDA-approved for treatment of nausea and vomiting associated with chemotherapy among patients who have not responded to conventional treatments.[395] Cesamet is a Schedule II controlled substance.

Other CBD and marijuana-related drugs may be in the pipeline, as evidenced by the numerous clinical trials that are ongoing, recruiting, or have been completed.[396] While not yet approved in the United States, GW Pharmaceuticals' Sativex—a cannabis-extract spray containing a 1:1 ratio of CBD and delta-9 THC—has regulatory approval in more than 25 countries for the treatment of spasticity (muscle stiffness/spasm) due to multiple sclerosis (MS).[397] For example, in Canada, Sativex is indicated as an adjunctive treatment for symptomatic relief of spasticity in patients with MS who have not responded adequately to other therapy.[398] Previously, Sativex was authorized as an adjunctive treatment for neuropathic pain in adult patients with MS and persistent background pain in adult patients with advanced cancer.[399] However, these indications were removed from the Sativex monograph after confirmatory trials did not support the therapeutic advantage

---

[394] Marinol was approved by FDA in 1985 and placed in Schedule II of the CSA. In July 1999, Marinol was moved to Schedule III after DEA found "that the difficulty of separating dronabinol from the sesame oil formulation and the delayed onset of behavioral effects due to oral route administration supported a lower abuse potential of Marinol as compared to substances in Schedule II." Syndros was approved by FDA in 2016, and due to its abuse potential it remains in Schedule II. See "Schedules of Controlled Substances: Placement of FDA-Approved Products of Oral Solutions Containing Dronabinol [(-)-delta-9-trans-tetrahydrocannabinol (delta-9-THC)] in Schedule II," interim rule, March 23, 2017, 82 *Federal Register* 14815, and final rule, November 22, 2017, 82 *Federal Register* 55504.

[395] FDA first approved nabilone in 1985 under the trade name Cesamet, which is registered to Meda Pharmaceuticals Inc. See http://www.accessdata.fda.gov/scripts/cder/ob/results_product.cfm?Appl_Type=N&Appl_No=018677.

[396] National Institutes of Health, National Library of Medicine, Clinicaltrials.gov, accessed January 13, 2022, https://clinicaltrials.gov/ct2/results?cond=&term=Cannabidiol&cntry=&state=&city=&dist=.

[397] GW Pharmaceuticals, "Information on Sativex," https://www.gwpharm.com/healthcare-professionals/sativex.

[398] Health Canada, Product Monograph Including Patient Medication Information SATIVEX® delta-9- tetrahydrocannabinol (THC) and cannabidiol (CBD) Solution, 27mg/mL / 25mg/mL, Buccal spray, revised December 11, 2019, https://pdf.hres.ca/dpd_pm/00054388.PDF.

[399] Product Monograph for SATIVEX, as authorized for marketing by Health Canada, https://pdf.hres.ca/dpd_pm/ 00016162.PDF.

of Sativex for neuropathic and cancer pain.[400] In 2014, GW Pharmaceuticals announced that the FDA had granted Fast Track designation to Sativex as a potential pain reliever for patients with advanced cancer.[401] However, Phase III clinical trials previously conducted by the company found that Sativex failed to show superiority over placebo in the treatment of pain in patients with advanced cancer who experience inadequate analgesia during optimized chronic opioid therapy.[402] Furthermore, while CBD is predicted to have anti-inflammatory properties, which may play a role in its analgesic effects, preliminary evidence suggests that the analgesia is mediated by THC, and it is unclear the extent to which CBD contributes to those therapeutic effects.[403] GW Pharmaceuticals reports that it is testing cannabinoid products for treatment of various conditions, including epilepsy, spasticity and PTSD, autism spectrum disorder, and schizophrenia, among others.[404]

Much of this research is in its nascent stages; therefore, conclusive evidence on the use of marijuana to treat various health conditions will likely not be available for some time. There are also still many unknowns regarding how marijuana would be used in medical treatment, including the individual and combined clinical benefits of THC, CBD, and other cannabinoids; proper dosage; and effects of different routes of administration, among others.[405] In addition, the short- and long-term health effects of marijuana use are largely

---

[400] Health Canada, Health Product InfoWatch, January 2020, https://www.canada.ca/en/health-canada/services/drugs-health-products/medeffect-canada/health-product-infowatch/january-2020.html#a4.1.

[401] GW Pharmaceuticals, "GW Pharmaceuticals Announces that Sativex Receives Fast Track Designation from FDA in Cancer Pain," press release, April 28, 2014, http://ir.gwpharm.com/releasedetail.cfm?ReleaseID=842890. For an explanation of FDA's Fast Track designation, see http://www.fda.gov/forpatients/approvals/fast/ucm20041766.htm.

[402] GW Pharmaceuticals, "GW Pharmaceuticals and Otsuka Announce Results From Two Remaining Sativex(R) Phase 3 Cancer Pain Trials," press release, October 27, 2015, http://ir.gwpharm.com/static-files/f2fc7456-a4a3-4d3b-a98c- 47954ec397dd.

[403] U.S. Congress, Testimony before the United States Senate Caucus on International Narcotics Control, *The Biology and Potential Therapeutic Effects of Cannabidiol*, prepared by Dr. Nora Volkow, National Institute on Drug Abuse, National Institutes of Health, 114th Cong., 1st sess., June 24, 2015.

[404] GW Pharmaceuticals, "Therapeutic Areas," https://www.gwpharm.com/healthcare-professionals/research/ therapeutic-areas#.

[405] National Academies of Sciences, Engineering, and Medicine, *The Health Effects of Cannabis and Cannabinoids: The Current State of Evidence and Recommendations for Research*, Washington, DC, 2017, p. 396, doi: 10.17226/24625.

unknown, in part due to the challenges of researching marijuana in the United States.[406]

Federal Research Requirements for Marijuana

For research involving controlled substances, many of the federal research requirements are standard across all schedules; however, some requirements vary according to the assigned schedule of the particular substance. Federal regulations are more stringent for Schedule I substances—including marijuana. Examples include the following:

- For Schedule I substances, such as marijuana, even if practitioners have a DEA registration for a substance in Schedules II-V, they must obtain a *separate* DEA registration for Schedule I substances.
- Individuals who seek to register to manufacture a controlled substance (for any purpose) in Schedule I or II are subject to production quota limitations as determined by DEA,[407] but registrants for substances in Schedules III-V are not subject to such quotas.
- Researchers are required to store Schedule I and II substances in electronically monitored safes, steel cabinets, or vaults that meet or exceed certain specifications[408]; they are required to store Schedule III-V substances by secure standards as well, but the requirements are less stringent.
- When researchers apply for a DEA registration to conduct research involving Schedule I controlled substances, they must comply with federal regulations specifying the form and content of the research protocols.[409] The DEA Administrator must forward a copy of the application and research protocol to HHS, which is responsible for determining "the qualifications and competency of the applicant, as well as the merits of the protocol."[410] The HHS Secretary delegates

[406] Ibid. See also, for example, L. Sanders, "The CBD Boom is Way Ahead of the Science," *Science News*, March 27, 2019.

[407] See 21 U.S.C. §826.

[408] 21 C.F.R. §§1301.72(a)(1)(i)-(iii) (specifications required for safes and steel cabinets storing Schedule I and II drugs or substances); see also 21 C.F.R. Sections 1301.72(a)(2) and 1301.72(a)(3)(i)-(vi) (specifications required for vaults storing Schedule I and II drugs or substances).

[409] 21 C.F.R. §1301.18(a).

[410] 21 U.S.C. §823(f); 21 C.F.R. §1301.32(a).

that responsibility to FDA. No equivalent process is required for Schedule II-V controlled substances.

Marijuana Supply for Researchers

Under the CSA, the Attorney General is required to register an applicant who would like to manufacture Schedule I or II controlled substances "if he determines that such registration is consistent with the public interest and with United States obligations under international treaties, conventions, or protocols in effect on May 1, 1971."[411] DEA thus seeks to balance the demands from researchers for a larger, more diverse supply of marijuana against the United States' obligations under international treaties.[412] Further, the supply of marijuana and other Schedule I and II controlled substances is subject to production quota limitations determined by DEA based on an annual assessment of need.

In the case of marijuana, the National Center for Natural Products Research at the University of Mississippi was previously the only registered manufacturer, operating under a contract administered by the National Institute on Drug Abuse (NIDA), which is housed in HHS's National Institutes of Health. For over 50 years, NIDA was the only official source of marijuana for research purposes—which some referred to as a "federal marijuana monopoly."[413] Some have contended that marijuana provided by NIDA to researchers is "both qualitatively and quantitatively inadequate."[414] For example, some of the issues researchers have raised regarding the Center for Natural Products Research marijuana include

- mold found in the samples of bulk marijuana,[415]

---

[411] 21 U.S.C. §823(a).

[412] DOJ, *Licensing Marijuana Cultivation in Compliance with the Single Convention on Narcotic Drugs*, June 6, 2018.

[413] See *NIDA's Role in Providing Marijuana for Research*, at http://www.drugabuse.gov/drugs-abuse/marijuana/nidas- role-in-providing-marijuana-research; and Marc Kaufman, "Federal Marijuana Monopoly Challenged," *Washington Post*, December 12, 2005.

[414] Marc Kaufman, "Federal Marijuana Monopoly Challenged," *Washington Post*, December 12, 2005; and DOJ, DEA, "Lyle E. Craker; Denial of Application," 74 *Federal Register* 2101, January 14, 2009.

[415] NIDA states there is currently no universally accepted standard for levels of mold and yeast on marijuana and "different health organizations set cutoffs for acceptable levels spanning an enormous range [from 500-200,000 colony forming units (CFU)/g]." See *NIDA's Role*

- excessive age of the samples,[416]
- lower THC potency compared to local products, and
- a lower number of product options compared to what is available elsewhere.[417]

Of note, NIDA states there is currently no universally accepted standard for levels of mold on marijuana, and NIDA's Certificates of Analysis for their marijuana state that NIDA may store marijuana for up to 10 years prior to shipment.[418] NIDA provides marijuana to researchers with a range of potencies.[419]

Over the last several years, both Congress and the executive branch have addressed the marijuana supply for researchers issue.

- In 2015, the Improving Regulatory Transparency for New Medical Therapies Act (P.L. 114-89) amended the CSA and imposed deadlines on DEA to issue notice of each application for a registration to manufacture Schedule I substances for research and then act on the application.[420]
- In August 2016, DEA announced a policy change "designed to foster research by expanding the number of DEA-registered marijuana manufacturers."[421] Under the new policy, DEA stated that it would register additional growers to "operate independently, provided the grower agrees (through a written memorandum of agreement with DEA) that it will only distribute marijuana with prior, written approval from DEA."[422] In addition, under the new policy these growers would only be permitted to supply marijuana to DEA-

in Providing Marijuana for Research, at http://www.drugabuse.gov/drugs-abuse/marijuana/nidas-role-in-providing-marijuana-research.

[416] NIDA indicates that it may store marijuana for up to 10 years prior to shipment.

[417] Heike Newman, "Cannabis Clinical Investigations in Colorado 2019," *Food and Drug Law Institute*, July/August 2019.

[418] National Institute on Drug Abuse, *NIDA's Role in Providing Marijuana for Research*, March 27, 2020; and Heike Newman, "Cannabis Clinical Investigations in Colorado 2019," *Food and Drug Law Institute*, July/August 2019.

[419] National Institute on Drug Abuse, *Marijuana Plant Material Available from the NIDA Drug Supply Program*, March 10, 2016.

[420] See 21 U.S.C. §823(i)(2).

[421] DOJ, DEA, *DEA Announces Actions Related to Marijuana and Industrial Hemp*, August 11, 2016.

[422] DOJ, DEA, "Applications To Become Registered Under the Controlled Substances Act To Manufacture Marijuana To Supply Researchers in the United States," 81 *Federal Register* 53846-53848, August 12, 2016.

registered researchers whose protocols have been determined to be "scientifically meritorious." This new approach, DEA stated, will allow individuals to obtain a DEA cultivation registration "not only to supply federally funded or other academic researchers, but also for strictly commercial endeavors funded by the private sector and aimed at drug product development."[423]

- Some attributed the delay in issuance of new registrations to a 2018 finding by the DOJ, Office of Legal Counsel (OLC) that DEA must change its current practices (registration of a single manufacturer) to adopt a framework in which it purchases and takes possession of the entire marijuana crop of each registrant after the marijuana is harvested. Further, the DOJ, OLC stated that DEA "must generally monopolize the import, export, wholesale trade, and stock maintenance of lawfully grown marijuana" to comply with the Single Convention on Narcotic Drugs.[424]
- In August 2019, former Attorney General Barr announced that DEA is "moving forward with its review of applications for those who seek to grow marijuana legally to support research."[425]
- In December 2020, DEA published a final rule that, among other things, requires all registered manufacturers who cultivate marijuana "to deliver" their total crops to DEA with limited exception;[426] however, the crops may remain at the manufacturers' registered locations. DEA is to purchase and take possession of such crops (not later than four months after harvest ends) by designating a secure

---

[423] Ibid.

[424] DOJ, Office of Legal Counsel, *Licensing Marijuana Cultivation in Compliance with the Single Convention on Narcotic Drugs*, June 6, 2018.

[425] An applicant for a registration petitioned the U.S. Court of Appeals for the D.C. Circuit (D.C. Circuit) for a writ of mandamus compelling DEA to issue notice of its application, and in July 2019 the D.C. Circuit ordered DEA to respond to the petition. On August 27, 2019, DEA published a notice in the *Federal Register* (1) providing notice of the 33 applications it has received to manufacture Schedule I controlled substances for research purposes and (2) announcing the agency's intent to promulgate regulations governing the manufacture of marijuana for research purposes. See Pet. for Writ of Mandamus at 16, *In re* Scottsdale Research Inst., No. 19-1120 (D.C. Cir. June 6, 2019); Order, *In re* Scottsdale Research Inst., No. 19-1120 (D.C. Cir. July 29, 2019; and DOJ, DEA, *DEA announces steps necessary to improve access to marijuana research*, August 25, 2019, https://www.dea.gov/press-releases.

[426] 21 C.F.R. §1318.04.

storage mechanism at the registered location and controlling access to the marijuana.[427]

These actions were precursors to DEA's announcement on May 14, 2021 that it would soon be registering additional manufacturers of marijuana.[428] As outlined in the announcement, DEA provided Memoranda of Agreement (MOAs) to multiple manufacturers pending final approval of their registration applications. As of April 1, 2022, DEA has five registered marijuana growers listed on their website.[429] Additional registrations to manufacture marijuana may increase the quantity and improve facets of marijuana research, and possibly contribute to future debate on rescheduling.[430]

Appendix C. Research on Effects of Cannabis Use

Some evidence suggests that cannabis may have therapeutic benefits, for example, in the treatment of chronic pain, chemotherapy-induced nausea and vomiting, and spasticity among patients with multiple sclerosis. Further, naturally occurring compounds found in cannabis called cannabinoids such as CBD and THC have proven therapeutic uses, as the Food and Drug Administration (FDA) has approved drugs that contain CBD and dronabinol (a synthetic THC) as active ingredients (see Appendix B). THC and CBD interact with specific cell receptors in the brain and throughout the body to produce their intended effects. While THC activates certain receptors that then produce euphoric or intoxicating effects,[431] CBD has low affinity for those same receptors and therefore does not produce intoxicating effects.[432] Some

---

[427] DOJ, DEA, "Controls To Enhance the Cultivation of Marihuana for Research in the United States," 85 *Federal Register* 82333-82355, December 18, 2020.

[428] DOJ, DEA, *DEA Continues to Prioritize Efforts to Expand Access to Marijuana for Research in the United States*, May 14, 2021.

[429] DOJ, DEA, Diversion Control Division, *Marihuana Growers Information*, https://www.deadiversion.usdoj.gov/ drugreg/marihuana.htm.

[430] Both FDA and DEA identified the lack of research as a significant factor in denying the rescheduling petitions in 2016.

[431] National Academies of Sciences, Engineering, and Medicine (NASEM), "The Health Effects of Cannabis and Cannabinoids: Current State of Evidence and Recommendations for Research" (Washington, DC: National Academies Press), 2017.

[432] U.S. Congress, Testimony before the United States Senate Caucus on International Narcotics Control, The Biology and Potential Therapeutic Effects of Cannabidiol, prepared by Dr. Nora Volkow, National Institute on Drug Abuse, National Institutes of Health, 114th Cong., 1st sess., June 24, 2015.

preclinical (e.g., animal model) research suggests that CBD may interact with other brain-signaling systems that can produce therapeutic effects, such as the reduction of seizures, pain, and anxiety.[433] Still, questions remain regarding the underlying mechanism of action for therapeutic benefits of these and other cannabinoids. For example, while CBD is predicted to have anti-inflammatory properties, which may play a role in its analgesic effects, preliminary evidence suggests that the analgesia is mediated by THC, and the extent to which CBD contributes to those therapeutic effects is unclear.[434]

According to the National Institutes on Drug Abuse (NIDA) at the National Institutes of Health (NIH), researchers generally consider therapeutics that use purified chemicals derived from or based on those in the cannabis plant, such as those approved by FDA (e.g., Epidiolex), "to be more promising therapeutically" than use of the whole plant or its crude extracts.[435] Scientific evaluations conducted separately by FDA and the National Academies of Sciences, Engineering, and Medicine (NASEM) may further support this assertion. These evaluations also illustrate the challenge of meeting the required standard of evidence (for FDA approval of a substance) or to demonstrate effective medical use of cannabis. While the purposes of the evaluations differed— resulting in different approaches being taken—both FDA and the NASEM found that the evidence base at the time the evaluations were conducted was, at least partially, elusive.

FDA's evaluation, called an eight-factor analysis,[436] was conducted in 2015 pursuant to a request by DEA. As statutorily required, DEA requested a scientific evaluation from the Secretary of Health and Human Services in response to petitions asking DEA to reschedule marijuana administratively.[437] FDA evaluated the research on marijuana only, not drugs containing a plant-derived chemical constituent of marijuana or drugs containing synthetic THC. FDA's analysis of the literature on marijuana's potential therapeutic effects was limited to 11 published studies that were considered "adequate and well-controlled clinical studies" (i.e., the studies were randomized controlled

---

[433] Ibid.

[434] Ibid.

[435] National Institutes of Health (NIH) National Institute on Drug Abuse (NIDA), "Marijuana Research Report," July 2020, https://www.drugabuse.gov/publications/research-reports/marijuana/marijuana-safe-effective-medicine.

[436] The term *eight-factor analysis* refers to the eight factors to be included pursuant to 21 U.S.C. Section 811(c).

[437] The request for a scientific and medical evaluation is required by 21 U.S.C. Section 811(b). The results of an earlier eight-factor analysis are available at DOJ, DEA, "Denial of Petition to Initiate Proceedings to Reschedule Marijuana," 76 *Federal Register* 40551-40589, July 8, 2011.

trials).[438] The studies examined marijuana's use to treat neuropathic pain (five studies), stimulate appetite in patients with HIV (two studies), treat glaucoma (two studies), treat spasticity in multiple sclerosis patients (one study), and treat asthma (one study).[439] As part of the evaluation, the FDA also assessed potential risks of marijuana use. Based on the data available at the time of the evaluation, FDA determined that marijuana met the criteria for placement in Schedule I of the CSA due its high potential for abuse, no currently accepted medical use in the United States, and a lack of accepted safety for use under medical supervision. NIDA concurred with this recommendation. Based on FDA's recommendation and other data, DEA determined that marijuana meets the criteria for Schedule I control.[440]

In January 2017, the NASEM published the findings of an almost year-long evaluation of cannabis, its constituents, and drugs containing synthetic THC. The NASEM focused on 11 groups of health topics and concerns: (1) therapeutic effects; (2) cancer; (3) cardiometabolic risk; (4) respiratory disease; (5) immunity; (6) injury and death; (7) prenatal, perinatal, and postnatal exposure to cannabis; (8) psychosocial effects, including cognitive domains of learning, memory, and attention and developmental implications among adolescents; (9) mental health; (10) problem cannabis use; and (11) cannabis use and abuse of other substances.[441] For each of these 11 health topics, the report assessed "fair- and good-quality" research, relying on systematic reviews published since 2011 (where available) and primary research published after the systematic review (or since 1999, if no systematic review exists).[442] The report presented nearly 100 conclusions, including some related to the challenges in conducting research with cannabis and cannabinoids. For example, the NASEM found conclusive or substantial evidence that cannabis or cannabinoids are an effective treatment for chronic

---

[438] Randomized controlled trials randomize patients into either an intervention group(s) or a placebo group. Randomization allows for differences observed between the groups to be attributable to the intervention, rather than differences between participants. For more information, see Leon Gordis, *Epidemiology*, 5th ed. (Philadelphia, PA: Elsevier Saunders, 2014).

[439] DOJ, DEA, "Denial of Petition to Initiate Proceedings to Reschedule Marijuana," 81 *Federal Register* 53689, August 12, 2016. Memorandum from the Acting Commissioner of Foods and Drugs to the Acting Assistant Secretary for Health, "Recommendation to Maintain Marijuana in Schedule I of the Controlled Substances Act," May 20, 2015.

[440] DOJ, DEA, "Denial of Petition to Initiate Proceedings to Reschedule Marijuana," 81 *Federal Register* 53689, August 12, 2016.

[441] NASEM, "The Health Effects of Cannabis and Cannabinoids: Current State of Evidence and Recommendations for Research" (Washington, DC: National Academies Press), 2017.

[442] Ibid.

pain, chemotherapy-induced nausea and vomiting, and self-reported symptoms of spasticity among patients with multiple sclerosis (but limited evidence for an effect on clinician-measured spasticity). The NASEM found insufficient or no evidence to support or refute conclusions regarding potential therapeutic effects of cannabis or cannabinoids for a variety of other examined health conditions (e.g., improving symptoms of posttraumatic stress disorder and certain cancers).[443]

There is interest in studying the potential utility of cannabis and its cannabinoids for various medical conditions, as evidenced by the numerous ongoing randomized controlled trials listed on clinicaltrials.gov, a database maintained by the NIH National Library of Medicine. However, researchers face several challenges in undertaking cannabis research programs. First are the challenges that are inherent to botanical drug development. As indicated by NIDA, botanicals such as the cannabis plant "may contain hundreds of unknown, active chemicals, and it can be difficult to develop a product with accurate and consistent doses of these chemicals."[444] In its 2015 evaluation, FDA identified eight methodological limitations of the marijuana studies in the published literature at the time, including a lack of consistent administration and reproducible dosing of marijuana.[445] FDA has issued guidance to assist researchers and drug manufacturers with development of plant-derived drugs, including from cannabis.[446] In addition, federal and state restrictions on cannabis research further make it difficult to study the safety and effectiveness of cannabis as treatment. As discussed in this report, individuals who seek to conduct research on any controlled substance must do so in accordance with the Controlled Substances Act and other federal laws, and DEA research requirements are more stringent for Schedule I and Schedule II substances than for substances in Schedules III-V (see Appendix B). In its 2015 evaluation, FDA identified several aspects of federal marijuana

---

443 Ibid.

444 NIH, NIDA, "Marijuana Research Report," July 2020, https://www.drugabuse.gov/ publications/research-reports/ marijuana/marijuana-safe-effective-medicine.

445 DOJ, DEA, "Denial of Petition to Initiate Proceedings to Reschedule Marijuana," 81 *Federal Register* 53689, August 12, 2016.

446 FDA, "Botanical Drug Development," Guidance for Industry, December 2016, https://www.fda.gov/media/93113/ download. FDA, "Cannabis and Cannabis-Derived Compounds: Quality Considerations for Clinical Research," Draft Guidance for Industry, July 2020, https://www.fda.gov/media/140319/download.

oversight that may warrant review to promote "efficient and scientifically rigorous research with marijuana and its constituents."[447]

Given these challenges, many uncertainties remain around the health benefits and risks of cannabis use. For example, some literature suggests that cannabis may be effective in treating certain conditions such as chronic pain, which is the most common condition cited by patients for the medical use of cannabis.[448] Other evaluations indicate there is limited evidence to recommend cannabis or cannabinoids for treatment of chronic pain.[449] Some research also has suggested an inverse relationship between state availability of medical marijuana and opioid analgesic overdose mortality.[450] For example, a 2014 NIDA-funded study found that from 1999 to 2010, states with medical cannabis laws experienced slower rates of increase in opioid overdose death rates compared to states without such laws.[451] However, another 2019 NIDA-funded study re-examined this relationship using data through 2017, finding that the trend reversed.[452] In particular, the 2019 analysis reported that states with medical cannabis laws experienced an increase in opioid morality deaths. Further, HHS agencies (e.g., FDA, NIH, the Centers for Disease Control and Prevention [CDC], Substance Abuse and Mental Health Services Administration [SAMHSA]) and NASEM have indicated that cannabis use is not without risks and may pose both short-term and long-term adverse health outcomes, particularly for certain groups.[453] See the text box below.

---

[447] Memorandum from the Acting Commissioner of Foods and Drugs to the Acting Assistant Secretary for Health, "Recommendation to Maintain Marijuana in Schedule I of the Controlled Substances Act," May 20, 2015, pp. 2-4.

[448] NASEM, "The Health Effects of Cannabis and Cannabinoids: Current State of Evidence and Recommendations for Research" (Washington, DC: National Academies Press), 2017, pp. 85-90.

[449] Jason W Busse, Patrick Vankrunkelsven, Linan Zeng et al., "Rapid Recommendations: Medical Cannabis or Cannabinoids for Chronic Pain: A Clinical Practice Guideline," *British Medical Journal (BMJ)*, September 2021, vol. 374, no. 2040, pp. 1-10.

[450] NASEM, "The Health Effects of Cannabis and Cannabinoids: Current State of Evidence and Recommendations for Research" (Washington, DC: National Academies Press), 2017, p. 87.

[451] Marcus A. Bachhuber, Brendan Saloner, Chinazo O. Cunningham et al., "Medical Cannabis Laws and Opioid Analgesic Overdose Mortality in the United States, 1999-2010," *JAMA Internal Medicine*, October 2014, vol. 174, no. 10, pp. 1668-1673.

[452] Chelsea L. Shover, Corey S. Davis, Sanford C. Gordon et al., "Association Between Medical Cannabis Laws and Opioid Overdose Mortality has Reversed Over Time," *Proceedings of the National Academy of Sciences (PNAS)*, June 2019, vol. 116, no. 26, pp. 12624-12626.

[453] Memorandum from the Acting Commissioner of Foods and Drugs to the Acting Assistant Secretary for Health "Recommendation to Maintain Marijuana in Schedule I of the Controlled Substances Act," May 20, 2015. DOJ, DEA, "Denial of Petition to Initiate Proceedings to Reschedule Marijuana," 81 *Federal Register* 53689, August 12, 2016. Centers for Disease Control and Prevention (CDC), "Health Effects of Marijuana," updated

Risks Associated with Marijuana Use

Marijuana can affect the central nervous system, the cardiovascular system, the respiratory system, and the immune system. Its effects may vary according to how it is consumed (e.g., inhaled or ingested), how much is consumed (including a range of THC content), how often it is consumed, over what time frame it is consumed, and other factors.

Some of marijuana's most widely recognized effects—which are largely due to the presence of THC—are among the reasons people use it recreationally: it can reduce inhibition, improve mood, enhance sensory perception, and heighten imagination, among other effects. Some common effects are more problematic: it can cause dizziness, confusion, ataxia (i.e., uncoordinated movements), delusions, and agitation, among other effects. Marijuana's acute effects can impair an individual's ability to perform daily activities, such as studying or driving. Chronic use of marijuana can lead to dependence and, in the case of heavy chronic use, the potential for withdrawal (with symptoms like insomnia, weight loss, and irritability).[454] Further, certain marijuana products, such as marijuana edibles, may present greater risk of adverse reaction, particularly for youth in situations of accidental exposure.[455]

Appendix D. Federal Regulation of Hemp and CBD

As mentioned in the main body of this report, hemp and its derivatives (including hemp-derived CBD) were removed from the CSA definition of marijuana. This cleared the path for legal production of hemp and CBD products, but federal control over production and distribution remains an issue.

June 2, 2021, https://www.cdc.gov/marijuana/health-effects/index.html. NIH, NIDA, "Marijuana Research Report," July 2020, https://www.drugabuse.gov/publications/research-reports/marijuana/marijuana-safe-effective-medicine. Substance Abuse and Mental Health Services Administration (SAMHSA), "Learn about Marijuana Risks," updated August 12, 2021, https://www.samhsa.gov/marijuana.

454 DOJ, DEA, "Denial of Petition to Initiate Proceedings to Reschedule Marijuana," 81 *Federal Register* 53689, August 12, 2016.

455 Jennifer M. Whitehill, Julia A. Dilley, and Ashley Brooks-Russell et al., "Edible Cannabis Exposures Among Children: 2017-2019," *Pediatrics*, vol. 147, no. 4 (April 1, 2021).

USDA Regulation of Hemp Production

The 2018 farm bill included a number of provisions intended to facilitate the commercial cultivation, processing, marketing, and sale of hemp in the United States, expanding on policies enacted in the 2014 farm bill (Agricultural Act of 2014, P.L. 113-79).[456] As defined in federal agricultural law,[457] hemp is

> the plant *Cannabis sativa* L. and any part of that plant, including the seeds thereof and all derivatives, extracts, cannabinoids, isomers, acids, salts, and salts of isomers, whether growing or not, with a delta-9 tetrahydrocannabinol concentration of not more than 0.3 percent on a dry weight basis.

As amended, the CSA now states "the term 'marihuana' does not include … hemp, as defined in section 1639o of title 7."[458] Accordingly, cannabis containing no more than a 0.3% concentration of THC is considered to be *hemp* and not *marijuana* for purposes of the CSA and DEA.[459] All cannabis and cannabis-derived products that do not fit the legal definition of *hemp* remain a Schedule I controlled substance under federal law and thus are subject to CSA regulations and DEA oversight (except for certain drug products approved by FDA). Prior to changes enacted in the 2018 farm bill, hemp cultivation, processing, marketing, and sale were subject to the CSA and DEA oversight.

Changes enacted in the 2018 farm bill now allow for the cultivation, processing, marketing, and sale of hemp and hemp-derived products that meet the statutory definition of *hemp*—if produced by an authorized grower in accordance with the 2018 farm bill, associated federal USDA regulations, and applicable state regulations.[460] The 2018 farm bill required that USDA

---

[456] For more background, see CRS In Focus IF11088, *2018 Farm Bill Primer: Hemp Cultivation and Processing*.

[457] 7 U.S.C. §1639o, codified in Section 297A of the Agricultural Marketing Act of 1946 (AMA). For more background on the definition of hemp, CRS Report R44742, *Defining Hemp: A Fact Sheet*.

[458] 21 U.S.C. §802(16)(B)(i).

[459] As stated in a legal opinion released by the U.S. Department of Agriculture (USDA), following enactment of the 2018 farm bill, "hemp has been removed from schedule I of the Controlled Substances Act and is no longer a controlled substance." See USDA, "Legal Opinion on Authorities for Hemp Production," May 28, 2019, https://www.ams.usda.gov/content/legal-opinion-authorities-hemp-production.

[460] Regulatory plans involving hemp under the oversight of states and tribes will need to include the following requirements: maintenance of relevant production information; THC testing; procedures for disposal of plants (and products from those plants) that exceed hemp THC levels; procedures to comply with USDA's enforcement provisions; procedures for

establish a regulatory framework under the Agricultural Marketing Act of 1946[461] making hemp production subject to USDA regulation and oversight as an agricultural commodity.[462] USDA published its final regulations in January 2021. It outlines the USDA process for approving plans submitted by states and tribes for the domestic production of hemp, and establishes a federal plan for producers in jurisdictions that do not have their own USDA-approved plan.[463] The 2018 farm bill further prohibited states and Indian tribes from interfering with the transport of hemp or hemp products produced in accordance with USDA's regulatory requirements.[464]

USDA's final hemp rule clarifies the role DEA will continue to play as part of USDA's regulatory oversight of hemp production in the United States. As required by the 2018 farm bill, USDA is to report any production of hemp without a license to the Attorney General, and report certain other information to federal, state, territorial, and local law enforcement.[465] Some in the hemp industry have objected to what they perceive to be the oversized role of DEA in USDA's hemp regulation.[466] USDA officials, however, have indicated that their interpretation of the 2018 farm bill provisions mandates DEA's role in the regulation of hemp, for both consultations with USDA and certain reporting requirements.[467]

According to USDA, because of changes enacted in the 2018 farm bill, "DEA no longer has authority to require hemp seed permits for import

---

conducting random, annual inspections of hemp producers; procedures for submitting hemp production information to USDA; and certification by state and tribal regulators that they have adequate resources and personnel to implement required procedures.

461 7 U.S.C. §§1621 et seq.

462 P.L. 115-334, §10113. For more background on USDA's forthcoming Hemp Production Program, see USDA's website: https://www.ams.usda.gov/content/hemp-production-program.

463 USDA, Agricultural Marketing Service, "Establishment of a Domestic Hemp Production Program," 86 *Federal Register* 5596-5691, January 19, 2021.

464 P.L. 115-334, §10114. USDA, "Legal Opinion on Authorities for Hemp Production," May 28, 2019, https://www.ams.usda.gov/content/legal-opinion-authorities-hemp-production. USDA's opinion further states that "States and Indian tribes also may not prohibit the interstate transportation or shipment of hemp lawfully produced under the 2014 Farm Bill."

465 P.L. 115-334, §10113.

466 Comments submitted to USDA are available at http://www.regulations.gov (docket No. AMS-SC-19-0042; SC19- 990-2IR). See also CRS In Focus IF12017, *Farm Bill Primer: Horticulture Title and Related Provisions.*

467 Verbal comments by Stephen Vaden, USDA General Counsel, at USDA's 96th Annual Agricultural Outlook Forum, February 20, 2020, https://www.usda.gov/oce/forum/2020/Program.htm#s03. See also 2018 farm bill language codified at 7 U.S.C. Section 1639r (Consultation with Attorney General) and 7 U.S.C. Section 1639q (Reporting to Attorney General).

purposes."[468] In addition, a May 2018 internal DEA directive clarified that certain "products and materials that are made from the cannabis plant and which fall outside the CSA definition of marijuana (such as sterilized seeds, oil or cake made from the seeds, and mature stalks) are not controlled under the CSA."[469] The 2018 directive does not apply to cannabis extracts and resins.[470]

FDA Regulation of CBD Products

While the 2018 farm bill removed cannabis and cannabis derivatives that are low in THC (i.e., hemp) from the CSA definition of marijuana, the law explicitly preserved FDA's authority to regulate cannabis and cannabis-derived compounds (including hemp-derived compounds) under the Federal Food, Drug, and Cosmetic Act (FFDCA) and Section 351 of the Public Health Service Act (PHSA).[471] Because the 2018 farm bill did not change FDA law, cannabis and cannabis-derived products are subject to the same regulatory framework as other FDA-regulated products containing any other substance. Hemp-derived products, particularly those claiming to contain CBD, are marketed in a wide range of consumer products—foods and beverages, dietary supplements, and cosmetics and personal care products, among others.[472]

Following enactment of the 2018 farm bill, FDA has maintained its position that it is "unlawful under the [FFDCA] to introduce food containing added CBD or THC into interstate commerce, or to market CBD or THC products as, or in, dietary supplements, regardless of whether the substances are hemp-derived."[473] There are several provisions of the FFDCA that FDA

---

468 USDA, "Importation of Hemp Seeds," https://www.ams.usda.gov/content/importation-hemp-seeds. In April, 2019, USDA announced that the Plant Variety Protection Office would start accepting applications of seed-propagated hemp for plant variety protection.

469 DOJ, DEA, "DEA Internal Directive Regarding the Presence of Cannabinoids in Products and Materials Made from the Cannabis Plant," May 22, 2018.

470 81 *Federal Register* 240: 90194-90196, December 14, 2016. See also DEA, "Clarification of the New Drug Code (7350) for Marijuana Extract," https://www.deadiversion.usdoj.gov/schedules/marijuana/m_extract_7350.html.

471 P.L. 115-334, §10113.

472 For more information, see CRS In Focus IF10391, *Hemp-Derived Cannabidiol (CBD) and Related Hemp Extracts*.

473 FDA, "Statement from FDA Commissioner Scott Gottlieb, M.D., on signing of the Agriculture Improvement Act and the agency's regulation of products containing cannabis and cannabis-derived compounds," December 20, 2018, https://www.fda.gov/news-events/press-announcements/statement-fda-commissioner-scott-gottlieb-md-signing-agriculture-improvement-act-and-agencys.

believes restrict the use of CBD and THC in food and dietary supplements. First, under FFDCA Section 301, it is a prohibited act to introduce into interstate commerce a food to which has been added an approved drug or a drug for which substantial clinical investigations have been instituted and made public.[474] There are several exceptions to this prohibition including, for example, if the substance was marketed in food before its approval as a drug or before clinical investigations were instituted. However, FDA has concluded that based on the available evidence these exceptions do not apply to CBD or THC.[475] FDA has the authority to promulgate regulations approving the use of a drug in food,[476] but has never done so for any substance. However, according to FDA, hemp-derived ingredients that do not contain CBD or THC may fall outside the scope of this prohibition.[477] More specifically, foods containing parts of the hemp plant that include only trace amounts of CBD or THC (e.g., hemp seed and hemp-seed derived ingredients) may be lawfully marketed under certain circumstances—pursuant to FDA approval as a food additive or a determination that the substance is generally recognized as safe (GRAS). FDA has not approved hemp as a food additive but it has evaluated three GRAS notices related to hemp seed-derived ingredients (hulled hemp seeds, hemp seed protein, and hemp seed oil), allowing them to be added to human food under specified conditions.[478]

The second FFDCA provision that FDA deems as restricting the use of CBD is specific to its use in dietary supplements. Under the FFDCA, an article that is an active ingredient in an approved drug, or that has been authorized for investigation as a new drug and the existence of such clinical investigations has been made public, is excluded from the definition of a dietary supplement and may not be marketed as such.[479] An exception to this is if FDA issues a regulation finding that use of such substance in a dietary supplement is lawful. According to FDA, CBD is an active ingredient in an FDA-approved drug

---

[474] FFDCA §301(ll); 21 U.S.C. §331(ll). See also CRS Report R46189, *FDA Regulation of Cannabidiol (CBD) Consumer Products: Overview and Considerations for Congress.*

[475] FDA, "FDA Regulation of Cannabis and Cannabis-Derived Products: Questions and Answers," updated January 15, 2020, https://www.fda.gov/news-events/public-health-focus/fda-regulation-cannabis-and-cannabis-derived-products- questions-and-answers.

[476] FFDCA §301(ll)(2); 21 U.S.C. §331(ll)(2).

[477] FDA, "FDA Regulation of Cannabis and Cannabis-Derived Products: Questions and Answers," updated January 15, 2020, https://www.fda.gov/news-events/public-health-focus/fda-regulation-cannabis-and-cannabis-derived-products- questions-and-answers.

[478] FDA, "FDA Responds to Three GRAS Notices for Hemp Seed-Derived Ingredients for Use in Human Food," December 20, 2018, https://www.fda.gov/food/cfsan-constituent-updates/fda-responds-three-gras-notices-hemp-seed- derived-ingredients-use-human-food.

[479] FFDCA §201(ff)(3)(B) [21 U.S.C. §321(ff)(3)(B)].

(i.e., Epidiolex) and was authorized for investigation as a new drug, for which substantial clinical investigations had been instituted and made public before its marketing as a dietary supplement; as such, CBD may not be sold as a dietary supplement unless FDA promulgates regulations concluding otherwise.[480] The agency maintains this is regardless of whether the CBD is hemp-derived or marijuana-derived. FDA has issued several public statements maintaining that it is unlawful to market CBD as, or in, dietary supplements.[481] Hemp-derived ingredients that do not contain CBD or THC may fall outside the scope of this exclusion.[482]

With regard to cosmetics, FDA has not made the determination that it is unlawful to add CBD to cosmetic products. FDA does not have the authority to conduct premarket review of cosmetic ingredients, and while FDA regulations prohibit or restrict certain cosmetic ingredients, the regulations do not apply to any cannabis or cannabis-derived ingredients (e.g., CBD).[483] FDA does have the authority to take certain enforcement action against adulterated or misbranded cosmetics. If a product makes therapeutic claims (i.e., that its intended use is to cure, mitigate, treat, or prevent a disease), FDA generally considers that product to be a drug and subject to premarket approval.

Delta-8 THC Products

Delta-9-THC is not the only psychoactive compound in cannabis, but it is the primary one. Other psychoactive compounds, such as delta-8-THC, are also found in cannabis, and recently, there has been a rise in delta-8-THC hemp and marijuana products available in state-authorized markets. Due to federal definitions' reference to Delta-9-THC only, these products are federally unregulated, and according to the FDA, some products may be mislabeled as hemp products given the volume of delta-8-THC and the psychoactive effects. In September 2021, both the FDA and the Centers for Disease Control and

---

[480] FDA, "Warning Letters and Test Results for Cannabidiol-Related Products," https://www.fda.gov/newsevents/ publichealthfocus/ucm484109.htm.

[481] FDA, "Statement from FDA Commissioner Scott Gottlieb, M.D., on signing of the Agriculture Improvement Act and the agency's regulation of products containing cannabis and cannabis-derived compounds," December 20, 2018, https://www.fda.gov/newsevents/newsroom/pressAnnouncements/ucm628988.htm.

[482] FDA, "FDA Regulation of Cannabis and Cannabis-Derived Products: Questions and Answers," updated April 2, 2019, https://www.fda.gov/news-events/public-health-focus/fda-regulation-cannabis-and-cannabis-derived-products- questions-and-answers.

[483] 21 C.F.R. Part 700.

Prevention (CDC) issued a warning about the dangers of using products containing delta-8-THC.[484]

United States Postal Service (USPS) Policy on Hemp and Hemp-Derived CBD

In June 2019, the U.S. Postal Service (USPS) revised its policies regarding mailing standards for hemp and hemp-based products, including hemp-derived CBD. USPS guidance provides that these produces may be mailed if the mailer "complies with all applicable federal, state, and local laws" pertaining to hemp production, processing, distribution, and sales; and if the mailer "retains records establishing compliance with such laws, including laboratory test results, licenses, or compliance reports, for no less than 2 years after the date of mailing."[485]

The Path Forward: Congressional Oversight of Federal Guidance on Hemp and CBD

Despite changes enacted in the 2018 farm bill, additional challenges remain for U.S. producers of hemp and hemp-derived products. Congress may exercise oversight over the USDA and FDA in their roles regulating the industry.

Oversight of USDA Regulation of Hemp Production

Two Senate committee hearings in July 2019 highlighted a range of issues.[486] These include hemp producers' uncertainty regarding the development and

---

[484] FDA, *5 Things to Know about Delta-8 Tetrahydrocannabinol – Delta-8 THC*, September 14, 2021, https://www.fda.gov/consumers/consumer-updates/5-things-know-about-delta-8-tetrahydrocannabinol-delta-8-thc; and CDC, *Increases in Availability of Cannabis Products Containing Delta-8 THC and Reported Cases of Adverse Events*, September 14, 2021, https://emergency.cdc.gov/han/2021/han00451.asp.

[485] U.S. Postal Service (USPS), "Publication 52 Revision: New Mailability Policy for Cannabis and Hemp-Related Products," Postal Bulletin 22521 (6-6-19), June 6, 2019. Revisions to Publication 52 (Hazardous, Restricted, and Perishable Mail), Section 453.37, "Hemp-based Products."

[486] Issues discussed and statements made by various Members of Congress at U.S. Congress, Senate Committee on Agriculture, Nutrition, & Forestry, "Hemp Production and the 2018 Farm Bill," July 25, 2019; and at U.S. Congress, Senate Banking, Housing and Urban Affairs Committee, "Cannabis Banking Challenges." July 23, 2019.

implementation of USDA's hemp regulations and market restrictions in some states and jurisdictions regarding hemp and hemp-derived products. Other issues include, but are not limited to, uncertainty about implementation of the 2018 farm bill's provision regarding convicted felons, regulators and enforcement officials' inability to readily and easily distinguish hemp from marijuana, and difficulty among hemp producers and businesses in obtaining financial services.[487] Additionally, some states and local jurisdictions have challenged the legality of hemp production and hemp-derived products, including hemp-derived CBD edible and ingestible products.[488] Some suggest that the 2018 farm bill's hemp provisions may be in conflict with state law, especially regarding enforcement and interstate commerce; they highlight the lack of reliable roadside testing/sampling, among other concerns.[489] Many states have established programs for hemp processors, requiring state-issued permits among other requirements, and may limit the manufacture of consumer products to regulated processors within their states.[490]

Some of these challenges may be addressed, in part, by USDA's new regulations governing U.S. hemp production.[491] In part, resolution of these challenges may hinge on the development of readily available technologies for regulators and enforcement officials to distinguish hemp from marijuana.[492]

---

[487] For additional information on ongoing banking and credit issues, see the letters from Senator McConnell and Senator Wyden to officials of the Federal Reserve System, the Federal Deposit Insurance Corporation, the Farm Credit Administration, and the Office of the Comptroller of the Currency, April 2, 2019; and the letter from the American Bankers Association to officials of the Federal Reserve System, the Federal Deposit Insurance Corporation, the Office of the Comptroller of the Currency, and the Financial Crimes Enforcement Network, June 21, 2019.

[488] Comments during USDA's 2018 Farm Bill Listening Session on Domestic Hemp Production Program, March 13, 2019, and a Congressional Dietary Supplement Caucus Briefing, "Cannabidiol (CBD): Understanding the Ingredient's Legal and Regulatory Status," May 7, 2019.

[489] See, for example, comments by Collin Mooney, "Commercial Vehicle Safety Alliance during USDA's 2018 Farm Bill Listening Session on Domestic Hemp Production Program, March 13, 2019 (minute 40:17). Also see *Transport Topics*, "Law Enforcement Officers Challenged to Enforce Bill Legalizing Transport of Hemp, CVSA Says," March 14, 2019.

[490] A summary of state laws is available through the National Conference of State Legislatures (NCSL), "State Industrial Hemp Statutes," http://www.ncsl.org/research/agriculture-and-rural-development/state-industrial-hemp- statutes.aspx. See also NCSL, "Regulating Hemp and Cannabis-based products," *LegisBrief*, Vol. 25, No. 37, October 2017.

[491] USDA, Agricultural Marketing Service, "Establishment of a Domestic Hemp Production Program," 84 *Federal Register* 58522-58564, October 31, 2019.

[492] USDA officials at a House Agriculture Committee briefing, April 5, 2019, indicated that such technologies are being reviewed within the department's Science & Technology Program; see https://www.ams.usda.gov/about-ams/programs-offices/science-technology-program.

Oversight of FDA Guidance on CBD

While the 2018 farm bill removed hemp and its derivatives from the definition of marijuana in the CSA, several obstacles may limit the marketing of hemp and its derivatives, including CBD. One of the obstacles is that many of these products remain subject to the FFDCA, and FDA has determined that, at this time, CBD cannot be added to any food that is sold in interstate commerce or be marketed as a dietary supplement. While FDA can initiate rulemaking to approve CBD as a food additive or to allow its use in dietary supplements, the agency has never issued such a rule for any substance (whether cannabis-derived or not) that is an approved drug or authorized for investigation as a new drug.[493]

In addition to FDA's position on CBD, some states and local jurisdictions have also decided to disallow the sale of hemp-derived CBD edible and ingestible products, given that hemp-derived CBD is not an FDA-approved food additive. Other cannabis-derived CBD that does not meet the definition of hemp remains illegal under federal law—except for marijuana-derived CBD approved by FDA as a pharmaceutical drug (i.e., Epidiolex).

Hemp and THC

The THC content of hemp remains a concern for those involved in hemp production. The process of hemp extraction can temporarily raise the THC content above the 0.3% THC threshold thereby temporarily qualifying a crop as marijuana under the CSA. In the next farm bill, Congress could consider whether to further amend the federal statutory definition of hemp (7 U.S.C. §1639o) to raise the allowable legal THC level from 0.3% to 1.0% and/or make an exception for hemp THC levels while it is being processed (e.g., H.R. 6645; S. 1005) to provide additional regulatory flexibility to hemp growers and businesses and to alleviate concern of potential intervention by federal law enforcement.

Although FDA has determined that it is currently unlawful to add CBD to food or to market CBD as or in dietary supplements, these products remain commercially available. In response, some Members of Congress have expressed support for a regulatory framework for hemp-derived CBD in

[493] See questions 9 and 10 in "FDA Regulation of Cannabis and Cannabis-Derived Products: Questions and Answers," updated April 2, 2019, https://www.fda.gov/news-events/public-health-focus/fda-regulation-cannabis-and-cannabis-derived-products-questions-and-answers#dietarysupplements.

certain FDA-regulated consumer products. In the absence of a regulatory framework for hemp-derived CBD products, Congress directed FDA in a joint explanatory statement to issue a policy of enforcement discretion with respect to CBD products that meet the statutory definition of hemp and come under FDA's jurisdiction.[494] While the statement does not explicitly require FDA to set a safe level or threshold for CBD in consumer products, the activities conducted pursuant to this directive may inform the establishment of such a level in the future.[495]

Appendix E. Federalism: Federal Preemption and the Anti-Commandeering Doctrine[496]

As briefly discussed in the report, the gap between the federal CSA[497] and certain state marijuana laws raises questions regarding "the proper division of authority between the Federal Government and the States"[498] under both the preemption and anti-commandeering doctrines. This appendix analyzes these two legal doctrines and their application to discordant federal and state marijuana laws.

General Preemption Principles[499]

The Constitution authorizes the federal government to preempt conflicting state laws as long as it is acting within the scope of its enumerated powers.[500]

---

494 Joint Explanatory Statement on Division B—Agriculture, Rural Development, Food and Drug Administration and Related Agencies Appropriations Act, 2020, p. 29, https://docs.house.gov/billsthisweek/20191216/BILLS-116HR1865SA-JES-DIVISION-B.pdf.

495 For additional discussion, see CRS Report R46189, *FDA Regulation of Cannabidiol (CBD) Consumer Products: Overview and Considerations for Congress.*

496 This appendix was authored by David H. Carpenter, Legislative Attorney in CRS's American Law Division (ALD). It uses citation and other editorial styles consistent with ALD's reports.

497 Comprehensive Drug Abuse Prevention and Control Act of 1970, Pub. L. No. 91-513, Title II, 84 Stat. 1236, 1242 (codified as amended at 21 U.S.C. §§ 801–904).

498 New York v. United States, 505 U.S. 144, 149 (1992).

499 For a general discussion of federal preemption, see CRS Report R45825, *Federal Preemption: A Legal Primer.*

500 Murphy v. NCAA, 138 S. Ct. 1461, 1479 (2019) (The Supremacy Clause "specifies that federal law is supreme in case of a conflict with state law. Therefore, in order for the [federal law in question] to preempt state law, it must satisfy two requirements. First, *it*

The doctrine of federal preemption is grounded in the Supremacy Clause of Article VI of the Constitution, which provides that "the Laws of the United States ... shall be the supreme Law of the Land; and the Judges in every State shall be bound thereby, any Thing in the Constitution or Laws of any State to the Contrary notwithstanding."[501] The Supreme Court has explained that "under the Supremacy Clause ... any state law, however clearly within a State's acknowledged power, which interferes with or is contrary to federal law, must yield."[502]

The Supreme Court has identified two general ways in which federal law can preempt state law. Federal law can preempt state law *expressly* where a federal statute or regulation contains explicit preemptive language—that is, where a clause in the relevant federal law explicitly states the extent to which state law is preempted.[503] Federal law can also preempt state law *impliedly*, "when Congress' command is ... implicitly contained in" the relevant federal law's "structure and purpose."[504] The Court has identified two subcategories of implied preemption. The broadest subcategory, "field preemption," occurs "where the scheme of federal regulation is so pervasive as to make reasonable the inference that Congress left no room for the States to supplement it."[505] The second subcategory, "conflict preemption," occurs when it is "physically impossible" to comply with both the state and federal law ("impossibility preemption") or where the state law "stands as an obstacle to the accomplishment and execution of the full purposes and objectives of Congress" ("obstacle preemption").[506] If a court concludes that state law is not preempted by an express preemption provision, the Court has indicated that the federal statute could still implicitly preempt state law.[507]

Several legal principles guide judicial preemption analysis. The Supreme Court has noted that, irrespective of preemption type, the "ultimate

---

must represent the exercise of a power conferred on Congress by the Constitution; pointing to the Supremacy Clause will not do. Second, since the Constitution 'confers upon Congress the power to regulate individuals, not States,' [the federal law] at issue must be best read as one that regulates private actors.") (emphasis added) (internal citations omitted).

501 U.S. CONST. art. VI, cl. 2.

502 Gade v. Nat'l Solid Wastes Mgmt. Assn., 505 U.S. 88, 108 (1992).

503 *Id.* at 98.

504 *Id.* (internal citations omitted).

505 *Id.*

506 Hillman v. Maretta, 569 U.S. 483, 490 (2013) (quoting Hines v. Davidovitz, 312 U.S. 52, 67 (1941)).

507 Freightliner Corp. v. Myrick, 514 U.S. 280, 288 (1995) (holding that the existence of an express preemption clause does not "foreclose[] any possibility of implied pre-emption."); Geier v. Am. Honda Motor Co., 529 U.S. 861, 869 (2000).

touchstone" of preemption analysis is congressional intent,[508] which is "primarily discerned" from the plain language of the legislative text.[509] Additionally, "[i]n all pre-emption cases, and particularly in those in which Congress has legislated ... in a field which the States have traditionally occupied," the Court "start[s] with the assumption that the historic police powers of the States were not to be superseded by" federal law "unless that was the clear and manifest purpose of Congress."[510] Furthermore, the Supreme Court has noted that matters of "health and safety ... are primarily[] and historically matters of local concern."[511]

Preemption and State Marijuana Laws

The Supreme Court has held that Congress has the constitutional authority under the Commerce Clause and Necessary and Proper Clause to criminalize marijuana, including even purely intrastate cultivation and possession of the substance.[512] Consequently, Congress has broad discretion to preempt state marijuana laws that conflict with the CSA.[513] Congress has most clearly expressed its preemptive intent through Section 903 of the CSA.

CSA Section 903 provides that

---

[508] Wyeth v. Levine, 555 U.S. 555, 565 (2009) (quoting Retail Clerks v. Schermerhorn, 375 U.S. 96, 103 (1963)).

[509] Medtronic, Inc. v. Lohr, 518 U.S. 470, 486 (1996) ("Congress' intent, of course, primarily is discerned from the language of the pre-emption statute and the statutory framework surrounding it.") (internal citations omitted).

[510] *Id.* at 485. *See also* Chateau Foghorn LP v. Hosford, 168 A.3d 824, 857 (Md. Ct. App. 2017) (in holding that Department of Housing and Urban Development-subsidized housing program lease requirements prohibiting the use of controlled substances does not preempt state landlord-tenant law, the court applied "a heightened presumption against preemption" because "[l]andlord-tenant law is an area traditionally regulated by state and local governments, and one that has never been federalized").

[511] *Id.* at 475 ("Throughout our history the several States have exercised their police powers to protect the health and safety of their citizens. Because these are primarily, and historically, matters of local concern, the States traditionally have had great latitude under their police powers to legislate as to the protection of the lives, limbs, health, comfort, and quiet of all persons.") (internal citations omitted). *See also* Gonzales v. Oregon, 546 U.S. 243, 270 (2006).

[512] Gonzales v. Raich, 545 U.S. 1, 22 (2005) (holding that, in criminalizing "the local cultivation and use of marijuana" through the CSA, "Congress was acting well within its authority to 'make all Laws which shall be necessary and proper' to 'regulate Commerce ... among the several States.'") (quoting U.S. CONST., ART. I, § 8).

[513] *See* Murphy v. NCAA, 138 S. Ct. 1461, 1479 (2019) (holding that a federal law can preempt conflicting state laws if the federal law both "represent[s] the exercise of a power conferred on Congress by the Constitution" and "regulates private actors," not states).

> No provision of this subchapter shall be construed as indicating an intent on the part of the Congress to occupy the field in which that provision operates, including criminal penalties, to the exclusion of any State law on the same subject matter which would otherwise be within the authority of the State, unless there is a positive conflict between that provision of this subchapter and that State law so that the two cannot consistently stand together.[514]

Courts agree that the opening phrase of Section 903 expresses Congress's intent *not* to exercise field preemption in this domain.[515] The Supreme Court has explained that, by declining "to occupy the field" in Section 903, Congress chose not to exercise the full extent of its preemptive power, but instead "explicitly contemplates a role for the States in regulating controlled substances."[516] However, courts have not consistently agreed on precisely what role Congress intended to leave to the states pursuant to Section 903's closing phrase—"unless there is a *positive conflict* between that provision of this subchapter and that State law *so that the two cannot consistently stand together*."[517]

Some have indicated that Section 903's closing phrase only evokes the narrow impossibility preemption rubric,[518] meaning that a state marijuana law is not preempted unless it is "physically impossible" to comply with both the state marijuana law and the CSA.[519] However, certain courts have also

---

[514] 21 U.S.C. § 903.

[515] Cnty of San Diego v. San Diego NORML, 165 Cal. App. 4th 798, 819 (2008) ("The parties agree, and numerous courts have concluded, that Congress's statement in the CSA [Section 903] ... demonstrates Congress intended to reject express and field preemption of state laws concerning controlled substances").

[516] Gonzales v. Oregon, 546 U.S. 243, 251 (2005).

[517] 21 U.S.C. § 903 (emphasis added). *See* Robert A. Mikos, *Preemption Under the Controlled Substances Act*, 16 J. HEALTH CARE & POL'Y 5, 23 (2013).

[518] *See, e.g.*, *Cnty of San Diego*, 165 Cal. App. 4th at 825–26 (2008) (concluding that Congress only intended impossibility preemption through CSA Section 903, but evaluating the relevant state marijuana law under obstacle preemption, nonetheless). *See also* Erwin Chemerinky, *et al.*, *Cooperative Federalism and Marijuana Regulation*, 62 UCLA L. Rev. 74, 106–07 (2015) ("There is a reasonable argument that this straightforward [impossibility preemption] analysis should entirely settle the preemption question in the context of all state marijuana laws ... [b]ut the Court has suggested in some of its preemption decisions that even when there is an express statutory preemption provision under which a reviewing court finds no federal preemption, courts should in some circumstances still undertake an 'implied preemption' analysis. Under this analysis federal law will preempt if the state law or action at issue creates an 'obstacle to the purposes and objectives' of the federal law").

[519] Hillman v. Maretta, 569 U.S. 483, 490 (2013).

analyzed state marijuana laws under the broader obstacle preemption rubric.[520] Under obstacle preemption, courts evaluate whether the state laws "stand[] as an obstacle to the accomplishment and execution of the full purposes and objectives of Congress."[521] The Supreme Court has noted that the "primary purpose of the CSA is to control the supply and demand of controlled substances in both lawful and unlawful drug markets."[522]

As discussed below, although some courts have held that the CSA preempts certain discrete provisions of state marijuana regimes,[523] more permissive state marijuana laws have largely withstood both impossibility and obstacle preemption review.[524] Courts have typically found that state marijuana laws survive impossibility preemption because generally it is possible for individuals to comply with both state marijuana laws and the CSA by abstaining from marijuana use.[525] However, a small subset of provisions of state marijuana laws have been successfully challenged under the impossibility preemption rubric to the extent that they have been interpreted as *requiring* CSA violations (e.g., a state law that requires an employer to

---

[520] *See, e.g.*, Qualified Patients Assn. v. City of Anaheim, 187 Cal. App. 4th 734, 758–763 (Cal. App. 2010); *Cnty of San Diego*, 165 Cal. App. 4th at 825–26; Ter Beek v. City of Wyoming, 495 Mich. 1, 12 (Mich. 2014).

[521] *Hillman*, 569 U.S. at 490.

[522] Gonazles v. Raich, 545 U.S. 1, 19 (2005).

[523] *See infra* notes 94 and 96.

[524] *See, e.g.*, Noffsinger v. SSC Niantic Operating Co. LLC, 273 F. Supp. 3d 326, 334 (D. Conn. 2017) (holding that a state prohibition on employment discrimination for medical marijuana use was not preempted by the CSA); Reed- Kaliher v. Hoggatt, 347 P.3d 136, 141 (Ariz. 2015) (holding that a state law that prohibits conditioning probation on compliance with CSA provisions that conflict with the state's medical marijuana laws was not preempted by CSA Section 903); White Mt. Health Ctr., Inc. v. Maricopa Cnty., 386 P.3d 416, 419 (Ariz. Ct. App. 2016) (holding that "the CSA does not preempt the AMMA [Arizona Medical Marijuana Act] to the extent the AMMA requires the County to pass reasonable zoning regulations for MMDs [Medical Marijuana Dispensaries] and process papers concerning zoning compliance or requires the State to issue documents to allow MMDs to operate"); Qualified Patients Assn. v. City of Anaheim, 187 Cal. App. 4th 734, 758–763 (Cal. App. 2010) (holding that the CSA did not preempt California's marijuana laws); *Cnty of San Diego*, 165 Cal. App. 4th at 809; Joe Hemp's First Hemp Bank v. City of Oakland, 2016 U.S. Dist. LEXIS 11668, *12 (N.D. Cal. 2016) (holding that the CSA does not preempt the city's marijuana dispensary permitting scheme); Ter Beek v. City of Wyoming, 495 Mich. 1, 12 (Mich. 2014) (holding that CSA does not preempt state medical marijuana law that immunized an individual's cultivation of marijuana for medical purposes). *See also* Erwin Chemerinky, *et al.*, *Cooperative Federalism and Marijuana Regulation*, 62 UCLA L. Rev. 74, 110 (2015) ("The federal government has never argued, however—nor has any court ever held—that the CSA completely preempts state marijuana laws that are more permissive than federal law").

[525] *See, e.g.*, *Ter Beek*, 495 Mich. at 14–15; City of Garden Grove v. Superior Court, 157 Cal. App. 4th 355, 385 (Cal. App. 2007).

reimburse an injured employee for the purchase of medical marijuana).[526] State marijuana laws have largely withstood obstacle preemption because courts have held that they do not protect individuals from prosecution under federal law and because the state laws in question address issues within a field traditionally occupied by the states that were not expressly addressed by the CSA.[527] However, at least one court has held that a discrete provision of state marijuana laws was preempted by the CSA under the obstacle preemption rubric.[528] In what is arguably an outlier due to the breadth of its interpretation of the CSA's preemptive effect,[529] the Oregon Supreme Court held that a provision of a state marijuana law was preempted "[t]o the extent that [it] affirmatively authorize[d]" marijuana use because it served "as an obstacle to the implementation and execution of the full purposes and objectives of the

---

[526] *See, e.g.*, Garcia v. Tractor Supply Co., 154 F. Supp.3d 1225, 1230 (D.N.M. 2016) (granting motion of dismissal, "Mr. Garcia does not merely seek state-law immunity for his marijuana use. Rather, he seeks the state to affirmatively require Tractor Supply to accommodate his marijuana use… To affirmatively require Tractor Supply to accommodate Mr. Garcia's illegal drug use would mandate Tractor Supply to permit the very conduct the CSA proscribes."); People v. Crouse, 388 P.3d 39, 43 (Col. 2017) (holding that a state law that "requires law enforcement officers to return medical marijuana seized from an individual later acquitted of a state drug charges" is preempted because it forces officers to violate and, thus, is in "positive conflict" with, the CSA); Bourgoin v. Twin Rivers Paper Co., LLC, 187 A.3d 10, 20 (Me. 2018) (holding, under the impossibility preemption rubric, that a state medical marijuana law that required a private employer to "reimburse [an employee] for the cost of []medical marijuana" was preempted because it would have required the employer to aid and abet marijuana use in violation of the CSA).

[527] *See, e.g.,* Noffsinger v. SSC Niantic Operating Co. LLC, 273 F. Supp. 3d 326, 333–34 (D. Conn. 2017) (holding that the CSA does not preempt a provision of Connecticut law that prohibits employment discrimination against individuals who are qualified to use medical marijuana under state law); White Mt. Health Ctr., Inc. v. Maricopa Cnty., 386 P.3d 416, 419 (Ariz. App. 2016) (holding that "the CSA does not preempt the AMMA [Arizona Medical Marijuana Act] to the extent the AMMA requires the County to pass reasonable zoning regulations for MMDs [medical marijuana dispensaries] and process papers concerning zoning compliance or requires the State to issue documents to allow MMDs to operate").

[528] Emerald Steel Fabricators, Inc. v. Bureau of Labor Indus., 230 P.3d 518, 529 (Or. 2010).

[529] *See generally* Kathleen Harvey, *Protecting Medical Marijuana Users in the Workplace,* 66 Case W. Res. L. Rev. 209, 222 (2015) ("The *Emerald Steel* decision was an outlier. Almost every case regarding termination of medical marijuana users for a positive drug test was decided on nonpreemption grounds. The courts in the cases decided on nonpreemption grounds made suggestions about what an appropriate employee protection statute would look like if the legislature were to amend its state's medical marijuana laws. This suggests that those courts would enforce a properly drafted statute that protects medical marijuana users. It is unlikely the statute proposed in this Note would be preempted").

Controlled Substances Act."[530] A sampling of these preemption cases are discussed below.

For example, a California appellate court in *County of San Diego v. San Diego NORML* ruled that state medical marijuana laws were not preempted by the CSA under either impossibility or obstacle preemption analysis.[531] The case involved a preemption challenge to California laws that require local governments to issue medical marijuana cards to qualified applicants to apprise state personnel "that [the cardholders] are medically exempt[] from the state's criminal sanctions for marijuana possession and use."[532] The court held that California laws were not vulnerable to impossibility preemption because the CSA did not outlaw the issuance of the medical marijuana cards that the California laws required.[533] Consequently, the laws survived impossibility preemption because it was possible for an individual to honor both the CSA and the California card laws.[534] Although, in the court's view, CSA Section 903 expresses congressional intent to evoke only impossibility preemption, the court also held that the relevant California laws survived obstacle preemption because they "regulate [the] state's medical practices"

---

[530] *Emerald Steel*, 230 P.3d at 529 (holding, under obstacle preemption analysis, that "[t]o the extent that [the Oregon statute] affirmatively authorizes the use of medical marijuana, federal law preempts that subsection leaving it without effect") (internal citations omitted). *But see* White Mt. Health Ctr., Inc. v. Maricopa Cnty., 386 P.3d 416, 430 (Ariz. Ct. App. 2016) ("We also decline to adopt *Emerald Steel*'s distinction between decriminalization and authorization of medical marijuana use. The authorization/decriminalization distinction itself seems to be primarily semantic and ultimately results in a circular analysis."); Noffsinger v. SSC Niantic Operating Co. LLC, 273 F. Supp. 3d 326, 333–34 (D. Conn. 2017) (holding that the CSA does not preempt a provision of Connecticut law that prohibits employment discrimination against individuals who are qualified to use medical marijuana under state law); Willis v. Winters, 253 P.3d 1058, 1064 n.6 (Or. 2011) (questioning the applicability of the *Emerald Steel* reasoning beyond the facts at the heart of that case); Callaghan v. Darlington Fabrics Corp., 2017 R.I. Super. LEXIS 88, *41–*42 (R.I. Super. 2017) (holding that the CSA does not preempt state marijuana law under either impossibility because employees can abstain from marijuana use on the job or obstacle preemption because the CSA is "too attenuated" from "the realm of employment and anti-discrimination law").

[531] Cnty of San Diego v. San Diego NORML, 165 Cal. App. 4th 798, 825 (Cal. App. 2008) ("Because Congress provided that the CSA preempted only laws positively conflicting with the CSA so that the two sets of laws could not consistently stand together, and omitted any reference to an intent to preempt laws posing an obstacle to the CSA, we interpret title 21 United States Code section 903 as preempting only those state laws that positively conflict with the CSA so that simultaneous compliance with both sets of laws is impossible").

[532] *Id.* at 827.

[533] *Id.* at 825–26.

[534] *Id.* at 826.

and do not serve as "a significant impediment" to the CSA's general goal of "combat[ing] recreational drug use."[535]

In contrast, the Supreme Court of Colorado struck down a marijuana-related provision of the Colorado Constitution, apparently under impossibility preemption. *People v. Crouse* involved a provision of the Colorado Constitution that "requires law enforcement officers to return medical marijuana seized from an individual later acquitted of a state drug charge."[536] A majority of the Colorado Supreme Court held that this marijuana "return provision" was "in positive conflict with and thus preempted by the federal Controlled Substances Act" because "when law enforcement officers return marijuana in compliance with [the Colorado law], they distribute marijuana in violation of the CSA."[537] Thus, the court held that police officers could not comply with both the state's marijuana return provision and the CSA. As a result, the court held that the state's marijuana return provision was preempted by the CSA.[538]

Maine's highest state court followed the same reasoning as the *Crouse* court in an analogous preemption challenge to Maine's medical marijuana law.[539] In *Bourqoin v. Twin Rivers Paper Co., LLC*, an individual received an

---

535 *Id.* at 826–27.

536 People v. Crouse, 388 P.3d 39, 40 (Colo. 2017).

537 *Id.* at 42. *See also id.* (Gabriel, J., dissenting) ("I perceive no conflict between the CSA and section 14(2)(e) of article XVIII of the Colorado Constitution, nor do I believe that it is impossible to comply with both the CSA and the Colorado Constitution, as the majority implicitly and the People expressly contend."). The majority further held that CSA Section 885(d), which immunizes from civil and criminal liability law enforcement officers "lawfully engaged in the enforcement of any law or municipal ordinance relating to controlled substances," does not protect officers who distribute marijuana in violation of the CSA, even if such activity is authorized under Colorado law. *Id.* at 40 ("The officers here could not be 'lawfully engaged' in law enforcement activities given that their conduct would violate federal law. We thus conclude that, because section 14(2)(e) [of the Colorado Constitution] positive[ly] conflicts' with the CSA, and because § 885(d) does not protect officers acting unlawfully under federal law, the return provision is preempted and rendered void.").

538 *Id.* at 43 ("We therefore hold that the return provision of section 14(2)(e) is in positive conflict with and thus preempted by the federal Controlled Substances Act."). A three-judge dissent in *Crouse* would have held that Colorado's marijuana return provision is not preempted by the CSA because CSA Section 885 immunizes law enforcement officers who return medical marijuana to patients in accordance with the Colorado Constitution and, consequently, it is not impossible to comply with both the Colorado law and the CSA. *Id.* (Gabriel, J., dissenting).

539 Bourqoin v. Twin Rivers Paper Co., LLC, 187 A.3d 10, 20 (Me. 2018) ("Analytically, there is no difference between the circumstances of *Crouse* and this case: Compelling an employer to subsidize an employee's medical marijuana will require the employer to commit a federal crime—aiding or abetting the distribution and possession of marijuana

administrative order from the state's Workers Compensation Board requiring his former employer to pay for medical marijuana the employee used to treat chronic back pain stemming from an injury sustained on the job.[540] The court held that if the former employer complied with the workers compensation administrative order, it would be aiding and abetting marijuana use in violation of the CSA.[541] Therefore, "[c]ompliance with both is an impossibility."[542] Consequently, the court held that Maine's medical marijuana law was preempted to the extent that it "is used as the basis for requiring an employer to reimburse an employee for the cost of medical marijuana."[543]

In contrast, a California appellate court came to the opposite conclusions as the Colorado Supreme Court in *Crouse* when it addressed a similar marijuana return provision of California law.[544] The California Court of Appeals held that "federal supremacy principles do not prohibit the return of marijuana to a qualified user whose possession of the drug is legally sanctioned under state law."[545] The court noted that the state law does not protect individuals from federal CSA enforcement, but merely "limits *state* prosecution for medical marijuana possession[, which] simply does not implicate federal supremacy concerns."[546] Consequently, the court held that the CSA did not preempt the state's marijuana return law.[547]

In *Ter Beek v. City of Wyoming*,[548] the Supreme Court of Michigan held that the Michigan Medical Marihuana Act (MMMA), which immunized an individual's cultivation of marijuana for medical purposes, withstood both impossibility and obstacle preemption.[549] As understood by the court, the MMMA escaped impossibility preemption because it was permissive and therefore "does not require anyone to commit" a CSA violation, "nor does it prohibit punishment of that offense under federal law."[550] Consequently, the court concluded that it was not "impossible to comply with both the CSA and

---

just as Colorado law would have required law enforcement officers to distribute drugs in violation of the CSA.") (internal citations omitted).

540 *Id.* at 12.

541 *Id.* at 17.

542 *Id.* at 19.

543 *Id.* at 22.

544 City of Garden Grove v. Superior Court, 157 Cal. App. 4th 355, 362 (Cal. App. 2007).

545 *Id.* at 386. The court also held that CSA Section 885 would immunize officers who comply with the state return law because they would be "handling controlled substances as part of their official duties." *Id.* at 390.

546 *Id.* at 385 (emphasis added).

547 *Id.* at 386.

548 495 Mich. 1 (Mich. 2014).

549 *Id.* at 12.

550 *Id.*

[] the MMMA."[551] The MMMA escaped obstacle preemption, according to the court, because it merely conveyed immunity from the consequences of *state* law.[552] The court explained that "the MMMA's limited state-law immunity for [medical marijuana] use does not frustrate the CSA's operation nor refuse its provisions their natural effect, such that its purpose cannot otherwise be accomplished."[553] In the court's view, the MMMA "does not ... alter the CSA's federal criminalization of marijuana, or [] interfere with or undermine federal enforcement of that prohibition."[554] As a result, the court concluded that the state's medical marijuana law does not serve as an obstacle to the CSA.[555]

The Oregon Supreme Court, in an opinion that was questioned, though not expressly overturned, by the same court a little over one year later,[556] adopted a broader interpretation of CSA Section 903 under an obstacle preemption analysis in the 2010 decision, *Emerald Steel*.[557] The case involved a state-based disability discrimination charge against Emerald Steel for firing an employee without engaging in a reasonable accommodation discussion because the employee used marijuana in accordance with the Oregon Medical Marijuana Act.[558] Emerald Steel argued that the firing was permissible because the state anti-discrimination law's reasonable accommodation requirements "do not apply to persons who are currently engaged in the illegal use of drugs."[559] While Oregon law explicitly allowed the employee in *Emerald Steel* to use medical marijuana, the employer argued that marijuana use nevertheless qualified as an "illegal use of drugs" because it was prohibited by the CSA.[560] Thus, the court had to determine whether the provision of state law that authorized the use of medical marijuana was preempted by the CSA.[561] If it was preempted, then the employee's medical marijuana use would qualify as the "illegal use of drugs," thus negating

---

[551] *Id.* at 14.
[552] *Id.*
[553] *Id.* at 15.
[554] *Id.* at 14–15.
[555] *Id.* at 14.
[556] Willis v. Winters, 253 P.3d 1058, 1064 n.6 (Or. 2011) (questioning the applicability of the *Emerald Steel* reasoning beyond the facts at the heart of that case).
[557] Emerald Steel Fabricators, Inc. v. Bureau of Labor and Indus., 230 P.3d 518 (2010).
[558] *Id.* at 520.
[559] *Id.* at 521.
[560] *Id.*
[561] *Id.* at 524.

Emerald Steel's duty to provide reasonable accommodation under the state's discrimination law.[562]

The Oregon court first held that, although "the two laws are logically inconsistent," "it is not physically impossible to comply with both the Oregon Medical Marijuana Act and the [CSA]" because individuals could simply abstain from marijuana use.[563] The court then turned to the broader obstacle preemption analysis.[564] The Oregon court concluded, based on its interpretation of U.S. Supreme Court preemption precedent, that "[a]ffirmatively authorizing a use that federal law prohibits stands as an obstacle to the implementation and execution of the full purposes and objectives of the Controlled Substances Act."[565] Thus, "[t]o the extent that [the Oregon statute] affirmatively authorizes the use of medical marijuana, federal law preempts that subsection leaving it without effect."[566] Consequently, the employee's medical marijuana use constituted the "illegal use of drugs" and Emerald Steel was relieved from its responsibility to provide a reasonable accommodation to the employee.

The continued viability of *Emerald Steel* may be open to question after the Oregon Supreme Court's 2011 decision in *Willis v. Winters*, which involved a preemption question under a federal gun control law rather than Section 903 of the CSA.[567] The *Willis* court suggested that *Emerald Steel*'s "affirmative authorization" obstacle preemption test should not be considered a generally applicable rule, but instead should be viewed as only applicable to the specific facts of that case.[568] The *Willis* court explained:

---

[562] *Id.* at 524–526.

[563] *Id.* at 528.

[564] *Id.*

[565] *Id.* ("To be sure, state law does not prevent the federal government from enforcing its marijuana laws against medical marijuana users in Oregon if the federal government chooses to do so. But the state law at issue in *Michigan Canners* did not prevent the federal government from seeking injunctive and other relief to enforce the federal prohibition in that case. Rather, state law stood as an obstacle to the enforcement of federal law in *Michigan Canners* because state law affirmatively authorized the very conduct that federal law prohibited, as it does in this case.") (citing Michigan Canners & Freezers Assoc. v. Agricultural Marketing and Bargaining Bd., 467 U.S. 461, 478 (1984)).

[566] *Id.*

[567] Willis v. Winters, 253 P.3d 1058, 1066 (2011) (holding that a state concealed gun law is not preempted because it does not prevent the federal government from enforcing the relevant provision of the federal Gun Control Act and, consequently, "does not pose an obstacle to the enforcement of [the federal] law").

[568] *Id.* at 1064 n.6.

> *Emerald Steel* should not be construed as announcing a stand-alone rule that any state law that can be viewed as 'affirmatively authorizing' what federal law prohibits is preempted. Rather it reflects this court's attempt to apply the federal rule and the logic of the most relevant federal cases to the particular preemption problem that was before it. And particularly where, as here, the issue of whether the statute contains an affirmative authorization is not straightforward, the analysis in *Emerald Steel* cannot operate as a simple stand-in for the more general federal rule.[569]

Other courts have also distinguished *Emerald Steel* or expressly rejected its reasoning.[570] For example, the Arizona Court of Appeals "decline[d] to adopt *Emerald Steel*'s distinction between decriminalization and authorization of medical marijuana use" in a preemption challenge to various zoning requirements under Arizona's medical marijuana law.[571] The court concluded that the state's marijuana law did not pose as an obstacle to the CSA because it in no way affects the CSA's enforceability.[572] The Arizona law merely "provide[s] immunity from state penalties for medical use of marijuana."[573] The appellants in the case, citing *Emerald Steel*, argued that the state law "goes beyond mere decriminalization to affirmatively authorize violations of the CSA."[574] According to the court, *Emerald Steel*'s "authorization/decriminalization distinction [] seems to be primarily semantic."[575] The court made clear that the preemption question before it was whether the zoning requirements of Arizona's medical marijuana law imposes "significant and unsolvable obstacles to the enforcement of the CSA."[576] The Arizona Supreme Court had previously held, and the appellants in this case conceded, that the CSA does not preempt state laws that decriminalize certain medical marijuana use.[577] If entirely decriminalizing medical marijuana use

---

569 *Id.*

570 *See, e.g.*, White Mt. Health Ctr., Inc. v. Maricopa Cnty., 386 P.3d 416, 430 (Ariz. Ct. App. 2016) ("We also decline to adopt *Emerald Steel*'s distinction between decriminalization and authorization of medical marijuana use. The authorization/decriminalization distinction itself seems to be primarily semantic and ultimately results in a circular analysis."); Noffsinger v. SSC Niantic Operating Co. LLC, 273 F. Supp. 3d 326, 334–35 (D. Conn. 2017) (noting a factual similarity to *Emerald Steel* but distinguishing the case from a legal perspective "because Oregon's medical marijuana statute contains no provision explicitly barring employment discrimination").

571 *White Mt. Health Ctr., Inc.*, 386 P.3d at 430.

572 *Id.* at 427.

573 *Id.* at 428.

574 *Id.* (internal citations omitted).

575 *Id.* at 430.

576 *Id.*

577 *Id.* at 240 (citing Reed-Kaliher v. Hoggatt, 347 P.3d 136, 141 (Ariz. 2015)).

does not pose as an obstacle to CSA enforcement, the court reasoned that state statutes that actually regulate certain medical marijuana use also are not preempted.[578]

Anti-Commandeering and State Marijuana Legalization Efforts

In a similar, though legally distinct, vein to the preemption discussion above, some have argued that the CSA's criminalization of the growth, sale, and possession of marijuana bars *states* from authorizing some of those same activities under state law.[579] For example, the Nebraska Attorney General, in an August 2019 memorandum assessing the legality of a proposed state bill (LB 110, the Medical Cannabis Act (MCA)), wrote

> In sum, we conclude that the MCA, by creating a state regulatory scheme that would affirmatively facilitate the cultivation, processing, wholesale distribution, and retail sale of federal contraband on an industrial scale, would frustrate and conflict with the purpose and intent of the CSA. Accordingly, we conclude that the MCA would be preempted by the CSA and would be, therefore, unconstitutional.[580]

However, as discussed below, Supreme Court interpretations of the anti-commandeering doctrine, which generally provides that the federal government cannot compel states to execute regulatory activities on the federal government's behalf, arguably undermine such broad-based preemption arguments.[581]

The Supreme Court has noted that "[t]he legislative powers granted to Congress are sizable, but they are not unlimited."[582] The Constitution, "rather than granting general authority to perform all the conceivable functions of

---

[578] *Id.* at 429 ("As we understand the Appellants' arguments, if the AMMA had merely decriminalized the manufacture, distribution, and sale of medical marijuana, the AMMA would not be preempted by the CSA any more than decriminalization of growth and possession for personal use would have been preempted. However, because the State decided to regulate MMDs, that regulation is preempted. The logic of that distinction escapes us.").

[579] *See, e.g.,* Nebraska Attorney General Legal Memorandum, CONSTITUTIONALITY OF LB 110 – ADOPTION OF THE MEDICAL CANNABIS ACT, 8 (Aug. 1, 2019), https://perma.cc/NXT2-RU2T.

[580] *Id.*

[581] Murphy v. NCAA, 138 S. Ct. 1461, 1476 (2018).

[582] *Id.*

government, ... lists, or enumerates, the Federal Government's powers."[583] The Supreme Court has explained that "[t]he Constitution's express conferral of some powers makes clear that it does not grant others. And the Federal Government can exercise only the powers granted to it."[584] These principles are reinforced by the Tenth Amendment, which provides that "[t]he powers not delegated to the United States by the Constitution, nor prohibited by it to the States, are reserved to the States respectively, or to the people."[585] The anti-commandeering doctrine derives from the Tenth Amendment and the other limitations imposed on the federal government by the Constitution,[586] and has been described as "a significant constitutional counterweight to the Supremacy Clause."[587]

Three Supreme Court decisions, in particular, have clarified the scope of the doctrine's limitations on congressional statutory authority.[588] In the 1992 decision *New York v. United States*, the Supreme Court invalidated under the anti-commandeering doctrine a federal law that would have forced states to either dispose of radioactive waste in accordance with federal standards or "take title ... [and] possession" of such waste.[589] The Court held that, although the federal government can preempt state laws that are "contrary to federal interests" and may "hold out incentives to the States as a means of encouraging them to adopt suggested regulatory schemes," the Constitution bars the federal government from "compel[ling] the States to enact or administer a federal regulatory program."[590]

In *Printz v. United States*, the Supreme Court reiterated the same constitutional principles articulated in *New York* to strike down a federal statute that would have compelled state law enforcement officers to perform background checks on potential firearm purchasers.[591] The Court held that the federal government "cannot circumvent" the *New York* holding by "issu[ing] directives requiring the States to address particular problems, nor command

---

583 Nat'l Federation of Ind. Business v. Sebelius, 567 U.S. 519, 534 (2012).
584 *Id.* at 534 – 35 (internal citations omitted).
585 U.S. CONST. AMD. 10.
586 Printz v. United States, 521 U.S. 898, 919–24 (1997).
587 Erwin Chemerinky, *et al.*, *Cooperative Federalism and Marijuana Regulation*, 62 UCLA L. Rev. 74, 102 (2015).
588 Murphy v. NCAA, 138 S. Ct. 1461 (2018); *Printz*, 521 U.S. at 898; New York v. United States, 505 U.S. 144 (1992).
589 *New York*, 505 U.S. at 149, 153.
590 *Id.* at 188.
591 *Printz*, 521 U.S. at 935.

the States' officers, or those of their political subdivisions, to administer or enforce a federal regulatory program."[592]

In the 2018 decision *Murphy v. NCAA*, the Supreme Court clarified that the anti-commandeering doctrine not only prohibits federal legislation that commands states to act, but also bars legislation that *prohibits* states from acting.[593] The *Murphy* Court struck down a federal law prohibiting both the "licens[ing]" and "state authorization of sports gambling."[594] The Court held that by "unequivocally dictat[ing] what a state legislature can and cannot do," the federal sports gambling law attempted to place a state "under the direct control of Congress" in violation of the anti-commandeering doctrine.[595] The Court distinguished the relevant statutory provision from a permissible preemption provision by the fact that it regulates *states*, rather than *private individuals*.[596] The *Murphy* Court explained that "regardless of the language sometimes used by Congress and this Court, every form of preemption is based on a federal law that regulates the conduct of private actors, not the States."[597] In contrast, the federal sports gambling provision in question, according to the Court, could only be interpreted as "a direct command to the States. And that is exactly what the anticommandeering rule does not allow."[598] The Court concluded that the federal sports gambling law "regulates state governments' regulation of their citizens. The Constitution gives Congress no such power."[599]

The Supreme Court's anti-commandeering precedent appears to undermine arguments, like those articulated by the Nebraska Attorney General, that the CSA broadly preempts *states* from legalizing certain marijuana-related activities.[600] Congress has the constitutional authority, under the Commerce Clause and Necessary and Proper Clause, to criminalize

---

[592] *Id.*

[593] *Murphy*, 138 S. Ct. at 1478.

[594] *Id.* at 1481–82 ("[The federal sports gambling law's] prohibition of state licensing ... suffers from the same defect as the prohibition of state authorization. It issues a direct order to the state legislature. Just as Congress lacks the power to order a state legislature not to enact a law authorizing sports gambling, it may not order a state legislature to refrain from enacting a law licensing sports gambling.") (internal citations omitted).

[595] *Id.* at 1478.

[596] *Id.* at 1478–79.

[597] *Id.* at 1481.

[598] *Id.* at 1481.

[599] *Id.* at 1485 (internal citations omitted).

[600] Nebraska Attorney General Legal Memorandum, CONSTITUTIONALITY OF LB 110 – ADOPTION OF THE MEDICAL CANNABIS ACT, 8 (Aug. 1, 2019), https://perma.cc/NXT2-RU2T.

the sale, distribution, and possession of marijuana by *individuals*.[601] By extension, the federal government can enforce the CSA against individuals in violation of federal law, even if the federal violations occur in states that have legalized the same behavior under state law.[602] However, the same legal principles delineated in *Murphy*, in which the Court held that Congress does not have the constitutional authority to prohibit states from enacting state legislation authorizing or licensing sports gambling in the state, arguably would also apply in the context of state-enacted marijuana legalization efforts.[603] In short, while federal laws may preempt state laws that "affirmatively interfere[e]" in regulated activities, under the anti-commandeering doctrine the federal government arguably lacks the constitutional authority to prevent states from legalizing marijuana-related activities, even if those same activities are unlawful under federal law.[604]

---

[601] Gonzales v. Raich, 545 U.S. 1, 22 (2005) (holding that, in criminalizing "the local cultivation and use of marijuana" through the CSA, "Congress was acting well within its authority to 'make all Laws which shall be necessary and proper' to 'regulate Commerce ... among the several States.'") (quoting U.S. CONST., ART. I, § 8).

[602] United States v. Oakland Cannabis Buyers' Coop., 532 U.S. 483, 486 (2001) (holding that there is no medical necessity exception under the federal CSA that could serve as a defense to the federal government's enforcement action for the cultivation and possession of marijuana in a state that has authorized such activity).

[603] *See* Robert Mikos, *Nebraska Attorney General Gives the State Some Bad Legal Advice Concerning Marijuana Legalization*, MARIJUANA LAW, POLICY, AND AUTHORITY, Vanderbilt University Law School (Aug. 4, 2019), https://my.vanderbilt.edu/marijuanalaw/2019/08/nebraska-attorney-general-gives-the-state-some-bad-legal-advice-concerning-marijuana-legalization/ ("Simply put, the anti-commandeering rule enables states to legalize/authorize marijuana possession and sales."). *See also* Cnty of San Diego v. San Diego NORML, 165 Cal. App. 4th 798, 825–26 (2008) ("Counties also appear to assert the identification card laws present a significant obstacle to the CSA because the bearer of an identification card will not be arrested by California's law enforcement officers despite being in violation of the CSA. However, the unstated predicate of this argument is that the federal government is entitled to conscript a state's law enforcement officers into enforcing federal enactments, over the objection of that state, and this entitlement will be obstructed to the extent the identification card precludes California's law enforcement officers from arresting medical marijuana users. The argument falters on its own predicate because Congress does not have the authority to compel the states to direct their law enforcement personnel to enforce federal laws.") (citing Printz v. United States, 521 U.S. 898 (1997)).

[604] *See* Brief of Constitutional Law Scholars as Amici Curiae in Support of Petitioners, Murphy v. NCAA, 138 S. Ct. 1461, 4-6 (2018) ("Properly understood, the Supremacy Clause empowers Congress to preempt only state action that interferes with activity—not state action that lets activity alone ...When a state 'authorizes' private activity merely by removing state-law impediments to it, the state is doing no more than allowing that activity to occur. Congress can no more forbid states to allow conduct than it could compel states to disallow that conduct in the first place. Although 'authorization' necessarily means allowing some activity to occur, the term is sometimes used more broadly to include state actions that go beyond mere grants of permission. If a state 'authorizes' conduct by

Appendix F. Monitoring Health Concerns Related to Marijuana in Colorado

The Colorado Department of Public Health and Environment (CDPHE) was given the responsibility to "monitor changes in drug use patterns, broken down by county and race and ethnicity, and the emerging science and medical information relevant to the health effects associated with marijuana use."[605] In the most recent report, the CDPHE presents the following trends in Colorado:

- From 2017–2019, CDPHE did not identify any *new* disparities in adult marijuana use by age, gender, race/ethnicity, or sexual orientation (although some continued, see below).
- Daily (or near daily) adult use of marijuana (9.1%) is lower than past-30-day binge drinking (18.2%).
- For adolescents, estimated prevalence of past-30-day marijuana use and frequencies of marijuana use have not changed since legalization.
- Adolescent (high school students) past-30-day marijuana use (20.6%) is similar to the national average (21.7%).
- Adolescent past 30-day-marijuana use (20.6%) continues to be lower than past- 30-day alcohol use (29.6%) and electronic vapor products with nicotine use (25.9%).
- The majority of homes with children do not have marijuana present or being used inside the home. Among homes that do have marijuana present (14.0%), the majority are storing marijuana safely (89.6%).

---

affirmatively interfering in that conduct, then its actions would be vulnerable to preemption. To clarify, imagine a state law that does two separate things: it repeals the state's prohibition on the possession of marijuana, and it also bars landlords from discriminating against tenants on the basis of their marijuana use. Both provisions might be understood to 'authorize' marijuana possession in some sense, but only the latter provision could be preempted, because only the latter provision interferes with activity."); Erwin Chemerinky, *et al., Cooperative Federalism and Marijuana Regulation*, 62 UCLA L. Rev. 74, 103 (2015) ("Because Congress has the authority under the Commerce Clause to prohibit even the intrastate cultivation and possession of marijuana, no state can erect a legal shield protecting its citizens from the reach of the CSA. But at the same time, states' decisions to eliminate state marijuana prohibitions are simply beyond the power of the federal government. The federal government cannot command any state government to criminalize marijuana conduct under state law. From that incontrovertible premise flows the conclusion that if states wish to repeal existing marijuana laws or partially repeal those laws, they may do so without running afoul of federal preemption.") (internal citations omitted).

[605] Colorado Revised Statutes, Title 25, §1.5-110. The most recent report is CDPHE, Retail Marijuana Public Health Advisory Committee, *Monitoring Health Concerns Related to Marijuana in Colorado: 2020*, January 2021.

- Adult marijuana use, both daily (9.1%) and past-month use (19.0%), increased since 2017.
- The gap is closing in the prevalence of women who discontinue marijuana use/consumption postpartum (marijuana consumption among postpartum-currently breastfeeding moms in Colorado increased from 3.5% in 2017 to 4.9% in 2018).
- Past 30-day marijuana use/consumption (19.0%) and daily or near daily (9.1%) use/consumption among adults in Colorado has increased in 2019.
- Adult past-30-day marijuana use (19.0%) is higher than the national average (11.9%). In Colorado, 28.8% of adults ages 18-25 reported use/consumption in the past 30 days and 14.1% reported daily or near daily marijuana use/consumption.
- Since 2017, significant increases in consumption were observed among older Colorado adults ages 35 to 64 (12.8% in 2017 to 17.3% in 2019) and ages 65 years and older (5.6% in 2017 to 9.3% in 2019).
- Since retail marijuana became available in Colorado in 2014, there have been significant increases in daily or near daily marijuana consumption among adults ages 26 and over.
- In 2019, smoking marijuana remained the most prevalent method of marijuana use/consumption among Colorado adults (14.4%), followed by eating/drinking (8.1%), vaporizing (6.1%), dabbing (3.7%), and other methods (2.2%).
- There continues to be disparities in marijuana use/consumption based on age, sex, race/ethnicity, and sexual orientation for both adults and adolescents, signifying health inequities in certain populations in Colorado.
- Since 2014, use/consumption among adults and use among adolescents has remained consistently higher in the southwest region of the state. In 2019, marijuana use/consumption among Colorado adults was highest in the southwest (19.8%) and northwest (19.2%) regions of the state.
- In 2019, more Colorado adults think daily marijuana use/consumption has slight or no risk of harm and fewer Colorado adults think daily use/consumption has a moderate or great risk of harm.
- Past 30-day marijuana use among middle school (5.2%) and high school students (20.6%) has remained stable.

- In 2019, more high school students drove a vehicle after recently using marijuana than in 2017 (9.0% in 2017; 11.2% in 2019).
- Colorado high school students dabbed (10.2%) and vaporized (6.8%) marijuana more in 2019 than previous years, however, smoking marijuana remained the most prevalent (15.3%) method of use/consumption.
- In 2019, 10.4% of homes with children in Colorado may not be storing marijuana products safely, which increases the risk of accidental ingestion of marijuana products by others, in particular children.
- Colorado children may be at risk of exposure to secondhand marijuana smoke in the home.
- In 2018, 8.2% of pregnant women used/consumed marijuana during pregnancy. This percentage is higher among those with unintended pregnancies, younger mothers, and mothers with 12 years or less of education.[606]

Author Information

Lisa N. Sacco, Coordinator Analyst in Illicit Drugs and Crime Policy	Renée Johnson Specialist in Agricultural Policy
Agata Bodie Analyst in Health Policy	Joanna R. Lampe Legislative Attorney
David H. Carpenter Legislative Attorney	Isaac A. Nicchitta Research Assistant
Anthony A. Cilluffo Analyst in Public Finance	Liana W. Rosen Specialist in International Crime and Narcotics
Kristin Finklea Specialist in Domestic Security	Jon O. Shimabukuro Legislative Attorney
Alexandra Hegji Analyst in Social Policy	

[606] Ibid.

Acknowledgments

CRS Graphics Specialist Amber Wilhelm and CRS GIS Analyst Calvin DeSouza contributed to the graphics used in this report. Former CRS Analysts Sean Lowry and Victoria Green contributed to this report.

Subject Matter Experts

Area of Expertise	Name
General Marijuana and Drug Enforcement Policy	Lisa N. Sacco
Marijuana Trafficking	Kristin Finklea
Financial Services for Marijuana Businesses and Federal Preemption	David H. Carpenter
Employment and Marijuana Use	Jon Shimabukuro
Hemp Production	Renée Johnson
FDA Policy on Marijuana	Agata Bodie
Higher Education and Marijuana Policy	Alexandra Hegji
International Marijuana Policy	Liana Rosen
The Controlled Substances Act	Joanna Lampe
Marijuana Tax Policy	Anthony Cilluffo

Disclaimer

Chapter 2

Marijuana Laws in America: Racial Justice and the Need for Reform*

Committee on the Judiciary

Wednesday, July 10, 2019
House of Representatives
Subcommittee on Crime, Terrorism, and Homeland Security
Committee on the Judiciary
Washington, DC.

The subcommittee met, pursuant to call, at 10:06 a.m., in Room 2141, Rayburn House Office Building, Hon. Karen Bass [chair of the subcommittee] presiding.

Members Present: Representatives Bass, Nadler, Jackson Lee, Cohen, Deutch, Jeffries, Cicilline, Lieu, McBath, Dean, Mucarsel-Powell, Collins, Chabot, McClintock, Reschenthaler, Cline, and Steube.

Also Present: Representative Gaetz.

Staff Present: David Greengrass, Senior Counsel; John Doty, Senior Adviser; Lisette Morton, Director, Policy, Planning, and Member Services; Moh Sharma, Member Services and Outreach Adviser; Susan Jensen, Parliamentarian/Senior Counsel; Joe Graupensperger, Chief Counsel; Milagros Cisneros, Detailee; Veronica Eligan, Professional Staff Member;

* This is an edited, reformatted and augmented version of Hearing before the Subcommittee on Crime, Terrorism, and Homeland Security, of the House of Representatives, Committee on the Judiciary, One Hundred Sixteenth Congress, First Session, Serial No. 116–33, dated July 10, 2019.

In: The Legal Issues Surrounding Marijuana
Editor: Sade W. Sato
ISBN: 979-8-89113-427-0

Tony Angeli, Minority Counsel; and Andrea Woodard, Minority Professional Staff Member.

Ms. BASS. The Subcommittee on Crime, Terrorism, and Homeland Security will come to order.

Without objection, the chair is authorized to declare recesses of the subcommittee at any time.

I welcome everyone to today's hearing on Marijuana Laws in America: Racial Justice and the Need for Reform.

I will now recognize myself for an opening statement.

In 2017, there were over 600,000 marijuana-related arrests reported in the United States. Of these almost 600,000 were arrests for marijuana possession in 1 year. Indeed, hundreds of thousands of people, the majority of whom are black and Latino, have had their lives impacted by arrests and convictions for marijuana offenses.

Since the time President Nixon declared a war on drugs in the early 1970s, the effect of this war on black and Latino communities has been severely disproportionate. The war on drugs was racially biased from its inception, and it has been carried out in a discriminatory fashion with disastrous consequences for hundreds of thousands of people of color and their communities.

Today, nearly 80 percent of people in Federal prison and almost 60 percent of people in State prison for drug offenses are black or Latino. A 2013 study by the American Civil Liberties Union found that on average a black person is 3.73 times more likely to be arrested for marijuana possession than a white person, even though blacks and whites use marijuana at similar rates. These racial disparities in marijuana possession arrests exist in all regions of the country, in counties large and small, urban and rural, wealthy and poor, and with large and small black populations.

In recent years, as a society we have begun to examine the issues surrounding the disproportionate impact of the war on drugs and to develop policies and legislation to work against the devastation wrought by this war in the black and Latino communities. Part of the devastation has been that we criminalize the health problem.

While it is not in the jurisdiction of this committee, I do want to register the fact that some people do become addicted to drugs, including marijuana. And while we poured millions of dollars into incarceration, we did not put adequate resources into drug treatment. And while legalization is the direction many States are going, we need to make sure that a percentage of the revenue targeted that is earned from commercialization will go toward needed treatment services.

In 1996, California became the first State to decriminalize marijuana for medicinal purposes, and more States have followed. Today, the majority of States, 33, and the District of Columbia have decriminalized medical marijuana. Beginning with Colorado and Washington in 2012, 11 States, including most recently Illinois, have also begun legalized marijuana for adult recreational use.

At the Federal level, the criminal laws that pertain to marijuana are governed primarily by the Controlled Substances Act, or CSA, as we often call it. The CSA was signed into law by President Nixon in 1971, and it established a scheduling system through which the Federal Government regulated the lawful production, possession, and distribution of controlled substances, including marijuana.

Marijuana was initially placed and today remains on Schedule I. As a result, a person who grows, possesses, uses, sells, transports, or distributes marijuana, even if it is done in a way that is consistent with State law or authorized by a State license, is nonetheless in violation of the CSA and remains subject to Federal prosecution. In addition, because marijuana is still a federally controlled substance, the application of various money laundering and banking laws leaves many marijuana dispensaries being totally cash-only business, which, in some instances, can be dangerous and vulnerable to robbery.

During the Obama administration, the Department of Justice issued guidance that made clear that the Federal Government would not pursue legal challenges against jurisdictions that authorize marijuana so long as those States and local governments maintained strict regulatory and enforcement control on marijuana cultivation, distribution, sale, and possession, limiting the risk to public safety, public health, and other law enforcement interests.

The Trump administration rescinded that guidance to Federal prosecutors and encouraged them instead to charge and pursue the most serious readily provable offense. There is, therefore, a growing interest for this subcommittee to examine the laws that regulate marijuana and how Congress should respond to the growing trend toward legalization.

The collateral consequences of even an arrest for marijuana possession can be devastating, especially if a felony conviction results. Those arrested can be saddled with a criminal conviction that can make it difficult or impossible to vote, obtain educational loans, get a job, maintain a professional license, secure housing, secure government assistance, or even adopt a child. These exclusions create an often permanent second-class status for millions of Americans.

Like drug war enforcement itself, these consequences fall disproportionately on people of color. Personally, I don't automatically believe that legalization will result in a decrease in the disproportionate arrest of people of color, in particular African Americans. But I do hope that those who use the disproportionate arrest as part of the campaign for legalization will be just as concerned and active if the disproportionate arrest rates continue years after legalization.

There is a growing consensus in this country that current marijuana laws are not appropriate, and we must consider reform. Today's hearing is a first step in that process. I look forward to hearing from all of our witnesses, and now I recognize the distinguished ranking member who is serving as ranking member today.

Mr. MCCLINTOCK. Acting ranking member, I suppose.

Ms. BASS. Acting ranking memberrom California, Mr. McClintock.

Mr. MCCLINTOCK. Thank you, Madam Chairman.

You know, marijuana decriminalization may be one of the very few issues upon which bipartisan agreement can still be reached in this session. It doesn't require endorsing cannabis. Quite the contrary. I think there is clear evidence that marijuana can cause long-term neurological problems in children and adolescents, and no one should approach the use of any drug without caution and moderation.

I believe we should do everything we can to prevent its use by children and warn of its use by adults. But it ought to be crystal clear to everyone that our laws have not accomplished their goals.

In fact, a deputy sheriff once said that if he were to choose two high school students anywhere in the country at random, give them each a $20 bill, send one to buy pot and the other to buy booze, the child he sent out to buy pot would always be the first one back. They know where to get it, and the dealer's entire business is built on ignoring the law. The youth sent to buy alcohol would visit one liquor store after another, get carded, and get thrown out precisely because the dealer's entire business depends on obeying the law.

I do worry about excessive use of marijuana by young adults, but excess is a trait of the young that is usually cured by experience. And against this, we need to balance how many millions of young people have had their lives ruined because of a marijuana conviction from their youth that follows them for the rest of their lives. Worse, like liquor prohibition in the 1920s and '30s, our marijuana laws have not only failed to curtail its use, they have created a violent underground economy and contributed to overall disdain for the rule of law in general. I mean, let us face it. Radish growers don't kill one another over their territory.

Furthermore, the essence of federalism is deferring to State legislatures on most domestic issues. Louis Brandeis famously observed that a State may, if its citizens choose, serve as a laboratory and try novel social and economic experiments without risk to the rest of the country. Many States are doing exactly that today, and the rest can learn from their example for good or for ill.

Last month, the House of Representatives approved a bipartisan amendment to protect State laws on marijuana commerce from interference by the Federal Government. I believe more permanent reforms are needed to allow individual States to control, regulate, and tax marijuana as each one sees fit. The present conflict between State and Federal law in this matter is no longer sustainable, and it must be resolved.

Now personally, I believe cannabis use in most cases is ill-advised, but many things are ill-advised that should not be illegal, but rather be left to the informed judgment of free men and women. Bruce Herschensohn, in discussing anti-tobacco laws, observed that for every pleasure in life, there is a concomitant risk. And usually, the greater the pleasure, the greater the risk.

"With enough force and regulation," he said, "we can create a nearly risk-free society, but it will also be the most miserable, colorless, tedious, boring society ever imposed upon a people."

I do regret that just as strong bipartisan consensus is emerging on this issue, the majority has decided to play the race card at today's hearing. We should have only one race in our free country, the American race, and the left does enormous harm every time it tries to divide Americans along racial lines.

The fact is that our marijuana laws have badly served all of us as a nation, and this realization could be used to bring us together rather than to tear us apart. When laws have been tried over many years and have not only failed to achieve their objectives but have created great harm in the process, I think it is time to revise and repeal them. I believe we have reached such a moment, and shame on those who would use it to inflame racial divisions.

I yield back.

Ms. BASS. I now recognize the committee chair, Mr. Nadler.

Chairman NADLER. Thank you. Thank you, Madam Chair.

Before I read my prepared statement, I want to say two things. Number one, until his last paragraph, I was preparing to say that I have the pleasure of agreeing with every word that the distinguished Member from California had said in all respects.

Let me just add, though, that enforcement of marijuana laws has been done in a racially disparate manner. The effects have been racially disparate. To point that out and to seek to cure that is not to inflame racial divisions, it is simply to point out a fact of life and to try to cure it.

I thank our Crime Subcommittee chair, the gentlelady from California, Ms. Bass, for holding this hearing today on the need to reform our marijuana laws. I have long believed that the criminalization of marijuana has been a mistake, and the racially disparate enforcement of marijuana laws has only compounded this mistake with serious consequences, particularly for minority communities.

Marijuana is one of the oldest agricultural commodities not grown for food. It has been continuously—it has been used medicinally all over the world since at least 2700 B.C., but its criminalization is a relatively recent phenomenon. The use of marijuana, which most likely originated in Asia, later spread to Europe and made its way to the Americas when the Jamestown settlers brought it with them across the Atlantic.

The cannabis plant has been widely grown in the United States and was used as a component in fabrics during the middle of the 19th century. During that time period, cannabis was also listed in the United States Pharmacopeia as a treatment for a multitude of ailments, including muscle spasms, headaches, cramps, asthma, and diabetes.

It was only in the early part of the 20th century that marijuana began to be criminalized, mainly because of misinformation and hysteria, based at least in part on racially biased stereotypes connecting marijuana use and minorities, particularly African Americans and Latinos. Unfortunately, the same racial animus motivating enactment of these laws also led to racially disproportionate enforcement of such laws, which has had a substantial negative impact on minority communities. The enforcement of the laws, I would also add, has also had a bad effect on nonminority communities.

As our chair, Ms. Bass, pointed out, the collateral consequences of conviction for marijuana possession and sometimes even for a mere arrest can be devastating. For those saddled with a criminal conviction, it can be difficult or impossible to vote, to obtain education loans, to get a job, to maintain a professional license, to secure housing, to receive government assistance, or even to adopt a child.

These exclusions create an often permanent second-class status for millions of Americans. This is unacceptable. It is also counter-productive, especially in light of the disproportionate impact enforcement of marijuana laws has had on communities of color.

It is not surprising, therefore, that over the past two decades, public support for legalizing marijuana has surged. States have led the way with reforms, and presently, medicinal or recreational marijuana use is legal in 33 States and the District of Columbia. However, our Federal laws have not kept pace with the obvious need for change. In my view, applying criminal penalties with their attendant collateral consequences for marijuana offenses is unjust and harmful to our society.

The use of marijuana should be viewed instead as an issue of personal choice and public health. An examination of our marijuana laws and potential reforms is long overdue. I should add that one of my first votes that I cast as a freshman member of the State Assembly in New York in 1977 was to decriminalize marijuana in New York.

I appreciate the chair for holding this important hearing today. I look forward to hearing from our witnesses, and I yield back the balance of my time.

Ms. BASS. Thank you, Chairman Nadler.

It is now my pleasure to recognize the ranking member of the full committee, the gentleman from Georgia, Mr. Collins, for his opening statement.

Mr. COLLINS. Thank you, Madam Chairwoman. I appreciate that.

And thanks for scheduling this hearing. You may recall some of my colleagues and I asked Chairman Nadler in April to promptly hold a hearing on legislative solutions to the conflict between Federal and State marijuana laws and to permit the committee to fully examine the issue. The scope of today's hearing is limited to the racial justice implication of marijuana laws, but many more factors must be explored before we change Federal law and establish protections for States that legalize marijuana.

As I wrote in April, the legal status of marijuana in the United States is in complete disarray. Over 30 States and the District of Columbia have legalized medicinal and/or recreational use of marijuana. More States have opted to decriminalize marijuana possession or legalize the consumption of extracts from the marijuana plant, yet some States prohibit the use of marijuana completely.

Marijuana remains a Schedule I under Federal law, and the Federal Drug Administration has never concluded that valid medical and scientific evidence exists to support the prescribed use of smoking marijuana. However, the FDA has approved some of the marijuana's derivative compounds for prescription use and should do more.

There are three primary international drug control treaties aimed at combating drug abuse. The United States is 1 of 186 state parties to these treaties, which seeks to combat drug trafficking and limit the manufacture, distribution, and sale of psychoactive drugs exclusively to medicinal and research purposes. Covered under these conventions include cocaine, heroin, marijuana, as well as opioids and other synthetic drugs.

This committee must be mindful of the conflict that already exists between Federal and State laws, and in drafting a solution, our treaty obligations must also be considered and evaluated for long-term purpose.

Since 2009, the Department of Justice provided amended and withdrawn guidance over the years in the form of memoranda to 94 U.S. attorneys about how to prioritize enforcement of the cultivation, distribution, and sale of marijuana in light of the conflict between Federal and State laws. I believe these changes in DOJ policy have added to the confusion.

Earlier this year, Attorney General Barr agreed, stating, "The current situation is untenable and really has to be addressed. It is almost like a back door nullification of Federal law. If we want a Federal approach, if we want States to have their own laws, then let us get there right away."

I agree. Federal and State laws, scientific evidence, international law, and a variety of enforcement policies have all combined to form an unsustainable state of affairs regarding marijuana. Numerous bills have been introduced over the years to address this situation. In April, I cosponsored the STATES Act. This bipartisan bill would ensure that each State has the right to determine the best approach to marijuana within its borders.

At the same time, the will of most of those States to limit or prohibit marijuana use must be respected. Regardless of how Members may feel about the proper approach, I believe the committee and Congress must clarify the rights, responsibilities of individuals, physicians, businesses, medical patients, law enforcement officials relative to marijuana. That is what this committee is for. That is what this committee should take up. And that is why we are here—to find good solutions.

The STATES Act, I believe, is an excellent foundation for legislative reforms and to begin in this committee or other committees. And with that, Madam Chair, I yield back.

Ms. BASS. Thank you, Mr. Collins.

It is now my pleasure to introduce today's panel. The Honorable Ms. Marilyn Mosby has been the State's attorney for Baltimore City since 2015, during which time she has put in place a number of initiatives to reform the criminal justice system in Baltimore. In January of this year, Ms. Mosby instituted a policy to stop prosecuting the possession of marijuana and move to vacate marijuana possession convictions dating back to 2011.

Dr. David Nathan is a psychiatrist, educator, and consultant. Dr. Nathan is an advocate for evidence-based changes in drug policy focusing on principles of public health and social justice. He is the founder and board president of Doctors for Cannabis Regulation.

Mr. Neal Levine is a national advocate for the cannabis industry. He cofounded and serves as the CEO of the Cannabis Trade Federation, which is a national coalition of cannabis-related businesses representing various aspects of the industry.

Dr. Malik Burnett is a physician, advocate, and entrepreneur. Dr. Burnett works on issues pertaining to drug policy reform, particularly relating to racial justice. He has worked on developing medical and adult use cannabis policy in the District of Columbia, Massachusetts, Maryland, Ohio, Pennsylvania, Tennessee, and Vermont.

We welcome our witnesses and thank them for participating in today's hearing. Please note that your written statement will be entered into the record in its entirety. Accordingly, I ask that you summarize your testimony in 5 minutes.

To help you stay within that time, there is a timing light on your table. When the light switches from green to yellow, you will have 1 minute to conclude your testimony. When the light turns red, it signals that your 5 minutes has expired.

Before proceeding with testimony, I hereby remind each witness that all of your written and oral statements made to the subcommittee in connection with this hearing are subject to penalties of perjury, pursuant to 18 U.S.C. 1001, which may result in the imposition of a fine or imprisonment of up to 5 years or both, as we talk about criminal justice reform.

Honorable Marilyn Mosby.

Statements of Hon. Marilyn Mosby, State's Attorney for Baltimore City, Baltimore, Maryland; David L. Nathan, M.D., DFAPA, Doctors for Cannabis Regulation, Princeton, New Jersey; Neal Levine, Chief Executive Officer, Cannabis Trade Federation, Denver, Colorado; and G. Malik Burnett, M.D., MBA, MPH, COO, Tribe Companies, LLC, Washington, D.C.

Statement of Hon. Marilyn Mosby

Ms. MOSBY. Thank you. Good morning, Chair Bass, Chairman Nadler, as well as Ranking Member Mr. McClintock—did I say that right?—

Mr. McClintock, as well as I believe Mr. Collins left, and the honorable members of the House Judiciary Subcommittee on Crime, Terrorism, and Homeland Security.

I am honored to be before you today. As the chief prosecutor of a major American city, it is my sworn ethical obligation as an administrator of justice to not only ensure the safety of my community, but to seek to reform and improve the criminal justice system where justice requires.

As was mentioned, on January 29th of this year, I announced that my office would stop devoting resources to the prosecution of marijuana possession charges, regardless of weight and criminal history. I mandated the referral of every first-time felony drug offender to my office's job training diversion program, and my office then moved to vacate the convictions of almost 5,000 marijuana possession convictions dating back to 2011.

In tandem with this announcement, my office released a white paper that enumerated the lack of public safety value in the prosecution of marijuana possession, the counterproductive outcomes of utilizing limited law enforcement resources with little to no public safety value, and racially disparate enforcement of marijuana laws resulting in adverse collateral consequences for poor black and brown communities in Baltimore.

The reason I am here today is because there is no better illumination of this country's failed war on drugs than the City of Baltimore, Maryland. A mere 45 minutes away from our Nation's capital, Baltimore, a city inextricably woven into the fabric our country's history, a city so critically important to the founding of this Nation, a proud city that boasts some of the greatest American legends from Justice Thurgood Marshall to the birthplace of the Star-Spangled Banner, unfortunately, last year, Baltimore led the Nation in per capita homicides, rising opioid deaths, and is one of the most segregated and impoverished cities in the Nation.

For decades, the State of Maryland has criminalized substance use disorders, as opposed to treating it as the public health crisis that we all recognize it to be. Meanwhile, over 20 million Americans have been arrested for violating marijuana laws that have imposed legal, social, and economic debilities and marginalization on every basic survival necessity of life for those not only convicted, but also those incarcerated.

From housing, healthcare access, welfare, immigration, employment, property rights, mobility, education, financial aid, and even voting, whole communities are being ravaged and have lost generations of mothers, fathers, brothers, sons, and daughters to incarceration in a cyclical poverty due to these convictions. And what is worse is that data shows the enforcement of these laws are overwhelmingly inflicted upon poor and black communities.

It has been reported, as was already mentioned, black people are almost four times more likely to be arrested for marijuana possession in the United States than white people, despite individuals of both races using marijuana at the same rate. In the City of Baltimore, prior to the decriminalization of 10 grams or less, black people were 6 times more likely to be arrested for simple possession.

And while many had hoped that decriminalization would offer a respite to communities of color, the flagrant racial disparities continue to exist. In our Nation's capital, black people are 11 times more likely to be arrested for public consumption of marijuana than whites. In the City of the Baltimore, my city, in 2017, 95 percent of all citations issued by the Baltimore police were issued to black people.

Forty-two percent of the citations issued citywide were issued in a single district that represents 9 percent of the total city population, which happens to be 95 percent black and disproportionately impoverished. Which is why I am here today, for three critically important reasons.

One, because I refuse to accept the status quo any longer, especially when there is so much evidence that proves that we can be smarter and do better as it relates to marijuana policy. Two, I refuse to be complicit in the continued decimation of poor black and brown communities, where we, as a community, irresponsibly continue to maintain and unfathomably seek to justify and defend a set of policies that without question are racist and discriminatory in implementation. And three, because it is the right thing to do, which is why I applaud Chair Bass for her leadership and her courage in convening today's hearing.

I implore Congress today to not only decriminalize marijuana, but to remove marijuana from the Controlled Substances Act, thereby federally legalizing it. Much like the regulation of alcohol and tobacco, let the States decide the legalization, regulation, and taxation of this substance because by doing so diminishing the black market distribution of it.

Furthermore, it is completely illogical to impose Federal interference or criminal penalties upon individuals that act in compliance with State law. This is especially pertinent to our immigrant population that already exists in a toxic and constant state of fear of deportation.

For decades, Congress has provided Federal economic incentives to States through grants and by way of task forces to encourage what we know was now a discriminatory enforcement of marijuana laws against black and brown people. I implore Congress to now provide the same economic funding opportunities to encourage States to create mechanisms to right the wrongs of the past, reinvest in not just the individuals hampered by these inequitable convictions, but I also implore you to reinvest in the communities that have been most adversely impacted.

You have the power to encourage the States to enact automatic and mass expungement and vacatur and post conviction. We spend an allocation of $4 billion federally every single year on marijuana enforcement. And I would encourage you all to please include creating and thinking about job opportunities, reentry and mental health services for formerly incarcerated individuals, and the inclusion of people of color in a billion-dollar industry that was shut out —

Ms. BASS. Thank you.

Ms. MOSBY [continuing]. That is including intentionally shutting them out. [The statement of Ms. Mosby follows:]

Marijuana Laws in America: Racial Justice and the Need for Reform, July 10, 2019, Written Statement, Marilyn J. Mosby, Baltimore City State's Attorney, Baltimore City State's Attorney Office

Introduction

Chairwoman Karen Bass, Vice Chair Val Butler Demings, Ranking Member John Ratcliff and members of the House Judiciary Subcommittee on Crime,

Terrorism, and Homeland Security, I am Marilyn Mosby, the State's Attorney for Baltimore City. It is an honor to appear before the Subcommittee today to discuss the need for federal decriminalization of marijuana, the need for criminal justice reform specific to marijuana enforcement, the necessity of second chances for those who have been involved in the justice system and the necessity for equitable economic participation and reinvestment in communities that have been disproportionately and most adversely affected by the discriminatory enforcement and criminalization of these laws. As the Chief prosecutor of Baltimore city, it is my sworn ethical obligation, as an administrator of justice, to not only seek justice and safety in my community, but to seek to reform and improve the fair administration of criminal justice. When inadequacies or injustices in the substantive or procedural law come to the prosecutor's attention, he or she should take action to remedy that injustice and create new practices that mitigate further harm.[1] That is the essence of the pursuit of justice and a proactive vision in my role as an elected prosecutor that fortifies community trust integral to the functioning of our justice system.[2] It is this vision that drove my recent implementation of a new marijuana policy, as well as my ongoing efforts to look at the integrity of past convictions and other areas where our justice system has fallen short.[3]

There's a growing number of prosecutors nationwide who are examining how best to implement criminal justice reform from within.[4] As part of this reform, many elected prosecutors' are reconsidering marijuana prosecution policies for several reasons including the need to address racially disproportionate punitive approaches to drug use, a desire to achieve more sensible use of scarce resources and the recognition that criminalizing drug use has not led to safer or healthier communities. This thinking is based on increasing evidence that "higher rates of drug imprisonment do not translate

---

[1] American Bar Association, fourth edition of the criminal justice standards for the prosecution function, part i. general standards, Standard 3-1.1.

[2] Fair and Just Prosecution. "21 Principles for the 21st Century Prosecutor," (2019), https://fairandjustprosecution.org/wp-content/uploads/2018/12/FJP_21Principles_ Interactive-w-destinations.pdf21rst%20century%20Principles and Bazelon and Krinsky, "There's a New Wave of Prosecutors. And They Mean Justice," New York Times, (2018) https://www.nytimes.com/2018/12/11/opinion/how-local-prosecutors-can-reform-their-justice-systems.html.

[3] National Public Radio, "Baltimore State's Attorney Will No Longer Prosecute Marijuana Possession," (2019), https://www.npr.org/2019/02/03/690975390/baltimore-states-attorney-will-no-longer-prosecute-marijuana- possession-cases.

[4] New York Times, "A Growing Chorus of Big City Prosecutors Say No to Marijuana Convictions," (2019), https://www.nytimes.com/2019/01/29/us/baltimore-marijuana-possession.html.

into lower rates of drug use, arrests, or overdose deaths."[5] Instead, mass incarceration for drug offenses has devastating consequences for those incarcerated and their families and communities. Excessive punishment of drug crimes perpetuates the cycles of generational trauma and socioeconomic marginalization that, in turn, intensify the social determinants of drug use.[6]

Based on these and other concerns, on January 29th of this year, I announced that I was utilizing my discretion as a prosecutor to stop devoting resources to the prosecution of marijuana possession charges, regardless of weight and criminal history. I mandated the referral of every first-time felony drug offender to my offices' job training diversion program.[7] My office moved to vacate the convictions of almost 5,000 marijuana possession convictions dating back to 2011. In tandem with the announcement of my policy, my office also released a detailed white paper entitled, *"Reforming a Broken System: Rethinking Marijuana Prosecution in the city of Baltimore,"* in which we enumerated the lack of public safety value in the prosecution of marijuana possession; the counterproductive nature of utilizing limited law enforcement resources for a crime with no public safety value; and the racially disparate enforcement of marijuana laws resulting in adverse collateral consequences for poor Black and Brown communities in Baltimore.

I am here today because there is no better illustration of this country's failed "War on Drugs" than the city of Baltimore, MD. A mere 45 minutes away from our nation's capital, Baltimore currently leads the nation in per capita homicides, rising opioid deaths and is one of the most impoverished cities in the nation. Once deemed the "Heroin capital of the World," for decades our government has criminalized substance use as opposed to treating it as the public health crisis we now recognize it to be. In fact, in 2015, the United States spent $3.96 billion on the enforcement and imprisonment of marijuana users and an additional $18.47 billion on all other substance users.[8] It is undisputed that the long-standing, well-established discriminatory

---

[5] The Pew Charitable Trusts, "More Imprisonment Does Not Reduce State Drug Problems," (2018), https://www.pewtrusts.org/-/media/assets/2018/03/pspp_more_imprisonment_does_not_reduce_state_drug_problems.pdf and Drug Policy Alliance, "The Drug War, Mass Incarceration and Race," (2018), http://www.drugpolicy.org/sites/default/files/drug-war-mass-incarceration-and-race_01_18_0.pdf.

[6] The Pew Charitable Trusts, "Collateral Costs: Incarceration's Effect on Economic Mobility," (2010), https://www.pewtrusts.org/~/media/legacy/uploadedfiles/pcs_assets/2010/collateralcosts1pdf.pdf.

[7] Baltimore City State's Attorneys Office, Full Term Report 2015-2018, (2019), https://www.stattorney.org/media-center/annual-reports/1676-2015-2018-full-term-report.

[8] Drug War Facts, "Economics of Drug Policy and The Drug War," https://www.drugwarfacts.org/chapter/economics.

enforcement of drug laws has disproportionately affected poor Black and Brown communities nationally and has led to widespread collateral consequences that not only severely and adversely impact an individuals' ability to find employment, secure housing and obtain student loans, but these barriers have led to the breakdown of families and the social and economic decimation of communities.[9]

National data has consistently shown that Black people are almost four times more likely to be arrested for marijuana possession in the United States than White people, despite individuals of both races using marijuana at the same rate.[10] In the city of Baltimore, prior to the decriminalization of 10 grams or less of marijuana, Black people were six times more likely to be arrested for the possession of marijuana.[11] While some had hoped that a movement toward decriminalization would offer a respite to communities of color, flagrant disparities continue to exist in Baltimore city. Since the decriminalization of possession of less than ten grams of marijuana to a civil infraction, Black people have continued to bear the disproportionate weight of enforcement. In 2017, 95% of the citations issued by the Baltimore Police Department were issued to Black people and shockingly, 42% of the citations issued city-wide were issued in a singled district out of nine that cover the city, the Western District. Unsurprisingly, 95% of the residents in this District are Black and disproportionately impoverished.[12]

For far too long, we all have stood by and allowed discriminatory policies and enforcement to destroy families and communities. We have allowed these practices to continue even as we have seen them strip communities of their health, prosperity, and hope. I am here today because I refuse to accept the status quo any longer. I refuse to be complicit in the destruction of our Black and Brown communities.

---

[9] Shawn M. Kneipp and Amanda Sheely, "The effects of collateral consequences of criminal involvement on employment, use of Temporary Assistance for Needy Families, and health," (2018), https://www.ncbi.nlm.nih.gov/pmc/articles/PMC5763494/.

[10] American Civil Liberties Union, "The War on Marijuana in Black and White," (June 2013), https://www.aclu.org/sites/default/files/field_document/1114413-mj-report-rfs-rel1.pdf at 21.

[11] Ethan McLeod, Andy Friedman and Brandon Soderberg, Baltimore Fishbowl, "Structural Racism and Cannabis: Black Baltimoreans still disproportionately arrested for weed after decriminalization," (2018), https://baltimorefishbowl.com/stories/structural-racism-and-cannabis-black-baltimoreans-still-disproportionately-arrested-for-weed-after-decriminalization/.

[12] Citation records obtained by Baltimore Police Department. Neighborhood ethnicity data found at: Statistical Atlas, "Race and Ethnicity in Baltimore City," (2018), https://statisticalatlas.com/place/Maryland/Baltimore/Race-and-Ethnicity#data-map/neighborhood.

I come before you today to share the impact of the failed "War on Drugs" that has ravaged my city and far too many other parts of our nation, which served as the impetus and support for the findings and proposals outlined in my white paper. As a prosecutor committed to equitable outcomes and the pursuit of "justice over convictions" in every instance, I welcome any discussions today and thank the members of the subcommittee for your willingness to continue to consider this critical issue.

Past and Present Consequences: War on Drugs

President Richard Nixon officially declared a "War on Drugs" in 1971. In the 1980s, President Ronald Reagan reinforced and expanded many of Nixon's "War on Drugs" policies. In 1984, First Lady Nancy Reagan later launched the "Just Say No" campaign with an effort to educate children on the dangers of drug use. As years passed, the "War on Drugs" continued and so did the policies designed to punish substance use. In 1994, President Bill Clinton solidified the United States' (U.S.) "Tough On Crime" and "War on Drugs" by way of his Violent Crime Control and Law Enforcement Act, which imposed three-strikes mandatory life sentencing, money to hire a 100,000 additional police officers, and funding for prisons, among many other policies.[13]

As a result of decades of escalating penalties and punitive approaches to substance use, from 1980 to 1997, the number of people behind bars for nonviolent drug offenses increased from 50,000 to over 400,000.[14] And between 1981 and 2006, the number of drug arrests in the United States quadrupled to nearly two million per year, disproportionately affecting people and communities of color.[15] Forty-six years since the official declaration of Nixon's drug war, as of 2017, 1.5 million arrests in the U.S. were due to drug law violations, where 85.4% of those arrested were related to drug

[13] Congressional Research Service, "Crime Control: Federal Initiatives IP310C, found at https://www.ncjrs.gov/pdffiles1/Digitization/148292NCJRS.pdf.

[14] Drug Policy Alliance, "Drug Policy Statistics," http://www.drugpolicy.org/issues/drug-war-statistics.

[15] Katherine Beckett, "The Uses and Abuses of Police Discretion: Toward Harm Reduction Policing," 10 Harv. L. & Pol'y Rev. 77, 81 (2016) and Brian Stauffer, "Every 25 Seconds: The Human Toll of Criminalizing Drug Use in the United States, Human Rights Watch" (2016), https://www.hrw.org/report/2016/10/12/every-25-seconds/human-toll- criminalizing-drug-use-united-states.

possession.[16] While the U.S. continues to lead the world with the highest rates of imprisonment for drug law violations, it is patently clear that drug-related arrests have had little impact on substance use, while having extremely deleterious impacts on communities of color. Although data is clear that the rates of drug use and even sales are comparable across racial and ethnic lines, Black and Latinx people are much more likely to be arrested for drug use and sales than White people. In fact, approximately 80% of people in federal prison and almost 60% of people in state prison for drug offenses are Black or Latinx.[17]

Precursors to Policy Development

No Demonstrable Public Safety Considerations

The test of time has provided us with ample data that there is little public safety value related to the current enforcement of marijuana laws. The data indicates that the disparate enforcement of marijuana laws and overall drug laws not only intensifies already existing racial disparities in the criminal justice system, but exacerbates distrust among communities and law enforcement without increasing overall public safety.

As further evidence that marijuana enforcement, in particular, is not creating a significant public safety benefit, one can look to states that have legalized recreational use of marijuana where no demonstrable increase in crime since legalization has been observed. The Manhattan District Attorney's Office released in 2018, *A Report on the Legalization of Recreational Marijuana in the United States*, and found no evidence of an increase in crime related to the legalization of recreational use of marijuana.[18] The report also looked at similar experiences in other jurisdictions, noting for example, that "Oregon's legalization law went into effect in July 2015, and the first stores opened in October 2016.[19] [However], the [Federal Bureau of Investigation]

---

[16] Drug Policy Alliance, "Drug Policy Statistics," http://www.drugpolicy.org/issues/drug-war-statistics - Cases include those with other charges where the defendant pleas to possession.

[17] Drug Policy Alliance, "Race and the Drug War," http://www.drugpolicy.org/issues/race-and-drug-war.

[18] The Office of Manhattan District Attorney Cyrus R. Vance Jr., "Marijuana, Fairness and Public Safety: A Report on the Legalization of Recreational Marijuana in the United States," (May 2018) https://www.manhattanda.org/wpcontent/uploads/2018/05/DANY-Report-on-the-Legalization-of-Recreational- Marijuana-Final.pdf.

[19] The Office of Manhattan District Attorney Cyrus R. Vance Jr., "Marijuana, Fairness and Public Safety: A Report on the Legalization of Recreational Marijuana in the United States," (May

FBI data shows that crime rates stayed largely the same between 2015 and 2016."[20]

In Nevada, the report found that there was an initial increase in burglaries at stores selling marijuana after legalization.[21] In response, these stores increased their security measures, and this substantially decreased the burglaries. The report also noted that in Las Vegas violent crimes did not increase after legalization.[22]

In Washington State, "...crime rates have remained...and continue on a downward trend after retail sales [of marijuana] began in mid-2014."[23] Interestingly, in Colorado where recreational use was legalized in 2014, there was an increase in crime reported in 2016.[24] State officials though - including the police department, the Department of Public Safety and the Governor - all agree that the evidence is inconclusive concerning whether the increase in crime is related to the legalization of marijuana or other factors.[25] Taken together, this national data fails to conclusively establish that the legalization of marijuana has resulted in any material increase in crimes related to its cultivation or sale.

2018) https://www.manhattanda.org/wpcontent/uploads/2018/05/DANY-Report-on-the-Legalization-of-Recreational-Marijuana-Final.pdf.

[20] The Office of Manhattan District Attorney Cyrus R. Vance Jr., "Marijuana, Fairness and Public Safety: A Report on the Legalization of Recreational Marijuana in the United States," (May 2018) https://www.manhattanda.org/wpcontent/uploads/2018/05/DANY-Report-on-the-Legalization-of-Recreational- Marijuana-Final.pdf.

[21] The Office of Manhattan District Attorney Cyrus R. Vance Jr., "Marijuana, Fairness and Public Safety: A Report on the Legalization of Recreational Marijuana in the United States," (May 2018) https://www.manhattanda.org/wpcontent/uploads/2018/05/DANY-Report-on-the-Legalization-of-Recreational- Marijuana-Final.pdf.

[22] The Office of Manhattan District Attorney Cyrus R. Vance Jr., "Marijuana, Fairness and Public Safety: A Report on the Legalization of Recreational Marijuana in the United States," (May 2018) https://www.manhattanda.org/wpcontent/uploads/2018/05/DANY-Report-on-the-Legalization-of-Recreational- Marijuana-Final.pdf.

[23] The Office of Manhattan District Attorney Cyrus R. Vance Jr., "Marijuana, Fairness and Public Safety: A Report on the Legalization of Recreational Marijuana in the United States," (May 2018) https://www.manhattanda.org/wpcontent/uploads/2018/05/DANY-Report-on-the-Legalization-of-Recreational- Marijuana-Final.pdf.

[24] The Office of Manhattan District Attorney Cyrus R. Vance Jr., "Marijuana, Fairness and Public Safety: A Report on the Legalization of Recreational Marijuana in the United States," (May 2018) https://www.manhattanda.org/wpcontent/uploads/2018/05/DANY-Report-on-the-Legalization-of-Recreational- Marijuana-Final.pdf.

[25] The Office of Manhattan District Attorney Cyrus R. Vance Jr., "Marijuana, Fairness and Public Safety: A Report on the Legalization of Recreational Marijuana in the United States," (May 2018) https://www.manhattanda.org/wpcontent/uploads/2018/05/DANY-Report-on-the-Legalization-of-Recreational- Marijuana-Final.pdf.

Marijuana Laws Drain Limited Law Enforcement and Criminal Justice Resources

In Baltimore, the lack of public safety benefits and the drain on the resources of our criminal justice system are easy to illustrate. Arrests for simple possession of marijuana are a drain on scarce resources and produce no apparent rehabilitative, deterrent or other public safety benefits. In 2017, Baltimore had the highest per capita murder rate of any American city with more than 500,000 people by way of 343 homicides and a year-end clearance rate of 31%.[26] In 2018, there were 309 homicides with a year-end clearance rate of 26%.[27] With the number of homicides that occur in Baltimore City annually, the majority of them going unsolved, limited law enforcement resources are far better utilized to address violent crime and target the perpetrators of that crime rather than continuing to enforce laws for behavior that has been shown to have no real public safety implications. The prosecution of marijuana possession does not make a city safer; instead, it uses scarce resources to implement ineffectual policies.

In contrast, there is increasing recognition of non-punitive harm reduction approaches as a proven response to substance use disorder globally, and numerous U.S. law enforcement organizations have similarly recognized that harm reduction strategies address substance use disorder and the overdose epidemic more effectively than arrests and prosecution. For example, 36 jurisdictions have implemented a Law Enforcement Assisted Diversion (LEAD) model, which enlists police and prosecutors to work with community groups and social service agencies to provide harm reduction interventions in lieu of a punitive criminal justice response.[28]

---

[26] Luke Broadwater & Ian Duncan, The Baltimore Sun, "Neighborhoods are crying out': Baltimore has highest homicide rate of U.S. big cities," (2018), found at https://www.baltimoresun.com/news/crime/bs-md-ci-fbi-data- 20180924-story.html. It is important to note that BPD utilizes a cumulative clearance rate in which the numerator is all cleared homicide cases that were cleared in a given year, including clearances for homicides that occurred in earlier years, and the denominator is only the number of homicides that occurred in the given year. Consequently, the actual clearance rate for murders that took place in that same year will always be lower than the cumulative rate.

[27] BPD utilizes a cumulative clearance rate in which the numerator is all cleared homicide cases that were cleared in a given year, including clearances for homicides that occurred in earlier years, and the denominator is only the number of homicides that occurred in the given year. Consequently, the actual clearance rate for murders that took place in that same year will always be lower than the cumulative rate.

[28] LEAD Bureau, www.leadbureau.org (last visited May 9, 2019).

Disparate Enforcement versus Non-Disparate Use

Along with the lack of legitimate public safety considerations and the resource drain that enforcing marijuana laws places on communities, national research consistently illustrates that Black people are almost four times more likely to be arrested for marijuana possession in the Unites States than White people.[29] This racial discrepancy remains despite the fact that individuals of both races use marijuana at the same rate.[30] Between 2001 and 2010 there were over eight million marijuana arrests in the United States, 88% of which were for possession.[31] Where marijuana arrests increased and accounted for over half (52%) of all drug arrests in the Unites States, Blacks accounted for nearly half (46%) of those same arrests.[32]

Even today when 11 States and the District of Columbia have legalized recreational use of marijuana and 33 States have legalized the use of marijuana for medicinal purposes, evidence suggests that racial disparities regarding enforcement of marijuana laws continue to exist. For instance, in Colorado after legalization of marijuana for recreational use, there was a 51% decrease in Whites being arrested but only a 33% decrease for Latinx and a 25% decrease for Blacks.[33] Comparatively, Washington State's post legalization arrest rate for Blacks is double the arrest rate for others and a Black person in Washington, D.C. is 11 times more likely than a White person to be arrested for public consumption of marijuana.[34]

Baltimore City, like other jurisdictions, shows alarming disparities in arrest rates and in the distribution of civil citations for marijuana possession. In 2010, the American Civil Liberties Union (ACLU) reported that Maryland's arrest rate for marijuana possession was the fourth highest in the nation.[35] In addition, while Black people only comprised 30% of the State's population in 2010, 58% of those arrested for marijuana possession were

---

[29] American Civil Liberties Union, "The War on Marijuana in Black and White," (June 2013), https://www.aclu.org/sites/default/files/field_document/1114413-mj-report-rfs-rell-pdf.

[30] American Civil Liberties Union, "The War on Marijuana in Black and White," (June 2013), https://www.aclu.org/sites/default/files/field_document/1114413-mj-report-rfs-rell-pdf at 21.

[31] American Civil Liberties Union, "The War on Marijuana in Black and White," (June 2013), https://www.aclu.org/sites/default/files/field_document/1114413-mj-report-rfs-rell-pdf.

[32] American Civil Liberties Union, "The War on Marijuana in Black and White," (June 2013), https://www.aclu.org/sites/default/files/field_document/1114413-mj-report-rfs-rell-pdf at 21.

[33] Colorado Department of Public Safety, "Marijuana Legalization in Colorado: Early Findings," (March 2016) http://edpsodocs.state.co.us/ors/docs/reports/2016-SB13-283-Rpt.pdf.

[34] Drug Policy Alliance, "From Prohibition to Progress: A Status Report on Marijuana Legalization," (January 2018) http://www.drugpolicy.porg/legalization-status-report.

[35] American Civil Liberties Union, "Blueprint for Smart Justice: Maryland" (2018) https://50stateblueprint.aclu.org/assets/reports/SJ-Blueprint-MD.pdf.

Black.[36] In that same time period, Baltimore City had the largest rate of disparity among marijuana arrestees, with Black people being almost six times more likely to be arrested for marijuana possession than Whites.[37]

Even with Maryland's October 1, 2014 decision to decriminalize possession of less than ten grams of marijuana to a civil infraction, racial disparities continue to exist in Baltimore City. According to BPD records, in 2015 89% of all citations issued were given to Black people. In 2016, records indicate that BPD issued 94% of the marijuana citations to Black people. In 2017, BPD issued 95% of the citations to Black people. Shockingly, approximately 42% of the aforementioned citations were issued in the Western District, where less than 9% of all city residents reside (one of the nine police districts in Baltimore City), and where approximately 95% of the residents in this District are Black and disproportionately impoverished.[38] When taken together, these statistics are incredibly alarming and elucidate the crisis of disparate treatment of Black people for marijuana possession.

Collateral Consequences

The disparate enforcement of marijuana laws is exacerbated when one considers the collateral consequences a marijuana possession conviction has on an individual and an individual's family. Collateral consequences are legal, social, and economic debilities that are imposed as a result of a criminal conviction regardless of whether a convicted individual serves any time incarcerated. These consequences create social and economic barriers for individuals reentering into society by denying or restricting benefits otherwise available to all citizens. Collateral consequences are known to adversely affect adoptions, housing, healthcare access, welfare, immigration, employment, professional licensure, property rights, mobility, education, voting rights, and other opportunities—the collective effect of which marginalizes the individual, extinguishes hope and a positive pathway forward, and thereby increases recidivism and undermines meaningful reentry of the convicted

---

[36] American Civil Liberties Union, "Blueprint for Smart Justice: Maryland" (2018) https://50stateblueprint.aclu.org/assets/reports/SJ-Blueprint-MD.pdf.

[37] American Civil Liberties Union, "Blueprint for Smart Justice: Maryland" (2018) https://50stateblueprint.aclu.org/assets/reports/SJ-Blueprint-MD.pdf.

[38] Baltimore city Population. (2019-05-12). Retrieved 2019-07-06, from http://worldpopulationreview.com/maryland-counties/baltimore-city/.

individual for a lifetime.[39] Neither the individual nor is the community benefitted as a result.

Instead of improving the safety of our communities, our marijuana laws make criminals out of millions of otherwise law-abiding individuals and impose a lifetime of punishment on those convicted. A minor marijuana possession conviction subjects an individual to a system of legal discrimination that makes it difficult or impossible to secure employment, housing, student loans, or even a driver's license. Even without a conviction, the collateral consequences of an arrest can include untold stigma, disruption and humiliation, the unmanageable financial burden of posting bail and hiring a lawyer, and lost hours at work or school. Employers frequently do not hire those with a criminal record, and it has been shown that individuals with a criminal record earn 40% less than those without.[40] Additionally, student financial aid can and is often denied to those convicted of marijuana possession. Federal law temporarily bars a student convicted of marijuana possession for the first or second time from receiving government-funded financial aid for higher education, and the third offense triggers a permanent disqualification.[41]

In Baltimore city, there is no better illustration of the blatant long-term collateral consequences that the disparate enforcement of marijuana laws have had on poor Black and Brown communities. While overall, 28% of Baltimore city residents live in poverty (16% more than the national average), the most impacted district regarding the enforcement of marijuana possession laws, is the Western Police District. Here 95% of the residents are Black, the median household income is $24,374, more than twice as low than the citywide median household income ($41,819) and the unemployment rate is 20% compared to the citywide unemployment rate of 13%. As cited above, 42% of the marijuana possession citations issued city-wide were issued in this district which means those most dependent on public housing, student aid, and living in poverty are the ones frequently targeted and most impacted.

---

[39] American Bar Association Criminal Justice Section "Collateral Consequences of Criminal Convictions Judicial Bench Book," (March 2018) https://www.ncjrs.gov/pdffiles1/nij/grants/251583.pdf.

[40] Drug Policy Alliance "Marijuana Reform Collateral Consequences," http://www.drugpolicy.org/sites/default/files/New_Solutions_Marijuana_Reform_Collateral_Consequences.pdf.

[41] Drug Policy Alliance "Marijuana Reform Collateral Consequences," http://www.drugpolicy.org/sites/default/files/New_Solutions_Marijuana_Reform_Collateral_Consequences.pdf.

A New Path Forward

While contemporary attitudes and public policies toward marijuana have changed dramatically in the past few years, the enforcement of marijuana laws- as well as drug laws more generally- remains grossly disproportionate in its impact on communities of color. My office understands this and, coupled with the overwhelming evidence showing that the "War on Drugs" has only served to further intensify existing racial biases across our country's criminal justice system without securing any significant net gains, I have utilized my prosecutorial discretion to change how marijuana laws are enforced in Baltimore City and, in so doing, have begun to rebalance the criminal justice system one individual, one family, at a time.

Marijuana Policy Reform Utilizing the Judicial Process

Because I am committed to holistic criminal justice reform, and in an effort to develop policies that better address systemic racial disparities and more efficiently allocate the scarce resources of the justice system, my office studied the national best practices and recommendations from accredited and innovative organizations to find ways to address what we saw as the uneven enforcement of marijuana laws borne, most significantly, by communities of color. Armed with the data, and using my discretion as an elected State's Attorney, I implemented the policy of no longer prosecuting individuals for marijuana possession (regardless of weight or of an individual's criminal history).

Concurrent with the implementation of this new policy, my office filed a *Writ of Coram Nobis (legal remedy to "right an extraordinary wrong")* in thousands of cases in both the Circuit and District Courts for Baltimore City, arguing that the discriminatory enforcement of marijuana laws violate the Equal Protection Clause of the 14th Amendment. Those writs sought to "right past wrongs" and vacate the convictions of almost 5,000 individuals dating back to 2011 that have suffered or continue to suffer the collateral consequences of the disparate enforcement of marijuana laws.

Unfortunately, both Courts denied our petition, but we have recently filed a Motion for Reconsideration, which is currently under review.

Marijuana Policy Reform Utilizing the State Legislative Process

Additionally, my office successfully advocated for the enactment of Maryland State HB 874 during the Maryland General Assembly's 2019 Legislative Session. The bill proposed to give prosecutors in the State of Maryland the legal ability to affirmatively file motions to vacate convictions where "fairness and justice" interests so warranted. Having passed, the law becomes effective October 1, 2019, but unfortunately was significantly revised and limited during the legislative process. In its original iteration, prosecutors across the State would have had a tool to vacate convictions (1) where a conviction was based on a crime that is no longer a crime, (2) in claims of actual innocence and (3) in those instances where, due to unforeseen circumstances, vacating a conviction would be in the "interest of fairness and justice."

The original language of Maryland State HB 874 also included a provision allowing the State to file a motion to vacate in instances where an individual had been convicted of possession of marijuana but where such possession was no longer a criminal offense. Unfortunately, the Maryland State's Attorney Association testified against the legislation and lobbied to add language to the bill to preclude prosecutors from utilizing it specifically for the purpose of vacating convictions for marijuana possession. I will continue, however, to advocate for the ability to vacate marijuana charges through any and all of the legal mechanisms available to my office.[42] These efforts parallel those of other prosecutors around the nation seeking to address post-conviction justice and create vehicles to revisit past unjust convictions or excessive sentencing.[43]

Recommendations: Congressional Considerations and Proposed Next Steps

Understanding Congress' fundamental role in leading the country in the right direction on issues of pressing national importance such as this one, knowing the trickle down effects of federal laws to state laws, and coupled with my own prosecutorial experience, I can imagine no better moment than now to significantly and positively impact communities of color by righting the wrongs of the past as it pertains to the disproportionate application of federal marijuana laws to those populations most affected and as it relates more generally to drug policies and mechanisms for correcting past injustices.

---

[42] Baltimore Sun Editorial, "If the courts won't allow Marilyn Mosby to throw out marijuana convictions, what about the legislature?," Baltimore Sun, 05012019, https://www.baltimoresun.com/opinion/editorial/bs-ed-0502-marilyn- mosby-marijuana-convictions-20190501-story.html.

[43] Ferner, Matt, Huffington Post, "Some Prosecutors Are Erasing Old Weed Convictions. Why Isn't Yours?," (2018), https://www.huffpost.com/entry/prosecutors-can-help-erase-old-weed-convictions-so-why-arent- they_n_5ae9e76fe4b06748dc8ed3da.

To that end, I respectfully offer the following proposals below as ideas to consider that I believe, if implemented, will begin to significantly undo past and present harm where the application of federal marijuana laws and other laws relating to drug policy are concerned.

1. First and foremost, I fully support the federal decriminalization of marijuana which should include the removal of marijuana from the schedule of Controlled Substances Act (CSA) outlined in the U.S. Code of Federal Regulations (C.F.R.) at 21 U.S.C. § 801 and elsewhere throughout the C.F.R. because I believe that matters of marijuana legalization, regulation, and taxation are best left to the states to determine for many reasons.
    a. Chief among them is the reality that the needs of a populous vary greatly from state to state. Thus, state legislators are in the best position to provide guidance and oversight on matters of marijuana policy because they know their constituents and constituents' needs on a direct and personal level.
    b. We must eliminate federal criminal penalties in states where marijuana has already been legalized. It is illogical to impose federal penalties upon individuals that act in compliance with state law under the 10th Amendment of the Constitution (this is especially pertinent to foreign nationals in fear of deportation or other federal reprisal for complying with state law).
2. The federal regulation of marijuana should be very much analogous to the federal regulation of alcohol to ensure public and consumer safety standards.
3. Federal economic incentives and relief are critical to addressing racial injustice resulting from the discriminatory enforcement of marijuana laws. It is unrefuted that when individuals cannot meet their basic needs due to the lingering collateral consequences of a conviction, we are all less safe. Hence, in furtherance of efforts to implement racial justice, and in an attempt to "right the wrongs of the past" wherever possible, I believe that another facet of this change must include consideration of creating federal economic incentives for states that create mechanisms for automatic or mass expungement, vacatur, post-conviction relief and/or re-sentencing opportunities for those already convicted. As previously discussed, the long-standing, well-established discriminatory enforcement of marijuana laws disproportionately affecting poor black and brown communities has

led to widespread collateral consequences severely and adversely impacting individuals' ability to find employment, secure housing and obtain student financial aid which have led to the breakdown of families and the social and economic decimation of communities.

a. Eliminate federal restrictions on school loans/Financial Aid
b. Eliminate federal restrictions in Housing

4. Finally, and working in tandem with the proposals outlined above, I would ask that Congress consider the swift reallocation of federal resources currently directed at continuing to sustain the United States' failed "War on Drugs" to those communities most adversely affected. This two-step approach of decriminalizing marijuana possession while, at the same time, providing much needed federal support and economic incentives to those communities most adversely affected by these failed policies – by:
   a. Creating job opportunities;
   b. Including equitable access and inclusion of people of color in the marijuana industry;
   c. Increasing reentry services for formerly incarcerated individuals;
   d. Promotion of harm reduction models/Pre-trial Diversion and approaches to substance use disorder, including medication-assisted treatment and other public health responses
   e. Developing community centers capable of providing educational support and wraparound health and social services for some of our nation's most at-risk youth – is key to creating lasting change.

Conclusion

These proposed legislative approaches are aimed at successfully addressing past injustices while providing better, brighter futures and more equitable outcomes. Because righting the wrongs of the past must be a priority when developing future approaches to reforming marijuana laws in this country, federal policy can and should start by working to address the collateral consequences facing individuals who have been impacted by disparate marijuana policy enforcement. No longer should the government be complacent or encouraging in the discriminatory enforcement of laws that hold no public safety value but, instead, affirmatively act to improve the lives of those who have been most deeply and disproportionately impacted.

Congress has the power and the ability to "right the wrongs" of a failed "War on Drugs," which we now know was really a "War on poor Black and Brown communities." I only hope that you will.

Thank you again for the honor of testifying before you today. I am happy to answer any questions that you may have.

Appendix

a. Marilyn Mosby, *Reforming A Broken System: Rethinking The Role of Marijuana Prosecutions In Baltimore City*, 01/29/2019, https://www.stattorney.org/images/MARIJUANA_WHITE_PAPER_FINAL.pdf.
b. Marilyn Mosby, *Full Term Report: 2015 – 2018*, 02/01/2019, https://www.stattorney.org/images/Annual_Report/2018_Full_Term_Report.pdf.

* * *

Ms. BASS. Thank you.
Dr. Nathan.

Statement of David L. Nathan, M.D.

Dr. NATHAN. Thank you, and good morning, Chair Bass, Chairman Nadler, Congressman McClintock, and honorable members of the House Judiciary Committee.

I speak to you today as the founder and board president of Doctors for Cannabis Regulation, or DFCR. DFCR is the leading national physicians association dedicated to the legalization, taxation, and above all, the effective regulation of cannabis for adults. DFCR has hundreds of respected physician members in nearly every U.S. State and territory.

As physicians, we believe that cannabis should never have been made illegal for consenting adults. It is less harmful to adults than alcohol and tobacco, and the prohibition has done far more damage to our society than the adult use of cannabis itself.

However, it is not harmless. People who are predisposed to psychotic disorders should avoid any cannabis use. Also, as with alcohol and other drugs, heavy cannabis use may adversely affect brain development in minors.

The cannabis prohibition for adults does not prevent underage use, nor limit its availability. For decades, preventive education has reduced the rates of alcohol and tobacco use by minors. At the same time, underage cannabis use rose steadily, despite its prohibition.

In the past several years, as more States legalize cannabis for adults, the rate of underage use has leveled off. Some have argued that if cannabis is legal for adults, then minors will think it is safe for them. But when cannabis is against the law for everyone, the Government sends the message that it is dangerous for everyone. Teenagers know that is not true.

By creating a legal distinction between use by adults and minors, we teach a respect for scientific evidence and the sanctity of the law. This may be why teen use has remained level or decreased in legalized States.

Cannabis use can impair driving, as can most psychoactive drugs, including antidepressants, antipsychotics, sedatives, opioids, and even stimulants, especially among inexperienced users. But driving under the influence of cannabis and other drugs is already a criminal offense in every jurisdiction, including in legalized States. And in legalized States, studies show no adverse impact on traffic safety resulting from legalization.

There is a persistent misconception that cannabis is a gateway drug. While users of hard drugs often try cannabis first, they are even more likely to try alcohol and tobacco, but not surprisingly, people generally try less dangerous drugs before trying more dangerous drugs. But the vast majority of those who try cannabis, alcohol, and tobacco never go on to use harder drugs. As we learned in high school, correlation does not imply causation.

In 2019, even those who oppose legalization generally believe that cannabis should be decriminalized, but cannabis is—but decriminalization is an inadequate substitute for legalization. In legalized States, government-licensed retailers scrupulously check IDs and only sell cannabis products to adults. But where it is merely decriminalized, the point of sale remains in the hands of drug dealers who sell cannabis, along with more dangerous drugs, to children.

Where cannabis is only decriminalized, the Government cannot regulate the production, testing, or labeling products, which means that users consume an untested and potentially adulterated product of unknown potency. According to the Controlled Substances Act, a Schedule I drug must meet three specific criteria—high potential for abuse, no currently accepted medical use, and a lack of accepted safety. Cannabis does not meet any of these criteria, and that is why today most States and a majority of physicians recognize the therapeutic value and relative safety of cannabis as a medicine.

But cannabis shouldn't simply be rescheduled. Like alcohol, it should be removed from the Controlled Substances Act completely. Even if it had no medical value, a free society should not punish competent adults for the personal use of this nonlethal plant. We must stop using a sledgehammer to kill a weed.

Informed physicians may disagree about the specifics of good regulation, but we can no longer support a prohibition that has done so much damage to public health and personal liberty. Members of the House Judiciary Committee, please work with us to advance public health and protect our children through effective, evidence-based regulation of cannabis in the United States.

My teenage children are growing up in a nation that does not regulate the cannabis industry. I want future generations of teenagers to grow up in an America that does.

I thank you for your time.

[The statement of Dr. Nathan follows:]

Testimony before the United States House Judiciary Committee, Subcommittee on Crime, Terrorism, and Homeland Security on "Marijuana Laws in America: Racial Justice and the Need for Reform"

David L. Nathan, MD, DFAPA

Founder and Board President, Doctors for Cannabis Regulation Clinical Associate Professor, Rutgers Robert Wood Johnson Medical School

July 10, 2019

Thank you and good morning Chairwoman Bass, Chairman Nadler, Ranking Member Ratcliffe, Ranking Member Collins, and honorable members of the House Judiciary Committee.

My name is Dr. David Nathan. I'm originally from Philadelphia, graduated *magna cum laude* from Princeton University, received my medical degree from the University of Pennsylvania School of Medicine, and completed my residency at McLean Hospital of Harvard Medical School. I am a board-certified private-practice psychiatrist based in Princeton, New Jersey, a Clinical Associate Professor at Rutgers Robert Wood Johnson Medical School, and a Distinguished Fellow of the American Psychiatric Association. I serve as the Chief Medical Advisor for 4Front Ventures, a multistate medical cannabis company founded by fellow social justice advocates.

I speak to you today as the founder and board president of Doctors for Cannabis Regulation (or DFCR). DFCR is the leading national physicians' association dedicated to the legalization, taxation and - above all - the effective regulation of cannabis for adults. DFCR has hundreds of respected physician members in nearly every US state and territory. DFCR physicians include integrative medicine pioneer Andrew Weil, former Surgeon General Joycelyn Elders, and retired clinical director of SAMHSA, H. Westley Clark.

In 1937, the American Medical Association sent Dr. William Woodward to the House of Representatives to testify against the proposed prohibition of cannabis.[44] Refuting hyperbolic tabloid claims, he testified that cannabis is not highly addictive, does not cause violence in users, and does not cause fatal overdoses. He reasoned that cannabis should, therefore, be regulated rather than prohibited. Scientific evidence now confirms that Dr. Woodward was correct.[45,46,47]

As physicians, we believe that cannabis should never have been made illegal for consenting adults. It is less harmful to adults than alcohol and tobacco, and the prohibition has done far more damage to our society than the adult use of cannabis itself.

However, cannabis is not harmless. People who are predisposed to psychotic disorders should avoid any cannabis use. Also, as with alcohol and other drugs, heavy cannabis use may adversely affect brain development in minors.[48] But cannabis prohibition for adults doesn't prevent underage use nor limit its availability. The government's own statistics show that 80-90% of

---

44 See Appendix B: "The Prescience of William C. Woodward."' Doctors for Cannabis Regulation, 2015. https:/dfcr.org/the-prescience-of-william-c-woodward/.

45 Joy, Janet E., et al. *Marijuana and Medicine: Assessing the Science Base.* Washington, DC: National Academy Press, 1999. http://medicalmarijuana.procon.org/sourcefiles/IOM_Report.pdf.

46 "Learn About Marijuana: Marijuana and Aggression." Alcohol and Drug Abuse Institute, University of Washington. 3/2015. http://learnaboutmarijuanawa.org/factsheets/aggression.htm.

47 Collen, Mark. "Prescribing cannabis for harm reduction." *Harm Reduct J.* 2012; 9: 1. http://www.ncbi.nlm.nih.gov/pmc/articles/PMC3295721/.

48 Schweinsburg, et al. "The Influence of Marijuana Use on Neurocognitive Functioning in Adolescents." *Curr Drug Abuse Rev.* 2008 Jan; 1 (1): 99-111. http://www.ncbi.nlm.nih.gov/pmc/articles/PMC2825218/.

eighteen-year-olds have consistently reported easy access to the drug since the 1970s.[49] For decades, preventive education has reduced the rates of alcohol and tobacco use by minors,[50] At the same time, underage cannabis use rose steadily despite its prohibition. In the past several years - as more states legalize cannabis for adults - the rate of underage cannabis use has stopped increasing.

Some have argued that if cannabis is legal for adults, then minors will think it's safe for them. But when cannabis is against the law for everyone, the government sends the message that cannabis is dangerous for everyone. Teenagers know that's not true. By creating a legal distinction between cannabis use by adults and minors, we teach our children a respect for scientific evidence - and the sanctity of the law. This may be why teen use has remained level or decreased in legalized states.[51,52]

Cannabis use can impair driving, as can most psychoactive drugs - including antidepressants, anti psychotics, sedatives, opioids, and even stimulants - especially among inexperienced users. But driving under the influence of cannabis and other drugs is already a criminal offense in every jurisdiction, including in legalized states. Numerous scientific studies exist showing only a weak correlation between marijuana-positive drivers and accident risk.[53] And in legalized states, studies show no adverse impact on traffic safety resulting from legalization.[54,55]

---

[49] Johnston, Lloyd. *Monitoring the Future: National Survey Results on Drug Use, 1975-2008. Volume II: College Students and Adults Ages 19-50.* Bethesda, MD: National Institute of Drug Abuse, 2009. http://monitoringthe future.org/pubs/monographs/vol2_2008.pdf.

[50] U.S. Department of Health and Human Services. *The Health Consequences of Smoking – 50 Years of Progress: A Report of the Surgeon General.* Atlanta, GA: U.S. Department of Health and Human Services, Centers for Disease Control and Prevention, National Center for Chronic Disease Prevention and Health Promotion, Office on Smoking and Health, 2014. http://www.ede.gov/tobacco/data_statistics/sgr/50th-anniversary/index.htm.

[51] Hasin et al. 2015. Medical marijuana laws and adolescent use in the USA from 1991 to 2014: results from annual, repeated cross-sectional surveys." Lancet Psychiatry 2: 601-608. http://www.ncbi.nlm.nih.gob/pubmed/26303557.

[52] Colorado Department of Public Safety. Impacts of marijuana legalization to Colorado, 2018. https://www.colorado.gov/pacific/publicsafety/news/colorado-division-criminal-justice-publishes-report-impacts-marijuana-legalization-colorado.

[53] U.S. Department of Transportation, National Highway Traffic Safety Administration. *Drug and Alcohol Crash Risk.* February 2015. https://www.nhtsa.gov/behabioral-reserch/drug-and-alcohol-crash-risk-study.

[54] Aydelotte et al., 2017. "Crash fatality rates after recreational marijuana legalization in Washington and Colorado." *American Journal of Public Health* 107: 1329-1331:https://www.ncbi.nlm.nih.gov/pubmed/28640679.

[55] Hansen, Benjamin, et al. "Early Evidence on Recreational Marijuana Legalization and Traffic Fatalities." National Bureau of Economic Research. Working Paper No. 24417. March 2018. https://www.nber.org/papers/w24417.

While a number of entities are trying to develop a blood, saliva, or breath test to assess impairment from cannabis intoxication, such a test is not presently available. The best method for assessing impaired driving is the use of specially trained police officers called Drug Recognition Experts (or DREs), and we support nationwide training of DREs in all jurisdictions.

There is a persistent misconception that cannabis is a "gateway" drug. While users of hard drugs often try cannabis first, they're even more likely to try alcohol and tobacco. People generally try less dangerous drugs before trying more dangerous drugs, but the vast majority of those who try cannabis, alcohol and tobacco never go on to use harder drugs. The risk of drug misuse and addiction is now known to be largely due to pre-existing genetic and environmental risk factors, not the use of cannabis, alcohol, or other so-called "soft" drugs. As we learned in high school, correlation does not imply causation.

In 2019, even those who oppose legalization generally believe that cannabis should be decriminalized. But decriminalization is an inadequate substitute for legalization. In legalized states, government licensed retailers scrupulously check IDs and only sell cannabis products to adults. But where cannabis is merely decriminalized, the point-of-sale remains in the hands of drug dealers who sell cannabis - along with more dangerous drugs - to children.

Legalization opponents often say: "This isn't your parents' cannabis." Cannabis cultivation has, in deed, led to the development of more potent strains.[56] In states where cannabis is legal, labeling enables adult users to make informed decisions about their intake based on potency. Where cannabis is decriminalized, the government cannot regulate the production, testing or labeling of products, which means that users consume an untested and potentially adulterated product of unknown potency.

According to the Controlled Substances Act, a Schedule I drug must meet three specific criteria: "high potential for abuse," "no currently accepted medical use," and "lack of accepted safety." Cannabis does not meet any of these criteria. Cannabis does not share the high abuse potential associated with other Schedule I drugs or other legal recreational substances. According to a comprehensive review by the National Academy of Medicine, cannabis's dependence liability is similar to that of caffeine (9 percent), and it is far lower

[56] Mehmedic, Z. et al. "Potency Trends of Δ9-THC and other cannabinoids in confiscated cannabis preparations from 1993 to 2008." J. Forensic Sci 2010 Sep; 55(5): 1209-1217. http://www/ncbi.nlm.gov/pubmed/20487147.

than dependence associated with alcohol (15 percent) and tobacco (32 percent).[57] Cannabis has a well-researched safety profile, and it possesses no documented risk of lethal overdose.[58] According to a United Nations Report, " The re are no confirmed cases of human deaths from cannabis poisoning in the world medical literature."[59] FDA-approved trials[60] and a comprehensive 2017 review by the National Academies of Science, Engineering, and Medicine[61] support the safety and efficacy of cannabis in various patient populations. Today, most states and a majority of physicians recognize the therapeutic value and relative safety of cannabis.[62]

But cannabis shouldn't simply be rescheduled. Like alcohol, it should be removed from the Controlled Substances Act completely. Even if it had no medical value, a free society should not punish competent adults for the personal use of this non-lethal plant. We must stop using a sledgehammer to kill a weed.

My teenage children are growing up in a nation that does not regulate the cannabis industry. I want future generations of teenagers to grow up in an America that does.

Informed physicians may disagree about the specifics of good regulation, but we can no longer support a prohibition that has done so much damage to public health and personal liberty. Members of the House Judiciary Committee, please work with us to advance public health and protect our children through effective, evidence-based regulation of cannabis in the United States.

---

[57] National Academies of Science, Engineering and Medicine. *Marijuana and Medicine: Assessing the Science Base.* Washington, DC: The National Academies Press, 1999. Page 95: Table 3.4:Prevalence of Drug Use and Dependence in the General Population. https://www.nap.edu/catalog/6376/marijuana-and-medicine-assessing-the-ecience-base.

[58] Calabria B, et al. (2010) "Does cannabis use increase the risk of death? A systematic review of epidemiological evidence on adverse effects of cannabis use." Drug Alcohol Rev 2010 May; 29 (3):318-30. https://www.ncbi.nlm.nih.gov/pubmer/20565525.

[59] Martin, B. R. and Hall, W. "The health effects of cannabis: key issues of policy relevance." United Nations Office on Drugs and Crime, December 1, 1999. https://www.unodc.org/unodc/en/data-and-analysis/bulettin/bulettin_1977-01_1page005.html.

[60] Grant, I., Atkinson, J. H., Gouaux, B., & Wilsey, B. (2012). "Medical marijuana: clearing away the smoke." *The Open Neurology Journal*, 6, 18-25. https://www.ncbi.nlm.nih.gov/pmc/articles/PMC3358713/.

[61] National Academies of Sciences, Engineering, and medicine. The health effects of cannabis and cannabinoids. The current state of evidence and recommendations for research. Washington, DC.: The National Academies Press, 2017. https:// www.nap.edu/catalog/24625/the-health-eefcts-of-cannabis-and-cannabinoids-the-current-state.

[62] Reppold, R. Scott. "Legalize Medical Marijuana, Doctors Say in Survey." WebMD, 2014. http://www.webmd.com/news/breaking-news/marijuana-on-main-street/20130225/webmed-marijuana-survey-web.

I thank you for your time.
Respectfully submitted,

David L. Nathan, MD, DFAPA
Board President, Doctors for Cannabis Regulation
dnalhan@dfcr.org
609-688-0400
601 Ewing Street, Suite C-10, Princeton NJ 08540

Appendices

Appendix A: "Declaration of Principles." Doctors for Cannabis Regulation, April 1 8, 2016.
https://dfcr.onr/wp-content/uploads/Declaration-of-principles.pdf

Appendix B: "The Prescience of William C. Woodward." Doctors for Cannabis Regulation, 2019.
https://dfcr.org/the-prescience-of-william-c-woodward/.

Appendix C: "Myth busting the Gateway Theory." Doctors for Cannabis Regulation, 2018.

Appendix A: A Declaration of Principles, by Doctors for Cannabis Regulation

We, the Board of Directors, Honorary Board, and Founding Physician Members of Doctors for Cannabis Regulation, with firm reliance on science and reason, hereby endorse this Declaration of Principles.

We believe cannabis prohibition is harmful.

- There are more than 700,000 cannabis arrests in the United States annually,[63] encumbering our overburdened criminal justice system and draining law enforcement's already limited resources.

[63] Federal Burau of Investigaion. *Uniform Crime Report: 2014 Crime in the United States*. New York, NY: 2015. https://www.fbi.gov/about-us/cjis/ucr/crime-in-the-u.s/2014/cime-in-the-u.s.-2014/persons-arrested/main.

- Nationwide, African-Americans are nearly four times more likely than whites to be arrested for cannabis possession, despite similar usage rates between the two groups.[64]
- Low-income individuals face disproportionate consequences from cannabis arrests due to inability to pay fines, inadequate access to counsel, and potential loss of employment, housing, and student loans.[65,66] Poverty reduces access to healthcare and undermines public health.,[67]
- Cannabis prohibition has led to the proliferation of dangerous synthetic cannabinoids.[68]
- Despite evidence that legal access to medical cannabis is correlated with a 25% reduction in opioid overdose deaths,[69] which currently number more than 28,000 per year in the U.S.,[70] prohibition prevents many patients from obtaining medical cannabis, even in states with medical cannabis laws.[71]

We believe cannabis prohibition is ineffective

---

[64] American Civil Liberties Union. *The War on Marijuana in Black and White.* New York, NY: June 2013. p. 17. https://www.aclu.org/report/war-marijuana-black-and-white.

[65] Laird, Lorelei. "Ex-offenders face tens of thousands of legal restrictions, bias and limits on their tights." *American Bar Association Journal,* June 1, http://www.abajournal.com/magazine/article/ex-offenders_face_tens_of_thousands_of_legal_restrictions.

[66] Csete, Joanne, et al. "Public Health and international drug policy." The Lancet special report. March 24, 2016. http://dx.doi.org/ =10.1016/S0140-676(16)00619-X.

[67] Mercado, Susan, et al. "Urban Poverty: An Urgent Public Health Issue." *Journal of Urban Health* 84, May 2007. pp. 7-15. http://www.ncbi.nih.gov/pmc/artiles/PMC1891652/.

[68] Fantegrossi, William E., et al. "Distinct pharmacology and metabolism of K2 synthetic cannabinoids compared to Δ^9-THC; Mechanism underlying greater toxicity?" *Life Science* (97)1. February 27, 2014. pp. 45-54. http://www/sciencedirect.com/science/article/pii/S0024320513005523.

[69] Bachhuber, Marcus A., et al. "Medical Cannabis Laws and Opioid Analgesic Overdose Mortality in the United States, 1999-2010." *JAMA Internal Medicine,* October 2014. http://archinte.jamanetwork.com/article.aspx?articleid-1898878.

[70] Rudd, Rose A., et al. "Increases in Drug and Opioid Overdose Deaths – United States, 2000-2014." *Morbidity and Mortality Weekly Report, Centers for Disease and Prevention,* January 1, 2016. http://www/cdc.gov/mmwr/preview/mmwrhtml/mm6450a3.htm?s_cid=mm6450a3_w.

[71] Pacula, Rosalie, et al. "Words Can be Deceiving: A Review of Variation among Legally Effective Medical Marijuana Laws in the United States." Journal of Drug Policy Analysis 7(1), 2014. Pp.1-19. http://www.ncbi.nih.gov/pmc/articles/PMC4314612/.

- More than 22,000,000 Americans currently use cannabis,[72] which represents 7% of the U.S. population.
- Cannabis prohibition has failed to prevent access by minors. Since the 197Os, 80-90% of American eighteen-year-olds have consistently reported that cannabis is "very easy" or "fairly easy" to obtain.[73]
- For decades, preventive education has reduced the rates of alcohol and tobacco use by minors, while underage cannabis use has risen.[74]

We believe cannabis prohibition is unnecessary

- The vast majority of adults are unharmed by the responsible use of cannabis.[75]
- The health risks of cannabis misuse are less than those of alcohol and tobacco.[76,77]
- Evidence does not support a causal "gateway" relationship between the use of cannabis and the later use of more harmful drugs.[78,79]

---

72 Center for Behavioral Health Statistics and Quality. *Behavioral Health Trends in the United States: Results from the 2014 National Survey on Drug Use and Health.* Substance Abuse and Mental Health Services Administration, 2015. P. 5. http://www.samhsa.gov/data/sites/default/files/NSDUH-FRR1-2014/NSDUH-FRR1-2014.pdf.

73 Johnston, Lloyd. *Monitoring the Future: National Survey Results on Drug Use, 1975-2008: Volume II: College Students and Adults Ages 19-50.* Bethesda, MD: National Institute on Drug Abuse, 2009. pp. 240-245. http://monitoringthefuture.org/pubs/monographs.vol2_2008.pdf.

74 Ingraham, Christopher, "Teen marijuana use falls as more states legalize." *Washington Post.* December 16, 2014. https://www.washingtonpost.com/news/work/wp/2014/12/16/teen-marijuana-use-falls-as-more-states-legalize/.

75 Alcohol and Drug Abuse Institute. "Learn About Marijuana: Adult Recreational Marijuana Consumers." University of Washington, March 2015. Htpp://leatnaboutmarijuanawa.otg/consumers.htm.

76 Fish, Jefferson. "Acute toxicity of drugs versus regulatory status." *Drugs and Society U.S. Public Policy.* New York: Rowman and Littlefield, 2006, Chapter 7. Pp. 149-162. https://books.google.com/books/about/Drugs_and_Society.html?id=xpZhkBuDkuwC.

77 Nutt, D. et al. "Development of a rational scale to access the harm of drugs of potential misuse." The Lancet 369(9566), 2007. Pp. 1047-1053. http://thelancet.com/journals/lancet/article/PIIS0140-6736(07)60464-4/abstract/.

78 Joy, Janet E., et al. *Marijuana and Medicine: Assessing the Science Base.* Washington, DC: National Academy Press, 1999. pp. 100-101. http://www/nap.edu/read/6376/chapter/5#100.

79 Levitan, Dave. "Is Marijuana Really a 'Gateway Drug'?" FactCheck: A Project of the Annenberg Public Policy Center. April 23, 2015. http://www.factcheck.org/2015/04/is-marijuana-really-a-gatewat-drug/.

We therefore support cannabis legalization for adults, preventive education of minors, and regulation of the industry.

- Legalization encourages honesty in patient-doctor communication about cannabis use.[80]
- Legalization facilitates research into the health risks and medical benefits of cannabis use.[81,82]
- Ending prohibition creates a legal distinction between underage and adult cannabis use. If we want our children to believe that cannabis can be harmful for them, then we must differentiate use by adults and minors.[83]
- Regulation benefits public health by enabling government oversight of the production, testing, labeling, distribution, and sale of cannabis.[84]
- Legalization takes the cannabis market out of the hands of illegal dealers, who do not pay taxes and sell cannabis-along with dangerous drugs-to minors as well as adults.[85]
- Tax revenues from cannabis can fund research, education, substance abuse treatment, and community reinvestment.[86]

---

[80] Mary Lynn Mathre R. N., M. S. N. (1988) A Survey o Disclosure of Marijuana Use to Health Care Professionals, Journal of Psychoactive Drugs, 20:1, 117-120. https://www/rescarhgate.net/publication/19762960_A survey_on_disclosure_of_marijuana_use_to_health_care_prodessionals.

[81] Coulter, Carol. "Is it time to legalise drugs?" *Irish Times,* July 12, 2008. http://www/irishtimes.com/news/is-it-time-to-legalise-drugs-1.944594.

[82] Nederlandse associate voor legale Cannabis en haar Stoffen als Medicatie. "The Dutch medicinal cannabis program." Retrieved March 20, 2016. http:/www.ncs.nl/English/the-dutch-medicinal-cannabis-program.

[83] Nelson, Steven. "Pot Use Among Colorado Teens Appears to Drop After Legalizaion." *U.S. News and World Report.* August 7, 2014. http://www.usnews.com/news/articles/2014/08/07/pot-use-among-colorado-teens-appears-to-drop-after-legalization.

[84] California Medical Association. "Cannabis and the Regulatory Void: Background Paper and Recommendations." http://www.cmanet.org/files/pdf/news/cma-cannabis-tac-white-paper-101411.pdf.

[85] Grillo, Ioan. "U.S. Legalization of Marijuana Has Hot Mexican Cartels' Cross Border Trade." *Time.* April 8, 2015. http://time.com/3801889/us-legalization-marijuana-trade/.

[86] Pabon, Rep. Dan, Chair. "Use of Recreational Marijuana Sales Tax Revenued Interim Study Committee." October 2014. https://www.colorado.gov/pacific/sites/default/files/14%20MarijuanaSummary Report.pdf.

- Legalization reduces the disproportionate impact of the criminal justice system on low-income and minority citizens.[87]

We call upon physicians and medical associations to promote cannabis regulation as an alternative to prohibition. Once supplied with the evidence, even physicians who vigorously oppose cannabis use may logically advocate its legalization for adults.

With confidence in the judgment of history, we commit our names to the support of this Declaration, published on the eighteenth day of April, 2016.

The Board of Directors, Honorary Board, and Founding Physician Members

DOCTORS FOR CANNABIS REGULATION

Doctors for Cannabis Regulation, April 2016

Board of Directors

Founder and Board President

David L. Nathan, MD, DFAPA, Princeton, NJ

Distinguished Fellow, American Psychiatric Association

Clinical Associate Professor of Psychiatry, Robert Wood Johnson Medical School

Executive Director

Brian C. Muraresku, JD, Washington, DC

DFCR Counsel and ex officio Board Member, Member, New York Bar

Sunil Kumar Aggarwal, MD, PhD, FAAPMR (BOARD TREASURER), Seattle, WA; *Fellow, American Academy of Physical Medicine and Rehabilitation; Member, American Academy of Hospice and Palliative Medicine; Associate Member, New York Academy of Medicine; Affiliated Faculty, MultiCare Institute for Research and Innovation; Invited Affiliate Professor University of Washington, Department of Geography*

Darby Beck, MA (BOARD SECRETARY), Dallas, TX; *Director of Media Relations and COO, Law Enforcement Against Prohibition*

---

[87] American Civil Liberties Union on Washington State. "Court Fillings for Adult Marijuana Possession Plummer." March 19, 2014. https://aclu-wa.org/news/court-filings-adult-marijuana-possession-plummet.

G. Malik Burnett, MD, MBA (DRUG POLICY AND PUBLIC HEALTH), Baltimore, MD; *Resident physician, Johns Hopkins General Preventative Medicine Program*

Julie Holland, MD (PSYCHJATRY), New York, NY; *Fellow, New York Academy of Medicine; farmer Assistant Clinical Professor, NYU School of Medicine; Editor, The Pot Book; Medical Monitor, Clinical Cannabis PTSD Research*

Udi Ofer, JD (ATTORNEY), Newark, NJ; *Executive Director of ACLU-NJ*

Sue Sisley, MD (INTERNAL MEDJCJNE AND PSYCHIATRY), Phoenix, AZ; *President, Scottsdale Research Institute; fanner Assistant Professor, Arizona Telemedicine Program, University of Arizona College of Medicine; Site principal investigator, FDA botanical cannabis trial far PTSD in military veterans*

Honorary Board

Donald I. Abrams, MD, *Chief of Hematology/Oncology, San Francisco General Hospital, Professor of Clinical Medicine, UCSF;·pioneer of HIV/AIDS research and treatment*

Chris Beyrer, MD, MPH, *Desmond Tutu Professor in Public Health and Human Rights, Johns Hopkin Bloomberg School of Public Health; President, International AIDS Society; various positions in scientific advisory committees for WHO, NIH, UNAIDS; researcher and author*

H. Westley Clark, MD, JD, MPH, CAS, FASAM, *Past Director, Center for Substance Abuse Treatment, Substance Abuse and Mental Health Services Administration (SAMHSA); author, researcher, educator*

Joycelyn Elders, *MD, former U.S. Surgeon General; Professor Emeritus of Pediatrics, University of Arkansas of Medical Sciences*

Lester Grinspoon, MD, *Associate Professor Emeritus of Psychiatry, Harward Medical School; Author, Marihuana Reconsidered; pioneer of cannabis legalization*

Carl Hart, PhD, *Associate Professor of Psychology and Psychiatry, Columbia University; author and social justice advocate*

David Lewis, MD, *Professor Emeritus of Medicine and Community Health, Donald G. Millar Distinguished Professor of Alcohol and Addiction Studies, Brown University*

Andrew Weil, MD, *Internationally renowned author and pioneer of integrative medicine*

Founding Physician Members

Joseph A. Adams, MD (INTERNAL MEDICINE, ADDICTION MEDICINE), Baltimore, MD; *Medical Director, Hampden Health Solutions; Past President, Smoke Free Maryland Coalition*

Bryon Adinoff, MD (ADDICTION PSYCHIATRY), Dallas, TX; *Editor-in-Chief, The American Journal of Drug and Alcohol Abuse; Founding Member, American Academy of Addiction Psychiatry; Fellow, American College of Neuropsychopharmacology*

David Barile, MD (INTERNAL MEDICINE, GERIATRIC MEDICINE, PALLIATIVE CARE AND HOSPICE MEDJCINE), Princeton, NJ; *Founder and CEO, NJ Goals of Care*

Richard Bayer, MD, FACP (INTERNAL MEDICINE) Portland, OR; *Co-author, Chief Petitioner and spokesperson, Oregon Medical Marijuana Act of 1998; Fellow, American College of Physicians*

David Bearman, MD (PAIN MANAGEMENT), Santa Barbara, CA; *Executive Director, American Academy of Cannabinoid Medicine; former Medical Director; Santa Barbara Regional Health Authority; former Health Officer and Director, Sutter County Health Department; former Officer, United States Public Health Service*

Craig Blinderman, MD, MA, FAAHPM (FAMILY MEDICINE, HOSPICE AND PALLIATIVE MEDICJNE), New York, NY;

Fellow, American Academy of Hospice and Palliative Medicine; Associate Professor, Department of Medicine, Columbia University College of Physicians and Surgeons; Director, Adult Palliative Medicine Service, Columbia University Medical Center

Carl J. Bonnett, MD, ADAAPM (EMERGENCY MEDICINE AND INTEGRATIVE MEDICINE), San Antonio, TX; *Lt. Col., Army National Guard (Ret'd); Co-founder and Medical Director, Klarisana; Advanced Diplomate, American Association of Pain Management*

Gregory T. Carter, MD, MS (PHYSICAL MEDICINE AND REHABILITATION), Spokane, WA; *Clinical Professor, University of Washington School of Medicine; Co-founder, MDA/ALS Center at University of Washington; Medical Director, St. Luke's Rehabilitation Institute*

James P. Crowley, MD, FACP (INTERNAL MEDICINE), Providence, RI; *Fellow, American College of Physicians; Past President, Rhode Island Medical Society; Professor of Medicine emeritus, Warren Alpert School of Medicine, Brown University*

Steve Daviss, MD, DFAPA (PSYCHIATRY, PSYCHOSOMATIC MEDICINE, AND MEDICAL INFORMATICS), Baltimore, MD;

Clinical Assistant Professor of Psychiatry, University of Maryland School of Medicine; Distinguished Fellow, American Psychiatric Association; Founding President, Fuse Health Strategies LLC

Gilbert J. Fanciullo MD, MS (ANESTHESIOLOGY AND PAIN MANAGEMENT), Lebanon, NH; *Director; Section of Pain Medicine, Dartmouth Hitchcock Medical Center; Professor of Anesthesiology, Geisel School of Medicine at Dartmouth*

Christopher G. Fichtner, MD, MDiv, MA, FACPE, FAPA (PSYCHIATRY AND NEUROSCIENCE), Riverside, CA; *Clinical Professor of Psychiatry, UCR School Medicine; Staff Psychiatrist, RUHS Behavioral Health*

Grace Forde, MD (NEUROLOGY, ANESTHESIOLOGY AND PAIN MANAGEMENT), Valley Stream, NY; *Board Secretary, New York State Pain Society; Director of Neurological Services, North American Partners in Pain Management*

Julia S. Golden, DO (UROLOGY), Sacramento, CA; *Chief, Urology, Mercy General Hospital*

Howard Grossman, MD (INTERNAL MEDICINE AND HIV MEDICINE), New York, NY; *Chair, Physicians for Compassionate Care NY; Clinical Assistant Professor of Medicine, NYU-Langone Medical Center; President, AlphaBetterCare*

S. Sutton Hamilton, III, MD, DLFAPA (PSYCHIATRY), Princeton, NJ; *Life Fellow, American Psychiatric Association; former Residency Director, Department of Psychiatry, University of Pennsylvania School of Medicine; Examiner, American Board of Psychiatry and Neurology*

S. Sutton Hamilton, IV, MD (FAMILY MEDICINE), Woodbury, NJ; *Assistant Professor, Department of Family Medicine, Thomas Jefferson University; Assistant Director; Inspira Family Medicine Residency*

Floyd Huen, MD (INTERNAL MEDICINE), Oakland, CA; *Member, Board of Trustees, Alameda County Health, system; former Chair, Strategic Planning, Board of Trustees, Alameda County Health System; Founder, California Physician Alliance; Founder, Health Access of California, former*

Medical Director, Highland Hospital; former Medical Director, Over Sixty Health Center; former Medical Director, Lifelong Medical Care

Stacey M. Kerr, MD (FAMILY MEDICINE), Santa Rosa, CA; *Author, Homebirth in the Hospital; Editor and Contributor, Clinical Cannabinoid Medicine Curriculum, The Medical Cannabis Institute; Past Executive Board member; Secretary and Treasurer, Society of Cannabis Clinicians*

Mikhail Kogan, MD (INTEGRATIVE MEDICINE, GERIATRICS AND PALLIATIVE CARE), Washington, DC; *Medical Director, CW Center far Integrative Medicine; Associate Director of the Geriatrics Fellowship Program; Assistant Professor of Medicine, George Washington University; Founder, AIM Health Institute; Founding board member, American Board of Integrative Medicine*

Donald O. Lyman, MD, DTPH (PREVENTIVE MEDICINE), Sacramento, CA; *Proponent, Adult Use of Marijuana Act (AUMA) of California, November 2016 ballot Proposition; Past President, California Academy of Preventive Medicine;* Chief *(Ret.), Division of Chronic Disease and Injury Control, California Department of Public Health; Deputy Director (Ret.), California Department of Public Health; Volunteer Clinical Faculty, University of California, Davis; Chair, Council on Science and Public Health, California Medical Association*

Deborah Malka MD, PhD (INTEGRATlVE MEDICINE), Santa Cruz, CA; *Faculty Director and Contributor, Clinical Cannabinoid Medicine Curriculum, The Medical Cannabis Institute; Past Secretary, Board of Directors, Society of Cannabis Clinicians*

Oscar A. Marcilla, MD, FACEP, FAAEM (EMERGENCY MEDICINE), New York, NY; *Fellow, American Academy of Emergency Medicine; Fellow, American College of Emergency Physicians; Board Member, Physicians for a National Health Program, NYC Metro Chapter*

John Molina MD, JD, LHD (OBSTETRJCS AND GYNECOLOGY), Guadalupe, AZ; *President/CEO, Four Directions; farmer Chief Executive Officer, Phoenix Indian Medical Center; farmer Medical Director, Arizona Health Care Cost Containment System; Tribal Affiliation, Pascua Yaqui and San Carlos Apache Tribes*

Dan K. Morhaim, MD (EMERGENCY MEDICINE AND INTERNNATIONAL MEDICINE), Baltimore, MD; *Delegate, Maryland House of Delegates; Adjunct Professor, Department of Health Policy and Management, Johns Hopkins Bloomberg School of Public Health*

Howard B. Moss, MD (PSYCHIATRY AND ADDICTION PSYCHIATRY), La Jolla, CA; *Clinical Professor of Psychiatry, University of*

California at Riverside School of Medicine; farmer Associate Director for Clinical and Translational Research, National Institute on Alcohol Abuse and Alcoholism, National Institutes of Health

David G. Ostrow, MD, PhD, LFAPA (ADDICTION PSYCHITRY AND HIV RESEARCH), Chicago, IL; *Life Fellow, American Psychiatric Association; Director, David Ostrow & Associates; Behavioral Investigator, Chicago Multi-Centered AIDS Cohort Study, Northwestern University Feinberg School of Medicine; Vice President for Community-Based Research, American Academy of Cannabinoid Medicine*

Thomas C. Patterson, MD (EMERGENCY MEDICINE), Mesa, AZ; *Former Majority Leader, Arizona State Senate; Past President, Arizona chapter, American College of Emergency Physicians; President and CEO, Eme1gency Physicians, Inc.*

Eugene Perlov, MD (FAMILY MEDICINE, INTEGRATIVE MEDICINE, PAIN MANAGEMENT, ADULT *AND* PEDJATRJC PALLIATIVE CARE), Kingston and New York, NY; *Regional Medical Director, VNSNY Hospice Care; Assistant Clinical Professor, Mount Sinai School of Medicine*

Josiah D. Rich, MD, MPH, FACP (INTERNAL MEDICINE, INFECTIOUS DISEASE, ADDICTION MEDICINE, EPIDEMIOLOGY), Providence, RI; *Professor; Medicine and Epidemiology, Brown University; Director, Center far Prisoner Health and Human Rights; Fellow, American College of Physicians*

Lauren Shaiova, MD (PHYSICAL MEDICINE AND REHABILITATION), New York, NY; *Chief of Palliative Care and Pain Medicine, Metropolitan Hospital Center; Associate Professor, Albert Einstein College of Medicine*

Jeffrey A Singer, MD, FACS (GENERAL SURGERY), Phoenix, AZ; *Fellow, American College of Smgcons; Board of Advisors, Arizona State University Center for Political Thought and Leadership; Instructor, Arizona State University Extension Program; Principal and Co-founder, Valley Surgical Clinics, Ltd.*

James Stoll, MD (ORTHOPEDIC SURGERY), Milwaukee, WI; *Board Certified, Fellowship trained reconstructive spinal surgeon; Senior Spinal Surgeon, Aurora Health Care*

Richard C. Strand MD (RADIOLOGY), Scottsdale, AZ; *Chairman, Substance Abuse, Education and Testing, USA Track and Field, 1992 to 2000; Team Physician USA Olympic Team, Sydney Olympics; Consultant, Arizona Department of Health Services, Arizona Medical Marijuana Physician*

Education Program; Co-investigator, PTSD Research Study sponsored by MAPS and the Colorado Department of Health and Environment

Allen Tien, MD, MHS (PSYCHIATRY, BIOINFORMATICS), Baltimore, MD; *Adjunct Associate Professor, Division of Health Sciences Informatics, John Hopkins University School of Medicine; Founder and President, Medical Decision Logic; Chief Science Officer, John W Brick Mental Health Foundation*

Eugene Tinelli MD, PhD (PSYCHIATRY), Syracuse, NY; *Associate Professor, Psychiatry and Behavioral Science, State University* of *New York, Upstate Medical University; Honorary Member, Law Enforcement Against Prohibition*

Carlos F. Tirado, MD, MPH, FABAM (GENERAL AND ADDICTION PSYCHIATRY), Austin, TX; *Fellow, American Board of Addiction Medicine; Board Member and Chair of Clinical Advisory Panel, SIMS Foundation; Advisory Board Member, CareFlash; President, Austin Psychiatric Society; Treasurer, Texas Society of Addiction Medicine*

John P. Vuchetich, MD, PhD (PSYCHIATRY), Minneapolis, MN; *Adjunct Associate Professor, Psychiatry and Psychology, University of Minnesota; Psychiatrist, Assertive Community Treatment (ACT) Team*

Mark S. Wallace, MD (ANESTHESIOLOGY AND PAIN MANAGEMENT), San Diego, CA; *Professor of Clinical Anesthesiology, University of California San Diego; Chair, Division of Pain Medicine, Department of Anesthesiology, University of California San Diego School of Medicine*

Charles Webb, MD (EMERGENCY MEDJCINE), Kailua-Kona, HI; *Former Fellow American College of Emergency Physicians. Founder MUM Clinic*

George Wilson, MD, DLFAPA (PSYCHIATRY), Princeton, NJ; *Distinguished Life Fellow, American Psychiatric Association*

Appendix B: The Prescience of William C. Woodward

William Creighton Woodward, M.D., LL.M., LL.D., was a physician, attorney, educator and public health advocate with a distinguished career spanning fifty years. As the Legal Counsel for the American Medical Association, his medical- legal perspective on cannabis in the 1930s was wise and prophetic, although his testimony was ridiculed and ultimately rejected by our nation's lawmakers. Seventy-eight years later, our experience with marijuana prohibition has vindicated his courageous decision to stand up for science and reason. In the 1937 hearings for the Marihuana Tax Act, Dr. Woodward defended the AMA's position that cannabis should be regulated but not prohibited. In his lengthy testimony, he refuted the hyperbolic claims put forward by the proponents of marijuana prohibition, offering a prescient view of how our society should handle drug addiction in general, and marijuana in particular. There is much we can learn from this early, learned proponent of an evidence- based national cannabis policy, and extracts of his testimony are included below.

Brief Biography

- 1867: Born in Washington, D.C.
- 1889: M.D. from Georgetown University School of Medicine
- 1894-1918: Health Officer, Washington, D.C.
- 1900: LL.D. from Georgetown University Law School
- 1918-1922: Commissioner of Public Health, Boston, Massachusetts
- 1922-1939: Legal Counsel for the American Medical Association
- 1949: Died in Washington, D.C.

Academic Appointments

- Professor of Medical Jurisprudence and State Medicine, Georgetown University School of Medicine
- Professor of Medical Jurisprudence, George Washington University, Department of Medicine

- Professor of Medical Jurisprudence, Howard University School of Medicine Instructor/Lecturer: School of Public Health, Harvard University and M.I.T. Faculty, Loyola University School of Law
- Professorial Lecturer in Medical Jurisprudence, Rush Medical College, University of Chicago

Selected Positions in Professional Societies

- Director, Bureau of Legal Medicine and Legislation, American Medical Association
- Secretary, Board of Medical Supervisors of Washington, D.C.
- Founding member, Health Administration Section of the American Public Health Association
- President, American Public Health Association

Selected Accomplishments

- 1908: Annual Report as health officer called attention to disproportionately high mortality rates of African-Americans in Washington, D.C.
- 1914: As the Georgetown delegate to the Annual Meeting of the Association of American Medical Colleges, called for minimum college requirements for medical school applicants, as well as creation of a national central examining and licensing board for U.S. physicians
- 1914: Assisted in drafting of the Harrison Narcotics Tax Act that regulated opiates and cocaine
- 1918-1920: Served as Boston's Commissioner of Public Health during the 'Spanish flu' pandemic 1937: Testified at Marihuana Tax Act hearings as Legal Counsel for the AMA
- 1938: Defended AMA against charges of violating the Sherman Antitrust Act

Excerpts from Dr. Woodward's testimony to the Ways and Means Committee, U.S. House of Representatives, MAY 4, 1937: [from *Ta-rntion of*

Marihuana, hearings before the House Committee on Ways and Means, 75th Cong., 1st Sess. (April 27-30 and May 4, 1937)]

"There is nothing in the medicinal use of Cannabis that has any relation to Cannabis addiction. I use the word 'Cannabis' in preference to the word 'marihuana', because Cannabis is the correct term for describing the plant and its products In other words, marihuana is not the correct term. It was the use of the term 'marihuana' rather than the use of the term 'Cannabis' or the use of the term 'Indian hemp' that was responsible, as you realized, probably, a day or two ago, for the failure of the dealers in Indian hempseed to connect up this bill with their business until rather late in the day. So, if you will permit me, I shall use the word 'Cannabis', and I should certainly suggest that if any legislation is enacted, the term used be 'Cannabis' and not the mongrel word 'marihuana.'

"I say the medicinal use of Cannabis has nothing to do with Cannabis or marihuana addiction. In all that you have heard here thus far, no mention has been made of any excessive use of the drug by any doctor or its excessive distribution by any pharmacist. And yet the burden of this bill is placed heavily on the doctors and pharmacists of the country; and I may say very heavily, most heavily, possibly of all, on the farmers of the country."

"To say, however, as has been proposed here, that the use of the drug should be prevented by a prohibitive tax, loses sight of the fact that future investigation may show that there are substantial medical uses for Cannabis."

"That there is a certain amount of narcotic addiction of an objectionable character no one will deny. The newspapers have called attention to it so prominently that there must be some grounds for these statements. It has surprised me, however, that the facts on which these statements have been based have not been brought before this committee by competent primary evidence. We are referred to newspaper publications concerning the prevalence of marihuana addiction. We are told that the use of marihuana causes crime.

"But yet no one has been produced from the Bureau of Prisons to show the number of prisoners who have been found addicted to the marihuana habit. An informed inquiry shows that the Bureau of Prisons has no evidence on that point.

"You have been told that school children are great users of marihuana cigarettes. No one has been summoned from the Children's Bureau to show the nature and extent of the habit, among children.

"Inquiry of the Children's Bureau shows that they have had no occasion to investigate it and know nothing particularly of it.

"Inquiry of the Office of Education- and they certainly should know something of the prevalence of the habit among the school children of the country, if there is a prevalent habit- indicates that they have had no occasion to investigate and know nothing of it.

"Moreover, there is in the Treasury Department itself, the Public Health Service, with its Division of Mental Hygiene. The Division of Mental Hygiene was, in the first place, the Division of Narcotics. It was converted into the Division of Mental Hygiene, l think, about 1930. That particular Bureau has control at the present time of the narcotics farms that were created about 1929 or 1930 and came into operation a few years later. No one has been summoned from that Bureau to give evidence on that point.

"Informal inquiry by me indicates that they have had no record of any marihuana or Cannabis addicts who have ever been committed to those farms."

Rep. Robert L. Doughton (D, NC), Chairman: If you want to advise us on legislation, you ought to come here with some constructive proposals, rather than criticism, rather than trying to throw obstacles in the way of something that the Federal Government is trying to do. It has not only an unselfish motive in this, but they have a serious responsibility.

Dr. Woodward: We cannot understand yet, Mr. Chairman, why this bill should have been prepared in secret for two years without any intimation, even, to the profession, that it was being prepared.

Rep. John D. Dingell (0, MI): We know that it is a habit that is spreading, particularly among youngsters. We learn that from the pages of the newspapers. You say that Michigan has a law regulating it. We have a State law, but we do not seem to be able to get anywhere with it, because, as l have said, the habit is growing. The number of victims is increasing each year.

Dr. Woodward: There is no evidence of that.

Rep. John W. McCormack (D, MA): There is no question that the drug habit has been increasing rapidly in recent years.

Dr. Woodward: There is no evidence to show whether or not it has been.
Mr. McCormack: In your opinion, has it increased?

Dr. Woodward: I should say it has increased slightly. Newspaper exploitation of the habit has done more to increase it than anything else.

Mr. McCormack: It is likely to increase further unless some effort is made to suppress it.

Dr. Woodward: I do not know. The exploitation tempts young men and women to venture into the habit.

"The Federal Government... would meet with the same difficulty that it met in prosecuting under the National Prohibition Act; the inadequacy of courts and the inadequacy of prosecuting attorneys, and I may say, the inadequacy of jails."

"I think the proper preparation of an adequate course of instruction originating in the Treasury Department and distributed, it may be, through the Office of Education, would be an effective means of limiting dangers of narcotic addiction.

"The trouble is that we are looking on narcotic addiction solely as a vice. It is a vice, but like all vices, it is based on human nature. The use of narcotics, as is trite at the present time in the medical profession, represents an effort on the part of the individual to adjust himself to some difficult situation in his life. He will take one thing to stimulate him and another to quiet him. His will is weakened in proportion as he relies on drugs of that sort. And until we develop young men and young women who are able to suffer a little and exercise a certain amount of control, even though it may be inconvenient and unpleasant to do so, we are going to have a considerable amount of addiction to narcotics and addiction to other drugs. So that we must deal with narcotic addiction as something more than a police measure."

Appendix C: Mythbusting the Gateway Theory, Correlation vs. Causation

We can trace the "gateway theory" to the 1930s, and even then public health experts knew it was based on anti-drug hysteria rather than science.[88] It's a destructive myth, and it hasn't aged well.

The gateway theory is the notion that cannabis use leads to use of more dangerous drugs. But for nearly 100 years, the public health community has confidently refuted these hyperbolic claims. Even in the darkest days of the drug war, there have always been physicians who spoke truth to propaganda: evidence does not support a causal link between cannabis and the later use of hard drugs.

People who use hard drugs often have tried cannabis earlier in their lives because of its wide availability and relative safety. They are even more likely to have tried alcohol and tobacco. For obvious reasons, people generally try less dangerous drugs before trying more dangerous drugs, which may be harder to obtain. But a simple observation reflects the reality: The vast

[88] Doctors for Cannabis Regulation. *"The Prescience of Willian C. Woodward."* https://dfcr.prg/the-prescience-of-william-c-woodward/.

majority of people who use cannabis, tobacco, and alcohol never go on to use more dangerous drugs.

Since the "reefer madness" of the 1930s, prohibitionists have made unfounded inferences from the unsurprising fact that people who use opioids have often consumed cannabis first. They' re also more likely to have tried alcohol, tobacco, caffeine, and cupcakes first. The fallacious gateway theory nonetheless influenced the U.S. Federal Government when it banned cannabis in 1937.

Over eighty years later, the gateway theory remains unsupported by scientific research. The Institute of Medicine, the health division of the National Academy of Sciences, has concluded that cannabis "does not appear to be a gateway drug to the extent that it is the cause or even that it is the most significant predictor of serious drug abuse."[89]

Simply put, cannabis does not *cause* people to use hard drugs. It's like your high school science teacher often said: "Correlation does not equal causation."

Studies show that other factors-including genetic predisposition, environment, and poverty-are highly correlated with and can predict substance use disorders. The misuse of so-called soft drugs are, at most, indicators of some people's predisposition to misusing other drugs. This more enlightened view of cause and effect in drug use is known as "common liability theory."

The gateway theory is a misleading explanation of the complicated set of factors that actually lead to substance misuse. Its reductive interpretation distracts from an important public health discussion, and this malignant misunderstanding has resulted in the many harms of cannabis prohibition.

Especially given the severity of the United States opioid crisis, we need research and preventive education that focuses on the demonstrable links to the use of hard drugs, including genetics, poverty, and social environment.[90]

According to the Oxford Dictionary, a theory is a "supposition or a system of ideas intended to explain something, especially one based on general principles independent of the thing to be explained.'"[91] By this definition, we should more properly speak of the "gateway myth."

---

[89] Joy, Janet E., et al. Marijuana and Medicine: Assessing the Science Base. Washington, DC: National Academy Press, 1999, pp. 100-101. https://www/nap/edu/catalog/6367/marikuana-and-medicine-assessing-the-base.

[90] Quenqua, Douglas. "A Comeback for the Gateway Drug Theory?" The New York Times, December 7, 2017. https://www.nytimes.com/2017/12/07/welllive/a-comeback-for-the-gateway-drug-theory.html?_r=0. See also: Valdez, Avelardo 2007; 33(4): 595-603. http://www/tandfonline.com/doi/full/10.1080/00952990701407637.

[91] "Theory" Oxford Living Dictionaries. https://en.oxforddictionaries.com/definition.theory.

One way cannabis *can* causally lead to the use of hard drugs is through its prohibition.

Wherever the cannabis trade is illegal, it is sold to anyone-including minors. In a legalized environment, cannabis sales arc separated from those of hard d rugs, and minors are excluded from purchases.

The bottom line: Legalization makes communities safer and actually separates the sales of cannabis from other, far more harmful drugs. This is just one of many reasons why America needs legalization now.

* * *

Ms. BASS. Mr. Levine.

Statement of Neal Levine

Mr. LEVINE. Chair Bass, Mr. McClintock, Chairman Nadler, honorable members of the subcommittee, I would like to thank you for the opportunity to testify today.

My name is Neal Levine, and I have been an advocate for the reform of cannabis laws for over 16 years. Today, I am the CEO of the Cannabis Trade Federation, a national coalition of cannabis-related businesses dedicated to professionalizing, diversifying, and unifying the cannabis business community.

Our members are some of the most successful and responsible operators in the United States cannabis market today, generating billions of dollars in sales while navigating complying with regulations that are not only comprehensive in scope, but vary significantly from State to State. So it is my honor to testify at this historic hearing today, representing our industry.

As an organization, CTF is dedicated to encouraging greater minority ownership and participation in the cannabis industry. In May of this year, we launched a ground-breaking task force centered on diversity, equity, and inclusion in the cannabis space. We are fortunate to have some of the most prominent civil rights leaders in the nation working with a diverse group of cannabis industry professionals, stakeholders, and the CTF board to develop and implement a strategy to diversify the cannabis industry.

The State-based cannabis industry today is not only serving consumers, but it has also become a driver of economic growth and tax revenue in States across the country. In Colorado, for example, sales of State legal cannabis have exceeded $6.5 billion since the first adult use sale in 2014, generating more than $1 billion in tax revenue and fees in Colorado alone.

Nationally, the Marijuana Business Daily's annual factbook estimates that State legal cannabis sales will exceed $12 billion in 2019. Conservative estimates have roughly 200,000 full-time workers in State legal cannabis industry today.

Despite all of this progress, there remains a troubling a frustrating dichotomy between the State and Federal cannabis laws that produces a broad range of problems. Most notably, cannabis businesses struggle to obtain and maintain accounts with financial institutions due to the underlying activity being illegal under Federal law.

The level to which cannabis businesses must rely on cash transactions as a result poses a hazard to both cannabis industry workers and the general public. Because of this dichotomy, cannabis businesses are denied almost all standard business deductions, meaning we are essentially taxed on our revenue, not our profits. This saddles the industry with an effective Federal tax rate of 70 percent or higher, pulling most of the profits out of the business.

Most cannabis businesses, unable to invest profits back into the business, invest in our workers. The cannabis industry consistently offers living wage entry-level positions that require little to no formal education. But this gap between State and Federal law also creates a tension for cannabis industry operators and employees who must show up to work every day knowing their activity could put them in danger of Federal prosecution.

Outside the threat of prosecution, our employees face a litany of issues in their daily lives, such as not being able to obtain mortgages, such as being denied car loans, sometimes having to be paid in cash, and having their personal bank accounts shut down, and on and on and on.

We are dedicated—these are dedicated and passionate workers acting in strict compliance with State law with the support of their State and local governments, who have families and should not be forced to live under the constant threat of arrest and punishment by Federal authorities for going to work. The great news is there are several pieces of legislature that would end Federal cannabis prohibition and address these issues, and today, this subcommittee is now tackling the issue head on.

This is amazing progress, and CTF supports all positive cannabis reform legislation. But as industry, we are not only concerned with how the policy is shaped, but how it impacts our businesses, our employees, and our State and local economies. And while some Members of Congress are having the debate of how we should end cannabis prohibition, there are still many Members who are struggling with should we end cannabis prohibition, not how.

Meanwhile, hundreds of thousands of American workers' daily lives continue to be impacted by this dichotomy between State and Federal law, and the situation has become untenable. The most immediate path to resolving the State-Federal conflict is the passage of the STATES Act currently sponsored by seven Democrats and Seven Republicans on the House Judiciary Committee, including ranking member of the full committee, Mr. Collins of Georgia.

The STATES Act would amend the Controlled Substance Act to exempt both individuals and businesses who are acting in compliance with State cannabis laws. We have a long way to go with respect to revising—reversing the harms caused by cannabis prohibition and the need to begin the process—and we need to begin the process as soon as possible.

The question before this subcommittee and before Congress is whether there is a willingness to advance a bill to the President's desk that will immediately address nearly all the issues that I have raised. With strong bipartisan support for the STATES Act, it is possible during the current session of Congress to take major steps toward respecting State cannabis laws, protecting workers, and advancing a more secure, vibrant, and equitable cannabis industry.

We hope that Congress will take advantage of this opportunity, and I would be honored to answer any questions.

Thank you for your time.

[The statement Mr. Levine follows:]

Testimony of Mr. Neal Levine, CEO of the Cannabis Trade Federation, before the U.S. House Committee on the Judiciary Subcommittee on Crime, Terrorism, and Homeland Security, Marijuana Laws in America: Racial Justice and the Need for Reform, July 10, 2019

Chairwoman Bass, Ranking Member Ratcliffe, and Members of this Subcommittee, I would like to thank you for the opportunity to testify today. My name is Neal Levine and I am the CEO of the Cannabis Trade Federation (CTF), a national coalition of cannabis-related businesses dedicated to professionalizing, diversifying, and unifying the cannabis business community. Our members are some of the most successful and responsible operators in the U.S. cannabis market today, generating billions of dollars in sales while navigating and complying with regulations that are not only comprehensive in scope, but vary significantly from state-to-state. These companies are doing everything in their power to follow the rules and regulations set for them.

Overview of CTF and the Cannabis Industry

I am in a unique position to understand these state laws, since I spent many years working for the Marijuana Policy Project (MPP) as the director of state policies and, later, director of state campaigns, helping to pass state cannabis laws and ballot measures. With that work in mind, I hope that Members on the Subcommittee who believe in the principle of federalism appreciate that cannabis reform in the country has been driven, as the Tenth Amendment provides, by "the States respectively." At a time when the federal government has largely suffered through cannabis policy inertia, 33 states, the District of Columbia, and numerous U.S. territories have passed effective medical cannabis laws and 11 of those states, DC, and two territories have made cannabis legal for all adults. In many of these states, reforms have been driven by the people, with strong majorities passing adult-use ballot measures in states as diverse as California, Nevada, Alaska, and Michigan.

In public polling, we now see majority support for cannabis legalization among all political persuasions. In a survey released last October, Gallup found support at 64 percent overall, with 51 percent of Republicans joining 72 percent of Democrats and 67 percent of Independents. Individuals have all kinds of reasons to support cannabis legalization. Some are concerned that criminalizing cannabis use has astronomical socials costs; some are concerned that cannabis prohibition enforcement disproportionately impacts communities and people of color; some have a passion for helping veterans or young children who derive therapeutic benefits from cannabis; some have concluded that, like alcohol, cannabis is better as a regulated product; and, finally, some just like cannabis. Whatever the reason, we urge Congress to respect the will of the people and of legislators in States that have chosen regulation over prohibition.

I worked closely at MPP with Heather Azzi, Steve Fox, and Mason Tvert, all of whom are now working with CTF as staff or retained advisors. The four of us collectively have dedicated more than 60 years to enacting more just and sensible cannabis laws in this country. And we bring that passion and determination to our work with CTF. Heather, Steve and myself are three of the five members of the CTF executive committee, along with former Republican congressman Carlos Curbelo and Linda Mercado Greene, owner of a Washington D.C. medical marijuana dispensary – the only dispensary east of the river in Historic Anacostia.

CTF represents an industry that has evolved dramatically over the past two decades. In fact, some of the earliest providers of medical cannabis in this country, whether they were on the west coast or elsewhere, would probably object to being considered "industry" participants at all, as they were driven primarily by a desire to bring the healing attributes of the cannabis plant to patients who were suffering from a variety of conditions. But whether cannabis providers were operating as non-profit cooperatives in California or vertically-integrated for-profit companies in Colorado, they were part of a system that was shifting the cultivation and sale of cannabis from the underground, illegal market and into markets that are highly regulated and monitored at the state level. These markets provide more reliable products in safer environments for customers of all types.

Today, the cannabis industry is not only serving patients and adult-use consumers, but it has become a driver of economic growth and tax revenue in states across the country. In Colorado, for example, since January 1, 2014, sales of state-legal cannabis have exceeded $6.5 billion, while tax revenue and fees at the state level just crossed the one-billion dollar mark. This does not include hundreds of millions of additional tax dollars garnered by Colorado localities. As of March 2019, there were more than 40,000 individuals in Colorado with active occupational licenses that allow them to work directly in the cannabis industry. Nationally, the Marijuana Business Daily's Annual Fact Book estimates state-legal cannabis sales will exceed $12 billion in 2019. It also estimates the state-legal cannabis industry currently employs the equivalent of 175,000 to 215,000 full-time workers.

The Challenge Current Federal Cannabis Laws Place on State-Legal Cannabis Activity

Despite these impressive figures, for more than two decades, there has been a troubling and frustrating dichotomy between state and federal cannabis laws. In the early days of state-legal medical cannabis, this often had extremely harsh ramifications, with the federal government conducting heavily-armed raids on caregivers and cooperatives, primarily in California.

Individuals acting in compliance with state law were investigated, arrested, prosecuted, and even imprisoned. More recently, since the passage of the first legalization ballot measures in Colorado and Washington in 2012 and the subsequent issuance of the Cole Memo by the Department of Justice in August 2013, direct federal law enforcement actions against state-compliant cannabis businesses have been rare. This has been true even after then-Attorney General Jeff Sessions rescinded the Cole Memo in January 2018. Nevertheless, the challenges stemming from the illegal status of cannabis at the federal level remain.

As most people are aware, one of the most significant issues related to the state-federal dichotomy is that cannabis businesses struggle to obtain and maintain accounts with financial institutions due to the underlying activity being illegal under federal law. Although the federal Financial Crimes Enforcement Network (FinCEN) issued guidance to financial institutions working with cannabis companies in February 2014, the majority of banks are still hesitant to engage in this space. The level to which cannabis businesses must rely on cash transactions as a result poses a hazard to both cannabis industry workers and the general public. To the extent there is good news to report, FINCen has maintained its 2014 guidance regarding banking cannabis businesses. From a law enforcement perspective, this makes eminent sense as it is always better for law enforcement to detect illicit activity if the proceeds of that activity are run through the regulated banking system. Our members support the anti-money laundering rules and regulations and believe bad actors will be more easily detected if the financial system is more readily available to state-legal cannabis businesses. To this end, we support passage of the SAFE Banking Act, which would enable financial institutions to have cannabis-related businesses as customers without fear of federal prosecution, forfeiture, or interference from their regulators.

Of course, the differences between state and federal law also create a tension for cannabis industry operators and employees, who must show up to work every day knowing that their activity could put them in danger of federal prosecution. These are dedicated and passionate workers acting in strict compliance with state laws, with the support of their state and local governments, and they should not be forced to live under the constant threat of arrest and punishment by federal authorities.

For some cannabis industry workers, the distinction between state and federal laws has even affected their ability to obtain U.S. citizenship. Recently, two Colorado residents were denied naturalization because of their work in the cannabis industry. Officials with the U.S. Citizenship and Immigration Services asserted that this work demonstrated a lack of "good moral character." In response, several members of the full Committee signed a letter to the Department of Justice and the Department of Homeland Security, urging them to reverse this practice of denying citizenship due to cannabis industry work. CTF applauds Members for taking action like this and hopes this letter will have an impact on current cannabis policy as it relates to immigrants. But the most effective means by which Congress can end this practice is by passing, as soon as possible, legislation that would bring state and federal cannabis laws in line.

The STATES Act: Resolving the State-Federal Conflict and Expanding Opportunity in the Industry

The most immediate path to resolving the state-federal cannabis conflict is passage of the STATES Act (H.R. 2093), currently sponsored by seven Democrats and seven Republicans on the House Judiciary Committee, including the Ranking Member of the full Committee, Mr. Collins of Georgia. The STATES Act would amend the Controlled Substances Act to exempt individuals and business that are acting in compliance with state cannabis laws. Even Attorney General William Barr, in recent testimony, suggested that he would prefer the approach encompassed by the STATES Act over the status quo of inconsistent state and federal laws.

Immediate passage of the STATES Act could also help spur economic activity in disadvantaged areas in our country. In a recent hearing before the Senate Appropriations Committee, Treasury Secretary Steven Mnuchin was asked whether cannabis businesses would qualify for certain tax credits under the Tax Cuts and Jobs Act of 2017, which established opportunity zones and provided financial incentives for businesses to locate in those areas. Due to the illegal status of cannabis, Secretary Mnuchin testified that cannabis businesses would not be eligible for these tax credits. In order to encourage greater investment in these depressed areas, we must exempt state-legal cannabis activity from the provisions of the Controlled Substance Act, as the STATES Act would do.

On the subject of taxes, it should also be mentioned that the STATES Act would bring tax fairness to cannabis companies. Under current law, specifically Section 280E of the Internal Revenue Code, cannabis businesses are prohibited from deducting expenses related to the trafficking of a federally illegal controlled substance. The result is that the effective federal tax rate on cannabis businesses is often between 70 and 90 percent, and at times higher. By making the underlying activity of these businesses legal under federal law, they will be treated like any other business and will pay the same tax rates that other businesses do.

Potential business owners could also benefit from passage of the STATES Act. Within the past few weeks, we have seen the introduction of legislation to make cannabis businesses eligible for Small Business Administration loans, including microloans for women, veterans, and minorities. CTF supports these kinds of efforts to advance a more inclusive industry, but know that the federal government will not be able to make loans to cannabis businesses as long as cannabis remains illegal under federal law.

As more and more states opt out of cannabis prohibition and allow highly regulated businesses to generate revenue selling cannabis, social equity programs designed to increase minority ownership in the cannabis industry are a major component of these new state cannabis laws. This is in recognition of the fact that enforcement of the war on drugs has disproportionately impacted communities and people of color, and the majority of arrests in the war on drugs have been for cannabis.

But the dichotomy between federal and state cannabis law are hindering these efforts at the state level. As reported in the Boston Globe late last year, John Barros, the City of Boston's Chief of Economic Development, “said the federal prohibition on marijuana has been a major obstacle to equity, since it prevents banks from loaning money to cannabis firms — and because most of the city’s small business assistance efforts are funded by federal dollars that cannot go toward [cannabis] companies.”

Passage of the STATES Act would benefit states and localities that are working to implement social equity programs in order to increase minority ownership in the cannabis industry. These programs are hampered by the fact that they are intended to inspire individuals, some of whom have been ensnared previously by the criminal justice system, to engage in activity that remains illegal under federal law. In addition, while I noted earlier the challenges associated with obtaining banking services in the cannabis industry, the situation is even worse when it comes to obtaining loans to operate cannabis businesses. As long as the state-federal conflict exists, it will be very difficult for social equity applicants to secure operating capital from most traditional sources of those funds.

As an organization, CTF is dedicated to encouraging greater minority ownership and participation in the cannabis industry. In fact, in May of this year, we launched a groundbreaking task force centered on diversity, equity, and inclusion in the cannabis space. The task force, which includes some of the most significant civil rights leaders in the nation, along with a diverse group of cannabis industry professionals, will work with members of the CTF board to develop and implement a strategy to diversify the cannabis industry and ensure that those communities that were disproportionately impacted by the War on Drugs derive a significant share of the benefits produced by the legal cannabis industry.

CTF also supports a broad range of reforms that have been proposed in Congress. From the grants to states and localities to cover the costs of expungements in the Marijuana Freedom and Opportunity Act to the community reinvestment provisions in the Marijuana Justice Act, we believe there is a role for the federal government to play in ensuring that those who have suffered due to marijuana prohibition are not left behind under legalization. Where progress on these bills is possible, we will be dedicating our resources toward encouraging their passage.

We have a long way to go with respect to reversing the harms caused by marijuana prohibition and need to begin the process as soon as possible. The question before this Subcommittee and before Congress is whether there is a willingness to advance a bill to the President's desk that will immediately address nearly all of the issues I have raised. With strong bipartisan support for legislation like the STATES Act, it is possible *during the current session of Congress* to take major steps toward respecting state cannabis laws, protecting workers, and advancing a more secure, vibrant, and equitable cannabis industry. We hope that Congress will take advantage of the opportunity.

I look forward to answering any questions you may have. Thank you.

* * *

Ms. BASS. Dr. Burnett.

Statement of G. Malik Burnett, M.D., MBA, MPH

Dr. BURNETT. Chair Bass, Chairman Nadler, Ranking Member McClintock, members of the Subcommittee on Crime, Terrorism, and Homeland Security, thank you for the opportunity to testify today.

My name is Malik Burnett. I am a physician by training and currently serve as the chief operating officer of Tribe Companies, a minority-owned, multi-State cannabis company with operations in California, Massachusetts, and Washington, D.C.

Over the past 7 years, I have provided testimony to many State and local legislatures on the regulatory aspects of medical cannabis and cannabis for adult use. But it is with great pleasure that I come before you today not to talk about whether ending cannabis prohibition at the Federal level is good public policy, but to discuss the best ways to go about ending cannabis prohibition and restoring communities devastated by the war on drugs.

It is an unmitigated fact that the state of cannabis policy today is best described as a tale of two Americas. In one America, there are men and women, most of them wealthy, white, and well-connected, who are starting cannabis companies, creating jobs, amassing significant personal wealth, and generating billions in tax dollars for States which sanction cannabis programs.

In the other America, there are men and women, most of them poor people of color, who are arrested for cannabis and suffer the collateral consequences associated with criminal conviction. Six hundred fifty-nine thousand Americans were subject to this reality in 2017, 91 percent of those for merely possessing the plant.

We have to do better. The status quo is not sustainable. Drug policy in America is and has always been a policy based on racial and social control. From the passage of the Marijuana Tax Act in 1937 with its race-based motivations to the passage of the 2018 farm bill legalizing commercial hemp cultivation and production, the laws and policies created in this legislative body have the power to shape the social determinants of health of every American.

With this in mind, you will hear arguments today that suggest when it comes to cannabis policy, this legislative body should take an incremental approach and do what is most politically expedient. This argument is not only intellectually lazy, but it is blind to both the historical and ongoing harms associated with current policy and will ensure that the vast majority of economic gains associated with this new industry goes to a select few. It is an effective white-washing of cannabis history in America.

Congress should instead take an intentional approach to cannabis policy reform with the concept of restorative justice as the guiding principle. This body should look to States like California, Massachusetts, and most recently, Illinois for policies that utilize tax revenue generated from the sale of cannabis to promote community reinvestment, including programs for record sealing, expungement, job training, the financing of public schools, parks, and recreational infrastructure, and medical and public health research.

Focusing legislative efforts to create incentives which ensure that the economic potential of this industry is shared across communities and that the employment bases are comprised of a diverse set of workers is a worthwhile goal and well within reach at the Federal level. Examples like the Marijuana Justice Act and the RESPECT Resolution provide a solid framework upon which more progress can be made.

In addition to more effectively utilizing tax revenue to restore harmed communities, Congress can take steps toward making the banking environment more friendly for small business development within the industry by removing cannabis from the Controlled Substances Act.

While most discussions on cannabis and banking rightfully revolve around the public safety issues associated with dealing in cash, a lack of banking access also plays a determinative factor in who can participate in the industry. Without small business lending, all cannabis companies must rely on angel investors, family offices, and high-interest debt financing vehicles in order to get the needed capital to start a business. The vast majority of this capital does not come from diverse sources and is a significant contributing factor to the lack of diversity in the industry.

By removing cannabis from the Controlled Substances Act, Congress would support the expansion of commercial banking access and could target Small Business Administration lending programs to promote diversity within the industry and across the country.

Finally, I would be remiss if I didn't highlight the immigration challenges associated with continued cannabis prohibition at the Federal level. America is fundamentally a nation of immigrants. However, the status quo prevents immigrants from working within the cannabis industry, as having a job in this space makes them and every noncitizen in their family inadmissible for naturalization. Furthermore, legal permanent residents who use cannabis medically or recreationally can be indefinitely detained and deported when attempting to return to the United States after traveling abroad.

The damage associated with breaking up immigrant families has been on full display in America as of late. Congress should not allow the legal use of cannabis or efforts to acquire gainful employment in the legal cannabis industry to contribute to this fundamentally un-American activity.

Overall, it is important that Congress make a concerted effort to provide legislative solutions to close both the economic and enforcement divides which exist in cannabis policy in America today. A successful legislative effort removes cannabis from the Controlled Substances Act and takes a comprehensive approach to addressing both the banking and taxation issues, as well as the criminal justice and economic issues involved, leaving no one behind.

Much has been made for the need of reparations in recent political times, and in the context of cannabis, the convenient argument of the Senate majority leader that none of us who are currently living are responsible goes out the window. All lawmakers currently living have a responsibility to right the wrongs associated with cannabis prohibition.

[The statement of Dr. Burnett follows:]

Marijuana Laws in America: Racial Justice and the Need for Reform, July 10, 2019

Chairwoman Bass and members of the Subcommittee on Crime, Terrorism and Homeland Security thank you for the opportunity to testify today. My name is Malik Burnett, I am a physician by training and currently serve as the Chief Operating Officer of the Tribe Companies, a minority owned multi-state cannabis company with operations in California, Massachusetts and Washington DC.

I have provided testimony to many state and local legislatures on the regulatory aspects of medical, cannabis, and cannabis for adult use but it is with great pleasure that I come before you today not to talk about whether ending cannabis prohibition at the federal level is good public policy; but to discuss the best ways to go about ending cannabis prohibition and restoring the communities devastated by the war on drugs.

It is an unmitigated fact that the state of cannabis policy today in best described as a tale of two Americas; in one America there are men and women, most of them wealthy, white and well connected, who are starting cannabis companies, creating jobs and amassing significant personal wealth, and generating billions in tax dollars for the states which sanction cannabis programs. In the other America, there are men and women, most of them poor, people of color, who are arrested and suffer the collateral consequences associated with criminal conviction. 659,700 Americans were subject to this reality in 2017, 91% of those for merely possessing the substance. We have to do better; the status quo is unsustainable.

Drug policy in America is, and has always been, a policy that is based on racial and social control. From the passage of the Marijuana Tax Act in 1937, with its race-based motivations, to the passage of the 2018 Farm Bill, legalizing commercial hemp cultivation and production; the laws and policies created in the legislative body have the power to shape the social determinants of health for every American. With this in mind, you will hear arguments today that suggest when it comes to cannabis policy, this legislative body should do what is most politically expedient. "Just get the federal government out of the way, and let the states handle the issue," is how the argument goes. This argument is not only intellectually lazy, but it is blind to the historical harms associated with the current policy, and will ensure that the vast majority of the economic gains associated with this new industry go to a select few. An effective "whitewashing" of cannabis history in America.

Congress should instead take an intentional approach to cannabis policy reform with the concept of restorative justice as the guiding principle. The body should look to states like California, Massachusetts, and most recently Illinois, for policies that utilize tax revenue generated from the sales of cannabis to promote community reinvestment including programs for record sealing and expungement, job training, financing public schools, parks, and recreational infrastructure, and medical and public health research. Make no mistake about it, the economic impact of legal cannabis markets is significant, for every one dollar spent within the cannabis industry, approximately $2.30 of economic activity is generated within a local economy.[92] Approximately 64,000 jobs were created nationwide in 2018, with just 20% of the US population living in states with adult use access.[93] Focusing legislative efforts to create incentives which ensure that the economic potential of this industry is shared across communities and that employee bases are comprised of a diverse set of workers is a worthwhile goal and well within reach at the federal level, examples like the Marijuana Justice Act and the RESPECT Resolution provide a solid framework upon which more progress can be made.

In addition to more effectively utilizing tax revenue to restore harmed communities, Congress can take steps towards making the banking environment more friendly for small business development within the industry. While most discussions on cannabis and banking, rightfully revolve

---

[92] Light et al. *The Economic Impact of Marijuana Legalization in Colorado.* Marijuana Policy Group. October 2016. p.5.

[93] Cox, J. *The marijuana industry looks like the fastest growing job-market in the country.* CNBC. March 14, 2019. https://www.cnbc.com/2019/03/14/the-marijuana-industry-looks-like-the-fastest-growing-job-market-in-the-country.html.

around the public safety issues of dealing in cash, a lack of banking access also plays a determinative factor in who can participate in the industry. Without small business lending, all cannabis companies must rely on angel investors, family offices, or high interest debt financing vehicles in order to get the needed capital to start a business. The vast majority of this capital does not come from diverse sources and this is a significant contributing factor to the lack of diversity in the industry. Some states, like Massachusetts are working to solve this problem by creating equity applicant programs and licenses earmarked for smaller footprint businesses. However, by opening up banking access and even developing SBA lending programs targeted towards diversifying the industry, the Congress can support these developments at a broader level.

Overall, it is important that Congress make a concerted effort to provide legislative solutions to close both the economic and enforcement divides which exist in cannabis policy in America today. A successful legislative effort takes a comprehensive approach to cannabis addressing both the banking and taxation issues, as well as the criminal and economic justice issues, leaving no one behind. Much has been made of the need for reparations in recent political times, in the context of cannabis, the convenient argument that "none of us currently living are responsible" goes out the window. All of the lawmakers currently living have a responsibility to right the wrongs associated with cannabis prohibition occurring today. This starts with passing legislation centered around restorative justice. Thank you for your time and I look forward to answering your questions.

Malik Burnett, MD MBA MPH
COO, Tribe Companies, LLC

* * *

Ms. BASS. Thank you.

We will now proceed under the 5-minute rule with questions, and I will begin by recognizing myself for 5 minutes.

I would like to ask unanimous consent to enter into the record a written testimony from Dr. Sabet, who is with the Smart Approaches to Marijuana, an organization that raises concerns over resources for drug treatment and also questions the disproportionate arrest rate going down with legalization.

So I ask unanimous consent. Without objection, I will enter it into the record.

[The information follows:]

Written Testimony for Marijuana Laws in America: Racial Justice and the Need for Reform, July 10th, 2019

Kevin A. Sabet, PhD
President & CEO of Smart Approaches to Marijuana (SAM)
Former White House ONDCP Staff member (Clinton, Bush, Obama)
and
Will Jones, III
Communication and Outreach Associate, Smart Approaches to Marijuana (SAM) http://www.learnaboutsam. org

While we are disappointed that this hearing has no witnesses who support alternatives to complete marijuana legalization and commercialization, we appreciate the opportunity to submit testimony to the Committee. We represent Smart Approaches to Marijuana (SAM), the leading non-partisan national organization offering a science-based approach to marijuana policy. SAM was founded by former Congressman Patrick Kennedy, senior editor of *The Atlantic* David Frum, and Dr. Kevin Sabet, a former White House advisor to the Obama Administration as well as two other U.S. Administrations.

In addition to his service to the past three White House administrations, Dr. Sabet is also an Affiliated Fellow at Yale University and has more than 25 years of drug policy experience.

Will Jones serves as the Communications and Outreach Associate at SAM and has had the privilege to work as community activist on issues of social justice at the local and national level. He later started the campaign against marijuana legalization and commercialization in Washington, DC. Mr. Jones is a proud husband, father, and also serves as a DC Firefighter/EMT and is completing his Master of Public Administration at George Washington University.

Many proponents of legalization have posited marijuana legalization as a solution for real issues that disproportionately affect communities of color. They cite the prevalence of minority groups jailed for minor possession charges as reason enough to legalize recreational marijuana.

They charge that legalizing marijuana would, in part, reduce the number of people of color whom are jailed for minor possession. The arguments are predicated on a mythology that woefully misrepresents the impact of marijuana through the lens of social justice.

In reality, there is a middle ground that could attract a bipartisan consensus: smart decriminalization instead of legalization. The goal of the overall policy should be to reduce drug use and connect those who are suffering from addiction with recovery resources. Instead, the goal of the marijuana industry is to increase the use of their products by increasing the potency, making appealing new products like candies and gummies, and aggressively marketing these products to young demographics (See Appendix A).

Marijuana Arrest Rates - Common Misconceptions

Many believe marijuana legalization will reduce the number of minorities imprisoned or arrested for marijuana-related offenses. Legalization advocates and the marijuana industry have worked diligently to ensure that legalization is perceived as a social justice issue, arguing that without full legalization, minority populations will continue to be targeted inappropriately by law enforcement officials. Proponents of legalization argue that this policy is vital to achieving social justice.

As is evidenced by New York state's recent legislation, decriminalization and legalization are not inextricably linked in the way that marijuana industry proponents have claimed they are. In June, New York passed legislation to decriminalize the drug without legalizing it for recreational use.[94] In perpetuating the false dichotomy that social justice cannot be addressed without full-scale legalization, proponents have ensured confusion around the underlying issue of social justice, seeking to legitimize legalization and commercialization by tacking it on to an entirely separate issue.

We have worked diligently to encourage and aid other states in creating decriminalization legislation to begin to address the socio-economic disparities in marijuana-related arrests. In New Jersey, proponents of legalization delayed any consideration of social justice reforms until they could profit from legalization. A pure decriminalization bill by the Chair of the Senate Black Caucus that did not include the commercialization of

---

[94] Reisman, N. (2019, June 21). Marijuana Decriminalization Bill Heads to Cuomo's Desk. Retrieved from https://spectrumlocalnews.com/nys/central-ny/news/2019/06/20/ marijuana-decriminalization-bill-passes-state- senate.

marijuana was ignored despite widespread outcry among state legislators regarding the impact of marijuana-related offenses on minority communities.[95]

Even still, in states that have legalized recreational marijuana under the premise of reducing social injustice, arrest rates for certain marijuana-related offenses have increased, particularly for minority groups.

In Washington D.C. for example, between 2015 and 2017 (the years immediately following legalization), although total marijuana-related arrests decreased, distribution and public consumption arrests more than tripled. Among adults, 89% of marijuana distribution or public consumption arrestees were African Americans.[96]

Additionally, the 2017 marijuana-related African American arrest rate in Colorado is nearly twice that of Caucasians (233 in 100,000 versus 118 in 100,000).[97] In Colorado, 39% of African American marijuana-related arrests in 2017 were made without a warrant, while only 18% of Caucasians were arrested without one.[98] In Denver, the average number of annual Hispanic arrests for marijuana increased by 98% since legalization (107 average annual arrests pre-legalization vs 212.25 post-legalization); the average number of arrests for African Americans increased 100.3% from 82.5 per year to 165.25 per year.[99] As pro-marijuana lobbyists argue that legalization will improve social justice in legalized states, disparities among use and criminal offense rates persist across race, ethnicity, and income levels.

Arrests of people of color have risen, contrary to what legalization proponents suggest. The evidence only bolsters the reality that the system itself is what warrants further investigation, not the legality of the drug. The charge that marijuana legalization will eliminate racial bias in the justice system is unfounded. The opposite has been proven.

The effect on young people of color in states that have legalized marijuana further exemplifies the alarming misconception that legalization reduces the

---

[95] Barchenger, S., & Racioppi, D. (2019, May 22). NJ Legal Weed: Top State Lawmaker Sweeney Rejects Marijuana Decriminalization. *APP.* Retrieved from https://www.app.com/story/news/local/new-jersey/marijuana/2019/05/22/nj-weed-sweeney-marijuana-decriminalization/3747328002/.

[96] DC Metropolitan Policy Department. (2018). Marijuana Arrest Data. Washington, District of Columbia. Retrieved February 2019, from https://mpdc. Dc.gov/node/1347766.

[97] Colorado Department of Public Safety. (2018). Impacts of Marijuana Legalization in Colorado: A Report Pursuant to Senate Bill 13-283. Division of Criminal Justice.

[98] Colorado Department of Public Safety. (2018). Impacts of Marijuana Legalization in Colorado: A Report Pursuant to Senate Bill 13-283. Division of Criminal Justice.

[99] Colorado Department of Public Safety. (2018). Impacts of Marijuana Legalization in Colorado: A Report Pursuant to Senate Bill 13-283. Division of Criminal Justice.

number of minorities being charged with violations of marijuana laws. Across Colorado, minority juveniles suffered. The average number of marijuana-related arrests among Hispanic juveniles increased 7.3% (770/year to 825/year), and the average number of marijuana-related arrests among African-American juveniles increased 5.9% (230/year to 243.5/year).[100] Additionally, drug suspension rates in Colorado schools with 76% or more students of color are over two times higher compared to Colorado schools with fewer than 25% students of color.[101] Colorado schools that had 25% or fewer youth of color had 313 marijuana-related suspensions per 100,000 students compared to 658 marijuana-related suspensions per 100,000 students for schools comprised of populations with 76% or more youth of color.[102] In Washington, DC juvenile marijuana-related arrests increased 114% between the three years before and after marijuana legalization.[103] The legalization of marijuana has served to further incriminate minority youth.

Economic Impact - the Marijuana Industry in Communities of Color

The marijuana industry has increasingly exploited minority communities with disastrous outcomes. Several consequences are borne of this.

First, higher crime rates follow areas in which marijuana stores set up shop. In 2017, the number of court filings charged with the Colorado Organized Crime Control Act that were linked to a marijuana charges increased 284% since 2012.[104] A study funded by the National Institutes of Health (NIH) showed that the density of marijuana dispensaries was linked to increased property crimes in nearby areas. Researchers found that in Denver, Colorado, neighborhoods adjacent to marijuana businesses saw 84.8 more

---

[100] Colorado Department of Public Safety. (2018). Impacts of Marijuana Legalization in Colorado: A Report Pursuant to Senate Bill 13-283. Division of Criminal Justice.

[101] Colorado Department of Public Safety. (2016). Marijuana Legalization in Colorado: Early Findings -A Report Pursuant to Senate Bill 13-283.

[102] Colorado Department of Public Safety. (2016). Marijuana Legalization in Colorado: Early Findings - A Report Pursuant to Senate Bill 13-283.

[103] DC Metropolitan Policy Department. (2018). Marijuana Arrest Data. Washington, District of Columbia. Retrieved February 2019, from https://mpdc. dc.gov/node/1347766.

[104] Colorado Department of Public Safety. (2018). Impacts of Marijuana Legalization in Colorado: A Report Pursuant to Senate Bill 13-283. Division of Criminal Justice.

property crimes each year than neighborhoods without a marijuana shop nearby.[105]

Second, marijuana store owners seek out lower-income and minority communities as prime locations for their shops. Just as Big Tobacco has targeted lower-income communities as an important consumer-base,[106] the marijuana industry seeks a similar bae to establish addiction- for-profit businesses. As reported by the Truth Initiative, an organization committed to exposing the truth about Big Tobacco, tobacco companies historically have targeted and advertised to lower-income communities and communities of color.[107] The marijuana industry has done the same.

In Los Angeles, the majority of dispensaries have opened in predominately African- American communities.[108] Additionally, an overlay of socioeconomic data with the geographic location of pot shops in Denver shows marijuana stores are located disproportionately in disadvantaged neighborhoods.[109] In Oregon, the state conducted an analysis on the distribution of state-sanctioned dispensaries and found that sites were disproportionately concentrated among low-income and historically disenfranchised communities.[110,111]

Yet these stores rarely employ members of the community or improve economic opportunities for the communities they target. In fact, nationally,

---

105 Freisthler, B., Gaidus, A., Tam, C., Ponicki, W.R., & Gruenewald, P. J. (2017). From Medical to Recreational Marijuana Sales: Marijuana Outlets and Crime in an Era of Changing Marijuana Legislation. The Journal of Primary Prevention, 38(3), 249-263.

106 Smith, S. (2010, August 30). Tobacco signs still target city's poorer areas. *Boston Globe.* Retrieved from http://archive.boston.com/news/health/articles/2010/08/30/tobacco_signs_still_target_citys_poorer_areas/?page=2.

107 Truth Initiative. (2017, January 31). Tobacco is a social justice issue: Low-income communities. Retrieved from https://truthinitiative.org/research-resources/targeted-communities/tobacco-social-justice-issue-low-income- communities.

108 Thomas, C., & Feisthler, B. (2017). Evaluating the Change in Medical Marijuana Dispensary Locations in Los Angeles Following the Passage of Local Legislation. The Journal of Primary Prevention, 38(3), 265-277.

109 Hamm, K. (20 I 6, January 2). Marijuana in Denver: Map of pot-related businesses by neighborhood with income data, school locations . *The Daily Post.* Retrieved from The Daily Post: https://www.denverpost.com/2016/01/02/marijuana-indenver-map-of-pot-related-businesses-by-neighborhood-with- income-dataschool-locations/.

110 McVey, E. (2017, July 31). Chart: Recreational marijuana stores are clustered in low-income areas of Denver, Seattle. *Marijuana Business Daily.* Retrieved February 2019, from https://mjbizdaily.com/chart-recreationalmarijuana-stores-clustered-low-income-areas-denver-seattle/.

111 Smith, P. (2017, August 9). Why Are Pot Shops Mainly in Poor Neighborhoods? *The Daily Chronic.* Retrieved February 2019, from http://www.thedailychronic.net/2017/75557/pot-shops-mainly-poorneighborhoods/.

less than 1% of all pot shops are owned by minorities of any community.[112] In Massachusetts, the phenomenon is further exemplified. Massachusetts requires that all "Marijuana Agents," persons who work at marijuana businesses, register with the state. Demographic analysis revealed that of 1,306 agents who applied in the city of Boston, 73% were Caucasian, 6% were Hispanic, and 4% were African- American.[113] This is unrepresentative of the city's population. According to recent census estimates, Caucasians comprise 44.9% of the population of Boston; Hispanics 19.4%; African-Americans, 25.3%.[114] The economic opportunities touted by the industry are missing in practice.

Furthermore, in efforts to curb the marketing practices of Big Tobacco, state governments acted to ensure that advertisements were limited, and the reach of tobacco companies was curbed. States like Massachusetts and New York imposed barrier rules restricting the ability of Big Tobacco to set up shop within a certain distance from schools, community centers, and churches.[115] The governments not only recognized that their youth were at risk, but that in particular, their minority youth were at risk.[116] Still, as communities attempt to impose barriers and distance marijuana from young people and young minority people, marijuana companies have expressed outrage. When the Kansas City government moved to restrict marijuana dispensaries from setting up shop within 750 feet of schools, churches, and child care centers, marijuana advocates were dismayed and promised to push back on the initiative.[117] Elsewhere, local governments have given the marijuana industry even greater

---

[112] McVey, E. (2017, September 11). Chart: Percentage of cannabis business owners and founders by race. *Marijuana Business Daily.* Retrieved from https://mjbizdaily.com/chart-19-cannabis-businesses-owned-founded- racial-minorities/.

[113] Schoenberg, S. (2018, December 4). Boston grapples with lack of diversity in marijuana industry. *Masslive.com.* Retrieved from https://www.masslive.com/politics/2018/12/boston _grapples_with_lack_of_ct.html.

[114] United States of America, Census Bureau. (n.d.). QuickFacts: Boston City, Massachusetts. Retrieved from https://www.census.gov/quickfacts/fact/table/bostoncitymassachusetts/RHI225218#RHI225218.

[115] Smith, S. (2010, August 30). Tobacco signs still target city's poorer areas. *Boston Globe.* Retrieved from http://archive.boston.com/news/health/articles/2010/08/30/tobacco_signs_still_target_citys_poorer_areas/?page=2.

[116] Smith, S. (2010, August 30). Tobacco signs still target city's poorer areas. *Boston Globe.* Retrieved from http://archive.boston.com/news/health/articles/2010/08/30/tobacco_signs_still_target_citys_poorer_areas/?page=2.

[117] Pepitone, J. (2019, June 27). Not everyone happy with KC's proposed rules for medical marijuana dispensaries. *Fox4 KC.* Retrieved from https://fox4kc.com/2019/06/27/not-everyone-happy-with-kcs-proposed-rules-for-medical- marijuana-dispensaries/.

leniency that is contradictory to the efforts that were initiated to curb the tobacco industry years ago.

Public Health - the Impact of Marijuana in Lower-Income Communities

In addition to the financial consequences for minority groups, minority women and children face a new risk. A study by the American College of Obstetricians and Gynecologists reported that young, urban women from lower income levels have a 15-28% rate of marijuana use during pregnancy. Between 34 and 60% of marijuana users continue marijuana use throughout pregnancy due to a decreased perception of risk and stigma.[118] The misrepresentation of marijuana effects has disproportionately impacted pregnant women in lower-income communities. The American Academy of Pediatrics tells us that pregnant women should not use marijuana due to widely established health harms associated with use.

An alarming mythology perpetuated by the marijuana industry is that marijuana-legal states have seen a decrease in opioid deaths. This claim is based loosely on a 2014 study that recently has been debunked by researchers at Stanford University.[119] The opioid epidemic has disproportionately impacted lower-income communities.[120] According to the Brookings Institution, this disproportionate impact is owed in part to the lack of education and the lack of treatment centers in these communities.[121] By taking over the messaging, the marijuana industry capitalizes on the vulnerability of the communities hit hardest by the epidemic.

The health risks of marijuana are lost amid confusing and misleading advertisements that target communities that lack educational resources.

---

[118] The American College of Obstetricians and Gynecologists. (2017, October). Marijuana Use During Pregnancy and Lactation. ACOG Committee Opinions, 722.

[119] Humphreys, K. (2019, JW1e 10). Medical marijuana does not reduce opioid deaths. *Stanford Medicine News Center*. Retrieved from http://med.stanford.edu/news/all-news/2019/06/medical marijuana-does-not-reduce-opioid- deaths.htrnl.

[120] Kneebone, E., & Allard, S. (2017, September 25). A nation in overdose peril: Pinpointing the most impacted communities and the local gaps in care. *Brookings Institution*. Retrieved from https://www.brookings.edu/research/pinpointing-opioid-in-most-impacted-commu-nities/.

[121] Kneebone, E., & Allard, S. (2017, September 25). A nation in overdose peril: Pinpointing the most impacted communities and the local gaps in care. *Brookings Institution*. Retrieved from https://www.brookings.edu/research/pinpointing-opioid-in-most-impacted-commu-nities/.

Today's high-potency marijuana is addictive,[122] and linked with serious mental health illnesses such as psychosis,[123] and lowers educational outcomes, especially for those who use it heavily.[124] These lower-income communities face a new threat to their health with inadequate resources to combat the effects.

Conclusion

The truth is, marijuana reforms can and should center on alternatives to incarceration, such as drug treatment courts, pre-arrest diversion, and more research. The full legalization and commercialization of marijuana will spawn Big Tobacco 2.0- and because of today's highly intoxicating THC levels, far worse social justice harms and impacts to targeted communities.

* * *

Ms. BASS. I would like to ask Ms. Mosby, when you were talking about Maryland, you mentioned the disproportionate arrest rate I think you were talking about in Washington, D.C. And I wanted to know if you could help me understand why you think that the disproportionate arrest rate of African Americans continues to be four times as high, even though marijuana is legalized for recreational use in Washington, D.C.

Ms. MOSBY. Thank you.

One of the issues that I see and I foresee is that even with the decriminalization, I think that it has to go—we have to go beyond decriminalization of marijuana. We have to actually legalize this drug. And the reason why, among many, including the fact that there should be a regulation that will allow the States to control it and a safe environment for our children.

But more importantly, it is what we have seen just with the mere decriminalization of marijuana —

---

[122] Wagener, D. (2019, June 21). Marijuana Addiction Facts: Is Marijuana Physically Addictive? *American Addiction Centers*. Retrieved from https://americanaddictioncenters.org/marijuana-rehab/is-it-addictive.

[123] Di Forti, et al. The contribution of cannabis use to variation in the incidence of psychotic disorder across Europe (EU-GEi): a multicentre case-control study. Lancet Psychiatry. March 19, 2019 doi:https://doi.org/10.1016/S2215-0366(19)30048-3.

[124] Fergusson DM, Boden JM. Cannabis use and later life outcomes. Addiction. 2008 Jun; 103(6): 969-76. doi: 10.1111/j.1360-0443.2008.0222l.x.

Ms. BASS. Isn't it —

Ms. MOSBY [continuing]. Is that discriminatory enforcement still exists.

Ms. BASS. But I thought in D.C., and I might be wrong, that it is legal. It is legal for recreational use. And I wanted to know if you knew about the arrest rates in California and Colorado, where it is legal for recreational use?

Ms. MOSBY. So recreational use in D.C., yes, it is. What I cited was that even with the legalization of it in D.C., what is happening is that these individuals are still being targeted 11 times—African Americans are being targeted 11 times more than white people for public consumption and being arrested for that.

Ms. BASS. So why is that? I mean, legalization was supposed to address that.

Dr. BURNETT. Chair Bass, can I jump in here? I ran the campaign to legalize cannabis in D.C.

Ms. BASS. Yes, go ahead. Go ahead.

Dr. BURNETT. And so the interesting dichotomy that exists in the District is that, you know, the Congress governs all of the funding provisions for the local government in D.C., and so we haven't actually been able to set up a regulated market. And so what you have in D.C. is a legal—it is legal to possess cannabis. However, there is no means through which you can actually acquire cannabis.

And so lots of—

Ms. BASS. What about California and Colorado?

Dr. BURNETT. In California and Colorado, you actually—the reality of the situation is that there is biased enforcement in criminal justice writ large, right? And so cannabis is the entryway in a large number of ways to the criminal justice system. And when you look at the overall number of arrests that are occurring within any State, if you end up legalizing cannabis, you significantly drop the total number of arrests.

But in all honesty, biased enforcement of the law is a reality that exists beyond cannabis.

Ms. BASS. Oh, okay. Okay. So in Maryland, what is the legal age that you can use marijuana?

Ms. MOSBY. So it is not based on legal age. It has been decriminalized for possession of 10 grams or less.

Ms. BASS. Okay.

Ms. MOSBY. So there is no legal age. And essentially, what has happened is that even with that decriminalization portion of it, it is now given to the police officers can issue civil citations. What we are finding is that even in the implementation of these civil citations, they are only targeting certain demographics and particular areas, which I have already cited.

Ms. BASS. Right, right. Yes. Thank you.

You know, one of the issues in California, and actually in the States where marijuana is legal, is driving under the influence and how you measure it since marijuana is stored in fat, and you know, it can be detected after 30 days.

I think, Dr. Burnett, have you done some research about how to—how to detect whether or not you are intoxicated while driving? Dr. BURNETT. So I haven't done research myself, but the research that is out there right now is still at a preliminary level. One of the main reasons for that is because of the Federal prohibition that prevents us from being able to conduct research more intentionally on the effects of operating motor vehicles under influence of cannabis.

However, what I would say is that —

Ms. BASS. Do you know about maybe—because of the Federal prohibition here, do you know anything about Canada?

Dr. BURNETT. In Canada? Yes —

Ms. BASS. If any places have been able to come up with ways to determine —

Dr. BURNETT. So, interestingly, Canada just ended up legalizing at the federal level in October of last year.

Ms. BASS. Okay.

Dr. BURNETT. And so we are still very much at the preliminary stages. There are some preliminary studies and devices out in the marketplace that look at impairment while driving under the influence. But as I believe my colleague Dr. Nathan said, you know, when you actually go about the business of legalizing cannabis in any State, it is still illegal to operate a vehicle under the influence. So —

Ms. BASS. Yes, yes, yes.

Dr. Nathan, you wanted to respond?

Dr. NATHAN. Absolutely, sure. And thank you.

I live in New Jersey, and New Jersey is the State that is proud to have the second-largest number of drug recognition experts, or DREs, that are specifically trained to detect impairment of any kind in drivers. And that is right now the state-of-the-art. There is no good "per se" test.

There is no sample of blood or saliva or breath that will give us a clear image of whether somebody has recently used cannabis, let alone is intoxicated. And that is even farther from being able to say that somebody is impaired.

So right now, it is really drug recognition experts that are the way to go, and we really should support that in every jurisdiction.

Ms. BASS. Thank you. Thank you. Mr. McClintock. Oh, Mr. Collins.

Mr. COLLINS. Thank you, Madam Chairwoman.

Just real quick. The last 2 minutes of this conversation is probably the one that needs to be focused on the greatest, in addition to changing, as I have said before, but I appreciate that conversation.

With that, I ask unanimous consent that Mr. Gaetz, a member of the full committee, be permitted to sit in during this subcommittee during this hearing.

Ms. BASS. Without objection.

Mr. COLLINS. Without objection, I yield him my time.

Mr. GAETZ. I thank the ranking member for yielding me his time. I had the privilege to write Florida's first two medical marijuana laws, along with my colleague Mr. Steube from Florida. And I really wanted to start with the STATES Act because it seems to me that that would give States like Florida and others who have implemented a regime not just of decriminalization, but that facilitates providing medical cannabis to patients in need a way to do so.

Among our panel, who supports the STATES Act? Would you just raise your hand?

[Show of hands.]

Mr. GAETZ. And then who opposes the STATES Act? [Show of hands.]

Mr. GAETZ. Okay. Two of you? Is that right? Dr. Burnett, did you oppose the STATES Act?

Dr. BURNETT. I don't oppose the STATES Act. I think that we should do much more than what goes on —

Mr. GAETZ. If it was up for a vote, would you vote for it, or would you vote against it?

Dr. BURNETT. I would vote for it to make progress.

Mr. GAETZ. Great. Well, that is great to hear because I was a little concerned. In your testimony, you seem to indict incrementalism a great deal. And in my State, it was that incrementalism that led to progress because if we kind of operate from our various political polls on the issue, nothing really gets done.

And when we initially legalized non-euphoric cannabis and then were able to go back and legalize euphoric cannabis, and then we were able to go back and provide minority access for licenses to grow cannabis, it took those multiple steps. And I am wondering why that is so concerning to you?

Dr. BURNETT. Thank you for the question.

I would say that if you actually went about the business of passing the STATES Act, you would actually create inherently more confusion inside of the marketplace than you would clarity.

Right now, just as an example for banking, right? There is actually very little problem with banks providing service to cannabis businesses, given the FinCEN guidelines that have been provided before. But banks are reluctant to do so because at the Federal level, cannabis remains on the Controlled Substances Act.

Through the STATES Act, that would still be true. There are provisions that provide some level of clarity for that, but it doesn't necessarily provide a wholesale solution for solving the problem. So we would just welcome a bit more —

Mr. GAETZ. I sense Mr. Levine is seeking an opportunity to respond to that.

Mr. LEVINE. Sure. Thank you, Congressman.

Yes, the American Bankers Association and Credit Unions Association have all endorsed the STATES Act and said that this would address banking. As somebody who is representing the industry, I can tell you that the STATES Act is clarity that we absolutely need to operate because of our tax issues, because of our banking issues. Because while we agree with the overarching goal absolutely to get to the full end of prohibition, we can't lose sight of the fact that we have over 200,000 Americans working in the industry today that are having all of these incredibly negative impacts on themselves and their families.

And so while we have something that can actually specifically address this now and help the industry get through some of these issues to resolve the conflict between Federal and State law, that does not end the conversation about what prohibition, the end of prohibition looks like. I think what we are —

Mr. GAETZ. Would you respond specifically to the assertion that the STATES Act would make things more confusing?

Mr. LEVINE. No, I think it would actually clarify it and would focus the conversation here because I have had a lot of conversation with Members of Congress and their staff, and there is a good chunk of the Congress that still isn't sure that we should legalize cannabis at all. It is not a debate about how we should do it, but there is a growing agreement that the conflict between —

Mr. GAETZ. I am going to reclaim my time because I only have about 90 seconds left. And I fear that is for all of us here gathered to move cannabis reform forward, and I am so grateful for the majority for scheduling this hearing and making this a priority. My deep concern is that concerns over how far to go on some of the restorative elements of our policy could divide our movement.

And as you have pointed out, it is already a divided Congress on this question. Though America is not divided, though America largely supports cannabis reform, Congress doesn't reflect the will of America. And so if we further divide out the movement, then I fear that we will continue to fall victim to that which has plagued other Congresses where we won't get anything done.

And Madam Chair, I know you will take great leadership in this, and so I want to take my remaining few seconds to point out a few areas of restorative justice just as categories that we might look to initially. License requirements for historically disadvantaged groups. We created minority licenses in the State of Florida to ensure that the industry better reflected the citizenry. Second, what you have heard the witnesses mention regarding plowing some of the resources generated from the industry back into the communities that have been most ravaged by the war on drugs.

But I would also highlight a third category. One of the major problems the industry has is that they are unable to take normal tax deductions. And if we were to fuse our goals on inmate reentry with restoring those tax benefits, potentially cannabis companies could earn the ability to take normal tax deductions if they hired people that were engaged in that reentry process.

Ms. BASS. Thank you.

Mr. GAETZ. I yield back.

Ms. BASS. Thank you very much.

Mr. Nadler.

Chairman NADLER. Thank you, Madam Chair.

Dr. Nathan, what advantages does cannabis have as composed to opioids as a treatment for chronic pain?

Dr. NATHAN. Thank you, Chairman Nadler, and that is a great question.

First, I should note that my father has very kindly given me permission to talk about the fact that he, too, is somebody who is using cannabis both for Parkinson's disease and for chronic pain that is a familial problem. And he has essentially discontinued his use of opioids.

Now I understand that is just a single example, but we don't need to go just by anecdote. The National Academies of Science, Engineering, and Medicine in 2017 released a comprehensive report, really a book, that is available for free online, and I encourage people to go and look for it because it outlines exactly how it is that cannabis can serve as an alternative to opioids.

It also really outlines the health effects, both positive and negative, of cannabis generally.

There are really two things I would say that make cannabis a good alternative to opioids. One is the lower potential for dependence and addiction, which is also related to a decreased level of tolerance. Opioids generally stop working in chronic use. Cannabis does not seem to have that same level of tolerance and decrease in efficacy.

So that is one advantage. The other advantage is that cannabis has fewer side effects and is nonlethal in overdose. To me, that is potentially the most important fact. Because even where opioids are prescribed properly, we still see overdose rates that contribute to what was last year over 70,000 Americans dying from opioids. Chairman NADLER. So, so in summary to this, cannabis is not— cannot be fatal in an overdose —

Dr. NATHAN. That is correct.

Chairman NADLER [continuing]. Unlike opioids. And are you saying it is not addictive, that you don't get the dependency?

Dr. NATHAN. No, there is dependency for cannabis, but it is far less than it is for opioids, for tobacco, for alcohol. The rate of dependence in adults is about 9 percent, which is similar to the rate of dependence of Americans on caffeine.

Chairman NADLER. Okay. Can you—well, it may be crazy, but it may be true.

Dr. NATHAN. Not maligning the coffee industry either.

Chairman NADLER. Can you explain how removing marijuana from the Controlled Substances Act would benefit medical research on cannabis?

Dr. NATHAN. Absolutely. See, right now, in theory it is possible to do research on cannabis with a Schedule I status with special permission from the DEA and if there is sign-off from the National Institutes for Drug Abuse and FDA. But as it stands, cannabis research simply cannot be done.

One of the honorary board members of our organization has been trying for years to do cannabis research. She has been granted a Schedule I license to do research, but when she is able to get cannabis, it is generally a very inferior quality, and the amount of THC is much closer to that of industrial hemp than it is to the kind of cannabis that is being used commonly today.

And so only by descheduling cannabis can you enable the research, both legally and also in terms of a patient's willingness to be honest with their physician about their use of cannabis when you decrease the stigma of its use by taking it off the CSA.

Chairman NADLER. Thank you.

Mr. Levine, could you explain whether or not the communities that have been harmed the most by decades of disproportionate marijuana enforcement have obtained their fair share of the benefits of marijuana legalization in the States that have legalized it?

Mr. LEVINE. I would maintain that nobody has maintained their fair share due to our taxation and the challenges that the industry faces. But no, I think that in our inception, as an industry, that the first adult use sales occurred in the beginning of January of 2014, that from the owner and the board level, we are not a very diverse industry to start.

Chairman NADLER. Thank you.

And finally, if Congress ends Federal marijuana prohibition without including provisions to help disadvantaged entrepreneurs, who will benefit the most? Small businesses who are more likely to have ties to the local economy or large businesses that are already the most advantaged to dominate the marketplace?

Mr. LEVINE. Well, we think that cannabis should be removed from the CSA entirely and agree with that point. But in regards to the STATES Act—

Chairman NADLER. Say that again.

Mr. LEVINE. We believe that it should be removed from the Controlled Substance Act entirely, and we agree with that point. In regards to the STATES Act, it would actually benefit small business owners.

The large business owners can amortize and run at very thin margins across multiple States, where small business owners under 280E, without any cogs to pack their costs back into, can't make any money. So they are all in jeopardy.

Chairman NADLER. And that would be true if Congress ends Federal marijuana prohibition or does the STATES Act, either one?

Mr. LEVINE. Yes, sir.

Chairman NADLER. Thank you. My time has expired.

Oh, Madam Chair.

Ms. BASS. Yes.

Chairman NADLER. I would like unanimous consent to enter the statement by the—statement of principles on Federal marijuana reform by the Marijuana Justice Coalition to the record.

Ms. BASS. Without objection. [The information follows:]

Statement of Principles on Federal Marijuana Reform, the Marijuana Justice Coalition

For decades, marijuana prohibition has devastated the lives of millions and disrupted the economic and social fabric of communities. The continued enforcement of marijuana prohibition laws results in over 600,000 arrests annually, disproportionately impacting people of color who are on average almost 4 times more likely to be arrested for marijuana possession than their white counterparts, despite equal rates of use across race.[125] Additionally, simple marijuana possession was the fourth most common cause of deportation for any offense and the most common cause of deportation for drug law violations.[126]

An ever-growing majority of American voters—68% percent—support marijuana legalization, according to a 2018 Center for American Progress and GBA Strategies poll.[127] Even higher, 73% of American voters support the automatic sealing of marijuana offenses.[128]

The nation has moved beyond the question of 'should we legalize marijuana?', and is now grappling with 'how do we legalize?' Thirty-three states plus the District of Columbia have adopted laws allowing legal access to medical marijuana with 10 states plus the District of Columbia allowing legal access to recreational marijuana.[129] Nationwide, the communities that have been most harmed by marijuana prohibition are benefitting the least from the legal marijuana marketplace.

Individuals who have suffered from the impact of a marijuana arrest or conviction are still languishing from the thousands of unique collateral consequences of over-enforcement of marijuana laws— collateral

---

[125] Federal Bureau of Investigations: Uniformed Crime Reporting. "2017 Crime in the United States." https://ucr.fbi.gov/crime-in-the-u.s/2017/crime-in-the-u.s.-2017/topic-pages/persons-arrested; American Civil Liberties Union. Report: The War on Marijuana in Black and White. June 2013. https://www.aclu.org/report/report-war-marijuana-black-and-white.

[126] Drug Policy Alliance. The Drug War and Mass Deportation. February 2016. https://www.drugpolicy.org/sites/default/files/DPA%20Fact%20Sheet_The%20Drug%20War%20 and%20Mass%20Deportation_%28Feb.%202016%29.pdf.

[127] Center for American Progress. Voters Across Party Line Support Clean Slate Legislation. https://www.americanprogress.org/issues/criminal-justice/news/2018/06/20/451624/ voters-across-party-lines-support-clean-slate-legislation/.

[128] Center for American Progress. Voters Across Party Line Support Clean Slate Legislation. https://www.americanprogress.org/issues/criminal-justice/news/2018/06/20/451624/ voters-across-party-lines-support-clean-slate-legislation/.

[129] National Organization for the reform of Marijuana Laws. "State Laws: Medical Marijuana" https://norml.org/legal/medical-marijuana-2; Leafly. "Where is Cannabis Legal?" https://www.leafly.com/news/cannabis-101/medical-recreational-cannabis-legal-states.

consequences that include difficulty securing or maintaining employment, housing, federal financial aid, nutritional assistance, the ability to vote, a valid driver's license, and harsh immigration-related consequences for noncitizens.[130]

Despite the fact that the harms of marijuana prohibition have not been borne equally across the nation and across specific populations, people of color are woefully underrepresented in the marijuana industry.[131] Historically disproportionate and racially biased arrests and convictions make it particularly difficult for Black and Brown people to enter the legal marijuana marketplace, as most states bar these individuals from participating because of their record. The Administration recently threatened that it will deny naturalization to lawful permanent residents, the great majority of whom are people of color, if they are employed in the industry.[132] Other barriers include exorbitant licensing fees and the need for large amounts of capital before gaining a license.

Ending prohibition on the federal level presents a unique and desperately needed opportunity to rightfully frame legalization as an issue of criminal justice reform, equity, racial justice, economic justice, and empowerment, particularly for communities most targeted by over-enforcement of marijuana laws.

As Congress considers the end of marijuana prohibition, the Marijuana Justice Coalition believes that any legislation that moves forward in Congress should be comprehensive. The provisions set forth below are agreed upon by the undersigned criminal justice, drug policy, civil rights, and anti-poverty groups as principles that should be considered as a part of any moving marijuana reform efforts in Congress:

---

[130] Berson, Sarah. National Institute of Justice. "Beyond the Sentence – Understanding Collateral Consequences." https://www.nij.gov/journals/272/Pages/collateral-consequences.aspx.

[131] Clarke, Kristen. USA Today. "Cannabis industry shouldn't expand until we fix marijuana's racial inequities, injustices." https://www.usatoday.com/story/opinion/2019/02/22/marijuana-legalization-exposes-cannabis-industry-racial-injustice-incarceration-minorities-column/2836449002/.

[132] Amendment effective April 19, 2019 to United States Customs and Immigration Services Policy Manual, Volume 12, Chapter 5, Part C.2, at https://www.uscis.gov/policy-manual/volume-12-part-f-chapter-5, effective April 19, 2019 ("[C]certain conduct involving marijuana, which is in violation of the CSA, continues to constitute a conditional bar to GMC for naturalization eligibility, even where such activity is not a criminal offense under state law … For example, possession of marijuana for recreational or medical purposes or employment in the marijuana industry may constitute conduct that violates federal controlled substance laws").

- Descheduling marijuana, as maintaining marijuana on the Controlled Substances Act serves to preserve federal criminalization and enforcement.
- Criminal justice reform provisions (e.g., expungement, resentencing).
- Provisions eliminating barriers to access to public benefits (e.g., nutrition assistance, public housing, etc.) and other collateral consequences related to an individual's marijuana use or previous arrest or conviction.
- Provisions eliminating unnecessarily discriminatory elements for marijuana use, arrests and convictions, including drug testing for public benefits or marijuana use as a reason for separating children from their biological families in the child welfare system.[133]
- Provisions that ensure that marijuana use or participation in the marijuana industry does not impact the immigration status of noncitizens nor their ability to naturalize.
- Marijuana tax revenue be directed to local units of government and community-based organizations to reinvest in individuals and communities most impacted by the war on drugs, particularly through programming that helps eliminate the collateral harms of marijuana prohibition, especially for individuals with systemic and structural barriers to employment and/or living in high-poverty communities.
- Marijuana tax revenue be directed to support entrepreneurs from communities directly impacted by the war on drugs with a process to provide them with the requisite capital to develop cannabis businesses, and encourage emerging licensing programs to be inclusive and reflective of their communities.

Signed by the members of the Marijuana Justice Coalition:

ACLU; Center for American Progress; Center for Law and Social Policy; Drug Policy Alliance; Human Rights Watch, Immigrant Legal Resource Center; Leadership Conference on Civil & Human Rights; NORML; Students for Sensible Drug Policy; Washington Lawyers Committee for Civil Rights and Urban Affairs

[133] Emma Ketteringham. New York Daily News. "Families torn apart over pot: As N.Y. moves to legalize marijuana, it must fix agonizing disparities that take children from black and brown mothers and fathers." https://www.nydailynews.com/opinion/ny-oped-families-ripped-apart-over-pot-20190508-qtrnmuyztzfr7let4vxjxga7zm-story.html.

* * *

Chairman NADLER. Thank you.

Ms. BASS. Mr. McClintock.

Mr. MCCLINTOCK. Thank you, Madam Chairman.

Mr. Levine, I mentioned Louis Brandeis' approach, States being laboratories. They experiment. We can all benefit from the results of the experiment. Could you briefly summarize the good and the bad that a State like Colorado has discovered as they legalized marijuana?

Mr. LEVINE. Yes. Well, the sky has not fallen. We have seen in Colorado, per the question Chair Bass was asking before, that arrest rates have fallen in Colorado since legalization, about 50 percent for African Americans, 50 percent overall. But the—

Mr. MCCLINTOCK. We keep hearing youth usage is up. Traffic accidents are up.

Mr. LEVINE. Teen usage is down. There is no statistical that— to my knowledge, there is nothing that shows in a statistically viable way that there has been any change in traffic accidents per—

Mr. MCCLINTOCK. What I had heard was that traffic accidents involving marijuana have gone up. But at the same time, traffic accidents involving alcohol have gone down, and the fatality rate has gone down because people who are driving under the influence of marijuana apparently tend to drive a little slower.

Mr. LEVINE. Well, not to get to wonky about it, but alcohol is water soluble, and cannabis is fat soluble. So it stays in your system for up to 30 days, and they weren't testing for it before. So the State of Colorado, CDOT started actually testing for cannabis after legalization.

So while you see an increase in the number, that doesn't necessarily mean that there has been an increase of people driving impaired. There might be an increase in people using cannabis because it is legal, but use does not mean impairment.

Mr. MCCLINTOCK. And you say that youth usage is actually down?

Mr. LEVINE. Teen usage is down.

Mr. MCCLINTOCK. Okay. And that is because the dealers are now carding them?

Mr. LEVINE. It is a factor. It is a number of factors. You have to be 21 years of age or older to enter any of our establishments. There is multiple identification checks. Your entire license is on the line if you sell or divert cannabis to a minor.

So regulation works better than prohibition, and we are seeing these impacts. But part of the issue is where you have got States that have full prohibition that border a State that doesn't have prohibition, you are running into some of these issues. So we do agree that cannabis should be removed from the Controlled Substance Act entirely. But in the interim, we have some real-world issues —

Mr. MCCLINTOCK. That is my next question is one of the things we hear from States that have prohibition is we are seeing all this marijuana coming in from the bordering State where it is legalized, and that is causing problems in our State. What role do you see the Federal Government involved in interstate commerce between States where it is legalized and States where it is still prohibited?

Mr. LEVINE. So to your earlier point, Congressman, the people have spoken. We have 33 States, plus the District of Columbia, plus the multiple territories that have opted out of prohibition in some form, 11 plus the District of Columbia and 2 territories that opted out entirely. And—

Mr. MCCLINTOCK. Do you dispute the prerogative of a State if its voters would like to keep it prohibited? States should be allowed to keep it prohibited?

Mr. LEVINE. Because of the inertia of Congress on cannabis policy reform, what we have seen here is that States have led because the people of the States have said that they want to do this. So, and a lot of that have been in ballot initiative States. And I think in a lot of these border States, if you take a look at the polling, that the vast majority of Americans want to see cannabis prohibition end. So I honestly think it is a little bit of a situation of maybe the people being ahead of their elected officials.

But yes, I believe that this is the issue—

Mr. MCCLINTOCK. Well, that may be. But if a State legislature elected by the people decides to keep it prohibited, do you have any problem with that?

Mr. LEVINE. This is a—

Mr. MCCLINTOCK. I mean, as a policy issue, they may be making a mistake, but do you dispute their right to make that mistake?

Mr. LEVINE. We support their right to opt out of prohibition until the Federal Government acts for sure.

Mr. MCCLINTOCK. All right. One concern I have is on the over taxation of marijuana. It is looked upon in some sectors of government as a tremendous cash cow. I mean, the profit margins are huge. Well, the reason the profit margins are huge is because our laws have terribly constricted competition.

As competition enters the marketplace, you are going to see those profit margins drop dramatically.

My concern is looking at the industry as a cash cow and applying all sorts of exorbitant taxes upon it is the same effect as prohibition. It will drive what should be legal commerce back into a violent underground economy. Are you concerned about that?

Mr. LEVINE. Very concerned about that. Our main competition are the criminal markets right now. And so these State-based laws, what they are doing is we are taking commerce out of the criminal markets and putting them to regulated and taxed markets. So the more tax, the higher the tax, the more restriction, the more regulation you place on that for the products that you ban from that, you are ceding those products to the criminal markets.

So regulation works better than prohibition, and we would like to see regulation nationwide. In the interim, we would like to see the Federal Government stop interfering with the State laws.

Mr. MCCLINTOCK. Thank you very much.

Ms. BASS. Ms. Jackson Lee.

Ms. JACKSON LEE. Thank you. Thank you to all the witnesses for your presence here today.

And as I was delayed, I managed to hear some of the discussion—delayed in the Homeland Security Committee, but I am very interested in the work that has been done by State's attorney in Baltimore City. We are certainly trying to work in the State of Texas without having the marijuana laws removed—marijuana removed from the Controlled Substance, but trying to on a county by county to be more reflective of dealing with simple possession by way of misdemeanor and/or citation.

So let me hear again, if I could, and I know that you have given it in your testimony, you have heard some of the commentary about the idea that taxation may shove some of the market into the underground. But let me hear directly from you on the issue of mass incarceration and what you have seen in your utilization of restorative justice.

And might I thank you for your leadership and your work.

Ms. MOSBY. Thank you. Thank you. And I would just say that, unfortunately, as a prosecutor in the City of Baltimore, it is incumbent on me to not just look at the laws and consider safety, but to understand that in the administration of justice, I have to pursue those wrongs and right those wrongs of the past, right?

And so what we have been able to see in Baltimore is that there has been discriminatory enforcement in the application of marijuana laws. And what I have done in utilizing my discretion as a prosecutor, in light of the fact that the legislature is considering the decriminalization/legalization of marijuana and have not yet acted, is that because of this discriminatory enforcement, because there is no public safety value, because there is—it is counter-productive to the limited resources that we have, is to utilize my discretion to say we are not prosecuting possession of marijuana cases in the City of Baltimore. And the reason why is because of those reasons, right?

And so what we have seen, unfortunately, is because of that discriminatory sort of enforcement, it has eroded public trust among—

Ms. JACKSON LEE. What has been the impact of your changes?

Ms. MOSBY. So what I can say is that, you know, the number of marijuana possession cases do not at this appear—I made the announcement in January, right? But the police department was not—did not agree with my decision initially.

And I can say that looking at the numbers, they have decreased the number of possession—of arrests that they are making.

I have made it very clear that, you know, as the State's attorney, I can never be complicit in discriminatory enforcement of laws against poor or discriminatory enforcement of laws against poor black and brown people—

Ms. JACKSON LEE. So it would help your work if this was removed federally from the Controlled Substance Act?

Ms. MOSBY. It would absolutely help my work because it would encourage the States to act. As I stated, this is something that they are considering that they have not yet done.

And the other thing that I think is also incredibly important and one that I would like to highlight just with the States—

Ms. JACKSON LEE. My time is short.

Ms. MOSBY. Oh, I apologize. I apologize.

Ms. JACKSON LEE. Do you want to just do 2 seconds and finish your sentence?

Ms. MOSBY. Is that the need to reinvest into those individuals and those communities that have been disproportionately impacted.

The STATES Act does not do that, and that is one of the reasons why I am opposed to it. We attempted to vacate—

Ms. JACKSON LEE. So we need new legislation that would reflect that concept of being able to be part of restorative justice?

Ms. MOSBY. Absolutely.

Ms. JACKSON LEE. Dr. Burnett, and then I want to ask Dr. Nathan, if I might. Dr. Burnett, can you talk about the value of having a community that has been—the material, the raw material for mass incarceration moved to a level of economic empowerment, but also restorative justice. Because we are still looking at—I don't know if someone has had a misdemeanor on marijuana and then they want to go into a business, I think that is something that we have to look at.

Dr. BURNETT. Right.

Ms. JACKSON LEE. And then, Dr. Nathan, again I think it is important. You made an important point about tobacco. But your question from me would be the impact on children. You decriminalize it. It is off the Controlled Substance. Is there greater access? And I would be interested in that.

So I have a short period of time, if you would answer, and then Dr. Nathan.

Dr. BURNETT. Sure. Really quickly, it is important that, you know, as we go about reforming cannabis laws that we actually ensure that the people who were historically criminalized have an opportunity to now participate in the economic opportunity. They can start local businesses in their local communities.

In all honesty, that is what they were doing before because they were shut out from being able to participate in a normal economy. And so being able to do that now with this new market is important.

Ms. JACKSON LEE. Thank you.

Dr. Nathan. And I would say that if you had a misdemeanor offense that you should not be barred from being able to participate.

Dr. BURNETT. Absolutely.

Ms. JACKSON LEE. Dr. Nathan.

Dr. NATHAN. Thank you, Congresswoman Jackson Lee.

You are asking about increased access for underage—potential underage users. I certainly share that concern. I have an 18-year-old and a 15-year-old, and in the 10 years that I have been working on this issue advocating, I have myself been very concerned about it. And of course, my concern is not just a personal one, but a professional one.

And reputationally, you know, I was holding my breath to see what was happening in the legalized States. And what we are seeing is seems to reflect decreased access. And this is actually the conclusion that was drawn in an article that just came out in JAMA Pediatrics, an esteemed journal, where they are looking at medical and recreational legalization. And what they are seeing is that to a degree, medical and especially in recreationally legal States, adult use States, that underage access appears to be going down.

And that is reflected in decreasing numbers of underage users, especially in the youngest and most vulnerable age range of 12 to 17 years old.

Ms. BASS. Thank you.

Ms. JACKSON LEE. Thank you.

Ms. BASS. Mr. Steube.

Mr. STEUBE. Thank you, Madam Chair.

Representative Gaetz and I were very involved in the legislation in Florida. I was in the State House and the State Senate and dealt with it in both chambers. And here are the two main challenges that Florida faces as it relates to we have medicinal marijuana through a ballot initiative.

We tried—well, I tried. I filed a bill in the House so that the legislature would have control over it because I thought that that was the best place statutorily that we could modify it and change it as we saw challenges with businesses and so on and so forth. But that never passed, and so there was a ballot initiative.

So now people in Florida have a constitutional right to medicinal marijuana, which I think causes other challenges from the legal spectrum. But here are the two challenges from a practicality standpoint that we face in Florida right now.

Number one is those that have a—and I can't say a prescription, but a recommendation for medicinal marijuana in Florida and working at, say, an air conditioning company or working heavy machinery or working on things that are dangerous implements or driving, the challenges is, as has been stated, is you can't test if the individual is under the influence at the time because marijuana stays in your body for 30 days.

That is the challenges that small businesses in Florida are facing right now. So I would ask Mr. Levine if there is a way, if there is some work that we can do as it relates to that? And then I will get to my second issue that is facing Florida.

Mr. LEVINE. So the question was specifically about people being barred from—

Mr. STEUBE. They are not barred because they have a medicinal use for it. The challenge is, is I have got—and I will give you an exact example. Just in the district a couple of weeks ago, I have an individual who is a friend of mine who owns an air conditioning company. So he obviously has a number of employees who are driving around his vehicles every day who may have a recommendation for medicinal marijuana but may also be under the influence of marijuana at the time that they are operating his vehicles that he is liable for.

Mr. LEVINE. Right.

Mr. STEUBE. Those are the challenges that we face in Florida, and I supported the bill. I support people being able to use it for medicinal purposes in Florida. But that is the challenge from a practicality standpoint that we face.

Is there a way that we as a State or country can try to address that specific issue for those that own small businesses that are hiring these individuals who may be under the influence while they are working?

Mr. LEVINE. Yes. So no one should drive impaired under any controlled substance, and we certainly don't support that. And when it comes to cannabis, use doesn't mean impairment. So you can detect it in your body.

So as an employer, nobody should be driving a vehicle or using any critical piece of equipment while they are impaired. And we need—as was said earlier, we need better testing. There is no "per se" test that currently exists to actually show impairment. And not look at metabolites because marijuana can stay in your system for up to a month, but actually look at levels of impairment.

Mr. STEUBE. Okay. The other big issue that we face in Florida is obviously something that has also been illustrated as it relates to the banking industry and the Federal laws as it relates to, you know, having all this money and all this going back and forth through the process.

I know that the STATES Act and discussion that Representative Gaetz and I just had doesn't address the "decriminalization" or the move from Schedule I to, say, a Schedule III. Would you support moving marijuana from a Schedule I to a Schedule III, and would that solve the problem that banks such in Florida are facing as it relates to medicinal marijuana?

Mr. LEVINE. It wouldn't solve banking. It would solve our 280E tax issue. We are in favor of cannabis being removed from the Controlled Substance Act entirely. But the STATES Act does for State-licensed businesses, their employees, their consumers, that all of that is removed from the Controlled Substance Act in the State system.

If you are not violating State law, you would no longer be violating Federal law. It just pulls the Federal Government out.

Mr. STEUBE. And I would support that moving from a Schedule I to Schedule III. I would encourage any of my colleagues that are interested on this issue. I know there was a bill filed last Congress. There doesn't appear to be one filed now.

I would love to work with any of those on the other side of the aisle to move that issue forward. And if you guys support that, I would be happy to work with you on that moving forward.

That is all the questions that I had. I yield the balance of my time to the ranking member.

Ms. BASS. Thank you. Mrs. McBath.

Mrs. MCBATH.

Thank you, Madam Chair.

And thank each of you for being here today with your expert— your expertise, sharing that with us.

As you may know, Georgia has taken measured and bipartisan approach and with respect to marijuana. 2015 then-Governor Nathan Deal signed a law allowing those with certain medical needs to possess cannabis oil. But legal access was still difficult since buying, selling, and transporting cannabis oil remained illegal until just a few months ago.

In April of this year, the legislature passed a law that will finally ensure a legal supply of cannabis oil for patients seeking to alleviate the effects of cancer, Parkinson's disease, and seizures. However, even these modest bipartisan efforts are at odds with Federal law that still impose a steep penalty even for the low THC cannabis oil legalized in Georgia.

With respect to criminal justice reform, Georgia has a similar pattern. Governor Deal led bipartisan efforts to reduce recidivism and keep nonviolent individuals out of the criminal justice system. Governor Deal's bipartisan reforms are saving Georgia taxpayers millions of dollars, and it is also just the right thing to do.

A major piece of these reforms are drug courts that find a better resolution to nonviolent marijuana offenses. Collectively, these reforms have begun to reduce the racial inequality in Georgia's criminal justice system. But here again, harsh Federal penalties for marijuana possession stand in sharp contrast from Georgia's efforts to do what is right for the people of Georgia, even when there is a bipartisan consensus.

Dr. Nathan, my question—I actually have two questions for you. How would Federal marijuana decriminalization enable doctors to better help patients in States like Georgia that allow cannabis for medical treatment?

Dr. NATHAN. In the answer to that question—and thank you, Congresswoman McBath—what you are alluding to is actually quite, quite noteworthy, which is that the Federal Government really needs to decriminalize. It doesn't itself need to legalize it. That is for the States, but to take it off of the Controlled Substances Act is to—is to expand by orders of magnitude patient access to cannabis, and it also has the effect of reducing stigma to individuals who want to use it.

It enables research. It enables honest discussions between doc- tors and patients about their cannabis use and their potential misuse of it. And it also puts it on a more level playing field with much more dangerous drugs for which it can act as a good substitute for medical use.

Mrs. MCBATH. Thank you.

My second question will be while Georgia has actually recognized the medical benefits of marijuana for certain patients, there are still concerns about the unintended consequences. A recent peer-reviewed study showed that in States with medical cannabis laws saw an increase in the cases or number of cases of opiate abuse addiction and overdose death. Can you address that concern for us?

Dr. NATHAN. Absolutely. Yes, and that is a recent article that you are referring to that came out that in its conclusion was saying that it contradicted earlier findings that showed an actual decrease in use.

But that study actually was much more inclusive of the definition of what a medically legalized State is. And what you were talking about earlier is important that it is not enough to legalize medical cannabis or cannabis oil or CBD. The benefits of cannabis legalization only occur in the States where they have actually implemented the program and where people can access it legally because it can be legal at the State level, and if there is no legal access, then patients really aren't seeing the benefit.

So where you see the rate of opioid use go down, and that is a 25 percent decrease in opioid overdoses, which can save tens of thousands of lives every year, that is only in States that have legal dispensaries. The study that you are referring to counted States that don't have a rolled out program for medical cannabis yet, that have just nominally legalized, and States for which only CBD is legal. And that, of course, is not the same thing as full-spectrum cannabis oil.

Mrs. MCBATH. Okay, thank you.

And Ms. Mosby, I have one question for you. How can Federal decriminalization of marijuana empower States to pursue criminal justice reforms that save money and align with local values?

Ms. MOSBY. So I would say that right now when we look at what we are spending just in the enforcement of marijuana laws federally, it is about $4 billion, right? If we were to actually utilize the incentive, the financial economic incentives that we use in the creation of these task forces that we once put into play that were enforcing these discriminatory laws, if we were to implement those resources and to utilize those resources for community investment.

Some of the things that we can do just in righting the wrongs of the past is to ensure that States are following or encouraging States to or incentivizing States to implement mass expungement, reentry services for formerly incarcerated individuals. There are a number of harm reduction strategies and models that we can employ that would create incentives for States to follow the Federal sort of rule and to provide and get the funding from the Federal Government.

Ms. BASS. Thank you. Mr. Cline.

Mr. CLINE. Thank you, Madam Chairman, for holding this hearing.

In Virginia, we have had similar circumstances as was shown in Georgia, and I took action similar to what we have seen in Georgia. So I appreciate the gentlelady's comments.

Studies have shown that cannabinoids have therapeutic effects in treating conditions such as chronic pain, nausea, symptoms from conditions such as multiple sclerosis and HIV-AIDS. As a former member of the Virginia House of Delegates, I introduced legislation to allow physicians to recommend cannabinoid oil to their patients, to create legal dispensaries, and to create an affirmative defense to possession of cannabinoid oil for medicinal use.

This non-hallucinogenic derivative can be given in drop form to help people suffering from a variety of debilitating medical conditions. And as we have witnessed the opioid crisis ravage rural America, I believe it is important to find alternatives for addictive painkillers, and I was surprised to hear of this study and do think it is counter to what we have seen from a lot of different studies related to the use of cannabinoids as a replacement for opiates.

As States have made changes to their own marijuana laws, conflicting policies from various administrations has placed a burden on law enforcement in States as they implement reforms. Congress must find a solution to alleviate the conflicts between State and Federal marijuana laws, and it is important to evaluate the role that the Federal Government should play when it comes to the regulation of marijuana.

The STATES Act is a promising step forward in giving States flexibility in addressing many of these issues. And furthermore, I am interested in reviewing ways to reclassify marijuana to a more appropriate classification in the Federal drug schedule.

In the meantime, however, we have Article VI of the U.S. Constitution. And in light of that, I would ask Mr. Levine how do you reconcile the actions of States like Colorado with Article VI?

Mr. LEVINE. Well, the only preemption action I am aware of didn't go through in the courts, which was the State of Arizona, I believe. And obviously, through the Tenth Amendment of the Constitution, the powers are not derived specifically to the Federal Government and reserved for the States. We now have 33 States plus the District of Columbia and multiple territories that have opted out of prohibition in some form, and these systems, outside of the conflict that we have with Federal and State laws —

Mr. CLINE. Does the Federal law give the States the right to opt out?

Mr. LEVINE. The power to prohibit cannabis is not enumerated in the Constitution.

Mr. CLINE. But it is a Federal law?

Mr. LEVINE. Yes, sir.

Mr. CLINE. And Article VI clarifies that Federal law is superior to State law?

Mr. LEVINE. Yes, sir.

Mr. CLINE. Okay. So your proposal then is to remove the Federal law completely?

Mr. LEVINE. No, the STATES Act would amend the Controlled Substance Act to say that if you are in compliance with State law, you would not be in violation of Federal law.

Mr. CLINE. Right. So you support the STATES Act, but you also support going further and removing it from classification altogether?

Mr. LEVINE. Yes. So we support Congress removing cannabis from the Controlled Substance Act entirely.

Mr. CLINE. Okay. Mr. Nathan, there is evidence legalization of marijuana has led to increased unintended exposure among young children. By 2011, rates of poison center calls for accidental pediatric marijuana ingestion has more than tripled in States that decriminalized marijuana before 2005. Have you seen youth access to marijuana increase as a result of legalization efforts?

I know Mr. Levine did mention teen rate is down. What about rates of accidental ingestion among children?

Dr. NATHAN. A great question—and thank you, Congressman Cline—because you are illustrating that there are two different issues here. One is the intentional use by teens and maybe older children, and then the unintentional ingestion not just by children, but also you have heard by pets. And indeed, those numbers have gone up in legalized States.

Now you have to remember that, first of all, that cannabis is not a drug that is lethal in overdose. So as scary and as unpleasant as an accidental ingestion may be, it is nothing compared to the countless household chemicals and other medications that kids can take that would, indeed, cause death.

I believe that all households that have any dangerous substances that can be contained should be contained in a drug safe, and then I think you will see a benefit. But also consider that in the legalized States, you actually have the ability to regulate the packaging to ensure that the packaging is more child-resistant. You don't see that in other States.

And there is actually a key factor that—well, two things. One is that the rate of accidental ingestion, though it has gone up quite a bit, is still a very small number compared to the ingestion of other chemicals and other drugs. And there is data to support that.

And the other point is that with the legal status of cannabis changing, families are much more comfortable bringing their young child or their pet to get some kind of help if there has been an accidental ingestion because there is no longer the fear of the criminalization and the stigma of them having had the drug in the household at the first place. So in a sense, that is a good thing that families would feel comfortable bringing their children to the emergency room in a legalized State.

Ms. BASS. Mr. Deutch.

Mr. DEUTCH. Thank you, Madam Chair.

I would like, first of all, to ask unanimous consent to enter for the record a statement from Randal Meyer, executive director of the Global Alliance for Cannabis Commerce, entitled "Racial Justice and Cannabis Prohibition and the Federal Role in the New Global Cannabis Economy."

Thank you, Madam Chair.

Ms. BASS. Without objection.

[The information follows:]

Racial Justice in Cannabis Prohibition and the Federal Role in the New Global Cannabis Economy, Testimony Submitted to the Committee on the Judiciary Subcommittee on Subcommittee on Crime, Terrorism, and Homeland Security, for the Hearing on "Marijuana Laws in America: Racial Justice and the Need for Reform"

By Randal John Meyer,
Executive Director of the Global Alliance for Cannabis Commerce

Chairwoman Bass and members of the Subcommittee on Crime, Terrorism, and Homeland Security, thank you for hosting this hearing on the pressing issues of racial justice and the need for reform in federal cannabis laws. The Global Alliance for Cannabis Commerce is honored to offer its testimony on these matters today.

The Global Alliance for Cannabis Commerce (GACC) is a California-based 501(c)(6) trade organization representing over a billion dollars of legal global cannabis businesses. GACC advocates in front of government policymakers and legislators to support legalizing and regulating the cultivation, manufacture, distribution, and use of medical and adult-use cannabis products globally. GACC further works to ensure that medical and adult users of cannabis are not improperly stigmatized for their ordinary needs and activities.

GACC members believe that it is impossible to talk about the inevitable end of federal cannabis prohibition without discussing a way to rectify the issues that cannabis prohibition has caused in American society. Indeed, it is our organization's Corporate Social Responsibility position that "it is the specific responsibility of the cannabis industry to support legislation and other measures to mitigate and compensate those most harmed by" cannabis prohibition.

Federal cannabis prohibition began in 1937 with the passage of the Marihuana Tax Act of 1937,[134] a federal law that was unanimously overturned by the Supreme Court in 1969 in *Leary v. United States* for requiring self-crimination under the Fifth Amendment—famously, hemp farmers had to bring their crop for inspection to D.C. to receive a license, only to be arrested upon presenting their crop for transporting "marihuana" in interstate commerce.[135]

The 1937 Act was passed over the objections of the American Medical Association and effectively de-listed cannabis from the *United States Pharmacopeia*, in which it had been listed since 1870.[136] Cannabis had, before 1937, been regulated as a drug in interstate commerce under the 1906 Pure Food and Drug Act and Harrison Narcotics Act of 1914.[137] As a consequence

[134] Marihuana Tax Act of 1937, Pub. L. 75-238, 50 Stat. 551 (Aug. 2, 1937).

[135] Leary v. United States, 395 U.S. 6, 17 (1969).

[136] *See,* e.g., Pharmecopœia of the United States (5th Decennial Rev., Philadelphia, J.B. Lippincott & Co. 1877); Pharmecopœia of the United States (11th Decennial Rev., Philadelphia, J.B. Lippincott & Co. 1936).

[137] *See* Harrison Narcotics Act, Pub. L. No. 223, 38 Stat. 785 (Dec. 17, 1914). Pub. L. 59-384, 34 Stat. 768 (June 30, 1906).

of the 1937 law, cannabis was excluded from the 1938 Food, Drug, and Cosmetic Act's regulatory scheme.

Cannabis prohibition took hold in 1937 on the heels of a propaganda campaign engineered by the Federal Bureau of Narcotics under Harry J. Anslinger and William Randolph Hearst's media empire, and aggrandized by media outlets jumping in on the "marihuana" frenzy.[138]

In response to the unanimous 1969 *Leary* decision striking down federal cannabis prohibition, in 1970 Congress passed and President Richard M. Nixon signed into law the Controlled Substances Act.[139] The Controlled Substances Act listed, and to this day lists cannabis as "marihuana," a Schedule I Controlled Substance, the most restrictive designation possible, and creates a nationwide cannabis prohibition.[140]

Members of Congress, in thinking about this history, should be cognizant that the federal government's agents in conducting their anti-cannabis propaganda campaign in the 1930s expressly linked the "'evil'" of cannabis to crime committed by "'Mexicans, Spaniards, Latin-Americans, Greeks, or Negroes'" in order to tie this lobbying effort to the racial tensions of the period—in government-printed public documents and in government-funded projects.[141] Federal cannabis prohibition was born in facial racism. Whatever one feels about the merits of cannabis legalization or federal drug policy in general today, that is a historical fact, and one Americans must confront as we work towards ending this misguided policy in recognizing its roots in deeply flawed public consensus. As one may predict of a policy born in demonstrable, facial government discrimination, it has effects which disproportionately harm those targeted by its original propaganda campaign. The American Civil Liberties Union has pointed out, statistically speaking "Blacks are 3.73 times

---

[138] *E.g.*, Richard J. Bonnie & Charles H. Whitehead, The Marihuana Conviction: A History of Marijuana Prohibition in the United States 100–02 (University Press of Virginia 1974).

[139] *See* Controlled Substances Act, Pub. L. 91-513, 84 Stat. 1236 (Oct. 27, 1970) (codified at 21 U.S.C. ch. 13).

[140] 21 U.S.C. §§ 802(16), 812; *see also generally Gonzales v. Raich*, 545 U.S. 1 (2005).

[141] BONNIE & WHITEHEAD, supra note 5, at 100 (discussing correspondence with and quoting an official Federal Bureau of Narcotics response to a reporter inquiry); *see also* Kyle Schmidlin, Column: 'War On Drugs' Merely Fights The Symptoms Of A Faulty System, *CBS News* (Sept. 13, 2008, 7:19am), https://www.cbsnews.com/news/column-war-on-drugs-merely-fights-the-symptoms-of-a-faulty-system/ ("Quotes attributable to [Commissioner] Anslinger include (and there are certainly more than these): 'Reefer makes darkies think they're as good as white men.' 'You smoke a joint and you're likely to kill your brother.' And my personal favorite, 'There are 100,000 total marijuana smokers in the U.S., and most are Negroes, Hispanics, Filipinos and entertainers. Their Satanic music, jazz and swing result from marijuana use. This marijuana causes white women to seek sexual relations with Negroes, entertainers and any others'").

more likely than whites to be arrested for marijuana."[142] This has led to higher incarceration rates for minorities for cannabis offenses.

The need for reform is clear. Thirty-four states allow and regulate medical-use cannabis; eleven more do so with adult use—numbers only expected to increase heading into 2020 based on polling data and political trends. The federal government's prohibitionist stance on cannabis is no longer a tenable position. The question now is not *if* reform will happen federally, but *how*.

Both parties should be congratulated and encouraged for their good-faith efforts in reaching bipartisan consensus on how to handle remedying those harms. In order to assist in those efforts, the Global Alliance for Cannabis Commerce has publicly released model U.S. federal cannabis legislation that comprehensively and wholly addresses how to regulate cannabis on a federal level, including components to ensure that communities disproportionately harmed by prohibition are not left out from the economic opportunities presented by its legalization.[143] GACC's model legislation takes from some of the best practices that have strong bipartisan support from proposals currently underway. It also adds to them by directing the Attorney General to individually review each and every federal marijuana conviction where the offender is currently serving and recommending action on clemency or pardon to the President.

True reform for the existing businesses in 33 states, the District of Columbia and communities of color means a framework that does not unnecessarily wreak havoc on existing relationships and business practices, and that adopts bipartisan best practices towards fixing the harms of cannabis prohibition, and that employs the constitutional powers of the federal government to ensure a functional, free, and fair market in cannabis. Improvident or ill-considered federal policy in legalizing cannabis can have dire, if unintended, consequences for minority-owned and non-minority-owned businesses alike.

The *sine qua non* of what industry and consumers need from the federal government for cannabis reform is clear: legalize and regulate interstate and international trade in cannabis products under its Article I, Section 8 Commerce Clause powers. In doing so, Congress could respect both the state

---

[142] American Civil Liberties Union, *Marijuana Arrests By the Numbers*, https://www.aclu.org/gallery/marijuana-arrests-numbers.

[143] *See generally* Model U.S. Federal Cannabis Reform Act (GACC 2019), *reprinted in* Appendix A; Appendix B (Section by Section of GACC Model Legislation).

right to choose to keep cannabis prohibited within its borders, and the state right to interstate trade of the thirty-four other states that legalized cannabis.

Right now, there are thirty-four balkanized legal state markets in the United States in cannabis. As Ilya Shapiro, Director of the Robert A. Levy Center for Constitutional Studies at the Cato Institute pointed out in his article *The Case for Allowing Interstate Trade Among Marijuana-Legal States*, "[b]y default, to succeed, any business has to be vertically integrated from seed to sale in each state. This limits competition and artificially inflates prices. Consumers, particularly elderly patients, many of whom rely on cannabis products to mitigate health concerns, will be at the mercy of businesses that don't have to respond to market forces."[144]

This balkanization has also lead to incredible supply-demand imbalances within the United States itself, threatening state-based cannabis markets, and remediable only by the federal government exercising its commerce powers. For example, on the supply side, according to a 2019 Cannabis crop projection, California cultivators "can produce up to 9 million pounds of crop every year, but the permitted wholesale market can realistically support 1.8 million to 2.2 million pounds," which potentially crash the market" in California.[145] Oregon has six-years' worth of stock,[146] and the state government has approved legislation for interstate commerce that only becomes effective upon only federal reform.[147]

Conversely, on the demand side, Canadian dispensaries continuously see shortages that could easily be filled by reducing excess West Coast stock.[148] Nevada has seen shortages as well.[149] Louisiana pharmacists—complaining of

---

[144] Ilya Shapiro, The Case for Allowing Interstate Trade Among Marijuana-Legal States, *The Federalist* (Mar. 13, 2019), https://thefederalist.com/2019/03/13/case-allowing-interstate-trade-among-marijuana-legal-states/, *reprinted in* Appendix C.

[145] Andrew Sheeler, California is growing so much marijuana it could crash the market, *Sacremento Bee* (Mar. 19, 2019 11:04am), https://www.sacbee.com/news/politics-government/capitol-alert/article228120439.html.

[146] Kristian Foden-Vencil, Oregon Is Producing Twice As Much Cannabis As People Are Using, *OPB* (Jan. 31, 2019, 12:00pm), https://www.opb.org/news/article/oregon-cannabis-surplus-2019/.

[147] S.B. 582, 80th Leg. Assemb., Reg. Sess. (Or. 2019); Suhauna Hussain, Oregon has too much cannabis. Two laws may help the state manage its surplus, *L.A. Times* (June 24, 2019, 3:00am), https://www.latimes.com/nation/la-na-oregon-legislature-tackles-supply-marijuana-20190624-story.html.

[148] *E.g.*, Paul Barach, What's Up With Canada's Nationwide Cannabis Shortages? *PotGuide.com* (Dec. 26, 2018), https://potguide.com/pot-guide-marijuana-news/article/whats-up-with-canadas-nationwide-cannabis-shortages/.

[149] *E.g.*, Melina Robinson, Nevada sold out of legal marijuana so quickly, the government used a 'statement of emergency' to bring in more weed, *Business Insider* (Jul. 13, 2017, 9:21pm),

watching "patients suffer…desperate for [cannabis] medication"— demanded their state allow medical cannabis to be available.[150] Illinois, the latest state to legalize, also is projected to face shortages for consumers.[151]

Legal operators in states operate without the benefits of federal regulation in the areas of agriculture, pesticide control, food and drug adulteration, and finance— areas where federal regulatory clarity has been a chief component of consumer confidence and commercial success. Without federal legalization and regulation, it is unlikely that legal businesses will be able to fully access the financial sector. As Dan Stipano recently told *American Banker*, "Anything short of legalization on the federal level will probably not be enough. Financial institutions are caught in the middle."[152] It is even less likely that U.S. businesses will be in a position to compete with the emerging international cannabis markets in Canada, Mexico, Europe, Israel, Africa, the Caribbean, and South America.

Moreover, as I recently pointed out in the *San Francisco Chronicle*, the federal government is setting these state-legal cannabis businesses up for failure by ensuring that they cannot compete with black market operators. It is an "inescapable consequence of supply and demand."[153]

"[B]usinesses cannot reduce prices by scaling up the production of cannabis and reaching a larger volume of the consuming population. This gap in federal law forces legal businesses to compete with black-market operators, which have the unfair advantages of both lower overhead costs per unit and a significantly larger market through their disregard of federal interstate commerce laws. Illegal producers' costs and prices are largely fixed by their illicit nature; they cannot build large, sustainable farms to reduce per-unit costs because of the inherently unstable nature of their business. Legal businesses in the United States, aided by the protections of the commerce clause, can

---

https://www.businessinsider.com/nevada-marijuana-shortage-statement-of-emergency-2017-7.

[150] Melinda Deslatte, Louisiana medical marijuana backers demand product by May 15, *AP News* (Mar. 25, 2019), https://apnews.com/d3de7002288148deb521be10c0f3eea1.

[151] Kris Krane, Illinois Legalization Is Historic, But Good Luck Finding Cannabis To Buy, *Forbes* (Jun 25, 2019, 12:03pm), https://www.forbes.com/sites/kriskrane/2019/06/25/illinois-legalization-is-historic-but-good-luck-finding-cannabis-to-buy/#16ce50c9e253.

[152] Neil Haggerty, Legalizing pot may be only way to lift cloud over pot banking, *American Banker* (June 11 2019, 9:00pm), https://www.americanbanker.com/news/legalizing-pot-may-be-only-way-to-lift-cloud-over-pot-banking, *reprinted in* Appendix D.

[153] Randal John Meyer, Feds must join California in getting #weedwise on black market, *San Fran. Chron.* (July 2, 2019), https://www.sfchronicle.com/opinion/openforum/article/Feds-must-join-California-in-getting-weedwise-on-14065415.php, *reprinted in* Appendix E.

easily compete with and replace the black market if given the chance. Federal law can easily be changed to reach this goal."[154]

Indeed, minority members of the community who take the steps to become legal operators face an economic environment where the black market has a competitive advantage based on outdated federal laws forcing legal operators to compete only within their own state, as opposed to black market operators which reach the full U.S. market by ignoring federal laws.

Congress also should not leave behind our Veterans, a community that would strongly benefit from access to cannabis to treat PTSD and long-term pain from battlefield injuries. As officials from the Veterans' Administration have testified in recent hearings, VA Doctors and programs operate on federal property, using federal resources, employing federal employees, on federal time. The concerns of veteran's access are not addresses by intra-state-only policies, such as the STATES Act or CARERS Act, or policies that do not create a federal framework for access.

Congress is no longer debating *if* federal cannabis prohibition will end— it is— but *how* to end it. Accordingly, Congress should be conscious of the racialized history and disparate effects of cannabis prohibition and take its cues from how the federal government ended alcohol prohibition in the Federal Alcohol Administration Act. Namely, by using its Commerce Clause powers to build a competitive and vibrant interstate and international trade in American goods.

* * *

Mr. DEUTCH. Thank you.

A report by the ACLU entitled "The War on Marijuana in Black and White" provides a startling statistic. Between 2001 and 2010, there were more than 8 million arrests involving marijuana. In 2010, there was 1 marijuana arrest every 37 seconds at a cost of about $3.5 billion to enforce our marijuana laws. Between 2012 and 2013, more than 13,000 people were deported for possessing marijuana, and a black person is 3.73 times more likely to be arrested for marijuana possession than a white person.

The damage caused by the enforcement of these laws, especially to minority communities, families, and individuals, is real. The collateral impacts of a criminal record are devastating for an individual. Having a past arrest

---

[154] *Id.*

record involving marijuana can pre- vent a person from finding a job, finding housing, and being eligible for a loan.

Two years ago in my State of Florida, 71 percent of voters supported legalization of medical marijuana. Since being legalized, more than 200,000 patients have signed up to be eligible to use medical marijuana, but implementing legalization of medical marijuana in Florida to ensure that people have access to the industry has been difficult.

The growing, processing, and distribution of medical marijuana has been limited to a few companies in Florida. In fact, as of the end of April, five licensed companies operated over 82 percent of the State's dispensaries. Expanding that number, the number of licensed companies and change in the status of marijuana at the Federal level could assist in diversifying participation in this developing industry.

The production, the processing, and selling of marijuana is still illegal at the Federal level, which creates significant limitations for businesses seeking capital to begin and maintain their operations as well as expand their business in States where it is legal. Banks are not permitted to extend loans to marijuana businesses. The SBA is not available to provide support.

Instead, marijuana business must rely upon capital investments from venture capitalists, private asset managers, or personal funds. And because of the disproportionately small number of minorities who work as venture capitalists and private asset managers, it limits the ability for people to participate in the legal business opportunities that exist.

Dr. Burnett, let me ask you, as more States legalize marijuana for recreational and medicinal use and the industry expands, what can be done to encourage diversity in the industry's production, processing, and selling?

Dr. BURNETT. Thank you, Mr. Deutch. That was very much in line with my comments around expanding capital.

Just to answer your question directly, when States go about the process of setting up legal regulated markets, by and large the trend has been to place a cap on the total number of available licenses within any particular State, automatically creating a very competitive environment for the acquisition of those licenses.

What we can do at a very base level is expand the number of total licenses available in any particular State and then, you know, if there is a concern about making sure that there are qualified actors, raise the regulatory requirements for you to be able to have that license. If we actually go about the business of removing cannabis from the Controlled Substances Act, as you rightly point out, there will be significantly more opportunities for the financing of traditional commercial loans or Small Business Administration loans that can support greater diversity across the market and ultimately expand the number of opportunities available.

Mr. DEUTCH. Great. Thank you very much.

Another critical issue that I think the committee should consider, Madam Chair, is the impact of marijuana legalization laws on American Indian tribes. Tribal nations are located within sovereign boundaries, and they must still comply with Federal laws. And under a 2014 DOJ memo, tribes were permitted to regulate the growing and selling of cannabis production on their land.

But the memo was repealed by Attorney General Sessions, and as we have seen in States that have legalized marijuana, the revenue generated from the production, processing, and selling of marijuana could provide a tremendous benefit for tribal nations desperate for economic support. And so I would just ask if any of the witnesses could speak to how tribal nations could be brought into the discussion of benefiting from a legalization of marijuana?

Ms. MOSBY. Do you want to do it?

Dr. BURNETT. Happy to jump in here. You know, within the current context of the Federal prohibition, there is a sizable number of tribes that are kind of sitting on the bench. And just as a writ large comments, here you as the Congress get to set the example to say, hey, if we take this cannabis out of the Controlled Substances Act, we are explicitly stating that it is okay for tribes or for any other parties to be able to get into the industry without fear of any sort of treaty violations or encroachment upon their rights as tribes.

Generally, when you see tribes getting in or just considering it, they automatically become concerned about, you know, well, is the Federal Government going to come in and violate our sovereignty, right? And so by removing cannabis from the Controlled Substances Act, you will immediately eliminate that concern and allow more tribes to be able to participate in the economic activity there.

Mr. DEUTCH. Thanks, Dr. Burnett.

Thanks, Madam Chair.

Ms. BASS. Mr. Jeffries.

Mr. JEFFRIES. Thank you, Madam Chair.

And I want to thank the distinguished witnesses for your presence, your advocacy, and your testimony here today.

Dr. Burnett, the origins of Federal marijuana prohibition date back to the 1930s. Is that right?

Dr. BURNETT. That is correct.

Mr. JEFFRIES. And it started with the Stamp Act of 1937?

Dr. BURNETT. The Marijuana Tax Act. Well, the Stamp Act preceded, but the Marijuana Tax Act was when it really jumped in.

Mr. JEFFRIES. Okay. And am I correct that that was driven by Harry Anslinger, who at the time I guess was the head of the U.S. Treasury's Department of Federal Bureau of Narcotics. Is that right?

Dr. BURNETT. That is correct.

Mr. JEFFRIES. And if you look at Dr. Anslinger's history, he seemed to have made claims about cannabis that were incorrect and that also targeted African Americans and Latinos as miscreants and the primary users of the drug. Is that right?

Dr. BURNETT. That is correct.

Mr. JEFFRIES. And I believe he said, "There are 100,000 total marijuana smokers in the U.S., and most are Negroes, Hispanics, Filipinos, and entertainers." Is that correct?

Dr. BURNETT. That is—that is correct.

Mr. JEFFRIES. He also stated, "Their satanic music, jazz and swing, result from marijuana use." Is that correct?

Dr. BURNETT. Yes, sir.

Mr. JEFFRIES. He also said, "This marijuana causes white women to seek sexual relations with Negroes, entertainers, and others." Is that correct?

Dr. BURNETT. Yes, sir.

Mr. JEFFRIES. And this is the individual who drove marijuana prohibition that we are living with today. Is that right?

Dr. BURNETT. That is right.

Mr. JEFFRIES. So would it be fair to say, and I know you have done a lot of work on this, that the origins of Federal marijuana prohibition are racially tinged, flawed, and stained with sort of the inhumane perspectives of the founding fathers of prohibition?

Dr. BURNETT. The foundations of marijuana policy are inherently racist.

Mr. JEFFRIES. Okay. Thank you.

Ms. Mosby, to sort of bring it into modern context, the failed war on drugs began in 1971. Is that right?

Ms. MOSBY. Yes, with President Nixon.

Mr. JEFFRIES. And that was when Richard Nixon declared drug abuse public enemy number one?

Ms. MOSBY. Yes.

Mr. JEFFRIES. And when you look at the Controlled Substances Act that I believe was enacted in 1970, that sort of is the foundation for the modern structure of Federal law with respect to drugs and substance abuse. Is that right?

Ms. MOSBY. That is correct.

Mr. JEFFRIES. And under that statute, marijuana is a Schedule I substance, the most restrictive category. Is that correct?

Ms. MOSBY. That is correct.

Mr. JEFFRIES. And that means it has the same classification as heroin and LSD and, in fact, a higher schedule than cocaine, meth, and fentanyl. Is that right?

Ms. MOSBY. That is correct.

Mr. JEFFRIES. And I believe that there was a commission at the time that recommended against classifying marijuana as a Schedule I drug, finding that the drug had no links to criminal behavior and recommended that cannabis be decriminalized nationwide. Is that right?

Ms. MOSBY. That is correct.

Mr. JEFFRIES. And that recommendation was obviously ignored. Is that correct?

Ms. MOSBY. It was.

Mr. JEFFRIES. Now Richard Nixon ignored that recommendation, I believe, at the time. Subsequently, one of his top advisers was John Ehrlichman. Is that true?

Ms. MOSBY. Yes.

Mr. JEFFRIES. And are you familiar with the fact that Ehrlichman has recently or in his latter years admitted that the war on drugs was created specifically to target black Americans?

Ms. MOSBY. That is correct.

Mr. JEFFRIES. In terms of how mass incarceration has devastated families, individuals, communities, having gone from a place where there were less than 100,000 people incarcerated about 50 years ago to more than 2.3 million, you have been a prosecutor who has promoted public safety but done it in a strong, in an ethical way, anchored in social and economic justice. Could you just give us a perspective on why decriminalization of marijuana or taking a different approach is in the best interest of both public safety and social, economic, and racial justice?

Ms. MOSBY. So it is in the best interest of racial justice because racial justice is the systemic fair treatment of people of all races resulting in the equitable opportunities and outcomes for all. And what we have seen through the enforcement of this war on drugs is that it has been a war on black and brown people. And specifically, the discriminatory enforcement against black—poor black and brown people.

And so from the perspective of criminal justice, we have criminalized what should have been a public health issue all of this time. And in light of the fact that these collateral consequences have had negative impacts not just on the individuals, but on the communities that these individuals come from. These debilitating social, political, economic debilities are something that have not just marginalized the individual, but have marginalized communities. And I see this each and every day as a prosecutor in one of the most impoverished cities in the Nation.

Mr. JEFFRIES. Well, thank you for your leadership.

The war on drugs has been a failure. It has been a stain on our society, our democracy, our country. It is time to end it. We can begin by dealing with marijuana decriminalization.

I yield back.

Ms. MOSBY. Thank you, Congressman.

Mr. COHEN [presiding]. Mr. Cicilline is recognized for 5 minutes.

Mr. CICILLINE. Thank you, Mr. Chairman, and thank you to Chair Bass and Ranking Member Ratcliffe for holding today's hearing.

And thank you to our witnesses for your very helpful testimony. As you all know, according to the Department of Justice, nearly 600,000 people are arrested for marijuana possession each year. However, it is also estimated that even though both white and black men and women use marijuana at roughly the same rate, African Americans are four times more likely to be arrested for marijuana offenses than white Americans.

This disparity in the enforcement of drug laws I believe is among the most critical issues that needs to be addressed in our reform efforts. This is further complicated by the fact that while marijuana is currently listed as a Schedule I drug at the Federal level, 11 States and the District of Columbia have legalized recreational marijuana use in some form while 22 other States have legalized marijuana use for medicinal purposes.

And while there might be some disagreement about how marijuana should be treated or regulated, it is, of course, unacceptable that marijuana laws are not enforced with the full equality that they should be and that both the origins of the marijuana laws, as just described by my colleague Mr. Jeffries, and their current application are disproportionately impacting communities of color, particularly poor communities of color. We have a responsibility to do something about it.

So, Ms. Mosby, I first want to ask you just to speak briefly about some of the collateral consequences of marijuana convictions because I was a former criminal defense attorney, and there were many young people who had a marijuana conviction that had implications for the rest of their lives in terms of employment, military service, a number of other—eligibility for programs. So if you could speak to that for a moment so that people understand the gravity of this?

Ms. MOSBY. Thank you, Congressman.

What I would say is the collateral consequences, as I stated before, are the legal, social, and economic debilities that are imposed as a result of a criminal conviction or even an arrest, regardless of that conviction. These individuals are known to have adverse sort of restrictions, and that goes and extends to adoptions, housing, healthcare access, welfare, immigration, employment, professional licensure, property rights, mobility, education, voting rights. The collective effect of these debilities marginalizes, as I stated earlier, the individuals, and it also extinguishes a level of hope and a positive pathway forward where it often at times increases recidivism and undermines meaningful reentry of that convicted individual for a lifetime. This not only affects the individual, but affects the communities.

And even without—and I said this earlier. Even without the conviction, the collateral consequences are still seen in the untold stigma that the disruption and humiliation, the unimaginable financial burden that is imposed on posting bail and hiring a lawyer, and even the lost hours at work or school. It is definitely something that is a problem.

Mr. CICILLINE. Dr. Nathan, you looked like you wanted to— thank you.

Dr. NATHAN. Yes. And this gives us an opportunity to really tie together the ideas of criminal justice reform, social justice, and public health. Because, you know, people have asked me what is a nice guy like you doing here? A doctor who is really interested in public health.

Well, to me, the criminalization of cannabis has been a far greater detriment to public health than it has been a benefit, and that is because for all the reasons the State's attorney Mosby was just listing, the cannabis prohibition perpetuates the impoverishment of the impoverished.

And that economic impoverishment we know is a major impediment to access to healthcare. And that being the case, that makes cannabis prohibition a truly negative public health issue, even if you set aside the actual harms of the drug itself.

Mr. CICILLINE. And for all the witnesses, is there any evidence in the States that have either decriminalized or legalized recreational use that there has been any significant increase in adolescent use of cannabis?

Mr. LEVINE. Just the opposite, Congressman. There is a new study out that Dr. Nathan referenced —

Mr. CICILLINE. Everyone agrees with that?

Mr. LEVINE. Yes, yes.

Mr. CICILLINE. Right. Finally, Ms. Mosby, you talked about your opposition to the STATES Act because of the omission of some restorative justice component. I am wondering if you would share with us what you think is the most effective way for us to think about those issues in terms of how do we ensure that the communities that have suffered the most because of our really obnoxious marijuana laws and have suffered disparate treatment as a consequence, that they might benefit from the economic value of a marijuana—cannabis operation? Are there other ways to compensate directly individuals who have suffered the consequences of this marijuana policy?

Ms. MOSBY. Thank you for your question, Congressman.

I do—I believe the Federal Government must create financial incentives to right the wrongs of the past and address the racial injustice that exists between and because of the criminalization and mass incarceration of poor black and brown people.

And by that, I mean the Federal Government pretty much endorsed and encouraged through the criminalization of what should have been a public health crisis, that war on drugs, and Congress funded task forces and funding the grant programs to use discriminatory—what we now know was discriminatory enforcement of these laws on poor black and brown people.

And what I think that the Federal Government needs to now do is to resolve these failed policies and then create financial incentives for the creation of automatic or mass expungement because this is an issue that even we are plagued with and has come up in the State of Maryland and other States, vacatur or post-conviction relief or resentencing opportunities for those already convicted. That is an individual.

But we also—the Federal Government also needs to extend resources to communities that have been most impacted by the discriminatory enforcement and collateral consequences of this enforcement. So we have to create financial reinvestment incentives that will create job opportunities for folks, increase reentry services for formerly incarcerated, advance harm reduction models and substance abuse disorder in line with public health. There is law enforcement assisted diversion. We can create incentives for States to adopt these policies and these models, develop community centers capable of educational support and wraparound services to some of our at-risk youth.

And last, but certainly not least, it is incredibly important, as we have already talked about, increasing the equitable access and inclusion of people of color in a billion-dollar industry that has attempted to shut out people of color. And Congress has that ability and that control —

Mr. CICILLINE. Thank you very much.

Ms. MOSBY [continuing]. Which is one of the reasons why I do not support the STATES Act, which, in my opinion, does not lend to that sort of investment in the community.

Mr. CICILLINE. Thank you. I yield back, Mr. Chairman.

Mr. COHEN. Thank you, sir.

Mr. Lieu is recognized for 5 minutes. Mr. LIEU. Thank you, Mr. Chair.

I want to start off by thanking the witnesses for being here today.

When I was in the California State legislature, I worked to decriminalize marijuana, and I was one of the ballot guide authors for their successful ballot initiative that eventually decriminalized marijuana in California. I want to touch on what my colleague Congressman Hakeem Jeffries said about the Controlled Substances Act and drill down into that some more.

So, Dr. Nathan, in your testimony, you stated that cannabis should have never been made illegal for consenting adults. It is less harmful to adults than alcohol and tobacco, and that prohibition has done far more damage to our society than adult use of cannabis itself.

So I agree with that. Are alcohol and tobacco within the Controlled Substances Act as regulated?

Dr. NATHAN. I am sorry. Are alcohol and tobacco —

Mr. LIEU. In the Controlled Substances Act?

Dr. NATHAN. They are not.

Mr. LIEU. Okay. Even though it is the generally accepted view that they—those substances are more dangerous than marijuana. Correct?

Dr. NATHAN. Correct on both counts.

Mr. LIEU. So the Controlled Substances Act has different schedules, and Schedule I is deemed to be the most harmful and potential to abuse. Is that correct?

Dr. NATHAN. That is correct.

Mr. LIEU. And marijuana is in Schedule I. Is that right?

Dr. NATHAN. Correct.

Mr. LIEU. Okay. And it is along with other drugs, such as heroin and LSD. Correct?

Dr. NATHAN. That is right.

Mr. LIEU. And your view is marijuana would also be less dangerous than either heroin or LSD. Correct?

Dr. NATHAN. Correct.

Mr. LIEU. All right. Schedule II is deemed to be less dangerous than Schedule I, and some of those drugs include cocaine and fentanyl. Would you agree that marijuana is less dangerous than either cocaine or fentanyl?

Dr. NATHAN. I agree with that.

Mr. LIEU. So what we have here is this completely irrational system where drugs are more dangerous, like alcohol and tobacco are not even in the act, and then drugs like heroin and LSD, which are far more dangerous, are in the same section as marijuana. And then you have got Schedule II, which has cocaine and fentanyl, which is classified as less dangerous than marijuana. The whole system to me seems irrational. So I think marijuana should be taken completely out of the Controlled Substances Act.

One of my colleagues on the Republican—a Republican had said earlier today that he would support moving marijuana to Schedule III. So, Mr. Levine, what would that do if it moved from Schedule I to Schedule III?

Mr. LEVINE. It would open up research, and it would solve our tax problem, which is specific to Schedule I and Schedule II. But it wouldn't open up banking, and it wouldn't do a lot of the other things that folks are talking about.

Mr. LIEU. And if it was simply moved to Schedule III, it would actually still not be authorized for consenting adults. Correct?

Mr. LEVINE. Correct.

Mr. LIEU. Okay. In terms of the banking issue, right now it is largely an all-cash industry. Is that right?

Mr. LEVINE. We are able to get some sort of commercial banking services through credit unions or community banks mostly, but it is hodge-podge and it is dicey at all times.

Mr. LIEU. Would you say the majority of businesses are banked or majority are not?

Mr. LEVINE. So the FinCEN guidance talks about establishing a relationship with the entity that you are banking with. So what we see in new, emerging markets like California and States that just opened up more recently, those are almost all cash businesses. And as the businesses exist for a couple of years, they can eventually get some sort of commercial banking services.

But it is we can't get loans. We can't do anything outside of get electronic deposits and payments.

Mr. LIEU. And for a business that has trouble accessing banks, they are relying on large amounts of cash, that poses certain elements that makes it riskier for that business in terms of just safety. Correct?

Mr. LEVINE. Yes, sir.

Mr. LIEU. It also would make it easier to avoid taxes. Isn't that right?

Mr. LEVINE. Yes, sir.

Mr. LIEU. Okay. So let me ask sort of this one last question, and I will ask it of Ms. Mosby. Thank you for your great work on it. Even if we were to remove marijuana from the Controlled Substances Act, States could still criminalize if they so choose to, right? Because States have vast discretion in criminal law matters.

Ms. MOSBY. They would still have the ability to legalize, tax, and regulate, or make a determination about the criminalization of marijuana.

Mr. LIEU. Thank you.

So my view is that it is a huge waste of Federal resources to criminalize marijuana. Our patriotic and outstanding FBI agents and prosecutors should be working on taking down child sex trafficking rings. They should be working on preventing interference from foreign agents in our elections. They should be rooting out corruption in Washington, D.C. They should not be investigating and prosecuting marijuana crimes.

And let me just end with this. My view is that everything in politics seems impossible until it happens. So 15 years ago, I were to tell you, hey, in 15 years we would have gay marriage in 50 States, and in some of those States we would be smoking weed, you would think I was crazy.

But that is, in fact, what is happening now. So I appreciate the fight. Keep on fighting, and I believe we can get this done.

I yield back.

Ms. MOSBY. Thank you.

Mr. COHEN. Thank you, sir.

Ms. Dean, you are recognized for 5 minutes.

Ms. DEAN. Thank you, Mr. Chair.

And thank you all for your testimony today. I am pleased the subcommittee chose to have this hearing.

I wanted to start with a couple of quick questions, but Dr. Nathan in particular. I was looking at your testimony, and this is the thing we hear all the time, and I will quote you. "There is a persistent misconception that cannabis is a gateway drug."

Could you speak to that misconception? Help me speak to that misconception.

Dr. NATHAN. Absolutely. This comes up time and time again in the debate over cannabis. You know, this is one of the most thoroughly debunked issues in this debate, and the reason is that although there is, indeed, a correlation between cannabis use and the use of other drugs, there is also a stronger correlation between alcohol and tobacco use and the use of other drugs.

And correlation does not equal causation. Just because the wind is—or just because the wind is blowing faster when windmills are turning faster doesn't mean that the windmills are creating the wind. And so you do see this sort of reverse directionality of causality.

What we do know, and this does and to some measure satisfy some of the observations that are made about cannabis and the use of other drugs—and alcohol and tobacco and the use of soft drugs and use of hard drugs—and that is this common liability theory. And that is that there are a common set of factors that tend to lead to all drug use, soft drugs and hard drugs.

And those factors are things like poverty, absence of parents in the home, not having dinner together at home, school failure, unsafe streets. And if you notice, a lot of these things are actually potential and real consequences of the drug war itself, so that there are many ways in which the prohibition of drugs generally is contributory to young people starting on a path that leads to drug use of all kinds and certainly not simply cannabis.

Ms. DEAN. And so beyond environment, also we know that substance abuse disorder has a genetic component as well. So thank you for helping me there, which leads me to Ms. Mosby.

You talked about the impact that criminalization of marijuana has had on you, your work directly, your communities directly. Can you describe maybe if the world turned around, and we actually recognized it is a public health issue, not a crime issue, what impact—what would your community—what would your work look like? What would law enforcement's work look like? What would your communities look like?

Ms. MOSBY. Thank you for your question, Congresswoman.

What would my work look like if we were to focus on safety? It would be great, right, if we were able to utilize our resources towards violent crime.

In Baltimore City in 2017, we had 343 homicides with a year-end clearance rate of 31 percent. Last year, we had 309 homicides with a year-end clearance rate of 26 percent. So what I would like to do as the prosecutor of a city and one of the most violent cities in the country is to focus my resources on solving those homicides and utilizing my prosecutors to work with the police.

You know, after I came out with my policy to say that we were not going to be enforcing marijuana possession laws, I worked with the police department. And I can tell you that, you know, from the numbers, what we have seen—and I am not attributing this necessarily to my marijuana policy. But you know, the nonfatal shootings of—and nonfatal shootings have—actually, the clearance rate has gone up this year. The overall crime numbers have gone down this year. However, the homicides and the nonfatal shootings are up.

So what I would like to utilize and what I would like to do to utilize my resources is to focus on violent crime, and that is what we should be doing, punishing those that have committed the most heinous offenses against those that are the most vulnerable within our society.

Ms. DEAN. And that is one of the most important public health crises in our country, the slaughter by gun violence.

Ms. MOSBY. Absolutely.

Ms. DEAN. It is stunning. So I agree with you. The resources ought to be directed there. And there is an economic connection there that we should so obviously make.

And maybe if I could end very briefly, I would like to go back to the sad roots of our marijuana policy. If you could just tell us a little bit more about the racial—racist, excuse me, roots of our marijuana policy?

Dr. BURNETT. Absolutely. If you look at the way the entire act, the Marijuana Tax Act was socialized in Congress, initially it didn't have public—it didn't have congressional support. But it was, you know, largely around the characterization and selling of the racist implications of the act that you were able to get enough support to impose a tax on cannabis.

Cannabis was in the United States Pharmacopeia. It was widely used as an elixir for—I mean, William Osler, the father of medicine, said it was one of the best cures for the common headache. But once we started criminalizing black and brown people in order to be able to gin up the number of votes, particularly amongst the Southern legislative body at the time, we were able to impose the Marijuana Tax Act. And from there, the criminalization, you know, has manifest over and over and gotten particularly pernicious.

Ms. DEAN. Thank you. I see my time is up. Thank you all.

Mr. COHEN. Thank you, Ms. Dean, for saying your time is up.

That is a rare congressional capability. Ms. Powell.

Ms. MUCARSEL-POWELL. Thank you, Mr. Chairman, and thank you for having such an important hearing.

I represent Florida's 26th District. It is a majority minority community. About close to 60 percent of the people living in my community are Hispanic, 12 to 13 percent African Americans. And I can tell you that I see how, Dr. Burnett, you mentioned in your testimony so eloquently that we have a tale of two Americas.

In Florida, they legalized medical cannabis, and that industry has been mainly managed and dominated by white, wealthy Americans. Yet marijuana is still considered—holding marijuana is still considered a crime, and it disproportionately affects communities of color, specifically in my community, and we need to break the cycle. I want to start with Dr. Nathan. Can you explain to us, and to everyone listening today, how incarceration of having possession of marijuana is a public health concern? Can you make that link for us, please?

Dr. NATHAN. Absolutely. First, I will note that a lot of people say that, well, you are not—you don't get incarcerated for cannabis possession, which on the face of it sounds like a true statement. But when you look at the details, what you find is particularly in communities of color, individuals who were arrested for cannabis and don't have the means to either get their record expunged or—or to necessarily pay the fines that are needed, they themselves can wind up in prison, and it all starts with an arrest for cannabis.

Prison itself is, of course, one of the most unhealthy environments for any person to live in. And America has over 2 million prisoners, greater than the number of incarcerated individuals of any country in the world, including totalitarian countries. And so, of course, prison itself is a terrible experience for an individual to undergo, both in terms of physical health and also in terms of mental health.

And what we find is that the United States penal system is the largest provider of mental healthcare in the world. And that statistic itself should tell you a lot about what incarceration does to the individuals who are incarcerated, and it doesn't even tell the story of what it does to the families of the individuals who are incarcerated who themselves suffer economically.

And that economic suffering all around leads, of course, to the limitations of access to healthcare. And in a country like ours where it really is an expensive endeavor to get healthcare, it will limit an individual's longevity.

Ms. MUCARSEL-POWELL. Interesting. So let me ask you, do you have any data on how much this is costing us to keep this population, which is about 60 percent of the people what are incarcerated are minority populations. How much is this costing America? How much can we save and invest in other programs like access to primary healthcare to our communities?

Dr. NATHAN. Right. How many billions is it? I am not sure. I can certainly get you that data, and Jeffrey Miron, who is an economist at Harvard, was one of the individuals who was influential for me in understanding the harm of cannabis prohibition because he outlined how much the drug war actually costs and how much legalization might save.

So, of course, legalization is not a panacea, and of course, cannabis itself is no panacea in medical use. But it is such an improvement and such a relief to a society that has been plagued by the failed war on drugs for decades.

Ms. MUCARSEL-POWELL. Thank you.

And Dr. Burnett, what do you think we need to do at the Federal Government to ensure that ownership is equitable —

Dr. BURNETT. Sure.

Ms. MUCARSEL-POWELL [continuing]. As we start legalizing medical cannabis across the States? Especially in Florida, how do we ensure that we have equal opportunities for minority populations?

Dr. BURNETT. One, I think that, you know, by simply going about the business of removing cannabis from the Controlled Substances Act. As I said before, you send a message to a large swath of people within the country that, you know, this is not a stigmatized plant.

It is okay to get into the business of participating in the cannabis industry.

Secondarily, at the Federal level, largely there are lots of incentives for economic empowerment zones, tax credits, Small Business Administration lending that can lower the barriers to entry for getting into and starting a cannabis business, which are significant. Largely because of the fact that right now there are no—no means through which you can go about financing the start-up capital necessary to get into a business other than by going to, you know, angel investors, hedge funds, venture capitalists, and the like, whom in and of themselves have a diversity problem.

And so if we are looking to ensure that the economic gains are spread across the country, and this is something that is, you know, the benefits are felt equitably, then the Federal Government can take the first step by sending the signal that this is not a stigmatized activity and then supporting that with economic resources and tax relief to ensure that in the places where harm has been most carried out that benefits can be received.

Ms. MUCARSEL-POWELL. Thank you so much. I have no more time.

Mr. COHEN. Thank you so much.

Ms. MUCARSEL-POWELL. Oh, can we allow the —

Mr. COHEN. No.

Ms. MUCARSEL-POWELL. I am sorry. That is fine.

Mr. COHEN. We are going to get this over with. This is a fried chicken day, and that is an important thing. [Laughter.]

Mr. COHEN. Firstly, without objection, I would like to introduce the testimony of Aaron Smith, executive director, National Cannabis Industry Association, into the record.

Without objection, so done. Thank you.

[The information follows:]

Testimony of Aaron Smith, Executive Director, National Cannabis Industry Association, before the United States House of Representatives, Committee on the Judiciary, Subcommittee on Crime, Terrorism, and Homeland Security, July 10, 2019

Introduction

Chairwoman Bass, Vice Chair Demings, Ranking member Ratcliffe, members of the subcommittee, good morning.

I am Aaron Smith, Executive Director and Co-Founder of the National Cannabis Industry Association (NCIA). NCIA is the largest national trade association dedicated to protecting state-regulated cannabis businesses and advancing policy reforms needed to harmonize federal marijuana law with the successful medical and adult-use state cannabis programs that exist throughout the country. Founded in 20 I 0, NCIA represents nearly 2,000 cannabis-related member-businesses and tens of thousands of cannabis professionals across the United States.

On behalf of our diverse membership, comprised of both large and small cannabis businesses as well as a variety of ancillary companies doing business in every U.S. state, we thank you for the opportunity to discuss our unwavering support for de-scheduling cannabis, social equity, and racial justice reforms, and responsibly regulating cannabis at both the state and federal levels. We are hopeful that social equity and racial justice reforms will be an integral part of any end-of-prohibition efforts.

I've been at this for a long time and I can't express how excited I am for this moment. To date, forty-seven states and the District of Columbia, as well as Guam, the Northern Mariana Islands, and Puerto Rico have passed legislation authorizing some form of cannabis for regulated medical or adult-use purposes and thirty-three states have enacted laws regulating the commercial production and sale of medical or adult-use marijuana. The time for comprehensive federal action is upon us.

There have been scores of cannabis-related bills introduced over the past few years, including the Marijuana Justice Act, the Strengthening The Tenth Amendment Through Entrusting States (STATES) Act, the Secure And Fair Enforcement (SAFE) Banking Act, the Small Business Tax Equity Act, and most recently, the Marijuana Freedom and Opportunity Act, to name a few. NCIA has been at the forefront, advocating in support of each and every one of these bills on behalf of our broad membership base. It is our sincere hope that Congress will take a more comprehensive, end-of-prohibition approach. Our NCIA member businesses, consumers, the American banking industry, and yes, the federal government, would benefit most from more comprehensive reforms that remove marijuana from the Controlled Substances Act and begin the process of regulating the substance at the federal level.

De-scheduling is the best approach that would immediately solve myriad problems related to banking, payment processing, tax parity, and other issues critical to the success of this burgeoning American industry. Because cannabis currently remains a Schedule I drug under the Controlled Substances Act, additional economic opportunity for states and localities is currently obstructed or has been lost to the illicit cannabis market. As a result, state-licensed cannabis businesses, as well as ancillary entities that serve cannabis-related businesses, are often blocked from accessing basic banking and payment processing services. Many of these businesses are forced to operate in an-all cash environment. creating a public safety risk for employees, consumers, and local law enforcement. Additionally, while state-licensed cannabis businesses pay upwards of an 80% effective tax rate to the federal government due to 26 USC 280E, they are not eligible to receive SBA small business and commercial loans, credit assistance, or technical assistance to spur economic development. These are the same loans that assist those in disadvantaged communities to access the resources necessary to become small business owners. The de-scheduling of cannabis immediately corrects all of these issues and is the first step toward a shared federal-state regulatory regime that works for policymakers, small and large entrepreneurs, and consumers alike.

De-scheduling cannabis at the federal level would also harmonize federal law with the successful medical and adult- use state cannabis programs that exist throughout the country. Most significantly, de-scheduling would also provide the federal government with an opportunity to tax and regulate cannabis products, much as it does with other products, such as alcohol or dietary supplements. NCTA wholeheartedly endorses the de-scheduling of cannabis in all forms and, as always, we stand ready to assist Congress with making sure that we get this right.

The Economic Benefits of De-Scheduling

Taxing and regulating cannabis sales has been an economic boon for states. From November 2018 to March 2019, it is estimated that seven states that taxed and regulated adult-use cannabis sales (Alaska, California, Colorado, Massachusetts, Nevada, Oregon, and Washington) collected more than $1 billion in state tax revenue and created thousands of jobs. Colorado alone generated $266,529,637 in legal marijuana taxes, licenses, and fees at the state level in 2018. That's just one year in one relatively small state. California, the most populous state and the nation's largest cannabis market, collected roughly $345,200,000 in taxes in the first year of adult-use sales. In Nevada, retail marijuana sales exceeded an average of $1 million per day through the first six months of operations. The windfall of state tax revenue from cannabis is only just beginning.

BDS Analytics and ArcView Market Research project that the U.S. sales of cannabis and hemp-derived CBD products are expected to surge to $20 billion by 2024 with the possibility of employing one million people. An analysis from New Frontier Data estimates that the cannabis industry could generate $131 billion in federal tax revenue if it is legalized for adult use in all 50 states. That same analysis found that if the U.S. were to legalize cannabis federally today, it would add 782,000 jobs to the economy.

Tax revenues derived from the state-regulated cannabis industry are used to fund a number of state and local priorities, such as: education (i.e., hiring more teachers and school infrastructure); mental health and substance abuse services; transpo1 1ation/infrastructure projects; and law enforcement initiatives aimed at more serious issues like the opioid crisis. However, the illicit cannabis market in the US is currently estimated to be valued near $30 billion.

This adverse ratio between the legal and illegal cannabis marketplace is a direct result of outdated federal policy toward a responsible industry operating at the state and local level.

Today's hearing, and a path forward on de-scheduling, marks a dramatic shift in those outdated federal policies. Imagine the day when cannabis is de-scheduled, and the federal government is able to tax and regulate retail purchases of cannabis. Those tax revenues would be a significant boon to the United States economy. And the federal government would retain control over how products are manufactured, marketed, and sold. It's a win/win.

De-Scheduling Is Good Politics

Not only is federal marijuana reform and de-scheduling good public policy, it is also good politics. The vast majority of the American public supports some legalization of cannabis. According to Gallop, support for legalizing marijuana possession and use for adults now regularly polls consistently above 64% nationally, including majorities among conservatives, liberals, and independents. According to a recent Quinnipiac poll, support for medicinal cannabis has achieved near unanimous backing, with national polls regularly showing support at about 90%, including supermajorities across age ranges and the political spectrum. At a time when nearly two-thirds of Americans live in a state with some form of comprehensive legal cannabis access, it now falls on Congress to determine when and how the federal government will end its conflict with these state programs. Congress should do what it can to allow states to create legal cannabis markets, enable access to banking services, bring about tax equity to businesses that abide by these laws, and allow their constituents to realize the full potential economic and societal benefits of legalized marijuana. De-scheduling is the best path forward to achieve these goals.

While the first and most important step of any comprehensive regulatory system would be to de-schedule marijuana and delta-9 tetrahydrocannabinol (THC) from the Controlled Substances Act, this would by no means be the end of the road. The Schedule I status of marijuana, THC, and until recently, hemp, criminalized their use, hindered research, and driven most cannabis product sales to the illicit market. It is for these reasons that NCIA strongly supports de- scheduling and subsequent taxation and federal regulatory regime that sets a roadmap for state-legal cannabis businesses to remain compliant with state and federal laws.

Social Equity and Expungement

We can't debate the merits of de-scheduling, or any other cannabis policy reform, without considering the historical consequences of cannabis' drug scheduling. We need to incorporate social equity provisions in any federal legalization effort. The fact is the cannabis prohibition inflicts severe and disproportionate damage to communities of color in multiple ways. It' s time that the industry, lawmakers, and federal and state regulators, make social equity a real priority. We can start with the expungement oflow-level cannabis-related offenses. But progress can't end there. We need to create the opportunity for people who have been historically disenfranchised.

One of the societal benefits of marijuana legalization is a reduction in arrests and law enforcement costs. Fewer arrests for marijuana offenses means that limited law enforcement resources can be re-directed toward preventing violent and other crimes involving victims. However, the reduction in marijuana arrests has not eliminated racial disparities in marijuana enforcement. In Colorado, marijuana arrests have dropped 51% for whites, but only 33% for Latinos and 25% for Black persons. This is more troubling when one considers that arrest rates for non-whites prior to legalization were proportionately greater than the arrest rates for whites at that time. Youth arrest rates have not dropped in proportion to the number of adult arrests despite teen use remaining stable or falling in states that have legalized cannabis. As the racial disparity numbers show, Latino and Black youths are dispropotionately the targets of those arrests. This demonstrates public officials need to examine ways to ensure that the benefits of legalization reach all Americans.

We have to acknowledge that cannabis prohibition was not only aimed to prevent individuals from possessing and using cannabis, but also to install a criminal punishment regime that enforced prohibition through federal, state, and local prosecutions. This regime did not affect everyone equally, as there is a clear history of racial disparities in cannabis arrests and convictions. Arrests happen far more frequently in heavily policed areas, which are disproportionately areas where people of color reside. Punishments, which tend to be harsher for people of color even when the underlying conduct is the same, include an elaborate array of collateral consequences that can hinder or eliminate future job prospects, educational opportunities, and other avenues for legitimate financial achievement.

A cannabis arrest stails a cycle of detrimental governmental action that can wreck families and communities across the country. When too many arrests occur in the same geographic location, the economic and social viability of entire neighborhoods can be negatively affected for generations.

Although cannabis legalization at the federal level ends prohibition, it does not stop or reverse the harm created by previous public policy decisions. As state-level legalization spreads, and the legal cannabis market expands, the individuals and communities most impacted by cannabis prohibition have all too often been left behind. To create a legal cannabis market accessible to all, the laws need to be designed and implemented with equity and fairness in mind. Thank fully, a number of states and jurisdictions are taking steps to ensure equitable participation in the state-legal cannabis industry by those communities that have been historically most harmed by prohibition enforcement. For example, Massachusetts is giving priority business licensing certification to applicants from areas with historically high rates of arrest, conviction, and incarceration related to marijuana crimes. Similarly, the city of Oakland, California is setting aside a minimum of half of all initial cannabis business permits to applicants from "police beats with a disprop01 lionately higher number of cannabis-related arrests." And countless bills on record expungement have been filed across the country. This is a good start, but we can do more -we need to do more. Federal de-scheduling efforts should incorporate some of these social equity best practices.

Some members of Congress are pushing to right the wrongs of racially disparate enforcement. One of the strongest advocates for marijuana reform and social equity is Representative Barbara Lee of California. Congresswoman Lee is the co-chair of the Congressional Cannabis Caucus and has co-sponsored multiple cannabis-related bills, including the Realizing Equitable & Sustainable Participation in Emerging Cannabis Trades (RESPECT) Resolution during the 116th Congress. This resolution proposes a set of best practices to address industry inequalities. Collectively, the best practices suggest that the legal cannabis market can be a force for justice, but only if implemented fairly. Congresswoman Lee also introduced the Marijuana Justice Act of 2019, which would withhold some federal funding from states with dispropo1 lionate cannabis arrest and incarceration rates and use the savings to reinvest in communities most affected by the war on drugs, by establishing a grant program to fund job training, libraries, community centers, and health education programs. That bill was referred to this Committee in April. NCIA strongly supports Representative Lee's effo1 ls. We have also worked closely with the Minority Cannabis Business Association (MCBA) to create the nation's first-ever Model Municipal Social Equity Ordinance, based on the recommendations in the RESPECT

Resolution, and we will continue to push for laws and regulations that embrace diversity and the inclusion of communities that disproportionately impacted by cannabis prohibition. The emerging cannabis industry must work for all people and we should endeavor to fix these problems right out of the gate, as this chamber considers broader reforms.

Recently, NCIA published a white paper on "Increasing Equity in the Cannabis Industry, Six Achievable goals for Policy Makers." We released the paper at a breakfast event in the House of Representatives this spring, where a number of members spoke about the impo1 1ance of social equity. That paper outlines six key goals for social equity programs: (I) repair the damage to individuals caused by discriminatory enforcement prohibition, (2) create more equitable licensing outcomes through the application process, (3) ensure the industry reflects the local community, (4) address financial barriers to market entry, (5) support companies and individuals entering the industly from dispropo1 1ionately-impacted communities, and (6) invest tax revenues in communities harmed by prohibition. We hope that members of this committee will seriously consider and incorporate our social equity recommendations, which can be found on our website at www.thecannabisindustrv.org, into any post-prohibition de-scheduling bill.

NCIA remains committed to working with the Minority Cannabis Business Association, the Congressional Black Caucus, the Congressional Hispanic Caucus and our new partner - the Last Prisoner Project, to find solutions to the myriad problems facing people of color, women, and other minorities and help them to realize opportunities in the cannabis industry and reverse unacceptable trends. We are hopeful that any de-scheduling legislation will include some, if not all, of NCI A's social equity goals for policymakers.

Public Health and Safety

A common concern that lawmakers have expressed when considering marijuana reform proposals is what impact legalization would have on crime. While there is no greater calling in public service than public safety, and lawmakers should always consider the health and safety of Americans in eve1ything that they do, data shows that legal marijuana businesses do not present a threat to public safety and they may even have a dampening effect on crime. A number of studies, including studies from *Preventative Medicine* and the *Journal of Urban Economics* from 2017, found that the presence of dispensaries actually reduces property crimes in the neighborhood. Data from

Colorado and Washington, two early adopters of legalized cannabis, showed drops in property and violent crimes post-legalization.

Notwithstanding this encouraging data, NCIA remains committed to finding solutions to some of the important public safety issues facing the industry, like youth use, impaired driving, and diversion. People should not be violating state law, they should not be selling cannabis to minors, they should not be consuming cannabis and driving, and they should not be transporting cannabis across state lines into states that have not legalized cannabis.

NCIA remains committed to working through these public policy issues that affect the health and safety of consumers and non-consumers alike. We are hopeful that with the end of prohibition will come a renewed sense of common purpose with the law enforcement community and that collaboration on public health and safety will be the norm. NCIA stands ready to work with the Fraternal Order of Police, the National Sheriffs Association, the International Association of Chiefs of Police, and any other law enforcement groups interested in finding public policy solutions to any public health and safety issues related to federal legalization of cannabis.

A Regulatory Path Forward Post De-Scheduling

With momentum building and public support increasing, the critical question is shifting from "should cannabis be legalized," to "how should we regulate the commercial cannabis market at the federal level?" The de-scheduling of cannabis would immediately bring us into the post-prohibition world, and we need to be ready. NCIA is proactively considering these important issues, and we will be releasing a white paper in the coming weeks with recommendations for how the federal government should regulate cannabis post-prohibition. It's important that we build the appropriate regulatory scheme right out of the gate because one thing remains clear: the current diversity of products that contain cannabis means that a "one size fits all" regulatory scheme would be ineffective and likely have unintended consequences.

In the coming weeks, NCIA will recommend that four different regulatory "lanes" be utilized, based on the characteristics and intended use of specific cannabis products. Because human consumables are already regulated by the federal government through a variety of lanes that are designed for these purposes, most cannabis products can simply follow analogous products already sold legally through these lanes. By building off existing systems and making modifications where necessary, all cannabis products can be properly regulated by existing federal agencies.

Currently, because of marijuana's status as a Schedule **1** drug, the Drug Enforcement Administration (DEA) is cannabis' primary regulator. This federal control consists entirely of criminal enforcement. Following the lead of similar products, NCJA believes that cannabis products should be regulated by the government agencies that regulate most human consumables, primarily the Food and Drug Administration (FDA) and the Alcohol and Tobacco Tax and Trade Bureau (TTB). This bifurcated system would allow the federal government to regulate the cannabis industry, based on the relative "dangers" of each product, with high THC products receiving the greatest regulatory oversight. stripping the DEA of its regulatory authority and replacing it with a consumer health and safety approach headed by the FDA would go a long way towards correcting the failed criminal enforcement approaches of the past.

Combined, these four lanes will allow cannabis products to be sold legally while providing for regulatory oversight dependent on public policy concerns. A comprehensive regulatory scheme that accurately tailors regulatory lanes to a product's risk profile is vital to creating a vibrant, competitive marketplace where products are effectively and efficiently cultivated, manufactured, and sold. We look forward to working with Congress on a regulatory approach post-de-scheduling that works for all Americans.

The SAFE Banking Act and Expanding Access to Capital

Companies that are transparent about providing ancillary services to the state-compliant cannabis industry have experienced their financial institutions shut off their banking and payment processing accounts, despite the fact that they don't operate "plant-touching" businesses. This even extends to law firms, accounting firms, and other professional organizations. In addition, other professionals like electricians, contractors, and plumbers are also at risk of losing their bank accounts for accepting payment from cannabis businesses. Other companies may be forced to choose between taking a job and generating revenue for their small business and doing business with a cannabis- related entity solely based on their geographic location. For instance, a plumbing company in Denver, Colorado may be called and offered a job to service a cannabis cultivation facility's water system. That plumbing company now faces a choice: service a cannabis-related business and risk losing SBA backed-loans – or lose the revenue from that job. Given a majority of states have some form of legalized medical or adult-use cannabis, this is a large customer base and revenue source that is not available to these small businesses. This situation is untenable and unfair for small businesses in states that have chosen to legalize cannabis in some form, and the issue can only be corrected at the federal level. De-scheduling cannabis in all forms would cure all of these woes in one fell swoop.

Since 2014, the U.S. Department of the Treasury's Financial Crime Enforcement Network (FinCEN) has maintained guidance regarding the conditions under which financial institutions may work with cannabis-related businesses. These conditions include a bevy of federal requirements financial institutions must meet in order to provide banking services to licensed cannabis-related business. However, the number of banks working with cannabis-related businesses remains marginal in the current context of an emerging global industry. Moreover, permitted cannabis-related businesses are always under threat of having their bank accounts and payment processing services closed without warning. Additionally, a cannabis-related business might be charged $10,000 to $1,000,000 annually for compliance and regulatory costs required for a financial institution to successfully follow obligations under federal anti-money-laundering laws. These excessive annual compliance fees could be otherwise invested to enhance business operations and expansion.

Earlier this year, Treasury Secreta1y Steve Mnuchin confirmed that the Department is reviewing existing FinCEN guidance and does not want to rescind the current guidance without having a replacement policy to address public safety concerns. Additionally, before the House Committee on Financial Services in May, the Treasu1y Secreta1y testified that banking regulators are currently constrained by conflicts between federal and state cannabis law and encouraged Congress to find a legislative solution. NCIA and its members appreciate the Secretary's decision to preserve FinCEN's 2014 guidance as the regulated cannabis industry continues to grow. And we agree that the indust1y needs a legislative solution, namely de-scheduling.

To operate safely and successfully, cannabis-related businesses must have access to working capital like any other legal enterprise in the United States. The regulated cannabis indust1y should also have full access to all federal resources, including SBA loans. By denying these basic financial services, we run the risk of hampering future economic development and job growth, including in areas that have been rejuvenated by the cannabis industry, and where tax revenue generated by the indust1y has helped fund infrastructure and transportation projects, expand education programs, and support public services. Without access to working capital, business owners may struggle to retain workforce talent and may be unable to create good-paying jobs in communities where they are needed most.

Because of continuing federal prohibition, many banks are reluctant to work with cannabis businesses out of fear of being prosecuted under federal money laundering statutes. As a result, many state-licensed cannabis businesses are forced to operate on a cash-only basis, which makes them targets for robberies. Ancillary businesses serving the industry, such as child-proof packaging manufacturers, compliance consultants, and law firms, are routinely denied basic financial services. A lack of access to financial services also means that cannabis businesses must pay their local, state and federal taxes in cash, creating logistical headaches for regulators and a security risk for employees of state and local tax agencies and cannabis entrepreneurs alike.

Since most small business entrepreneurs, particularly those in low-income and minority communities, have traditionally had limited access to wealth networks and large investors, access to financial services in the form of bank loans would provide much-needed capital options for smaller operators and those who have been most harmed economically by prohibition. Legislation to address issues faced by small businesses in the cannabis industry has been introduced by the Chairwoman of the Committee on Small Business, Nydia Velazquez. The Ensuring Safe Capital Access for All Small Businesses Act (H.R. 3540), which was introduced by the Chairwoman of the Committee on Small Business, which would not only deschedule cannabis, but would also prohibit the Small Business Administration (SBA) from declining to provide a loan guarantee under the 7(a) Loan Guaranty Program, the Disaster Assistance Program, Micro loan program, or the 504/Certified Development Company program to a cannabis-related legitimate business or service provider. That legislation also seeks to be inclusive by ensuring that minority, women, and veteran entrepreneurs in the legitimate cannabis industry are able to fairly and affordably access capital from the Small Business Administration.

As of May 2019, a measure to provide safe harbor for financial institutions that want to work with state-legal cannabis businesses and their employees, known as the Secure and Fair Enforcement (SAFE) Banking Act, has been introduced in both chambers of Congress and most recently was approved by the House Financial Services Committee while garnering 206 co-sponsors in the House and 30 co-sponsors in the Senate. We should not delay action on that bill while we await action on legalization through de-scheduling or another means. The industry needs access to banking services as soon as possible, and we hope that we will see action in both chambers later this month, with passage soon after the August recess.

280E Tax Reform

Notwithstanding the significant economic and related contributions delivered by these small businesses, company owners are facing fierce headwinds. While some of these headwinds are no different in the cannabis industry than those facing other state-legal small business owners (i.e., payroll, employee health insurance, etc.), the cannabis businesses (including ancillary businesses) must also deal with significant challenges such as staying compliant with stringent state/local laws and finding creative ways to access capital (and even rudimentary banking services). Perhaps the most difficult challenge is section 280E of the federal tax code, which results in state-legal cannabis businesses paying an effective 80% tax rate, which would be unsustainable for any business.

Section 280E of the Internal Revenue Code prohibits businesses engaged in the "trafficking" of Schedule I or Schedule II control led substances in contravention of state or federal law from deducting normal business expenses, including payroll, employee benefits, and rent from gross income. While 280E was originally intended to penalize drug cartels, it now applies to licensed cannabis businesses that operate in compliance with state laws and regulations. This amounts to a significant financial burden for legitimate cannabis producers, processors, and retailers who often pay effective tax rates of 60% to 90% because of this arcane provision in the federal tax code. And because businesses are not able to make federal tax deductions, they sometimes end up paying higher rates at the state level as well.

Reforming 280E for businesses engaged in state-legal cannabis activities would generate revenue through expanded operations by enabling them to hire more employees and make capital improvements to their businesses, which reinvests money back into the local economy. States are further harmed by 280E because it provides an incentive to those seeking to sell cannabis for profit to do so outside of the regulated system. Entities that complete the arduous state licensing process, comply with stringent state regulations, and pay a variety of taxes imposed at each level of government are at an economic disadvantage relative to the criminal market operators for whom 280E was truly intended. Of course, fundamental fairness dictates that businesses that play by the rules should not be subject to excessive financial burdens that are not faced by untaxed illicit operations that do not adhere to the requirements of licensing and regulation. While it is possible that 280E reform could lead to some short-term losses in federal tax revenue from state-licensed businesses because of newly allowed deductions, however, these losses would likely only last for a handful of years. Within five years of reforming 280E, the federal government could potentially see increased tax revenues under cautious low-growth assumptions for the industry. Again, it is our hope that Congress will move quickly to find a permanent fix to 280E, even while it debates the merits of de-scheduling. Of course, de-scheduling cannabis in all forms would immediately cure the problems associated with section 280E of the tax code.

Conclusion

The cannabis industry has evolved into a national commercial enterprise generating significant tax revenue, generating hundreds of thousands of jobs, and providing people access to plant-based medicines that work to alleviate pain and treat symptoms of myriad diseases. State laws that have replaced the criminal markets with systems that provide for tightly regulated production and sale of cannabis to patients and adults over 21 are improving public safety. But, the unnecessary burdens caused by outdated federal policies must be resolved to benefit our communities' entrepreneurs.

De-scheduling cannabis cures most of the problems plaguing the industry all at once, rather than an incremental approach that leaves significant problems remaining. It's time to look ahead, move forward, balance the needs of small and large businesses alike, and legislate toward an approach that leaves no significant issues for tomorrow. De-scheduling is the only viable solution to the issues facing the cannabis industry at large. And it's the right public policy solution for an end to failed federal prohibition policies that have not worked for anyone, but pal licularly for small businesses.

I want to thank the Chair, Vice Chair, Ranking Member, and members of the Subcommittee for your time to discuss the de-scheduling of cannabis and a path forward. As always, NCIA remains ready to work with Congress on public policy solutions that will benefit the burgeoning American cannabis industry, small and large businesses, lawmakers, and the American public.

* * *

Mr. COHEN. Ms. Mosby, your testimony has been interesting in the context of all affected minorities. I proposed for years, I think since my first year in Congress, the Fresh Start Act, and I have introduced it again. It would say that if you had a nonviolent offense and you had gone 7 years without any other offenses in the Federal system, you could get your record expunged. Hopefully, we will have a chance to get that done.

Tell me your perspective on expungement of records and how that can affect people's lives.

Ms. MOSBY. So I would love to tell you—actually, in filing the motions to vacate over 5,000 convictions, the actual court actually denied our request. We do not have automatic expungement for marijuana possession cases in the State of Maryland. But what we do have is it is, unfortunately, I deem this a second-class sort of remedy to righting the wrongs of the past.

I think the number-one priority would be a vacatur. And the different between a vacatur and an expungement is that a vacatur is where you set aside a conviction, where the expungement merely seeks to remove the conviction from public view. And so what we are essentially saying is that these—based upon these discriminatory enforcement, these judgments should have been set aside.

But there are hurdles to that without sort of Federal enforcement or incentives to encourage the States to create these automatic expungements. In Maryland, there is a 4-year waiting period, right? People are suffering from collateral consequences not 4 years from now as a result of a marijuana conviction or not even 7 years, but actually now in the current, present day.

Mr. COHEN. And some of those consequences, they can't get jobs because they have had a —

Ms. MOSBY. Exactly.

Mr. COHEN. And they can't get maybe housing in Federal programs?

Ms. MOSBY. I mean, the collateral consequences —

Mr. COHEN. College loans.

Ms. MOSBY [continuing]. Extend to Federal loans. It extends to housing. It extends to adoptions. It extends to the access of healthcare. These collateral consequences extend to employment, professional licenses. I mean, every sort of basic necessity of life.

Mr. COHEN. These restrictions, disabilities are all as a result of Harry Anslinger back in 1939, which was a stupid, foolhardy, racist, race-based policy that J. Edgar Hoover endorsed and has been the public policy of the United States since and then politically was continued in 1971 with Ehrlichman's decision on the Southern strategy, right?

Ms. MOSBY. It is.

Mr. COHEN. So it is insane. This week, I will be introducing the Safer Streets Act, which will provide high crime areas—and Baltimore would be one, and Memphis would be another, unfortunately—more opportunities to get more monies. And how could— if we had such a program, what would you suggest communities could use for better policing efforts in reallocating the priorities?

Ms. MOSBY. So, I mean, again, I think that that is huge. I think that the introduction of that could be major for a city like Baltimore, but it would encourage us to utilize our resources not for marijuana possession, but for those violent offenses.

It also can better community-police relations. Because what the discriminatory enforcement has pretty much resulted in is an erosion of trust among communities and the law enforcement, police department that are there to serve them.

Mr. COHEN. Thank you.

Dr. Nathan, I have sponsored a bill called CARES, which I think Cory Booker is my Senate sponsor. It is the Compassionate Access, Research Expansion, and Respect States Act of 2019.

This current administration hasn't been as good as they have talked. The past administration wasn't as good as they talked either. Why do you think we haven't had more efforts to get research on marijuana in basically our whole history?

Dr. NATHAN. It has been through no lack of effort of the part of researchers, particularly in recent history. You know, you would like to think that we are at an age where we at least are willing to ask the questions that need to be answered.

Now we have had quite a bit or research on cannabis over the years that has been allowed, as it needs to be, by the National Institute of Drug Abuse. But that research is almost exclusively on the harms of cannabis. So when we hear that we really don't know the harms of cannabis, that is simply not the case.

Mr. COHEN. Doesn't cannabis—you said it is not a gateway drug. Does not cannabis cause people to try more than chocolate and vanilla at Baskin-Robbins? [Laughter.]

Dr. NATHAN. It is debatable, actually. The literature is mixed on that question. So —

Mr. COHEN. Okay. Let me ask Ms. Mosby this question. In jurisdictions where banks—marijuana businesses can't use banks, does that contribute to other crime, or are the people in the marijuana business potentially subject to robberies or burglaries or other things because they are using cash?

Ms. MOSBY. It absolutely is because knowing that, I mean, the criminals nowadays are very sophisticated, right? And understanding that there are these discrepancies and these conflicts between State and Federal laws, they are—the dispensaries are actually targeted, and we have seen some of those cases where individuals have been robbed.

Mr. COHEN. Thank you.

And my last question, and my time is up, too, but there is nobody here except Mr. McClintock to object, and he is kind enough not to.

Mr. MCCLINTOCK. Well, thank you for the opportunity.

Mr. COHEN. Overruled. [Laughter.]

Mr. COHEN. Mr.—is it Levine or Levine?

Mr. LEVINE. Levine.

Mr. COHEN. Mr. Levine, how does the banking policies, if you could explain why incrementally amending marijuana policy under the Controlled Substance Act, as the STATES Act proposed, is more beneficial than just totally ending marijuana prohibition outright?

Mr. LEVINE. Well, I don't think we view it as incremental as that we are representing 200,000 workers in the industry today, that we need it as vital. But that is not in opposition to removing cannabis from the Controlled Substance Act entirely, which we fully support. Our position is that we have real-world issues today that this piece of legislation would fix.

And to take, I appreciate that State's attorney Mosby said that it was her opinion that there was absolutely no equity provision of STATES Act. A lot of this stuff is happening on the State level. Ninety-nine percent of all expungements have to happen at the State and local level. And we have Illinois just passed a law, 25 percent of all revenue set aside to restore, reinvest, and renew programs.

Also, social equity applicants have lower application fees. In Massachusetts, where they have done equity applicants, not a single one has opened their doors because of lack of access to equity, and the head of Boston's chief of economic development said that the conflict between Federal and State law is an obstacle to the local equity program.

So we don't view this as competitive pieces of legislation. We would like to see it all passed as fast as we can get it passed.

Mr. COHEN. Thank you, sir. I appreciate your testimony.

I appreciate all of the witnesses today.

This has been an historic hearing. I don't think the Judiciary Committee has had a hearing on marijuana. And so I thank Chair Bass for scheduling the hearing. I thank her for allowing me to close it.

I have been working on this issue for 40 years, and it is just crazy that we don't just get it all done.

I appreciate Mr. Gaetz's work on the issue, but—and I understand incremental. But after 40 years, it is time to just zap straight up, get it all done, Schedule I gone.

So thank you for this historic hearing. Thank all of our witnesses for appearing.

Without objection, all Members will have 5 legislative days to submit written questions for the witnesses and additional materials.

And with that, and without objection, this hearing is adjourned. [Whereupon, at 12:16 p.m., the subcommittee was adjourned.]

Appendix

July 17, 2019

Chairwoman Karen Bass
Ranking Member John Ratcliffe
Subcommittee on Crime, Terrorism, Homeland Security
House Judiciary Committee
2138 Rayburn House Office Building
Washington, D.C. 20515

Dear Chairwoman Bass and Ranking Member Ratcliffe:

On behalf of The Leadership Conference on Civil and Human Rights (The Leadership Conference), a coalition of more than 200 national advocacy organizations, we write to express our continued strong support for the reform of cannabis laws and policy in the United States. We commend the Judiciary Committee for holding a hearing on this critical issue and especially applaud this committee's emphasis on highlighting the disparate impact of cannabis policies on communities of color, particularly African Americans. We urge the committee to only put forward legislation that includes the de-criminalization (i.e., de-scheduling) of cannabis at the federal level and provides relief to currently incarcerated individuals and those with prior arrests and conviction histories.

The hearing — *Marijuana Laws in America: Racial Justice and the Need for Reform* — has come at a particularly auspicious time. There is a critical need for reform because current federal cannabis laws and policies continue to disparately punish Black and Brown people and contribute to mass incarceration, penal institution overcrowding, and a costly criminal legal system. As a member of the Marijuana Justice Coalition, we ask that any legislation moving forward in Congress be comprehensive and address the impact of these draconian policies on people of color. The Marijuana Justice Coalition's full list of principles was released yesterday and can be found at the link here.

Future cannabis legislation must provide a mechanism through which the United States government can atone for the War on Drugs. Ultimately, comprehensive cannabis legislation will help to better facilitate the dismantling of structural racism and inequity within the criminal legal system that resulted from the War on Drugs. Federal drug laws and the drug policies adopted by this administration and previous administrations continue to undermine civil and human rights, disproportionately impact people of color, and contribute to mass incarceration. Adopting a policy position that focuses on lowering or eliminating federal penalties for medicinal and recreational cannabis use, possession, and/or sale would promote a public health, rather than punishment, approach to drugs.

Historical Context and War on Drugs

Cannabis was first categorized as a Schedule I drug during the Nixon administration through the Comprehensive Drug Abuse Prevention and Control Act of 1970 as part of Nixon's War on Drugs.[155] Even so, the administrations of Presidents Nixon, Ford, and Carter all focused on drug rehabilitation and treatment, with the majority of drug enforcement actions directed toward substances with greater health risks than cannabis, like heroin, fentanyl and cocaine.[156] Enforcement against cannabis increased dramatically, however, when the Reagan administration adopted a punishment-based

---

[155] "The War on Marijuana in Black and White." *The American Civil Liberties Union*. June 2013. Pg. 86. https://www.aclu.org/report/report-war-marijuana-black-and-white.

[156] *Ibid*. Pg. 87.

approach to the War on Drugs and emphasized arrest and incarceration as the primary means to combat drug use.[157] The Reagan administration imposed mandatory minimum sentences for drug offenses under the Anti-Drug Abuse Act of 1986 and dedicated more than a billion dollars to law enforcement efforts to increase drug arrests.[158] The subsequent administrations implemented even harsher enforcement tactics, emphasizing a "zero-tolerance" approach to drugs and calling upon law enforcement to channel its efforts against street-level drug sales and use in local neighborhoods.[159]

The "arrest-first" policy of the early 1990s led to an increase in drug arrests overall, but it had an especially large impact on cannabis arrests. FBI reports show that total drug arrests increased by 41 percent between 1991 and 1995, with cannabis arrests increasing by 80 percent.[160] The FBI called cannabis the "fastest growing drug category" in the 1990s. The emphasis on neighborhood-focused eradication led to a large increase in arrests of persons of color, largely due to the emphasis on street searches within low-income communities of color. FBI reports show that drug arrests for persons of color increased by 98 percent between 1990 and 1995, compared with a 62 percent increase for White people.[161] The increasing arrest rates and racial disparities continued into the 2000s and still exist today. The majority of these cannabis-related arrests were for simple possession.[162] Of the 8.2 million marijuana arrests between 2001 and 2010, 88 percent were for simply possessing cannabis.[163]

The punishment-based approach to the War on Drugs also led to a dramatic increase in incarceration and a corresponding racial disparity in incarceration rates. The total incarceration rate in the United States remained relatively stable throughout the 20th century, but it began to increase around the same time the focus of the War on Drugs turned from treatment and rehabilitation to arrest and incarceration.[164] The number of people incarcerated

---

157 *Ibid.*

158 *Ibid.*

159 *Ibid.* Pg. 89.

160 "Crime in the United States 1996. Section V. Drugs in America: 1980-1995." *FBI Uniform Crime Reporting*. 1996. Pg. 280. https://ucr.fbi.gov/crime-in-the-u.s/1996/96sec5.pdf.

161 *Ibid.* Pg. 282.

162 Angell, Tom, Marijuana Arrests Increasing Despite Legalization, New FBI Data Shows, Forbes, September 2018, https://www.forbes.com/sites/tomangell/2018/09/24/marijuana-arrests-are-increasing-despite-legalization-new-fbi-data-shows/.

163 Marijuana Arrests by the Numbers, ACLU, https://www.aclu.org/gallery/marijuana-arrests-numbers.

164 "Trends in U.S. Corrections." *The Sentencing Project*. Last Updated June 2019. Pg. 1. https://sentencingproject.org/wp-content/uploads/2016/01/Trends-in-US-Corrections.pdf.

in prisons and jails for drug offenses in the United States was 40,900 in 1980,[165] but steadily climbed to reach a total number of 469,545 in 2015. The exponential increase is largely due to the War on Drugs and mandatory sentencing laws.[166]

Cannabis Reform Will Impact Communities of Color because Punishment for Cannabis Use Historically and Currently Has Been Disproportionately Burdensome to these Groups

Overincarceration and racial disparities created by the enforcement of cannabis laws are still a significant issue in the United States. The continued enforcement of cannabis prohibition laws results in over 600,000 arrests annually, disproportionately impacting people of color. These cannabis arrests continue to punish low-level street dealers and users more severely than the high-level members of drug organizations.[167] On average, Black people are more 3.73 times more likely to be arrested for possession of cannabis than White people.[168] This is the case despite studies that indicate Black people only use cannabis at 1.3 times the rate of White people.[169] Further, in addition to disproportionate arrest rates, people of color have been historically targeted by discriminatory sentencing practices. On average, Black men receive drug sentences that are 13.1 percent longer than sentences imposed for White men, and Latinos are nearly 6.5 times more likely to receive a federal sentence for cannabis possession than non-Hispanic Whites. For example, in 2013, simple cannabis possession was the fourth most common cause of deportation for all offenses and the most common cause of deportation for drug law violations.

---

165 *Ibid.* Pg. 3.
166 *Ibid.*
167 King, Ryan and Mauer, Marc. "A 25-Year Quagmire: The War on Drugs and its Impact on American Society." *The Sentencing Project.* September 1, 2007. Pgs. 12-13. https://www.sentencingproject.org/publications/a-25-year-quagmire-the-war-on-drugs-and-its-impact-on-american-society/.
168 "Criminal Law Reform." *ACLU.* 2018. https://www.aclu.org/issues/criminal-law-reform.
169 *Ibid.*

Cannabis Reform Can Positively Impact the Economic and Social Fabric of Communities of Color and the Country at Large

Discriminatory drug enforcement has structural barriers to building economic wealth.[170] While people of color suffer the disparate burden of the punishment for cannabis violations, the economic benefits predominantly flow to others. Currently, it is estimated that less than one percent of the cannabis industry is owned or operated by people of color.[171] Therefore, any meaningful cannabis reform legislation must be developed using a racial justice lens. The War on Drugs and cannabis criminalization have caused economic devastation and led to the perpetuation of poverty in America, especially for communities of color. Many impacted individuals are burdened by bail and fees that they cannot afford because of an offense and often times end up spending additional time in confinement because of an inability to pay.[172] The money-bail system bars many cannabis users and dealers who are low-level offenders and awaiting trial to be released. Research shows that Black defendants receive higher bail amounts and are less likely to be released without bail.[173] The majority of people in jail, 60 percent, are there because they can't afford bail.[174] Bail and fees, discriminatory policies that have led to mass incarceration and over incarceration, prevent many people of color from benefiting from the cannabis industry and increasing their economic opportunities.

Full legalization is also likely to result in cost-savings and tax benefits for federal and state governments. The total amount that cannabis prohibition costs states and the federal government each year by pursuing cannabis offenses is an estimated four billion dollars.[175] Legalizing cannabis use and possession would save money by eliminating associated law enforcement and court filing fees, as demonstrated by the savings experienced by states that have already legalized it. Studies have found that crime dropped in each state

---

[170] Using Marijuana Revenue to Create Jobs, Center for American Progress, May 2019, https://www.americanprogress.org/issues/criminal-justice/reports/2019/05/20/470031/using-marijuana-revenue-create-jobs/.

[171] *Ibid.*

[172] Harriot, Michael, Money Bail Might Be the Most Racist, Immoral Part of America's Criminal Injustice System, The Root, Dec. 2018, https://www.theroot.com/money-bail-might-be-the-most-racist-immoral-part-of-am-1831241786.

[173] *Ibid.*

[174] Lam, Bourree, Is Bail Causing Convictions?, The Atlantic, May 2016, https://www.theatlantic.com/business/archive/2016/05/money-bail/484034/.

[175] Statement of Principles on Federal Marijuana Reform, The Marijuana Justice Coalition, http://www.drugpolicy.org/sites/default/files/mjc-principles_0.pdf.

after legalization.[176] Some proponents for legalization of cannabis argue that reform can eliminate hostile interactions and even improve community trust with law enforcement to ultimately decrease violence, increase the solving of more violent crimes, and positively affect reentry outcomes.[177]

Furthermore, governments would be able to regulate and tax the industry, generating revenue and shifting limited law enforcement resources toward issues that present more of a threat to public safety. Federal and state governments could also direct cost savings and revenue toward rehabilitation and treatment programs for other drug users and to programs that benefit and reinvest in communities. For example, Colorado distributed $230 million of cannabis tax revenues to the Colorado Department of Education between 2015 and 2017 to fund school construction, early childhood literacy, bullying prevention, and behavioral health.[178] Washington also dedicates 25 percent of its cannabis tax revenues to substance use disorder treatment, education, and prevention, and distributes 55 percent of its cannabis tax revenues to fund basic health plans.[179] Oregon allocates 40 percent of cannabis tax revenue to its state school fund, depositing over $34 million into the fund, and also distributes 20 percent of the revenue to alcohol and drug treatment.[180]

Cannabis Reform Will Positively Affect the Public Health of America

Many public health concerns are part of the cannabis reform debate. Anti-legalization proponents argue that cannabis is a gateway drug and any potential reform can lead to substance misuse, addiction, accidental ingestion by children, and intentional consumption by adolescents.[181] In contrast, evidence suggests medicinal marijuana use can also benefit those undergoing chemotherapy, epilepsy, and those suffering from wasting syndrome as a

---

[176] From Prohibition to Progress: A Status Report on Marijuana Legalization, Drug Policy Alliance. Jan. 2018. http://www.drugpolicy.org/legalization-status-report.

[177] Jaeger, Kyle, Legalizing Marijuana Helps Police Solve Other crimes, New Study Shows, Marijuana Movement, Jul. 2018, https://www.marijuanamoment.net/legalizing-marijuana-helps-police-solve-other-crimes-new-study-shows/.

[178] From Prohibition to Progress: A Status Report on Marijuana Legalization, Drug Policy Alliance. Jan. 2018. http://www.drugpolicy.org/legalization-status-report.

[179] *Ibid.*

[180] *Ibid.*

[181] *McFarland, A. Finn,* Weeding through the Public Health Implications of Marijuana Legalization, Tufts Public Health, December 18, 2018. https://publichealth.tufts.edu/news/2019/02/weeding-through-public-health-implications-marijuana-legalization.

result of AIDS.[182] Further, there is now evidence that cannabis can even serve as an "exit drug," in that it reduces or eliminates use of more harmful drugs such as opiates or alcohol by easing withdrawal symptoms.[183] Experts say medical marijuana may also help reduce opioid overdoses because it can be prescribed to treat pain instead of highly addictive opioids.[184] In addition, states with medical marijuana laws have lower rates of deaths from drug use.[185] Cannabis reform can also improve trust and strength in doctor-patient relationships,[186] and patients may be willing to be more candid about their drug use because of its decreased stigma.

Cannabis Reform Will Eliminate Barriers to Access to Public Benefits

Arresting and incarcerating individuals for cannabis leads to serious consequences that affect the person who was convicted, their family, and society as a whole. People convicted of felony cannabis offenses suffer from the same, if not worse, consequences as those convicted of non-felony level "violent" crimes. Federal law requires that the states revoke the driver's license of a person who was convicted of any felony for at least six months, and permits states to revoke their license for even longer.[187] Under federal law and under the law of 31 states, people with felony convictions are not allowed to participate in jury service,[188] and many states restrict their voting rights.[189] Individuals with felony convictions also experience limited access to

---

182 *Ibid.*

183 Is marijuana a gateway drug?, Drug Policy Alliance, http://www.drugpolicy.org/marijuana-gateway-drug.

184 *McFarland, A. Finn,* Weeding through the Public Health Implications of Marijuana Legalization, Tufts Public Health, December 18, 2018. https://publichealth.tufts.edu/news/2019/02/weeding-through-public-health-implications-marijuana-legalization.

185 Marijuana Legalization and Public Health: The Great Debate, MPHonline, https://www.mphonline.org/marijuana-legalization-public-health/.

186 Grinspoon, Peter, Medical marijuana Harvard Health Publishing, Harvard Medical School, January 2018, https://www.health.harvard.edu/blog/medical-marijuana-2018011513085.

187 23 U.S. Code § 159.

188 "Every 25 Seconds the Human Toll on Criminalizing Drug Use in the United States." *ACLU* and *Human Rights Watch.* October 2016. Pg. 156. https://www.aclu.org/sites/default/files/field_document/usdrug1016_web.pdf.

189 *Ibid.* Pgs. 150-51.

employment opportunities, and often struggle to find a job after release.[190] When coupled with current efforts to increase work requirements for government assistance with basic need, reentry becomes even more complicated for already vulnerable individuals impacted by drug convictions.

Lifting federal bans that disproportionately affect low-income communities and persons of color would help to reduce racial disparities in reentry. People convicted of drug offenses, including cannabis offenses, are often targeted under criminal law and subject to exclusions that do not impact other people returning to their communities after a period of incarceration. They face barriers to actively participating in their children's lives (i.e., prohibited from volunteering at schools or chaperoning field trips). Impacted individuals are often ineligible for certain public benefits, for example, Supplemental Nutrition Assistance Program (SNAP) and Temporary Assistance for Needy Families (TANF) based on the jurisdiction they live in. They also can't access affordable public housing and can be prohibited from receiving public education loans. Cannabis reform can also lead to the development of community services and provide additional wraparound services to impacted individuals.

These impacted individuals are also subject to drug testing for public benefits. Conviction or continued marijuana use by returning citizens has also led to family separation by removing children from their biological families and placing them in the child welfare system. Additional limitations include barriers to acquiring business loans, access to health care, or even inability to legally adopt. In totality, individuals leaving prison face stigma, and research shows that these barriers present themselves even further because of spotty work history, low education levels, and untreated substance abuse and mental health issues. Collateral consequences like those listed create barriers for individuals attempting to re-integrate back into society.[191] Therefore, dismantling these collateral consequences would help reduce the likelihood of recidivism.

---

[190] "'Ban the Box' is a Fair Chance For Workers With Records." *National Employment Law Project*. Aug. 2017. https://s27147.pcdn.co/wp-content/uploads/Ban-the-Box-Fair-Chance-Fact-Sheet.pdf.

[191] Laird, Lorelei, Ex-offenders face tens of thousands of legal restrictions, bias and limits on their rights, ABA Journal, Jun.2013, http://www.abajournal.com/magazine/article/ex-offenders_face_tens_of_thousands_of_legal_restrictions.

Cannabis Reform Will Increase Equity in a Society Shaped by Racial Discrimination in the Criminal Justice System

The Leadership Conference advocates for the complete removal of federal penalties for the use and possession of cannabis, including recreational and medicinal cannabis, with provisions that focus on reparative justice, and removal of cannabis from the Controlled Substances Act. Public sentiment supports legalization: a majority of American voters — 68 percent — are in support of cannabis reform, according to a 2018 Center for American Progress and GBAO Strategies poll.[192] Additionally, 73 percent of American voters support the automatic sealing of marijuana offenses.[193] More importantly, ending prohibition would eliminate any racial disparities resulting from cannabis-related arrests and convictions and would likely help decrease the overall number of incarcerated persons of color. Federal reform would also result in the dismantling of federal collateral consequences in education, employment, and housing that disproportionately harm communities of color and low-income communities. Several states have already legalized cannabis, including Alaska, Illinois, Maine, Michigan, Nevada, Vermont, Washington, Washington, D.C., California, Colorado, Massachusetts, and Oregon.

We urge action through legislative reform to increase equity within the legal cannabis marketplace and provide industry access to people of color. This country must reckon with its legacy of racial and ethnic injustices, including the disproportionate collateral consequences of 80 years of cannabis prohibition enforcement that now limits participation in the industry. Both disproportionate arrest and conviction rates have made it particularly difficult for people of color to enter the legal cannabis marketplace. The communities that have been most harmed by cannabis prohibition are benefiting the least from the legal cannabis marketplace. One way to increase equity within the cannabis industry is to provide loans and capital for cannabis businesses to individuals who are disproportionately impacted minority small business owners.

Cannabis legislative reform must benefit individuals who were formerly incarcerated or have prior drug law violations and criminal convictions. Creating a process that will provide the expungement or sealing of criminal records for cannabis offenses and eliminating broad felony restrictions for

---

[192] Center for American Progress. Voters Across Party Line Support Clean Slate Legislation. https://www.americanprogress.org/issues/criminal-justice/news/2018/06/20/451624/ voters-across-party-lines-support-clean-slate-legislation/.

[193] *Ibid.*

licensing will benefit these individuals, as well as individuals who are currently on parole or under any probationary agreement, for cannabis offenses. Any meaningful cannabis reform should also establish resentencing for individuals serving sentences for cannabis convictions and redesignate penalties for persons previously convicted of cannabis-related crimes for which the penalties have been reduced or removed. This should also apply to those currently under parole, probation, state supervision, or released on bail awaiting trial.

Any meaningful cannabis reform must provide opportunities where tax revenue from cannabis sales can be reinvested in communities that have been most affected by cannabis arrests and the War on Drugs. Tax revenues should also be used to establish a special fund to provide small business investments to support people of color entering the legal cannabis industry. Moreover, profits made through the cannabis industry should support local jurisdictions and community leaders in developing programs in order to serve impacted individuals with job training, reentry services, expungement expenses, public libraries, community centers, programs and opportunities dedicated to youth, and health education programs.

Conclusion

Federal drug laws and the drug policies adopted by this administration and previous administrations continue to undermine civil and human rights, disparately impact persons of color, and contribute to mass incarceration. Adopting a policy position that focuses on lowering or eliminating federal penalties for medicinal and recreational cannabis use, possession, and/or sale would harmonize well with the "public health rather than punishment" approach to drug reform that The Leadership Conference has already adopted.

Moreover, given the evolving public sentiment towards cannabis, recent state-level reforms, and the increasingly vocal support for reform from even more moderate coalition members, the issue of cannabis reform is ripe for action. We urge you to advance cannabis drug reforms that finally respect the civil and human rights of all communities. If you have any questions, please feel free to contact Sakira Cook at cook@civilrights.org or (202) 263-2894. Thank you for your support for this critical legislation.

Sincerely,
Vanita Gupta
President & CEO

* * *

July 15, 2019

Dear Chairman Bass, Ranking Member Ratcliffe and Members of the House Judiciary Committee,

The federal government's heavy-handed influence on the everyday choices made by Americans is alarming, and Congress should seek to inhibit federal encroachment on state issues. However, the federal government maintains a legitimate interest in enforcing federal laws relating to dangerous drugs, including marijuana. As the House Judiciary Committee considers marijuana legislation, Concerned Women for America strongly urges you to resist the aggressive push for liberalization of federal marijuana laws.

The Strengthening the Tenth Amendment Through Entrusting States Act, or the STATES Act (H.R. 2093), seeks to amend the Controlled Substances Act of 1970[194] to exempt the production or sale of marijuana from the Controlled Substances Act in accordance with state or tribal law. This will exempt marijuana from federal enforcement and federal oversight in states where marijuana has been legalized. This equates to the federal legalization of marijuana.

During the 2019 legislative session, the marijuana industry suffered defeat after defeat on the state level; in Vermont, New Hampshire, Connecticut, New Mexico, New Jersey, New York, and in many other states, legislatures declined to enact pro-recreational marijuana measures. Although the legalization conversation is ongoing around the nation, the marijuana industry is relentlessly pushing their pro-legalization agenda on the federal level for their own financial gain. The STATES Act is a crucial element in this legalization strategy.

The STATES Act would wrongfully give states the ultimate governing authority, and liability, over marijuana policy, but drug enforcement is not a state issue. Congress passed the Controlled Substances Act of 1970 (CSA) because the black market does not honor state lines. Its rationale for passing the CSA in 1970, the effect of drugs on interstate commerce and concern of the effects of psychotropic substances, still stand today. By arguing that states should be the ultimate governing authority over marijuana policy, proponents ignore legalization's effects on neighboring states and the nation as a whole. In order to support this bill from a states' rights perspective, supporters must

[194] 21 U.S.C. ch. 13 § 801 et seq.

either conclude that the entire Controlled Substances Act is unconstitutional, thus states are solely responsible for handling all activity relating to all drugs, including heroin, fentanyl, and other illicit drugs or that marijuana is completely harmless with no potential for addiction or abuse and should be legal in all cases.

The federal government has a legitimate interest in overseeing interstate commerce, as expressed by the Founders in Article I, Section 8 of the U.S. Constitution. This federal interest has been reinforced by the Supreme Court of the United States many times. In *Gonzales v. Raich*, a 2005 case regarding federal enforcement of laws concerning medicinal marijuana plants in someone's yard, the Supreme Court affirmed 6 to 3 that federal law supersedes state law in enforcing drug statutes – even in states where marijuana is legal. Marijuana use in intrastate commerce was determined to be part of the national marijuana market, and thus under "essential" federal regulation, because local use has an effect on the national market.

What happens in legalized states doesn't stay there, and legal recreational use states provide exceptional cover for criminal organizations who want to exploit addiction for profit. In 2018, NBC News published an extensive piece on foreign cartels in Colorado taking advantage of recreational legalization.[195] According to federal and local officials, "Chinese, Cuban and Mexican drug rings have purchased or rented hundreds of homes [to cultivate and grow marijuana] and use human trafficking to bring inexperienced growers to the U.S. to tend them …"[196] These cartels target legalized states to shield black market operations in a legal environment, grow more marijuana than the entire state could consume, ship marijuana out of the state to states where recreational use is illegal, and then turn a massive profit. The federal government should not make it easier for foreign drug cartels to flourish in the United States.

Since Colorado has legalized recreational use, marijuana has poured into nearby states[197], so much so, that neighboring states Nebraska and Oklahoma

[195] Romero, D., Gutierrez, G., Blankstein, A., & Powell, R. (2018, May 29). Black-market marijuana is big business, even in states where pot's legal. Retrieved February 1, 2019, from https://www.nbcnews.com/news/us-news/foreign-cartels-embrace-home-grown-marijuana-pot-legal-states-n875666.

[196] Romero, D., Gutierrez, G., Blankstein, A., & Powell, R. (2018, May 29). Black-market marijuana is big business, even in states where pot's legal. Retrieved February 1, 2019, from https://www.nbcnews.com/news/us-news/foreign-cartels-embrace-home-grown-marijuana-pot-legal-states-n875666.

[197] Hughes, T. (2016, May 17). When smuggling Colo. pot, not even the sky's the limit. Retrieved February 1, 2019, from https://www.usatoday.com/story/news/2016/05/13/when-smuggling-colo-pot-not-even-skys-limit/83623226/.

have sued Colorado for exacerbating their in-state marijuana trafficking operations.[198] One does not need to travel to Colorado for Colorado marijuana, it exists in virtually every state.[199] The Colorado Attorney General's office said that legalization "has inadvertently helped fuel the business of Mexican drug cartels … cartels are now trading drugs like heroin for marijuana."[200] The Drug Enforcement Administration's (DEA) 2018 National Drug Threat Assessment repeatedly states that "traffickers are transporting their marijuana across states lines, into states where it is not legal to grow it, and/or the laws are different."[201] In 2018, the DEA found that the majority of marijuana in the U.S. is illicitly produced on United States soil by state-licensed medical growers and drug trafficking organizations.[202]

Unsurprisingly, the overgrowth of the black market in legalized states is not isolated to Colorado. A report from the Oregon State Police found that the black market in Oregon has skyrocketed since the state legalized marijuana, including significant trafficking operations to states that have not legalized marijuana as well as foreign countries.[203] In 2019, California Governor Gavin Newsom asked for help from the federal government to eradicate the state's massive black market.[204] The California State Legislature considered a tax break during its 2018 session for legal operations so that they can compete with black market prices.[205] Legalization in a high-tax, highly regulated environment like that of California, Oregon, and Colorado does not eliminate the black market, rather, according to the DEA, it enables it.[206]

---

[198] *Nebraska, et al. v. Colorado*, No. 144, Orig., https://caselaw.findlaw.com/us-supreme-court/144-orig.html.

[199] Hughes, T. (2016, May 17). When smuggling Colo. pot, not even the sky's the limit. Retrieved February 1, 2019, from https://www.usatoday.com/story/news/2016/05/13/when-smuggling-colo-pot-not-even-skys-limit/83623226/.

[200] Mamdooh, S. (2016, April 08). Cartels cashing in on Colorado's pot industry. Retrieved February 1, 2019, from http://www.thedenverchannel.com/news/local-news/marijuana/mexican-drug-cartels-are-taking-full-advantage-of-colorados-marijuana-laws.

[201] United States of America, Department of Justice, Drug Enforcement Administration. (2018). *2018 National Drug Threat Assessment* (pp. 77-88).

[202] United States of America, Department of Justice, Drug Enforcement Administration. (2018). *2018 National Drug Threat Assessment* (pp. 77-88).

[203] Oregon State Police, Drug Enforcement Section. (2017). *A baseline evaluation of cannabis enforcement priorities in Oregon*. Oregon State Library.

[204] Daniels, J. (2019, April 03). California wages war against illegal weed farms; Gov. Newsom wants Trump to pay some costs. Retrieved February 1, 2019, from https://www.cnbc.com/2019/04/03/california-wages-war-against-illegal-marijuana-farms-retailers.html.

[205] C.A. Legis. Assemb. AB-3157. Reg. Sess. 2017-2018 (2018).

[206] United States of America, Department of Justice, Drug Enforcement Administration. (2018). *2018 National Drug Threat Assessment* (pp. 77-88).

All of this translates to cost, and marijuana legalization does not serve as an income-generator for states. In Colorado, one comprehensive study found that for every $1 in revenue marijuana brings in, the state spends $4.50 countering the effects.[207] This number includes health care costs, traffic fatalities, DUIs, high school dropouts, and poison control calls.[208]

The enactment of the STATES Act would hurt states economically, while simultaneously legitimizing the marijuana industry financially, granting marijuana businesses, including drug trafficking organizations, access to the federal banking system. This would be the first time the banking industry was opened to schedule I drug operations and would set an alarming and dangerous precedent of granting banking access to criminal activity.

Keeping marijuana operations separate from the banking system has helped limit the rate of growth of the marijuana industry.[209] Furthermore, there is no assurance that drug trafficking organizations would be unable to access the banking system for marijuana-related businesses. Drug trafficking organizations are willing to exploit what is legal to accomplish what is illegal.

Opening up the banking system to marijuana operations will no doubt abet foreign drug trafficking operations in the United States and abroad. Canada, which legalized recreational marijuana nationwide in late 2018, has already seen offshore investments infiltrate their marijuana operations, some with ties to organized crime.[210]

Marijuana is a multibillion-dollar a year industry. Allowing the banking industry access to this underground industry would lead to unprecedented Wall Street investment.[211] Former big tobacco executives are already

---

207 *Economic and Social Costs of Legalized Marijuana*[Study]. (2018, November 15). In *Centennial Institute*. Retrieved February 1, 2019, from http://www.ccu.edu/centennial/policy-briefs/marijuana-costs/.

208 *Economic and Social Costs of Legalized Marijuana*[Study]. (2018, November 15). In *Centennial Institute*. Retrieved February 1, 2019, from http://www.ccu.edu/centennial/policy-briefs/marijuana-costs/.

209 Smart Approaches to Marijuana. (2019, March 28). *House Financial Services Committee Approves Marijuana Banking Bill* [Press release]. Retrieved May 29, 2019, from https://learnaboutsam.org/house-financial-services-committee-approves-marijuana-banking-bill/.

210 Smart Approaches to Marijuana. (2019, March 28). *House Financial Services Committee Approves Marijuana Banking Bill* [Press release]. Retrieved May 29, 2019, from https://learnaboutsam.org/house-financial-services-committee-approves-marijuana-banking-bill/.

211 Smart Approaches to Marijuana. (2018, June 7). *Statement from SAM President Kevin Sabet Regarding Senator Cory Gardner's Legislation Shielding Addiction-For-Profit Industry From Federal Law* [Press release]. Retrieved May 1, 2019, from https://learnaboutsam.org/statement-sam-president-kevin-sabet-regarding-senator-cory-gardners-legislation-shielding-addiction-profit-industry-federal-law/.

aggressively investing in marijuana[212] and former big tobacco companies have already invested in Canadian legal marijuana markets.[213] Allowing the tobacco industry, with its proven record of complete disregard for public health and safety, access to Wall Street marijuana investment on a massive scale would all but assure that marijuana is the next big tobacco. State legal marijuana markets have already seen immense investment from tobacco titans like The Altria Group and Phillip Morris, the maker of Marlboro.[214]

The STATES Act not only legalizes marijuana use but legitimizes its use even though marijuana legalization has had a documented negative impact on mental health, violence, and adolescent behavior and development. Study after study continues to show conclusively that marijuana does have a high potential for abuse, which reinforces the need for its schedule 1 categorization.[215] In 2016, President Obama's Department of Health and Human Services along with the DEA, reiterated this and refused to reschedule marijuana from a schedule I drug because of its high potential for abuse and lack of current acceptable medical use.[216] Furthermore, because of obligations outlined in international drug treaties, the United States cannot reschedule marijuana to a schedule less restrictive than schedule II.[217]

Marijuana is not FDA approved to treat any disorder, disease, or condition, and medical legalization always serves as a foothold for recreational legalization. In fact, the FDA has fined the marijuana industry for making counterfeit, off the rail, medical claims, mostly claims relating to

---

[212] Marijuana Business Daily. (2017, June 21). MPP chief ready to barter for marijuana campaign donations. Retrieved May 29, 2019, from https://mjbizdaily.com/mpp-chief-ready-barter-marijuana-campaign-donations/.

[213] Hirsch, L. (2018, December 07). Altria to invest $1.8 billion in cannabis company Cronos Group, exits some e-cig brands. Retrieved June 8, 2019, from https://www.cnbc.com/2018/12/07/altria-to-invest-1point8-billion-in-cannabis-company-cronos-group.html.

[214] Smart Approaches to Marijuana. (2019, February 8). *Senator Ron Wyden Introduces Bill to Legalize Marijuana; Big Tobacco Rejoices* [Press release]. Retrieved from https://learnaboutsam.org/senator-ron-wyden-introduces-bill-to-legalize-marijuana-big-tobacco-rejoices/.

[215] Drug Enforcement Administration, Department of Justice; Denial of Petition to Initiate Proceedings to Reschedule Marijuana, 81 Fed. Reg. 53767 (Aug. 12, 2016) (codified at 21 C.F.R. Pt. II).

[216] Drug Enforcement Administration, Department of Justice; Denial of Petition to Initiate Proceedings to Reschedule Marijuana, 81 Fed. Reg. 53767 (Aug. 12, 2016) (codified at 21 C.F.R. Pt. II).

[217] Drug Enforcement Administration, Department of Justice; Denial of Petition to Initiate Proceedings to Reschedule Marijuana, 81 Fed. Reg. 53767 (Aug. 12, 2016) (codified at 21 C.F.R. Pt. II).

marijuana's treatment or even "curing" of terminal cancer.[218] Legitimate scientific research does not support the industry's claims. If marijuana or its derivatives provide any hope for patients, the FDA should regulate marijuana like any other drug instead of a recreational activity.

The costs of marijuana use on the health care system cannot be easily dismissed and purporting marijuana use as a legitimate health care remedy is irresponsible and reckless. Marijuana has a high potential for abuse and daily or near daily marijuana users are 25-50% more likely to develop cannabis use disorder.[219] In Colorado, it cost $31,448,905.88 to treat cannabis use disorder in 2017 alone.[220] Research continues to show that "the higher the use of marijuana, the greater the risk" for long-term health issues and adverse reactions.[221] Long-term marijuana use is linked to health and behavior problems later in life[222], including heart attacks[223], violence[224], and schizophrenia.[225] Furthermore, marijuana doesn't treat mental illnesses such as anxiety or depression. At best, it serves as a coping mechanism to emotionally numb the pain, rather than addressing the root cause of it, at worst, it exacerbates existing issues.[226]

---

218 Smart Approaches to Marijuana. (2017, November 1). *SAM Applauds FDA Action on Medical Pot Companies Making Dishonest Medical Claims* [Press release]. Retrieved May 29, 2019, from https://learnaboutsam.org/sam-applauds-fda-action-medical-pot-companies-making-dishonest-medical-claims/.

219 *Economic and Social Costs of Legalized Marijuana* [Study]. (2018, November 15). In *Centennial Institute*. Retrieved February 1, 2019, from http://www.ccu.edu/centennial/policy-briefs/marijuana-costs/.

220 *Economic and Social Costs of Legalized Marijuana* [Study]. (2018, November 15). In *Centennial Institute*. Retrieved February 1, 2019, from http://www.ccu.edu/centennial/policy-briefs/marijuana-costs/.

221 National Academies of Sciences, Engineering, and Medicine. 2017. *The health effects of cannabis and cannabinoids: Current state of evidence and recommendations for research.* Washington, DC: The National Academies Press.

222 Sarlin, E., M.Ed., M.A. (2018, February 08). Long-Term Marijuana Use Is Associated With Health Problems Later in Life. Retrieved February 1, 2019, from https://www.drugabuse.gov/news-events/nida-notes/2018/02/long-term-marijuana-use-associated-health-problems-later-in-life.

223 Singh, A., Saluja, S., Kumar, A., Agrawal, S., Thind, M., Nanda, S., & Shirani, J. (2017). Cardiovascular Complications of Marijuana and Related Substances: A Review. *Cardiology and Therapy,* 7(1), 45-59. doi:10.1007/s40119-017-0102-x.

224 Berenson, Alex. (2019). *Tell Your Children: The Truth about Marijuana, Mental Illness, and Violence* (pp. 166). New York, New York: Free Press.

225 Berenson, Alex. (2019). *Tell Your Children: The Truth about Marijuana, Mental Illness, and Violence* (pp. 168). New York, New York: Free Press.

226 Berenson, Alex. (2019). *Tell Your Children: The Truth about Marijuana, Mental Illness, and Violence* (pp. 168). New York, New York: Free Press.

Although the STATES Act sounds like an appealing compromise, especially for states' rights advocates and proponents of small government, it is logically inconsistent and dishonest. The STATES Act would hurt law enforcement efforts to end drug trafficking in the U.S., irreparably compromise the integrity of the U.S. banking system, and damage the physical and economic health of the American public. The marijuana industry has invested significant time and resources on specific messaging strategies aimed to garner as much support for incrementalism as possible. Both the states' rights approach and the medical push bring hesitant parties into the fold and are crucial steps to the overall goal of full legalization with as little industry oversight as possible.

The STATES Act does not decriminalize marijuana or address any of the legitimate criminal justice concerns that legalization creates because decriminalization is not the industry objective, full legalization is the objective. The STATES Act would exacerbate current state marijuana legalization issues while simultaneously ignoring the scientific and economic data that shows legalization is harmful. Pushing legislation like the STATES Act further advances the reckless legalization trend. The STATES Act is not about states' rights, it is a blatant attempt to deceive the public to legalize marijuana on the federal level in the name of state autonomy. The marijuana industry has spent millions lobbying and drafting this legislation for their own personal gain, all at the expense of public health, safety, justice, and common sense.[227] This bill plunges the U.S. into a real-time human experiment on marijuana use and should be opposed.

Sincerely,

Penny Young Nance CEO and President

Concerned Women for America Legislative Action Committee

---

[227] Smart Approaches to Marijuana. (2019, February 8). *Senator Ron Wyden Introduces Bill to Legalize Marijuana; Big Tobacco Rejoices*[Press release]. Retrieved from https://learnaboutsam.org/senator-ron-wyden-introduces-bill-to-legalize-marijuana-big-tobacco-rejoices/.

Testimony before the United States House of Representatives, Committee on the Judiciary, Subcommittee on Crime, Terrorism, and Homeland Security Hearing on: "Marijuana Laws in America: Racial Injustice and the Need for Reform," July 10, 2019, Statement (for the Hearing Record), Richard Brumfield, Founder and Chief Executive Officer, Full Spectrum Omega, Inc.

Chairwoman Bass, Ranking Member Ratcliffe, and Members of the House Subcommittee on Crime, Terrorism, and Homeland Security. My name Is Richard Brumfield, Founder and CEO, Full Spectrum Omega, Inc. (FSO). FSO is a privately held Service-Disabled Veteran-Owned Small Business (SDVOSB) phytocannabinoids company based in Los Angeles, CA focused on development of FDA approved phytocannabinoids to address unmet medical conditions while improving patients' lives.

I am a service disabled African American Veteran.

The Committee may be interested in learning that the company that manages FSO's unique structured molecular product line, MJRx, has been notified by the Medical Cannabis Safety Bureau/Department of Health that due to its high standards and excellent reviews its extraction company, la India Inc., has been chosen as a "state of the art" example of a California Manufacturing facility.

MJRx Corp. is an owner-executive management team with over 100 years combined legal cannabis experience and is comprised of ZO California professionals, managers, and cannabis operators that own and manage 13 city and 10 state MAUCRSA licenses since 2016.

MJRX provides professional services and resources, legal compliance, CCTT documentation, funding, start-up, personnel, training, education, operations and auditing.

For the past decade my company has developed a cannabis extract product line that has shown unique and remarkable positive results for a wide variety of medical conditions in patient use under California State Medical Cannabis provisions. FSO's products contain less than 0.3% (il9-THC) and are reported to be non-euphoric by patients. Results to date have generated significant Interest and support for further development as U.S. Food and Drug Administration (FDA) approved products.

FSO currently has signed agreements with the Federal government to test its products as wound healing treatments secondary to burns and radiation as well as non-opioid analgesics for the treatment of pain. The government laboratories and FSO are actively engaging with the Drug Enforcement Administration (DEA) to secure the required federal waiver to initiate the studies. As of to date, FSO's Federal partner has already received the necessary permit to conduct the studies. FSO's application Is currently under review by the DEA.

The Committee should be aware that U.S. small biotech companies involved In cannabis R&D for drug development are struggling with the conflicted policies and convoluted processes that must be navigated In order to obtain the required schedule I registrations from the Drug Enforcement Administration (DEA).

Currently, U.S. provisions for access to cannabis plants and products are limited to a single source, the NIDA contracted farm at the University of Mississippi.

Stakeholders and we believe that term includes the FDA, understand the fundamental mismatch between the current single source model for both Industry needs and the needs of academic research.

However, DEA Docket 447 with its focus on NIH grants and post-IND activities, as well as current proposed legislative language, does not clearly provide access to cannabis strains from sources sufficient to meet the requirements for all the research and development activities of product development by U.S. industry. Stakeholders understand that the intent of DEA Docket 447 and legislation is to provide expanded access to cannabis, but absent shared understanding of the differing needs of federal research institutions, academia and industry the path to effective solutions is still unclear. Rescheduling is a step in the clarification process, but It not the only step required.

I recently was asked to make a presentation to the Federal Food and Drug Administration hearing, "to obtain scientific data and Information about the safety, manufacturing, product quality, marketing, labeling, and sale of products containing cannabis or cannabis-derived compounds" held in May 31 to talk about how the Federal government could help facilitate opportunities for cannabis businesses, and I would assume the majority of enterprises in this industry, like Full Spectrum Omega, are qualified small businesses.

I presented a series of issues, challenged and proposed solutions.

Issue: The FDA requested recommendations on data sources useful in providing safety and efficacy information.

Problem: The legal restriction to the type of product available from current sources (NIDA Mississippi Farm) does not allow for well-controlled studies of medical cannabis products in use in State programs or developed by US industry, even if suitable for most academic research on cannabis and cannabis components.

Solution 1: Many States are establishing patient registries that either are or could be sources of fully documented Real World Data (RWD). FDA and Congress should work on ways to facilitate leveraging of this RWD for Real World Evidence (RWE).

Solution 2: FDA should work with DEA to facilitate approval of interstate transport of low THC products made under State program licenses for the purposes of research required for FDA approval without requiring DEA to approve the source (e.g., use hemp exclusion}.

Issue: The new definition of hemp, when incorporated into the Controlled Substance Act (CSA), will not exempt from schedule I those products only made from plants that meet the % THC limit. The definition confers non-schedule I status to products containing no more than 0.3% THC as made from ANY type of cannabis. Hemp-derived Is only a sub-class.

Problem: Lack of understanding of the 2018 Farm Bill definition of hemp. The new hemp definition applies to Cannabis Sativa plants, parts of Cannabis Sativa plants, products of Cannabis Sativa plants, etc. that meet the% limit as defined in the Farm Bill.

Solution: WHO (0.2%) and FDA (0.1%) have already made recommendations for products at low THC levels to be de- or re-scheduled. FDA needs to be proactive in working with the DEA on rescheduling actions to facilitate R&D supporting FDA approval of low THC products.

Alignment with 0.3% THC hemp limit should be actively considered.

Issue: Product development research requires industry control of plant varieties and manufacturing processes. Most historic medical cannabis products are botanical blends of multiple components as determined by plant variety and extraction/manufacturing processes. Those are the majority of products already in use in State programs, with demonstrated, but not fully documented, positive results. Such products are not available from NIDA Drug Supply Program.

Problem: Congressional supporters of medical research are embracing the position that medical products are best derived from generic cannabis/cannabis components supplied by a few bulk suppliers. There is a lack of understanding of Industry requirements for product development activities vs. research activities and the viability of FDA approval under FDA drug development guidelines.

Solution: FDA should work to educate Congressional members and staff on the botanical drug approach and press Congress and DEA to provide access to industry developed products for the purposes of product development "research" activities leading to FDA approval.

Issue: The FDA doesn't want patients to forgo appropriate medical treatments by substituting unapproved products for approved medicines used to prevent, treat, mitigate or cure a particular diseases or conditions.

Problem: The timelines for approval are long and patients will continue to demand access to State program products. Significant amounts of epidemiological data are available on the safety and efficacy of cannabinoids, but additional data is being generated every day that is not available to the FDA.

Solution: While companies go through the FDA regulatory process, the FDA should use an expedited review process and consider making products available to, and data from, patients under the Right-to-Try and/or Expanded Access/Compassionate Use - i.e., FDA "Project Facilitate."

The FDA should work with industry to establish protocols, so as to make accommodations to utilize existing epidemiological data to reduce unnecessary study size and duration of clinical trials.

Issue: The FDA has pathways and guidelines that support seeking approval of cannabis- derived products but can't make access to US-made products legal. The DEA has provisions to make foreign made medical cannabis products legally available for medical R&O supporting FDA approval (import provisions), but no clear provisions for US industry made products.

Problem: The path to FDA approval of U.S. made cannabis-derived products are far more difficult than approval of foreign made products.

Solution: FDA and all federal agencies join In supporting a change to DEA policies and/or legislation that would fulfill their responsibilities to support US based companies as they seek FDA approval for cannabis-derived products.

As a small business I am concerned about the trends I see and implore the Small Business Administration to take steps to develop policies and guidelines that allow the growth of small entrepreneurs. The cannabis community is not afraid of hard work. Evolving the industry's ethos will take time, yes, but if done right, we may accomplish our goals and create a kinder and more compassionate society.

Finding our footing in this new era of big business may take longer, as stakes are high and competition is tough. But one thing Is certain: 2019 will be a stellar year for the Industry, especially for those who thrive on grit and grind.

Legalization process must be fair to everyone.

Legalizing marijuana must come with reinvestment In the communities most harmed by enforcement, with limitations on how police can Interact with people who they suspect of a marijuana offense, with legal nonpublic spaces for smoking marijuana for those who cannot smoke in their residence, with a prohibition on deportation for people with marijuana convictions, and with full inclusion of those most Impacted by criminalization of marijuana in the new marijuana Industry.

While progress in reforming our nation's drug laws is vital, we must remember that if we legalize without righting the wrongs of past marijuana enforcement, we risk reinforcing the decades of disproportionate harm communities of color face and endure. People in the United States use and sell marijuana at roughly the same rate regardless of their race, yet a black person is almost four times more likely than a white person to be arrested for marijuana possession nationwide.

Having a marijuana conviction on your record can make it difficult to secure and maintain employment, housing, or secure government assistance for the rest of your life. This is why clearing people's records of marijuana convictions is a necessary addition to any legalization measure. If we believe that marijuana is not worthy of criminal intervention, then it is only right we stop the suffering inflicted on people by a marijuana prosecution. Especially since we know this disproportionately falls on the shoulders, and families, of low-income communities and communities of color.

Such efforts to extend racial justice must explicitly be tied to a program of economic justice.

Once again, I thank the Committee for allowing me to make my views and experience available to the hearing record. Full Spectrum Omega, Inc. intends to remain a viable SDVOSB and is looking forward to working with the Committee to assist in the development of appropriate legislative solutions.

Written Testimony for: The House Judiciary Subcommittee on Crime, Terrorism, and Homeland Security, Regarding: Marijuana Laws in America: Racial Justice and the Need for Reform, Submitted by Justin Strekal, Political Director for the National Organization for the Reform of Marijuana Laws, July 10th, 2019

Esteemed Members of the Committee and Interested Parties:

This is the first time in a generation that members of Congress have held a hearing specifically to address the failures of marijuana criminalization in the United States. Such a conversation is long overdue.

Right now, many states are light-years ahead of Congress when it comes to addressing and amending marijuana policy.

To date, 11 states and Washington, DC have legalized the use and possession of cannabis by adults. All but one of these states also regulates commercial cannabis production and retail sales. In June 2019, Illinois became the first state to pass legislation regulating adult cannabis use and retail sales via legislative action rather than by the passage of a voter initiative. In 2019 alone, an additional 18 states considered legalization and regulatory proposals in Statehouses across the country.

In addition, 33 states and Washington, DC have enacted regulatory access laws that allow qualified patients to obtain and use cannabis therapeutically, and many of these states continue to pass significant expansions to their programs. In 2019, an additional twelve states considered medical cannabis program proposals in Statehouses across the country.

Another 13 states have passed laws specific to the possession of cannabidiol (CBD) extracts for therapeutic purposes. CBD is an organic compound in the cannabis plant.

In total, 46 states have enacted statutory laws specific to the possession and use of either whole-plant cannabis or extracted cannabinoids that are in direct violation of the Schedule 1 status of marijuana.

Yet despite these changes in state-level policies, federal marijuana policy – and the status as a Schedule I controlled substance – remains unchanged.

This untenable contradiction in state and federal policy undermines the very premise of the uniquely American belief in the rule of law.

Modern Consequences of Federal Cannabis Prohibition

According to the FBI's Uniform Crime Report, police made 659,700 arrests for marijuana-related violations in the United States in 2017, the last year for which data is available. Over the past decades, well over 20 million Americans have been arrested for violating marijuana laws. As a result, whole communities have lost generations of citizens to cyclical poverty and incarceration due to the collateral consequences of having a cannabis-related conviction on their record. These consequences include the loss of access to higher education, the inability to qualify for government-subsidized housing, employment discrimination, the loss of child custody, homelessness, etc. In large part due to the modern War on Drugs, the United States' prison population has skyrocketed by over 500 percent over the last 40 years, with nearly 2.3 million people incarcerated in the United States at the beginning of 2019.

Additionally, cannabis possession is the second most common reason for a drug-related deportation infraction, and the US Citizen and Immigration Services recently released a policy alert, stating that immigrants seeking citizenship who use cannabis or work with a state-legal and regulated cannabis company, even in states where it is legal, may be denied citizenship due to their "lack of good moral character."

In addition to the human cost of prohibition, there continues to be a massive financial cost to the federal government as well. On average, federal prohibition enforcement costs US taxpayers nearly $4 billion annually. This does not include the over $6 billion spent in states that continue to criminalize cannabis. In contrast, a recent study published earlier this year concluded that legal marijuana nationwide would add over $132 billion in federal tax revenue and add over one million jobs to the economy in the next decade.

The prohibition of marijuana has crippled the civil rights and liberties of communities across the country, leading to an exorbitant increase in incarceration rates, particularly among communities of color. Although whites and blacks have been found to consume marijuana at similar rates, a 2013 report by the ACLU found that a "black person is 3.73 times more likely to be arrested for marijuana possession than a white person," leading to disparate incarceration rates of black Americans. Additionally, a whopping 77% of all federal sentences for marijuana crimes went to Latinx people, who represent less than 20% of the country's population.

Congress must not turn its back on the millions of Americans nationwide who rely on access to marijuana for their health, wellness, or private, personal purposes. According to recently released nationwide survey data, the majority of Americans strongly support patients' access to medical cannabis and oppose federal interference in these matters.

A recent poll shows a whopping 93 percent support the medical use of marijuana, and the most recent Gallup poll on the subject found that American voters' support of legal marijuana is at an all-time high, with 66% of respondents indicating their support for legalization and regulation.

Perhaps most importantly, the poll shows a majority of voters in both major political parties and Independents now believe that marijuana should be legal, with the most dramatic jump in support observed in Republican respondents.

Consideration for Statutory Changes

NORML opines that comprehensive legislation to end the federal policy of prohibition and criminalization of cannabis should include the following components:

Reform the Approach

The criminalization of cannabis is a disproportionate public policy response to personal behavior that is, at worst, a public health matter – not a criminal justice concern. Cannabis should be removed completely from the Controlled Substances Act and regulations should be created regulating its use by adults, and discouraging its misuse.

Restoration of Rights

Although cannabis prohibition enforcement has negatively impacted nearly every community in the United States, the adverse effects of this policy have been especially concentrated in economically-disadvantaged communities. It is imperative that legislation addresses this disparity by providing funding for the review and automatic expungement of records of those with low-level cannabis convictions.

Restabilization of the Marketplace

Much of the cannabis market today continues to be controlled by illicit market players. While some states have successfully implemented regulated and transparent marketplaces, it has yet to completely crowd out the preexisting unregulated marketplace. Any legislation that seeks to end federal cannabis prohibition should incentivize realistic, pragmatic, and enforceable framework that is socially and economically inclusive for the safe, lawful production, manufacture, transportation, and distribution of cannabis.

Reinvestment for the Impacted

In legal cannabis states, revenues generated from licensed cannabis sales have been used for social programs ranging from new school construction to substance abuse treatment programs. Given the dramatic personal and generational implications of the criminalization of cannabis, action to direct these new revenues toward those communities most adversely affected by the failed policy of cannabis prohibition should be considered. This ensures that individuals and communities that have been most harmed by cannabis prohibition are able to benefit from its legalization.

In closing, it is time that members of Congress openly embrace the need for reform and end the senseless and cruel policy of the national criminalization of cannabis.

Thank you for your consideration,

Justin Strekal
NORML Political Director
Justin@norml.org
202-483-5500

Congressional Testimony, Marijuana Laws in America: Racial Justice and the Need for Reform, Testimony before Subcommittee on Crime, Terrorism and Homeland Security, Committee on the Judiciary, United States House of Representatives, July 10, 2019, Saphira Galoob, Executive Director, National Cannabis Roundtable

On behalf of the National Cannabis Roundtable (NCR), I appreciate the opportunity to submit written testimony for the Subcommittee on Crime, Terrorism and Homeland Security's historic hearing on the need for comprehensive cannabis reform. NCR applauds the subcommittee's leadership in addressing the long-simmering conflict between federal law and laws in forty-seven states, the District of Columbia and several US territories with regard to the use of cannabis. We are particularly gratified by the subcommittee's acknowledgement of social and racial injustices perpetuated by the inclusion of cannabis as a Schedule I drug in the Controlled Substances Act.

NCR promotes common sense federal regulation, tax equality and financial services reform for regulated cannabis businesses by advocating for changes to federal law that acknowledge states' rights to regulate and manage cannabis policy. We are proud to be part of a growing debate about how to transform and modernize our national cannabis policy safely, thoughtfully and comprehensively.

NCR's membership represents every aspect of the cannabis supply chain, including growers, processors, retailers, wellness centers, investors, entrepreneurs and publicly traded companies.

Our members have an established commercial presence in 23 states, including the District of Columbia, serving more than 172 million Americans.

In the last decade, 47 states have enacted comprehensive medical cannabis regimes, laws permitting full adult cannabis consumption, or laws otherwise decriminalizing some aspect of cannabis access or use. As this subcommittee is aware, cannabis is now a robust and sophisticated industry in 33 states, and there is broad popular support for ending prohibition. Sixty-two percent of Americans favor comprehensively regulated cannabis for medical and adult consumption, and 93 percent of Americans favor regulated access to cannabis for medical purposes. Based on these trends – and as the title of this hearing suggests – congressional action appears increasingly inevitable. It is now a matter of identifying the best legislative approach.

As NCR joins in the chorus calling for reform of the nation's cannabis policies, it is critical to move forward without further delay. Each day, hundreds of individuals are arrested for cannabis offenses, a disproportionate majority of whom are African American and Latinx. In 2017, the most recent year with a complete data set available, the FBI reported that there were over 659,000 arrests for cannabis offenses.[228] Unfortunately, those arrests are continuing, and the individuals who continue to be adversely impacted by the war on drugs cannot wait for the perfect piece of legislation to emerge.

---

[228] U.S. DEP'T OF JUSTICE, UNIVERSAL CRIME REPORT 2017, (2018), *available a t*https://ucr.fbi.gov/crime-in-the-u.s/2017/crime-in-the-u.s.-2017/topic-pages/persons-arrested.

For better or worse, legislation in Washington moves slowly. However, over the last two decades, states have developed cannabis policies that reduce criminal penalties, address the malignancies of the drug war and set up flourishing industries. States have developed mandatory expungement programs and have awarded licenses - and established access to capital - for those impacted by cannabis prohibition, as well as created robust medical cannabis programs for patients in need. If anything, the development of cannabis policies in states has shown that one size does not fit all. States vary widely in their geographic, socioeconomic and political differences, and have developed policies that make sense for their residents.

Recognizing this progress, a reasonable first step towards reconciling the conflict between state and federal laws would be adoption of the Strengthening the Tenth Amendment Through Entrusting States (STATES) Act. The STATES Act recognizes the reform efforts that states have already implemented and will act as a foundation for further drug reform. By removing the federal government from the equation, states can have full discretion over their police powers granted to them under the 10th Amendment. As we have seen, when cannabis prosecutions are not a priority, states can focus their limited resources on reducing violent crime - and increasing clearances of non-drug related offenses - ultimately making communities safer. The STATES Act would ensure that individual states can continue to regulate cannabis use in the manner deemed appropriate by their constituents. States in which majorities favor legalization would be permitted to do so, and states that prefer a slower approach – including those committed to prohibition solely because of existing federal policy – would be allowed to choose their own path. Unsurprisingly, this commonsense approach enjoys the broadest bipartisan and public support of any of the federal cannabis reform proposals. It also has the clearest path to passage in both chambers. Accordingly, we urge the House Committee on the Judiciary to take up the STATES Act for consideration.

While passage of the STATES Act is an important first step as it removes the threat of federal prosecution for those complying with state law, we acknowledge that it will not be enough. Tens of millions of lives have been upended by the war on drugs, especially when it comes to cannabis. While legalization has brought tremendous social and economic benefits in several states, we recognize that few of those benefits have gone to those individuals and communities harmed by decades of prohibition.

The National Cannabis Roundtable stands ready to work with the subcommittee – and with social and racial justice advocates – to craft additional legislation to address past injustices and ensure that the growing cannabis industry benefits all those who wish to participate.

Criminal justice reform and cannabis reform are issues that transcend party lines. As we work toward viable solutions, we must balance the critical need for near-term progress with the long-term goal of correcting the injustices of the past. Tangible incremental reform is obtainable.

Passage of the STATES Act is something we can do *right now* to benefit tens of millions of Americans that want safe and legal access to cannabis. As the cannabis industry matures, it can - *and should* - play a leading role in redressing past wrongs. But it can only do so if it is given a chance to prosper. The STATES Act will provide that chance.

The momentum for cannabis reform is undeniable. Even the most ardent opponents recognize the dramatic shift in public opinion. The question now for most federal lawmakers is not whether we must harmonize federal and state laws regarding cannabis reform, rather what legislative mechanisms are the most pragmatic - and politically achievable – for addressing the gross criminal and social injustices that have been caused by our current federal drug policy.

We applaud the subcommittee for holding today's hearing and look forward to working with Members of Congress to ameliorate the issues created by the federal government's policy of prohibition.

Increasing Equity in the Cannabis Industry: Six Achievable Goals for Policy Makers, MARCH 2019

Introduction

With cannabis now fully legal for adults in ten U.S. states and the District of Columbia - and more elected officials considering legalization in other states every day - it appears as if the complete end of cannabis prohibition is nearly upon us. As we reach this milestone, we must acknowledge that cannabis prohibition was not only an attempt at preventing individuals from possessing and using cannabis, but also an accompanying criminal punishment regime that enforced this prohibition through government force. This system, like most other law enforcement regimes, did not affect everyone equally.

There is a clear history of racial disparities in cannabis arrests and convictions.[229] Arrests happen far more frequently in heavily policed areas, which are disproportionately areas where people of color reside. Punishments, which tend to be harsher for people of color even when the underlying conduct is the same, include an elaborate array of collateral consequences that can hinder or eliminate future job prospects, educational opportunities, and other avenues for legitimate financial achievement. A cannabis arrest, often a person's first interaction with the criminal justice system, starts a cycle of detrimental state action that can wreck families. When too many arrests occur in the same geographic location, the economic and social viability of entire neighborhoods can be destroyed.

Although cannabis legalization ends prohibition, it does not necessarily stop or reverse the harm created by the punishment regime. As state-level legalization spreads and the legal cannabis market expands, the individuals and communities most impacted by cannabis prohibition have all too often been left behind. Early legalization efforts were fighting decades of stigma and the psychological linkage of cannabis and crime. To counteract this ingrained belief and create a clear difference with their illegal predecessors, new state-legal cannabis markets often feature invasive background checks, elaborate and expensive security systems, and bans on those with criminal histories from operating or even working in the industry. These laws and regulations related to entry into the industry, like cannabis prohibition before it, have disproportionately impacted people of color.

To create a legal cannabis market accessible to all, the laws need to be designed and implemented with equity and fairness in mind. Three trends recently converged to make policy makers more comfortable with this proactive approach. First, public support for cannabis legalization continues to rise.[230] Second, awareness of racial disparities and inequalities built into the criminal justice system has grown. Third, the evidence from early legalization states shows that a very small portion of the economic benefits resulting from legalization have gone to people of color, women, or lower-income individuals.[231]

---

[229] See American Civil Liberties (2013). The War on Marijuana in Black and White. Available at: https://www.aclu.org/report-war-marijuana-black-and-white?redirect=criminal-law-reform/war-marijuanablack-and-white.

[230] McCarthy, J. (2018). Two in Three Americans Now Support Legalizing Marijuana. Gallup. Available at: https://news.gallup.com/poll/243908/twp-three-americans-support-legalizing-marijuana.aspx.

[231] See, e.g., Comeau, Z. (Jan. 7, 2019) Left Behind: Minorities are hard to find in the legal pot industry. The Worcester Business Journal. Available ar http://www.wbjournal.com/article/

These trends are leading to progress. Some states and localities are trying to implement social equity programs to help redress the situation. Massachusetts gives priority license review to entities promoting economic empowerment in communities disproportionately impacted by past law enforcement practices related to cannabis and other drugs, and has created a social equity program to build pathways into the cannabis industry.[232] At the time of this writing, New Jersey appears poised to pass social justice reforms like expungement alongside cannabis legalization.[233] There is a strong push to include social equity provisions in any legalization bill in New York. California cities like Los Angeles, Oakland, Sacramento, and San Francisco are all in the process of implementing local social equity programs. Countless bills on record expungement have been filed around the country.

Additionally, some members of Congress have been fierce advocates for coupling cannabis legalization with strong social equity provisions. One of the strongest advocates is Rep. Barbara Lee (D-CA). Rep. Lee is the co-chair of the Congressional Cannabis Caucus and has filed multiple cannabis-related bills, including the Realizing Equitable & Sustainable Participation in Emerging Cannabis Trades (RESPECT) Resolution (H.Res. 163, during the 116th Congress). This resolution proposes a set of best practices to address industry inequalities. Collectively, the best practices suggest that the legal cannabis market can be a force for justice, but only if implemented justly.

NCIA strongly supports these efforts. We have worked closely with the Minority Cannabis Business Association to create the nation's first- ever Model Municipal Social Equity Ordinance based on the recommendations in the RESPECT Resolution,[234] and will continue to push for laws and

---

20190107/PRINTEDITION/301049997/left-behind-minorities-are-hard-to-find-in-the-legal-pot-industry; Margolls, A. (Sep. 20, 2018) The top cannabis companies are dominated by men. We must do better. Forbes. Available at https://www.forbes.com/sites/amymargolis/2018/09/20/and minority-run businesses want in on it. The Chicago Tribune. Available ar https://www/chicagotribune.com/business/ct-biz-illinois-marijuana-industry-diversity-20190215-story.html.

[232] Massachusetts Cannabis Control Commission, Social Equity Guidance. Available ar: http://mass-cannabiscontrol.com/wp-content/uploads/2018/03/UPDATED-Guidance-Summary-of-Equity-Provisions-with-6th-criterionadded-1.pdf.

[233] See, e.g., Corasaniti, N. (Nov. 28, 2018) How a Push to Legalize Pot in N.J. Became a Debate on Race and Fairness. The New York Times. Available at: https://www.nytimes.com/2018/11/28/nyregion/legalization-marijuana-newjersey.html.

[234] The MCBA Model Municipal Social Equity Ordinance was drafted by NCIA Board Vice Chair and MCBA Policy Committee Co-chair Khurshid Khoja; NCIA Policy Council Staff and MCBA Policy Committee Member Chloe Grossman; NCIA and MCBA Policy Committee Member Jesse Stout; and Drug Policy Alliance Attorney and MCBA Policy Committee Member Rodney Holcombe, The Ordinance is available at

regulations that embrace diversity and the inclusion of communities disproportionately- impacted by cannabis prohibition. The emerging cannabis industry must work for all people.

Opportunities to right structural wrongs that have caused multi-generational injustice emerge infrequently and must be embraced when they arise.

6 Key Goals for Social Equity Programs

Implementing the best practices of the RESPECT Resolution and building on the achievements of early states through social equity programs can create a fair and equitable cannabis industry. As states and localities establish systems for the production, distribution, and retail sale of cannabis, they should strive for six key goals:

Repair the damage to individuals caused by discriminatory enforcement of prohibition

Create more equitable licensing outcomes through the application process

Ensure the industry reflects the local community

Address financial barriers to market entry

Support companies and individuals entering the industry from disproportionately-impacted communities

Invest tax revenue in communities harmed by prohibition

Together these key goals create a strategy to correct the negative impacts of cannabis prohibition on low-income and minority communities and to address the under-representation of minorities, women, and other groups in the legal cannabis industry. In the remainder of the paper, we expand upon these goals and include the best practices from the RESPECT Resolution that correspond to each one.

Repair the Damage to Individuals Caused by Discriminatory Enforcement of Prohibition

- create an automatic process, at no cost for the individual, for the expungement or sealing of criminal records for cannabis offenses that

---

https://minoritycannabis.org/wp-content/up- loads/2019/03/Final-Draft-of-MCBA-Model-Municipal-Social-Equity-Ordinance-v.1.pdf.

is inclusive of individuals currently on parole or under any probationary agreement, for cannabis offenses

- establish a process for resentencing persons serving sentences for cannabis convictions and redesignating of penalties for persons previously convicted of cannabis-related crimes for which the penalties have been reduced or removed
- eliminate punishment or other penalization for persons currently under parole, probation, or other State supervision, or released on bail awaiting trial, for conduct otherwise allowed under State cannabis laws

The damage created by criminalizing cannabis use and possession can never be erased. However, the legalization moment provides an opportunity to begin repairing the damage. The RESPECT Resolution emphasizes the need to grasp this opportunity to invest in and begin the process of rebuilding communities. This starts with erasing the criminal sanctions remaining from the prohibition era. The criminalization of cannabis was a mistake and the government should stop punishing those harmed by that mistake. People currently incarcerated for non-violent, cannabis- related convictions should be resentenced.

People with past convictions should have access to expungement so their past conviction does not continue to haunt them. Those under correctional supervision, like parole or probation, should have the terms of their supervision revised to better reflect the state laws.

This effort should be coupled with a robust outreach effort to help the individuals affected. People need to be connected to services and assisted with cleaning up their criminal records. As Rep. Lee's Best Practice #6 notes, expungement should be automatic. Individuals who recently lost their liberty through the court system may be hesitant to reengage with that same system to expunge their record. It would also be helpful to advise individuals on how to handle questions relating to their criminal history after their records are expunged. This is vital to helping impacted individuals find jobs and live productive lives after their incarceration, whether in the cannabis industry or any other industry.

Create More Equitable Licensing Outcomes through the Application Process

- create a system where licensing is to be obtained at the city or county level and should be based on regulations determined by the local jurisdiction that meet the State's minimum requirements, which allows the community to determine the type and number of businesses, avoids arbitrary caps on licenses, and results in an industry more representative of the local market
- create more equitable licensing by (A) eliminating broad felony restrictions for licensing; (B) focusing restrictions on entering the market to those, determined on a case-by-case basis for both licensees and employees, with criminal convictions that are relevant to the owning and operating of a business; and (C) prohibiting previous cannabis convictions from consideration as justification for a denial of a license

All states legalizing cannabis should strive to have a diverse industry that is representative of their consumer base and the state more broadly. To achieve this diversity, laws and regulations must not create explicit or implicit barriers that continue to disproportionately affect certain communities. Many early state cannabis programs explicitly prohibited people with criminal records from entering the industry. As noted earlier, the criminal punishment regime attached to prohibition did not affect everyone equally. People of color were disproportionately targeted under the enforcement regime and are therefore disproportionately excluded now under these new collateral consequences. The most basic step lawmakers can take is to stop banning people with drug convictions from the cannabis industry. Society is recognizing that the punishment regime attached to prohibition was unjust and we should not carry over the harms of the previous system to the new, legal regime.

Merely refraining from banning individuals from the industry through collateral consequences, however, is far from sufficient. Licensing processes that appear facially neutral can still lead to unequal results if applicants are starting from different places. These implicit barriers are more pervasive and, thus, harder to address. While direct legal barriers only affect certain individuals, implicit barriers affect entire communities, particularly communities of color and lower-income communities with limited access to business capital.

Systems with a limited number of licenses and competitive assessments of qualifications typically encourage large, capital-intensive operations that often do not recoup start-up costs for several years. This scale of operation and the associated capital requirements will be much harder to achieve for businesses owned by low-income individuals and victims of systemic inequality. These systems generally also require applicants to submit financial documentation or meet minimum financial requirements. Businesses with less capital or limited access to banking will look comparatively worse than a business that can provide start-up capital, place large sums in escrow, and fulfill other financially burdensome requirements. If this sort of competitive licensing system was used in other industries, national chains would lock up most of the licenses, effectively blocking out the locally-owned, independent shops or restaurants that build character in so many neighborhoods. Any artificially limited market with competitive bid licensing will guarantee the success of the large and national over the small and local. Therefore, any licensing system intended to promote an inclusive industry should be based upon minimum standards that all applicants must meet and should grant licenses to those who can meet those standards (as well as other local considerations, such as zoning).

Ensure the Industry Reflects the Local Community

- in States where license caps are completely unavoidable, establish local oversight and control of cannabis licenses by allowing local cities and municipalities to prioritize licenses for local citizens and residents, especially individuals most impacted by the War on Drugs, by taking into account and prioritizing (A) long-term residency within the State or locality; (B) individuals whose income is less than 80 percent of the median household income within a county; (C) individuals who have been fom,erly incarcerated; (D) individuals with prior drug law violations; and (E) individuals living within a jurisdiction that is heavily policed
- establish cannabis regulatory and oversight bodies and commissions that reflect the racial, ethnic, economic, and gender makeup of the surrounding community

As mentioned in the previous section, an optimal system is one in which applicants are not competing against each other for licenses, but rather compete against each other as licensed businesses in a free market. If a limited license system is nevertheless required, localities should strive to advance an inclusive industry. Prioritizing long-term residents, those with lower-incomes, and those affected most by the criminal punishment systems that accompanied prohibition will create a more inclusive, local industry that benefits the entire community.

It is worth noting a bit of caution regarding RESPECT Resolution Best Practice #3. Establishing local control of licensing does not necessarily increase diversity of the industry. In some jurisdictions, particularly Massachusetts, we are seeing that allowing local control can actually work against an inclusive industry. This happens when municipalities use local licensing caps to make companies compete for a license.

While some municipalities in Massachusetts are prioritizing social equity and local applicants, others are prioritizing aspects like revenue generation which favor large multi-state operators. The problem exists because of the artificially limited nature of the license process. In an ideal system both the small, local operator and the large, multi-state operator should be able to open, just like most towns have both chain stores and restaurants and local small businesses competing against each other. Again, **it** is best to allow the market to decide the number of licenses awarded. But if licenses caps are required, the preferences should be set in such a way that will allow small businesses to compete.

Creating an industry that reflects the community goes beyond just ensuring people of color hold some of the licenses and jobs. The regulatory structure should also reflect the community. Regulatory and oversight bodies that are comprised of individuals with diverse backgrounds, experiences, and socio-economic status will create a more just system and will be less susceptible to group think.

Address Financial Barriers to Market Entry

- establish licensing and application fees that are reasonable to cover only the costs of program implementation and necessary regulation

Probably the most significant and difficult to overcome barriers to a diverse and inclusive industry are the high costs of entry and a lack of access to capital. The RESPECT Resolution addresses this by pointing out the problem of high licensing and application fees. But policy makers should go further; the government fees are only part of the problem.

High licensing and application fees create a major barrier to entry for individuals from lower income communities. Raising government revenue through fees on applicants rather than taxes from consumers distorts the market in favor of the largest and richest companies. Those with less access to capital and banking will be kept from even applying to enter the industry. The fees should be kept low and in proportion to the costs of the program. If the government wants to raise additional revenue from legal cannabis, it should be done through taxes, so the cost burden remains proportional, allowing small companies to survive.

In addition to application fees, policy makers should avoid laws and regulations that artificially inflate costs. Again, anything that makes it more expensive to enter the market makes it difficult for small, local companies to get a foothold hold in the industry. Compliance costs associated with hyper-specific and unnecessarily burdensome regulations regarding matters such as security equipment, personnel, and facilities may be prohibitive for businesses with less access to capital. The higher the compliance costs, the more it benefits the largest operators.

Certain populations, particularly people of color, have been systematically denied employment and wealth creation opportunities for generations. In other industries, borrowing and using small business programs can help offset a lack of capital. Cannabis companies, however, have a notoriously difficult time securing banking services. They cannot obtain small business loans from major financial institutions, nor are they eligible for any federal assistance. The fact that people of color are already more likely to be underserved by the financial services sector and are subjected to inequitable treatment in terms of fees and loan access only exacerbates the problem.[235] A major effort to increase access to banking is needed.

Support Companies and Individuals Entering the Industry from Disproportionately-Impacted Communities

- adopt laws and implement regulations that will allow small cultivators to thrive in the legal market
- use a percentage of tax revenue to establish a special fund to provide small business investments to support people of color entering into the legal marijuana industry

---

[235] Faber, J. & Friedline. T. (2018), The Racialized Costs of Banking. New America Available at: https://www.newamcrica.org/family-centered-social-policy/reports/racialized-costs-banking/overview/.

- create employment and subcontracting requirements for cannabis licensees in order to use the ancillary business activity generated by the cannabis industry to employ people of color

Beyond just breaking down barriers to entry, regulations should be set up to promote inclusion in the new industry. Entering the industry in the first wave of cannabis legalization states often required a large amount of capital, an expansive network of potential investors and vendors, and advanced business skills. New regulatory structures should chip away at this by providing opportunities to low-income and minority communities. To actually give historically disadvantaged populations a fair shot at becoming owners and operators in the new, legal cannabis market, the platitudes and good intentions must be coupled with a significant financial investment in programs that support these communities.

There are many forms that this support can take and some combination of many of them will probably be necessary to establish a successful social equity program. First, the laws need to be designed with equity in mind. This can involve specialized licenses for smaller or local businesses, employment and subcontracting requirements that ensure diversity in ancillary businesses, and a tax system that encourages diverse licensees. Second, these equity provisions should be accompanied by equity programs.

Training and mentorship programs, programs to help connect prospective entrepreneurs with sources of capital, programs to help individuals procure and afford real estate, and many other forms of assistance can help prospective applicants feel comfortable moving forward with their businesses and help eliminate the head start that experienced multi-state operators have over new entrants to the industry. These programs should also be accompanied by outreach efforts so potential entrepreneurs know what kind of support exist. Part of the tax revenue generated by legal sales should go into building and funding these programs. Third, legislators and regulators should be vigilant in protecting these potential entrepreneurs from bad practices like predatory lending and leases. The current federal scheduling of marijuana should not be a license for unscrupulous actors to take advantage of potential cannabis entrepreneurs.

Invest Tax Revenue in Communities Harmed by Prohibition

- set aside a percentage of the tax revenue from cannabis sales to be reinvested in communities that have been most affected by cannabis arrests and the drug war, which most frequently have been communities of color, including programs for job training, reentry services, expungement expenses, public libraries, community centers, programs and opportunities dedicated to youth, and health education programs

State and local cannabis laws can and should provide pathways for licensed adult-use cannabis businesses to fund reinvestment in communities that lack economic opportunity, resources, or have otherwise been disproportionately impacted by the war on cannabis and other drugs. Both government-managed and private community reinvestment funds should be considered, as well as an appropriate system of incentives and mandates to generate sufficient financial resources for real impact.

One approach is for a state legislature to enact a statutory mandate requiring that all adult-use cannabis businesses contribute to a community reinvestment fund to be allocated to select communities by an appropriate government body. Tax revenues would eventually provide a reasonably stable funding stream, but initial funding would have to be borrowed or the launch of the fund could be delayed by a year or more while the regulatory system is established and operators are licensed and become operational.

Providing incentives for businesses that voluntarily contribute to a government-managed community reinvestment fund is likely to be a less controversial approach than requiring that all or some businesses contribute through taxes or special fees. Voluntary contributions may be encouraged by offering participating businesses priority application processing, reduced renewal fees for the period in which contributions are made, and other similar benefits.

Similarly, a privately-managed community reinvestment fund could be established and supported by cannabis business contributions, whether mandated or incentivized. For example, the state could engage in a competitive procurement process in which non-profit organizations submit proposals to provide comprehensive community reinvestment fund management on a contract basis. Alternatively, states and localities could identify eligible neighborhoods (or some other geographic unit) and provide incentives for businesses that work directly with those neighborhoods to fund reinvestment efforts that target specific community concerns. The latter option gives communities more say in how the funds are used for their benefit and encourages real engagement between businesses and impacted communities.

Potential licensees could also be required to submit community reinvestment plans, describing selected reinvestment projects that fall within approved categories or impact qualified communities. A monitoring framework would be established to ensure that licensees fulfill their obligations. Though it could be beneficial to provide the option for licensees to enter into agreements with localities or pre-established community-level governing bodies to provide funds to support approved projects in target areas, policy makers must take steps to ensure this model is not exploited by localities. This has been the case in Massachusetts, where significant demands associated with host community agreements have given businesses with deep pockets a competitive advantage. To encourage robust investment and constructive collaboration between impacted communities and cannabis businesses, temporary fee reductions, a seat on a rulemaking working group, or other exclusive benefits could be awarded to the businesses with top scoring community reinvestment plans.

Conclusion

The activity over the next few years will shape the cannabis market for decades. Prohibition and the enforcement of that prohibition caused pain for many, particularly communities of color. While this new legal system is being developed, policy makers should strive to reach these six goals in order to ensure that those harmed the most by the system of the past have a chance to benefit from the system of the future.

Using Marijuana Revenue to Create Jobs

By Maritza Perez, Olugbenga Ajilore, and Ed Chung
May 20, 2019

Today's national policy debate around marijuana stands in sharp contrast to the debate of the past. Current elected leaders as well as those running for office now are asked not only if they believe marijuana should be legalized, but also when and how. Much of this is due to a shift in public opinion. A 2018 Center for American Progress poll showed that 68 percent of Americans believe that marijuana possession should be legalized.[236] The momentum is evident in states as well: 33 states and the District of Columbia have loosened their marijuana laws, while 10 of these states and the District of Columbia have specifically legalized marijuana for recreational use.[237] This year, states such as Illinois and Connecticut have also indicated that marijuana legalization will be a top priority.[238]

The reasons behind why lawmakers are considering marijuana legalization vary, but one of the overarching motivations is to take advantage of what appears to be a windfall to state budgets for public projects. In Colorado, for example, the first $40 million received from the excise tax on retail marijuana in fiscal year 2017–2018 was used for public school construction, while the remaining $27.8 million was transferred to a fund for public schools.[239] In Washington state, marijuana sales surpassed $1 billion in FY 2017, and the state collected $314.8 million in excise tax revenue.[240] The revenue was primarily used to fund Medicaid which secured health insurance for many low-income Washington residents.[241]

But as lawmakers decide how and for what priorities the tax revenue from marijuana sales will be used, they must not ignore the history and damage that past public policies surrounding marijuana have caused. For decades, the war on drugs—which includes the war on marijuana[242]—disproportionately criminalized African American and Latinx individuals for engaging in marijuana activity that is increasingly legal in the majority of the United States. The criminal records that stem from marijuana-related arrests and

---

236 John Halpin and Karl Agne, "Voters Across Party Lines Support Clean Slate Legislation," Center for American Progress, June 20, 2018, available at https://www.americanprogress.org/issues/criminal-justice/news/2018/06/20/451624/voters-across-party-lines-support-clean-slate-legislation/.

237 Governing, "State Marijuana Laws in 2018 Map," November 7, 2018, available at https://www.governing.com/gov-data/safety-justice/state-marijuana-laws-map-medical-recreational.html.

238 Tom Angell, "These States Are Most Likely To Legalize Marijuana In 2019," *Forbes*, December 26, 2018, available at https://www.forbes.com/sites/tomangell/2018/12/26/these-states-are-most-likely-to-legalize-marijuana-in-2019/#53257ecc5add.

239 Colorado Department of Revenue, "Disposition of Marijuana Tax Revenue," available at https://www.colorado.gov/pacific/revenue/disposition-marijuana-tax-revenue (last accessed May 2019).

240 Jake Whittenberg, "Where Does Washington's Marijuana Tax Money Go?," KING 5 News, August 10, 2018, available at https://www.king5.com/article/news/local/where-does-washingtons-marijuana-tax-money-go/281-581833195.

241 Ibid.

242 German Lopez, "Marijuana Legalization is a Response to the Failures of the War on Drugs," Vox, November 14, 2018, available at https://www.vox.com/identities/2018/8/20/17938342/marijuana-legalization-war-on-drugs-failure.

convictions can have lifelong consequences that systematically excludes people of color from equal access to jobs and economic opportunity.

Correcting these injustices by using marijuana-related tax revenue to create specific opportunities for affected communities must come first—not at some later, undefined time. Below are several proposals offered by or implemented in jurisdictions across the country that provide communities most harmed by the war on marijuana with access to the benefits of creating a regulated marijuana market. These proposals include automatically clearing the records of people arrested or convicted of marijuana offenses; supporting businesses owned and operated by people of color entering the regulated marijuana market; and encouraging equitable licensing practices in the market.

Jurisdictions, however, should also offer broader solutions that are not necessarily connected directly to the regulated marijuana market. This issue brief, therefore, proposes using tax revenue from marijuana sales to create public sector jobs specifically for communities affected by the war on marijuana. The proposal uses the model laid out in CAP's 2018 report, "Blueprint for the 21st Century: A Plan for Better Jobs and Stronger Communities," that makes major investments in employment for long-term residents of targeted distressed areas who want to work.

Discriminatory Drug Enforcement Created Structural Barriers to Building Economic Wealth

As documented in a previous CAP report, the war on drugs created a vast network of laws that systematically excluded generations of African American and Latinx individuals from equal access to economic opportunity.[243] The consequences of unequal enforcement in these communities are still evident today, even in states where marijuana restrictions have been loosened. New York City, for example, deprioritized marijuana prosecutions in 2018, after *The New York Times* reported that black and Hispanic New Yorkers were arrested on low-level marijuana charges at eight times and five times the rate

[243] Betsy Pearl and Maritza Perez, "Ending the War on Drugs" (Washington: Center for American Progress, 2018), available at https://www.americanprogress.org/issues/criminal-justice/reports/2018/06/27/452786/ending-war-drugs/; Angela Hanks, Danyelle Solomon, and Christian E. Weller, "Systematic Inequality: How America's Structural Racism Helped Create the Black-White Wealth Gap" (Washington: Center for American Progress, 2018), available at https://www.americanprogress.org/issues/ race/reports/2018/02/21/447051/ systematic-inequality/.

of white New Yorkers, respectively—despite continued evidence of equal usage rates of marijuana across races.[244] Nonetheless, in the same year the new policy was announced, nearly 90 percent of all New Yorkers arrested for smoking marijuana were black or Hispanic, even as overall marijuana arrests were drastically reduced.[245]

In addition to the overrepresentation of African Americans and Latinx individuals in arrest rates, the war on drugs led to harsh sentencing laws that contributed to greater incarceration rates and depleted these communities of breadwinners and workers. A 2016 analysis placed the unemployment rate for black men in the United States at 11 percent but concluded that this rate would jump to 19 percent if it accounted for incarcerated individuals.[246] For those who are formerly incarcerated, a recent analysis by the Prison Policy Initiative showed that more than 27 percent are unemployed, which is higher than the overall unemployment rate during the Great Depression.[247] These results are compounded for African Americans due to existing racial discrimination present in employment practices; indeed, one study found that white job applicants with a criminal record were more likely to be called for a job interview than black applicants without a criminal record.[248]

Increased incarceration rates cycled more families and children into poverty, particularly African American and Latino children, who are seven and two times more likely than white children, respectively, to have an incarcerated parent.[249] Children who experience the incarceration of a parent

---

[244] Benjamin Mueller, Robert Gebeloff, and Sahil Chinoy, "Surest Way to Face Marijuana Charges in New York: Be Black or Hispanic," *The New York Times*, May 13, 2018, available at https://www.nytimes.com/2018/05/13/nyregion/marijuana-arrests-nyc-race.html?module=inline.

[245] Reuven Blau, "Nearly 90% of New Yorkers busted for marijuana last year were minorities despite major drop in pot arrests," *New York Daily News*, January 8, 2019, available at https://www.nydailynews.com/new-york/ny-metro-pot-racial-disparity-20190107-story.html.

[246] Hanks and others, "Systemic Inequality"; Jeff Guo, "America has locked up so many black people it has warped our sense of reality," *The Washington Post*, February 26, 2016, available at https://www.washingtonpost.com/ news/wonk/wp/2016/02/26/america-has-locked-up-so-many-black-people-it-has-warped-our-sense-of-reality/?noredirect=on&utm_term=.0d4c3455fe41.

[247] Lucius Couloute and Daniel Kopf, "Out of Prison & Out of Work: Unemployment among formerly incarcerated people," Prison Policy Initiative, July 2018, available at https://www.prisonpolicy.org/reports/outofwork.html.

[248] Bruce Western, "The Inspiring Life and Career of Devah Pager," The Marshall Project, November 13, 2018, available at https://www.themarshallproject.org/2018/11/13/the-inspiring-life-and-career-of-devah-pager.

[249] The Annie E. Casey Foundation, "A Shared Sentence," (Baltimore: 2016), p. 2, available at https://www.aecf.org/m/resourcedoc/aecf-asharedsentence-2016.pdf.

tend to be socioeconomically disadvantaged prior to their parent's incarceration, as individuals who have limited access to resources or face structural barriers are at greater risk of becoming justice-involved. But incarceration worsens these disadvantages due to the loss of a family member and provider.[250] A 2015 research project on incarceration's economic effect on families showed that nearly 2 in 3 families with an incarcerated loved one could not afford basic needs due to the financial costs of losing a wage earner and paying fees associated with incarceration.[251] Communities that experience high incarceration rates are left with fragmented social networks and a smaller workforce, both of which can contribute to continued contact with the criminal justice system.

Providing Access to Employment Opportunities and the Regulated Marijuana Market

To begin to ameliorate these harms, lawmakers must lead with proposals that incorporate equity and inclusivity into marijuana legalization policy, particularly around employment and business opportunities. At the outset, states must reduce the collateral consequences that are associated with marijuana arrests and convictions; these include prohibiting a person from obtaining an occupational license, public housing, and student loan assistance for college. The American Bar Association (ABA) has identified more than 40,000 state and federal regulations that impose collateral consequences on criminal convictions.[252] One analysis of the ABA data found that at least 84 percent of collateral consequences were related to employment, and 82 percent did not have an end date.[253] For non-U.S. citizens, the collateral consequences of a drug conviction can also include the inability to naturalize, which can

---

[250] Siobhan Montgomery O'Keefe, "Incarceration and Child- hood Disadvantage," *Poverty Facts* 1 (1) (2018), available at https://poverty.ucdavis.edu/sites/main/files/file-attachments/incarceration_and_childhood_disadvantage_0.pdf.

[251] Saneta deVuono-powell and others, "Who Pays?: The True Cost of Incarceration on Families" (Oakland, CA: Ella Baker Center, Forward Together, Research Action Design, 2015), pp. 8–9, available at https://ellabakercenter.org/sites/default/files/downloads/who-pays.pdf.

[252] National Institute of Justice, "National Inventory of the Col- lateral Consequences of Conviction," available at https:// www.nij.gov/topics/courts/pages/collateral-consequenc-es-inventory.aspx (last accessed May 2019).

[253] Stephen Saltzburg, "Testimony Before the Equal Employment Opportunity Commission to Examine Arrest and Conviction Records as a Hiring Barrier," July 26, 2011, available at https://www.eeoc.gov/eeoc/meetings/7-26-11/ saltzburg.cfm#fn9.

exclude people from opportunities only available to citizens.[254] These hindrances make it more difficult for people with arrest or conviction records to find and maintain employment, including in the regulated marijuana market, where past drug convictions are often used to bar people from receiving a marijuana business license.[255]

In order to assist people who have been arrested or convicted of marijuana crimes with securing employment, states must provide automatic and cost-free expungements. An expungement is a legal process by which a person's record of arrest or conviction is erased, meaning that the individual will not need to disclose their arrest or conviction, and a background search will not reveal a record of arrest or conviction. It provides a clean slate[256] to people with arrest and conviction records and mitigates the effects of collateral consequences. In 2018, for example, California passed legislation requiring prosecutors to expunge certain marijuana-related convictions. And earlier this year, San Francisco District Attorney George Gascón partnered with Code for America, a technology solutions nonprofit, to automate the cumbersome expungement process, leading to the clearing of thousands of records.[257] Other major California counties such as Los Angeles and San Joaquin have followed San Francisco's lead.[258]

Jurisdictions must also consider the forces keeping low-income individuals of color from joining and profiting from the regulated marijuana market. A 2017 survey of marijuana business owners found that only 19 percent identified as nonwhite.[259] One reason for this underrepresentation is

---

254 Aaron Reichlin-Melnick, "USCIS Says Immigrants Who Use Legal Marijuana Can Be Denied Citizenship for 'Lacking Good Moral Character,'" American Immigration Council, April 23, 2019, available at http://immigrationimpact. com/2019/04/23/uscis-immigrants-use-marijuana-citizenship-character/.

255 Mona Zhang, "Cannabis Industry Struggles With Hiring People With Past Pot Convictions," *Forbes*, October 4, 2017, available at https://www.forbes.com/sites/mon-azhang/2017/10/04/cannabis-industry-hiring-people-past-pot-convictions/#89b911c5cd4a.

256 Aloha Backenstose and others, "Introducing Clean Slate," Center for American Progress, April 12, 2019, available at https://www.americanprogress.org/issues/criminal-justice/news/2019/04/12/468633/introducing-clean-slate/.

257 Matthew S. Schwartz, "San Francisco To Expunge Thou- sands of Marijuana Convictions," NPR, February 26, 2019, available at https://www.npr.org/2019/02/26/698045482/san-francisco-to-expunge-thousands-of-marijuana-convictions

258 Alene Tchekmedyian, "Prosecutors move to clear 54,000 marijuana convictions in California," *Los Angeles Times*, April 1, 2019, available at https://www.latimes.com/local/lanow/la-me-ln-la-county-marijuana-convictions-20190401-story.html.

259 Marijuana Business Daily, "Women & Minorities in the Marijuana Industry" (2017), p. 10, available at https://mjbizdaily.com/wp-content/uploads/2017/10/Women- and-Minorities-Report.pdf.

that access to capital is a barrier for business owners of color.[260] To enter the marijuana market, owners must usually pay a large fee in addition to the start-up costs associated with opening a business.[261] Thus, jurisdictions should create grant programs that support minority-owned businesses and underrepresented people who want to enter the industry. An example is included in the Marijuana and Freedom Opportunity Act, a bill recently reintroduced by Senate Minority Leader Chuck Schumer (D-NY).[262] The bill would establish a fund from revenue collected from regulated marijuana businesses under existing federal tax laws to support the small-business concerns of marijuana businesses owned and controlled by socioeconomically disadvantaged people.[263]

Additionally, states can reduce barriers to the regulated marijuana market by prioritizing people directly affected by the war on drugs in receiving marijuana business licenses. An initial application fee to receive a license can cost up to $120,000, a figure that excludes associated business costs such as legal fees, insurance, taxes, and marketing.[264] Further, many jurisdictions exclude people with drug convictions from receiving a license to sell marijuana. Some states and cities have taken steps to solve this problem such as Oakland, California, whose Equity Permit Program reserves half of its licenses for "equity applicants."[265] Participants in the program can have their licensing fees waived and receive technical and financial assistance. To qualify, equity applicants must earn less than 80 percent of the city's median income and have been convicted of a marijuana offense or lived for 10 years in an area where people were disproportionately arrested for marijuana offenses.[266]

---

260 Benjamin Goggin, "Black People Face Big Barriers Entering the Legal Weed Industry," Vice, September 20, 2018, available at https://free.vice.com/en_us/article/yw4pkw/weed-industry-equity-black-business.

261 Ibid.

262 Marijuana Freedom and Opportunity Act, 116th Cong., 2nd sess. (May 9, 2019), available at https://www.democrats. senate.gov/imo/media/doc/Marijuana%20Freedom%20 and%20 Opportunity%20Act.pdf.

263 Ibid.

264 Goggin, "Black People Face Big Barriers Entering the Legal Weed Industry."

265 Max Blau, "Legal Pot Is Notoriously White. Oakland Is Changing That," *Politico Magazine*, March 27, 2018, available at https://www.politico.com/magazine/ story/2018/03/27/ oakland-legal-cannabis-hood-incubator-217657.

266 City of Oakland, California, "Become an Equity Applicant or Incubator," available at http://www2.oaklandnet.com/government/o/CityAdministration/cannabis-permits/OAK 068455 (last accessed May 2019).

Creating Public Sector Jobs for Communities Affected by the War on Marijuana

In addition to proposals focused on providing access to the regulated marijuana market, policymakers should use marijuana-related tax revenue to provide broader opportunities for people who have been adversely affected by disproportionate marijuana enforcement actions over the years. One possibility is outlined in Sen. Cory Booker's (D-NJ) Marijuana Justice Act of 2019, which proposes a community reinvestment fund that would provide grants to communities most affected by the war on drugs.[267] The grants would support programming focused on job training, re-entry services, expungement of convictions, health education, and other community initiatives. This month, Illinois Gov. J.B. Pritzker (D) included a similar proposal in his plan to legalize recreational marijuana in his state.[268] The plan calls for 25 percent of all revenue from regulated marijuana sales to fund the Restoring Our Communities grant program, which would be used to repair communities most harmed by "discriminatory drug policies."[269]

A more direct approach, however, would be to use marijuana-related revenue to fund the creation of public sector jobs for people in communities most affected by harsh marijuana enforcement. This proposal is based on a concept in CAP's "Blueprint for the 21st Century," which calls for a nationwide investment in millions of new jobs in the country's hardest-hit areas to meet pressing social and economic needs.[270] As the Jobs Blueprint notes, certain communities have been left especially far behind in today's economy, including those that have experienced persistent poverty or decades-long lack of opportunities.[271]

For communities in which harsh marijuana enforcement has contributed to the enduring lack of opportunities, using marijuana revenue to create jobs would provide a boost to the local economy as well as address broader community needs. Actual jobs created under the Jobs Blueprint and the

---

[267] Marijuana Justice Act of 2019, S. 597, 116th Cong. (February 28, 2019), available at https://www.congress.gov/bill/116th-congress/senate-bill/597?q=%7B%22search %22%3A%5B%22marijuana+justice+act%22%5D%7D&s=2 &r=2.

[268] Sara Burnett, "Illinois Governor Announces Plan to Legalize Marijuana," *Time*, May 4, 2019, available at http://time. com/5583289/illinois-governor-legalize-marijuana-plan/.

[269] Ibid.

[270] Center for American Progress, "Blueprint for the 21st Century: A Plan for Better Jobs and Stronger Communities" (Washington: 2018), available at https://cdn.american-progress.org/content/uploads/2018/05/05055049/ JobsBlueprint-report1.pdf.

[271] Ibid.

proposal in this brief could include: support services in schools and libraries; outreach and peer support to people struggling with substance misuse by trained and certified graduates of treatment programs; support for after-school or summer enrichment programs; and delivery of meals to seniors and other homebound individuals.[272]

To determine which communities should benefit from this proposal, policymakers could use essentially the same formula outlined in the Jobs Blueprint—a weighted index of communities' poverty rate, median earnings, and nonemployment.[273] However, they must also determine which communities have experienced disproportionate arrest rates for marijuana offenses. This can be accomplished using historical data on marijuana arrests from data inputted into the FBI's Uniform Crime Reporting (UCR) database or similar state-based data collections whereby areas that experienced high marijuana arrest rates relative to their population will be program targets.

Using the calculations in the Jobs Blueprint,[274] the authors find that thousands of jobs could be created using marijuana revenue in highly distressed communities with disproportionate rates of marijuana arrests. Colorado's 2017–2018 excise tax revenue could have created nearly 2,000 jobs, and Washington state could have added almost 10,000 jobs with their 2017 excise tax revenue. Similarly, California's tax revenue from its regulated marijuana market in 2018 totaled $345 million, which could have created an additional 10,000 jobs in highly distressed communities. The federal government could use this same model by taking the revenue that the U.S. Department of the Treasury currently collects from marijuana businesses and regranting it to states to create jobs in communities that have historically been adversely affected by harsh marijuana enforcement policies.

Conclusion

Today, states are raking in billion-dollar profits for activity that sent millions of African American and Latinx individuals into the criminal justice system, trapping their families and communities in poverty for generations. The

---

[272] Ibid, p. 53.

[273] Ibid, p. 45.

[274] Ibid, footnote 185. CAP's Jobs Blueprint estimated that the 900,000 jobs could be guaranteed at a cost of $32 billion—or $35,555 per job—which includes 25 percent for nonlabor costs. The 900,000 jobs figure does not include the 300,000 additional jobs estimated to be created separately from the other public investments described in the Jobs Blueprint.

movement to legalize marijuana presents an opportunity both to achieve justice for and to build economic opportunity in these communities. Creating public sector jobs and other policies outlined in this issue brief acknowledge the economic impact that the war on drugs has had on low-income people of color. With these policies, elected leaders can begin to address the structural barriers that states must rupture so that individuals from some of their most vulnerable communities have equal access to economic opportunity.

Maritza Perez is a senior policy analyst for Criminal Justice Reform at the Center for American Progress. Olugbenga Ajilore is a senior economist at the Center. Ed Chung is the vice president for Criminal Justice Reform at the Center.

Office of the State's Attorney for Baltimore City, Reforming a Broken System: Rethinking the Role of Marijuana Prosecutions in Baltimore City, Marilyn J. Mosby, State's Attorney for Baltimore City, January 2019

Introduction

Prosecutors around the country are examining how best to implement criminal justice reform from within. As part of this reform, prosecutors' offices are reconsidering marijuana prosecution policies and their impact on reducing crime. Widespread and reliable data suggests that there is little public safety value related to the current enforcement of marijuana laws. In fact, the data indicates that the disparate enforcement of marijuana laws not only intensifies already existing racial disparities in the criminal justice system but exacerbates distrust among communities and law enforcement without increasing overall public safety.

Moreover, given the legitimate public safety concerns that do exist in our nation's cities, when resources are expended to address marijuana possession cases (from docketing to finger printing and general processing of those arrested to the ultimate resolution of charges), those same resources are no longer available to address significant criminal activity. This leaves those communities most affected by serious crime with no punitive, rehabilitative or public safety value gained from the prosecution of marijuana possession cases.

National research has consistently shown that Black people are almost four times more likely to be arrested for marijuana possession in the United

States than White people despite individuals of both races using marijuana at the same rate. Between 2001 and 2010 there were over 8 million marijuana arrests in the United States, 88% of which were for possession. Where marijuana arrests increased and accounted for over half (52%) of all drug arrests in the United States, Blacks accounted for nearly half (46%) of those same arrests.[275]

Today, racial disparities regarding enforcement of marijuana laws continue to exist even where marijuana use has been legalized. In Colorado after legalization of marijuana for recreational use, there was a 51% decrease in Whites being arrested but only a 33% decrease for Latinx and a 25% decrease for Blacks.[276] Comparatively, Washington State's post-legalization arrest rate for Blacks is double the arrest rate for others and a Black person in Washington, D.C. is 11 times more likely than a White person to be arrested for public consumption of marijuana.[277]

Given the lack of a demonstrable public safety benefit, the resource drain that resolving marijuana possession cases places on prosecutors, and the racially unjust manner in which these laws have been, and continue to be, enforced nationally and in Baltimore City specifically, the Office of the State's Attorney for Baltimore City (BCSAO) has reconsidered how we prosecute marijuana cases. This paper outlines our research into national and local enforcement policies and their effects on public safety and minorities in Baltimore City and concludes with our policies for a new path forward.

Historical Context

As history demonstrates, the roots of the disproportionate impact of marijuana criminalization on people of color in the United States can be traced beyond the War on Drugs. A sordid history of marijuana prohibition lies in ethnic and racial bigotry. It has been observed that, "Marijuana gives rise to insanity –

---

[275] American Civil Liberties Union, "The War on Marijuana in Black and White," (June 2013), https://www.aclu.org/sites/default/files/field_document/1114413-mj-report-rfs-rel1.pdf at 21.

[276] Colorado Department of Public Safety, "Marijuana Legalization in Colorado: Early Findings," (March 2016) http://cdpsdocs.state.co.us/ors/docs/reports/2016-SB13-283-Rpt.pdf.

[277] Drug Policy Alliance, "From Prohibition to Progress: A Status Report on Marijuana Legalization," (January 2018) http://www.drugpolicy.org/legalization-status-report.

not in its users but in the policies directed against it."[278] The genesis of this insanity began in the early part of the twentieth century which brought forth a large influx of Mexicans into America seeking to escape the violence of the Revolution of 1910.[279]

A History of Stigmatization with the Recreational Use of Marijuana

Immigrants coming to America as a result of the Revolution of 1910, as part of their culture, smoked cannabis on a recreational basis which they referred to as "marihuana." Although cannabis was used by Americans at this time as a purported tonic for a variety of ailments, it appears that recreational use was limited.

Marijuana, on the other hand, became the basis of a xenophobic campaign of government-sponsored fear mongering against the new immigrants. Dire warnings were published of the "Marijuana Menace" and of crimes committed by Mexican immigrants while ostensibly under the influence of marijuana. By 1931, twenty-nine states had passed laws outlawing the possession of marijuana.[280] The 1933 repeal of alcohol prohibition did nothing to slow the train of marijuana criminalization. Driving that train was one Harry Anslinger, commissioner of the then-nascent National Bureau of Narcotics. Anslinger described marijuana users as follows, "most are Negroes, Hispanics, Filipinos, and entertainers. Their Satanic music, jazz, and swing, result from marijuana use." Furthermore, "the primary reason to outlaw marijuana is its effect on the degenerate races."[281]

In 1937, largely in response to testimony provided by Commissioner Anslinger, Congress passed the Marijuana Tax Act, effectively outlawing marijuana by imposing heavy taxes on the sale, possession, and transportation of cannabis. The final descent into legislative madness occurred in 1970 when the United States Congress passed the Controlled Substances Act,[282] which repealed the Marijuana Tax Act, but classified cannabis in the same category

---

[278] Eric Shlosser, The Atlantic, "More Reefer Madness," (April 1997) https://www.theatlantic.com/magazine/archive/1997/04/more-reefer-madness/376827/.

[279] Marijuana is the term used in this paper, as this is the term used in current laws. The BCSAO acknowledges that while the terms marijuana and cannabis are used interchangeably, the term marijuana is associated with past racial and ethnic injustices.

[280] See www.pbs.org/wgbh/pages/frontline/shows/dope/etc/cron.html.

[281] Common Sense for Drug Policy, "The Devil Weed and Harry Anslinger," www.csdp.org/publiscservice/anslinger.htm.

[282] Title II of the Comprehensive Drug Abuse Prevention and Control Act of 1970.

as heroin, as a Schedule 1 drug. Maryland thereafter followed suit and maintains this schedule I classification to this very day.[283]

Continued Stigmatization with the "War on Drugs"

President Richard Nixon officially declared a "War on Drugs" in 1971. In the 1980s, President Ronald Reagan reinforced and expanded many of Nixon's War on Drug policies. In 1984, his wife Nancy Reagan later launched the "Just Say No" campaign with an effort to educate children on the dangers of drug use.

As years passed, the War on Drugs continued and so did the policies designed to punish drug users. By 1997, the number of people behind bars for nonviolent drug offenses increased from 50,000 in 1980 to over 400,000 within a span of only seventeen years. Forty-six years since the official declaration of Nixon's Drug War, as of 2017, 1.5 million arrests in the United States (U.S.) were due to drug law violations, where 85.4% of those arrested were related to drug possession.[284]

And while the U.S. continues to lead the world with the highest rates of imprisonment for drug law violations, it is patently clear that drug related arrests have had the most impact on communities of color. Although data suggests that the rates of drug use and even sales are comparable across racial and ethnic lines, Black and Latinx people are much more likely to be arrested for drug use and sales than White people. In fact, approximately 80% of people in federal prison and almost 60% of people in state prison for drug offenses are Black or Latinx.[285]

Public Safety and the War on Marijuana

While racial disparities are evident when considering the manner in which marijuana laws are enforced, the problem is even more compounded when such enforcement produces no demonstrable public safety benefit. For example, since 2014 the BCSAO has closed 1,128 District Court cases for simple marijuana possession. Seventy three of those individuals were found guilty, five not guilty, 49 cases were stetted, and 1,001 (88%) cases were nolle

[283] See §5-402(d) (23) of the Criminal Law Article of the Maryland Code.

[284] Drug Policy Alliance, "Drug Policy Statistics," http://www.drugpolicy.org/issues/drug-war-statistics - Cases include those with other charges where the defendant pleas to possession.

[285] Drug Policy Alliance, "Race and the Drug War," http://www.drugpolicy.org/issues/race-and-drug-war.

prosequi.[286] As a matter of consequence, no public safety benefit was seemingly gained in the overwhelming majority of these cases, yet they required the extensive use of limited city resources, including resources from not only the BCSAO but also resources from the Baltimore Police Department (BPD), the Department of Public Safety and Correctional Services (DPSCS) and the Baltimore City Circuit and District Courts.

Even in the instances where civil citations are issued pursuant to the 2014 law that decriminalized the possession of less than 10 grams of marijuana, if an individual is without identification when cited for possession of marijuana, the extensive use of limited resources still exist; whereby this individual is arrested, booked and processed within the criminal justice system.

As further evidence that marijuana enforcement is not creating a significant public safety benefit, states that have legalized recreational use of marijuana do not exhibit an increase in crime since legalization. The Manhattan District Attorney's Office released in 2018 *A Report on the Legalization of Recreational Marijuana in the United States* and found no evidence of an increase in crime related to the legalization of recreational use of marijuana.[287] The report noted, for example, that, "Oregon's legalization law went into effect in July 2015, and the first stores opened in October 2016. [However], the [Federal Bureau of Investigation] FBI data shows that crime rates stayed largely the same between 2015 and 2016."[288]

In Nevada the report found that there was an initial increase in burglaries at stores selling marijuana after legalization. In response, these stores increased their security measures, and this substantially decreased the

---

[286] BCSAO data collected regarding closed simple marijuana possession cases is reflective only of convictions captured within the Judicial Information Systems (JIS). We do not profess to have captured every case, this is only what our data illustrates. In a recent article published in Baltimore Fishbowl (2018) it was found that there were a total of 3,200 misdemeanor marijuana possession charges filed between 2015 and 2017 in Baltimore City, of which 95% were issued to Black people. https://baltimorefishbowl.com/stories/structural-racism-and-cannabis-black-baltimoreans-still-disproportionately-arrested-for-weed-after-decriminalization/.

[287] The Office of Manhattan District Attorney Cyrus R. Vance Jr., "Marijuana, Fairness and Public Safety: A Report on the Legalization of Recreational Marijuana in the United States," (May 2018) https://www.manhattanda.org/wp-content/uploads/2018/05/DANY-Report-on-the-Legalization-of-Recreational-Marijuana-Final.pdf.

[288] The Office of Manhattan District Attorney Cyrus R. Vance Jr., "Marijuana, Fairness and Public Safety: A Report on the Legalization of Recreational Marijuana in the United States," (May 2018) https://www.manhattanda.org/wp-content/uploads/2018/05/DANY-Report-on-the-Legalization-of-Recreational-Marijuana-Final.pdf.

burglaries. The report also noted that in Las Vegas violent crimes did not increase after legalization.[289]

In Washington State, "...crime rates have remained... and continue on a downward trend after retail sales [of marijuana] began in mid-2014."[290] Interestingly, in Colorado where recreational use was legalized in 2014, there was an increase in crime reported in 2016. State officials though - including the police department, the Department of Public Safety and the Governor - all agree that the evidence is inconclusive concerning whether the increase in crime is related to the legalization of marijuana or other factors.[291] Taken together, this national data fails to conclusively establish that the legalization of marijuana has resulted in any material increase in crimes related to its cultivation or sale.

In sum, arrests for simple marijuana possession are a drain on limited resources and produce no rehabilitative, deterrent or other public safety benefit. In a city where there were 343 homicides in 2017 and a year-end clearance rate of 31% of homicides that occurred that year, and in 2018 there were 309 homicides with a year-end clearance rate of 26% for homicides that occurred in 2018, resources are scarce.[292] The scarcity of resources is being wasted to deter a problem that is not threatening the safety or security of Baltimore City residents.

---

[289] The Office of Manhattan District Attorney Cyrus R. Vance Jr., "Marijuana, Fairness and Public Safety: A Report on the Legalization of Recreational Marijuana in the United States," (May 2018) https://www.manhattanda.org/wp-content/uploads/2018/05/DANY-Report-on-the-Legalization-of-Recreational-Marijuana-Final.pdf.

[290] The Office of Manhattan District Attorney Cyrus R. Vance Jr., "Marijuana, Fairness and Public Safety: A Report on the Legalization of Recreational Marijuana in the United States," (May 2018) https://www.manhattanda.org/wp-content/uploads/2018/05/DANY-Report-on-the-Legalization-of-Recreational-Marijuana-Final.pdf.

[291] The Office of Manhattan District Attorney Cyrus R. Vance Jr., "Marijuana, Fairness and Public Safety: A Report on the Legalization of Recreational Marijuana in the United States," (May 2018) https://www.manhattanda.org/wp-content/uploads/2018/05/DANY-Report-on-the-Legalization-of-Recreational-Marijuana-Final.pdf.

[292] BPD utilizes a cumulative clearance rate in which the numerator is all cleared homicide cases that were cleared in a given year, including clearances for homicides that occurred in earlier years, and the denominator is only the number of homicides that occurred in the given year. Consequently, the actual clearance rate for murders that took place in that same year will always be lower than the cumulative rate.

Public Health and Marijuana

Marijuana decriminalization and legalization as a public health concern is an evolving debate with little irrefutable evidence on marijuana's effects – good or bad. While there is limited data-driven research beyond anecdotal reports on the public health risks and benefits of marijuana decriminalization and legalization, marijuana remains illegal under federal law -prohibiting its sale, use or transport - and is classified as a Schedule 1 drug with zero medicinal value and high probability for abuse.[293]

According to the Centers for Disease Control and Prevention with data from the Substance Abuse and Mental Health Services Administration, marijuana is the most commonly used illegal drug in the United States, with 37.6 million users in 2017.[294] Marijuana is believed to possess a wide range of health effects, including: addiction; brain health; cancer; chronic pain; heart health; lung health; mental health; poisoning; and is also an alleged risk for the use of other drugs. In fact, opponents of decriminalization and legalization argue that marijuana is a "gateway drug," that fuels the prospective use of heroin and other drugs and increases the accessibility and likelihood of youth consumption. According to the data, these arguments are not founded in fact. The Drug Policy Alliance notes, the majority of marijuana users do not go on to use other drugs, but instead cease drug use with marijuana.[295]

And while opponents of reform assert that the decriminalization and legalization of marijuana promotes alcohol abuse, impaired driving and that marijuana stores are criminally enticing, supporters of reform argue that marijuana decriminalization and legalization dissolves racial injustices in drug arrests; weakens the black market associated with violent crime; decreases crime, whereby police resources are reallocated to pressing public safety concerns; improves doctor-patient relations (where patients are more willing to openly communicate marijuana use); and reduces alcohol use (where alcohol is a substance with severe direct and collateral consequences).[296]

Notwithstanding this public health debate, there is widespread consensus that the criminalization of marijuana possession significantly impacts

---

[293] 21 U.S.C § 801 et seq.

[294] Center for Disease Control and Prevention, "Marijuana: How Can It Affect Your Health" https://www.cdc.gov/marijuana/health-effects.html.

[295] Drug Policy Alliance, "Is Marijuana a Gateway Drug" http://www.drugpolicy.org/marijuana-gateway-drug.

[296] Drug Policy Alliance, "Is Marijuana a Gateway Drug" http://www.drugpolicy.org/marijuana-gateway-drug.

communities of color often without addressing any public health-related concerns in a meaningful way. The American Civil Liberties Union (ACLU), relying on federally collected data and broad accredited references, found that Black men are four times more likely to be arrested for marijuana possession than Whites, even though both groups use the drug at similar rates.[297] Furthermore, the ACLU Maryland's *Blueprint for Smart Justice: Maryland* Report argues that Maryland over relies on incarceration, particularly for offenses that are best treated as public health concerns.[298]

Enforcement of Marijuana Laws in Baltimore City

In 2010, the American Civil Liberties Union (ACLU) reported that Maryland's arrest rate for marijuana possession was the fourth highest in the nation. In fact, police arrested one out of every 250 Maryland residents for possession of marijuana. In addition, while Black people only comprised 30% of the State's population in 2010, 58% of those arrested for marijuana possession were Black.[299]

In that same time period, Baltimore City had the largest rate of disparity among marijuana arrestees, with Black people being almost six times more likely to be arrested for marijuana possession than Whites.[300] And even with Maryland's October 1, 2014 decision to decriminalize possession of less than ten grams of marijuana to a civil infraction, racial disparities continue to exist in Baltimore City.

According to Baltimore Police Department BPD records, in 2015 45 citations were issued and 39 of those were given to Black people (89%). In 2016, records indicate that BPD issued 199 citations for marijuana possession and 187 (94%) were issued to Black people. In 2017, BPD issued 431 citations for marijuana possession, where 410 (95%) were issued to Black people. Shockingly, approximately 42% of the aforementioned citations were issued in the Western District, where approximately 95% of the residents in this District are Black.

When taken together, these statistics are incredibly alarming and elucidate the crisis of disparate treatment of Black people for marijuana possession and

---

297 American Civil Liberties Union, "Blueprint for Smart Justice: Maryland" (2018) https://50stateblueprint.aclu.org/assets/reports/SJ-Blueprint-MD.pdf.

298 American Civil Liberties Union, "Blueprint for Smart Justice: Maryland" (2018) https://50stateblueprint.aclu.org/assets/reports/SJ-Blueprint-MD.pdf.

299 American Civil Liberties Union, "Blueprint for Smart Justice: Maryland" (2018) https://50stateblueprint.aclu.org/assets/reports/SJ-Blueprint-MD.pdf.

300 American Civil Liberties Union, "Blueprint for Smart Justice: Maryland" (2018) https://50stateblueprint.aclu.org/assets/reports/SJ-Blueprint-MD.pdf.

other offenses without any seeming regard for the possible adverse public health effects resulting from such enforcement. As such, these statistics provide further support for creating policies that offer alternatives to incarceration for individuals who commit offenses that have not been shown to have a significant impact on the overall health and well-being of communities.

Collateral Consequences

Collateral consequences are legal, social, and economic debilities imposed as a result of a criminal conviction regardless of whether a convicted individual serves any time incarcerated. These consequences create social and economic barriers for individuals reentering into society by denying or restricting benefits otherwise available to all citizens. Collateral consequences are known to adversely affect adoptions, housing, welfare, immigration, employment, professional licensure, property rights, mobility, education and other opportunities—the collective effect of which increases recidivism and undermines meaningful reentry of the convicted for a lifetime.[301]

Although sweeping adverse ramifications flowing from collateral consequences exists, defendants are generally not entitled, as a matter of due process, to be warned of these consequences, either before entering a guilty plea or upon conviction.

In a city like Baltimore, the collateral consequences of an inequitable criminal justice system are apparent. According to the United States Census Bureau, in 2017 an estimated 39.7 million (12%) of the country's 327.16 million Americans lived in poverty.[302] In Baltimore City - home to 622,454 residents, 62% of which are Black – 28% of families live in poverty.[303] Specifically, Baltimore's Western District, home too much of the city's Black population and where health and wellness indicators sit well below the city's total performance, 42% of marijuana citations were issued despite the reality of unsupported human capital.

---

301 American Bar Association Criminal Justice Section "Collateral Consequences of Criminal Convictions Judicial Bench Book," (March 2018) https://www.ncjrs.gov/pdffiles1/nij/grants/251583.pdf.

302 United States Census Bureau https://www.census.gov/en.html.

303 Baltimore City Health Department, "Baltimore City 2017 Neighborhood Health Profile" https://health.baltimorecity.gov/sites/default/files/NHP%202017%20-%2047%20 Sandtown-Winchester-Harlem%20Park%20(rev%206-9-17).pdf.

Moreover, data from the Baltimore City Health Department's *Baltimore City 2017 Neighborhood Health Profile*, shows that in Baltimore's Western district (comprised of several historic neighborhoods such as Sandtown-Winchester, Penn-North, and Druid Hill) – where approximately 95% of the residents are Black – the median household income is $24,374 compared to the city's overall median income of $41,819.[304] In addition, the unemployment rate in this district is 20% as compared to a 13% city rate overall, and the poverty rate is 50% as compared to a 28% rate citywide.[305] Despite these numbers, or maybe because of them, the BPD disproportionately issued over approximately 42% of its 2017 marijuana citations to Black people in this District.

These statistics are staggering evidence of an intimate and vivid relationship between discriminatory marijuana law enforcement and the absence of investment in human capital where the root causes of poverty are not alleviated. If individuals are provided quality education, workforce development, housing and income stability, they become productive, contributing and law-abiding citizens not simply for society but themselves and families – both of which are mutually benefiting. If, however, large swatches of the community are disproportionately and negatively impacted by having to engage with the criminal justice system to address marijuana possession charges that show no significant public safety threat and, instead, cause prosecutors' offices to expend extensive resources, then the cost/benefit analysis is clear and those disproportionately-effecting policies should be changed.

The Prosecutor's Role

Given the foregoing statistics, many in the United States are progressively rethinking and reconsidering how the "War on Drugs" has impacted the country on personal and systemic levels. A survey conducted by the *Pew Research Center* found that 67% of Americans believe that drug policy should

---

[304] Baltimore City Health Department, "Baltimore City 2017 Neighborhood Health Profile" https://health.baltimorecity.gov/sites/default/files/NHP%202017%20-%2047%20 Sandtown-Winchester-Harlem%20Park%20(rev%206-9-17).pdf.

[305] Baltimore City Health Department, "Baltimore City 2017 Neighborhood Health Profile" https://health.baltimorecity.gov/sites/default/files/NHP%202017%20-%2047%20 Sandtown-Winchester-Harlem%20Park%20(rev%206-9-17).pdf.

focus more on treatment and less on prosecution.[306] The continued criminalization of marijuana possession and use has become even more troubling as states decriminalize and legalize these activities.[307]

Prosecutors have a sworn duty to "seek justice, not merely convict."[308] Also, they are expected to improve the criminal justice system. This duty to seek justice, not simply convict, and to improve the system in which they work, has led many District Attorneys across the country to change how they prosecute, whether they prosecute, and how they address marijuana enforcement in their districts. Manhattan, Brooklyn, Philadelphia, Nueces County (TX), and others, are declining to prosecute marijuana possession, diverting marijuana drug violators, and implementing many other progressive policies surrounding enforcement of marijuana violations.

Prosecutors are beginning to address the War on Marijuana and offer more effective solutions to the problems that marijuana violations cause in the communities they affect. In this way, prosecutors can begin to change the narrative surrounding marijuana violations by recognizing and remedying the conscious and collateral impact it can have on individuals, particularly people of color. Certainly, prosecutors decide what charges to bring, when to bring them, which plea deals to offer, when to divert, and when to not charge enhancements.[309] This immense amount of power is best utilized to socially, politically and behaviorally reform and mandate marijuana legislation and policy.

Alternatives to Incarceration

Diversion programs refer to programs that redirect individuals away from incarceration. These programs are an important tool in criminal justice reform. Diversion programs limit expenditure of resources, reduce rates of recidivism

---

[306] Pew Research Center: U.S. Politics and Policy "America's New Drug Policy Landscape," (April 2014) http://www.people-press.org/2014/04/02/americas-new-drug-policy-landscape/.

[307] Mike Males & Lizzie Buchen, "Reforming Marijuana Laws: Which Approach Best Reduces the Harms of Criminalization: A Five State Analysis, Center on Juvenile and Criminal Justice," (Sept. 2014), http://www.cjcj.org/uploads/cjcj/documents/cjcj_marijuana_reform_comparison.pdf.

[308] Fair and Just Prosecution "Marijuana Policy Reform," (2017) https://fairandjustprosecution.org/wp-content/uploads/2017/09/FJPBrief.Marijuana.9.25.pdf.

[309] Fair and Just Prosecution "Marijuana Policy Reform," (2017) https://fairandjustprosecution.org/wp-content/uploads/2017/09/FJPBrief.Marijuana.9.25.pdf.

and decrease the collateral consequences of entanglement in the criminal justice system.[310] Diversion programs decrease the likelihood of people entering the prison system and help people access much needed resources.

Drug Treatment Courts

In Baltimore City there exist both Circuit and District Drug Treatment Courts. These are specialized court dockets to serve criminal defendants who have alcohol and other drug dependency barriers.[311] These courts require cooperative relationships among drug court team members. Collaboration must exist from beginning through end of the process. The court, through the designated judge, provides the overall leadership of the team and represents the court's authority to drug court participants.[312]

The goal of Drug Treatment Court Programs is to offer nonviolent offenders, who are identified as being drug-dependent, fully integrated and comprehensive substance abuse treatment services, with close criminal justice supervision and judicial monitoring. These programs strive to enhance public safety, provide cost-effective alternatives to incarceration, give offenders the tools and skills necessary to maintain sobriety, reward positive life changes and maintain accountability for negative conduct, with an overarching goal to rehabilitate drug offenders to become productive, self-sustaining members of society. Participants are held accountable for negative conduct, and consequences resulting from negative conduct are decided by the team on an individual basis.

Mental Health Courts

In Baltimore there exist both Circuit and District Mental Health Courts. A Mental Health Court is a specialized court docket established for defendants with mental illness. Participants can have a co-occurring substance use disorder. Participants are identified through mental health screening and assessments and voluntarily participate in a judicially supervised treatment plan developed jointly by a team of court staff and mental health professionals. The overarching goal of the Mental Health Court is to decrease the frequency of participants' contacts with the criminal justice system by providing participants with judicial leadership to improve the social functioning,

---

[310] Fair and Just Prosecution "21 Principles for the 21st Century Prosecutor" https://www.brennancenter.org/sites/default/files/publications/FJP_21Principles_FINAL.pdf .

[311] Maryland Courts "Drug Treatment Courts," https://www.courts.state.md.us/opsc/dtc.

[312] Maryland Courts "Drug Treatment Courts," https://www.courts.state.md.us/opsc/dtc.

employment linkage, housing needs, treatment, and support services of participants.[313]

Mental Health Courts rely on individualized treatment plans and ongoing judicial monitoring to address both the mental health needs of offenders and public safety concerns of communities. These courts also seek to address the underlying problems that contribute to criminal behavior, and to assist with the avoidance of recurring correctional visits, as well as to overall lower the recidivism of this population. Both the Drug Treatment Courts and the BCSAO diversion programs described below have borrowed heavily from the assessment, treatment, and supervision aspects of the Mental Health Courts.

BCSAO's AIM to B'More (AIM) Diversion Program

Created in 2015 by and operated under the administration of State's Attorney Marilyn J. Mosby, AIM to B'More (AIM) is an alternative to incarceration that improves the quality of life for low-level felony drug offenders. Merging accountability with real opportunities for self and situational development and sustainability, amenable and successful participants graduate without a criminal record and with a career. While it is recognized that certain criminal offenses may require confined and secure settings, problem solving initiatives and approaches, similar to AIM, provide choices to initial or continued formal processing in the criminal justice system. Equally, diversion programs reduce crime, improve practices and coordination across agencies, enhance client and victim services, reduce repetitive care and increase public trust in the pursuit of justice.

Fundamentally, AIM was modeled after former San Francisco District Attorney Kamala Harris's evidence-based *Back on Track: A Problem Solving Reentry initiative.* Existing in partnership with 24 public and private agencies, including the Division of Parole and Probation in the Department of Public Safety and Correctional Services, AIM to B'More fills a critical void within the criminal justice system for offenders who sell drugs for income. First, participants submit to an amenability assessment of serious or chronic behavioral, social and psychological disorders and barriers; undergo treatment deemed necessary; and are encouraged to work with the program's licensed certified clinical social worker to develop a tentative action plan based on his or her evolving needs. Participants are offered a two-year supervised

---

[313] Maryland Courts "Mental Health Courts," https://mdcourts.gov/opsc/mhc.

probation, including 100 hours of community service, career coaching, and are required to maintain consistent full time employment for one year. Upon successful completion of AIM, including full compliance with the terms of a 2-year supervised probation, the state will initiate and facilitate the defendant's timely petition for expungement.

Overall, AIM services a population that is 98% Black and predominantly (86%) male. Sixty (60%) of participants have their high school diploma or are under 24 years old and 80% are working full-time. Remarkably, AIM's success rate is 68% and its recidivism rate (32%) is well below the national average (68%). To date, 98% of AIM graduates have full time employment.

Reform

The BCSAO is committed to holistic criminal justice reform. In an effort to develop new policies that better address and remedy the systemic racial disparities resulting from the uneven enforcement of marijuana laws borne by communities of color in Baltimore City, the BCSAO has studied the national best practices and recommendations from accredited and progressively innovative agencies, including: *Fair and Just Prosecution*, *The Brennan Center for Justice*, *PEW Charitable Trust*, and other District Attorneys across the country. Collectively, the efforts guide the BCSAO's new policies, particularly in relation to marijuana, and these policies will begin to address the disproportionate effects from the War on Drugs.

Many of the BCSAO's current policies and programs are progressive and strive to reduce rates of mass incarceration, especially when it comes to incarceration for conduct that is primarily a public health concern. The City's neighbor, Washington, D.C., and states across the country have decriminalized marijuana while Maryland has yet to follow suit. The new policies outlined below are intended to further address the injustices of the past and ensure that justice always prevails.

BCSAO Will Not Prosecute Marijuana Possession Regardless of Weight and Criminal History

Effective immediately, the BCSAO will not prosecute individuals for the possession of marijuana regardless of weight and/or criminal history.[314]

[314] In instances where there are extraordinary circumstances, Executive approval must be gained in order to prosecute possession, and such approval must be noted in all case files.

BCSAO Will Prosecute Marijuana Possession with Intent to Distribute (PWID) and Distribution if Articulation of indicium of Distribution Exists

Effective immediately, the BCSAO will continue to prosecute felony Possession with Intent to Distribute and/or Distribution Charges if those charges are based on articulated evidence of intent to sell or distribution of marijuana exists, in addition to the amount possessed.

BCSAO Mandates Referrals of All First Time Felony Drug Distribution Offenses to AIM to B'MORE Diversion Program

Effective immediately, Assistant State's Attorneys for Baltimore City must refer all first time felony drug distribution defendants to AIM to B'More Diversion Program.

Correcting Past Convictions

In addition to the reforms above, this office will work to right the wrongs of the past. In light of the disproportionate enforcement of marijuana possession laws and the collateral consequences of such convictions on communities of color, the BCSAO has moved to vacate marijuana possession convictions in 1,050 Circuit Court cases and in 3,778 District Court cases, dating back to 2011.[315] Removing the aforesaid convictions is in line with the BCSAO's mission of pursuing "justice over convictions" in every case.

Expungement motions were not filed in these cases because of the numerous hurdles in the expungement statutes that would require expenditure of enormous resources to determine whether expungement might be possible.[316]

---

[315] The BCSAO collected the number of cases dating back to the year 2000 from JIS, but we do not contend that the Office has captured all cases. The Administrative Office of The Courts possesses the comprehensive data, but we have been unsuccessful in obtaining this information.

[316] Barriers to expungement motions include: The Unit Rule, The Pending Case Exception, The Waiting Period and having to pull the controlled dangerous substance analysis for each case.

Conclusion

While contemporary attitudes and public policy toward marijuana have changed dramatically in the past few years, the enforcement of marijuana laws remains grossly disproportionate in its impact on communities of color. Moreover, prosecuting marijuana possession has not been shown to significantly improve public safety or public health outcomes in communities, and the resources saved from prosecuting such cases can be redirected to prosecuting drug kingpins and addressing other significant crimes, including crimes of violence.

The BCSAO understands this and, coupled with the overwhelming evidence showing that the War on Marijuana has only served to further intensify existing racial biases across our country's criminal justice system without securing any significant net gains, the Baltimore City State's Attorney stands ready to use her prosecutorial discretion to change how marijuana laws are enforced in Baltimore City and, in so doing, re-balance the justice system one individual, one family, at a time.

The Failures of the States to Regulate Marijuana. Studies Show That Marijuana Products Have High Levels of Contaminants Including Pesticides, Fungus, Heavy Metals and Solvents

*By: David G. Evans, Esq., CIVEL**

Introduction

The marijuana industry referred to here are those who illegally, negligently or fraudulently produce, market, or distribute marijuana. The marijuana industry claims that the states should regulate "medical" and recreational marijuana. They desire this because they know that they will largely be unrestrained in making a profit. State regulation of marijuana has been a sorry spectacle especially in the states that have been at this for the longest time.

Many studies and news exposes show that marijuana products can contain high levels of chemical contamination, pesticides, heavy metals, mold and fungus. This is true even in "regulated" marijuana states such as Alaska,

Colorado, California, Massachusetts, Michigan, Oregon and Washington. The states are not doing a good job of regulating "medical" marijuana that is sold to sick people. They are not doing any better with recreational marijuana. Here are some examples from studies and news stories.

Alaska

Alaska has had "medical" marijuana for about 20 years (1998) yet, in addition to selling moldy products, a new story reported that a marijuana manufacturer in Alaska was found to be selling untracked marijuana and selling more than 114,000 untested edibles.[317] That they were not even tested is a danger to public health.

California

California had to call out the troops to deal with 22 years of growing "medicine." In 1996 California passed a "medical" marijuana law. They recently legalized recreational marijuana. They had over 22 years to get this under control. It is a disaster. Governor Gavin Newsom, an early backer of recreational marijuana use in the state, is now having to stamp out California's black market. Newsom announced in February 2019 he would "boost the National Guard's statewide Counterdrug Task Force by redeploying up north to go after illegal cannabis farms, many of which are run by cartels." He said the illegal crops "are devastating our pristine forests, and are increasingly becoming fire hazards themselves." "We still have an overwhelming, and what I would characterize as a, catastrophic illegal marijuana problem in Siskiyou County and really the region," said Sheriff Jon Lopey of Siskiyou County, which borders Trinity and Humboldt counties. "So the black market hasn't been curtailed, but it's probably been accelerated."[318]

California has had "medical" marijuana for about 22 years. They have been dispensing marijuana products under the following conditions:

---

317 Available from http://www.thecannabist.co/2017/12/15/alaska-frozen-budz-moldy-marijuana-edibles/94698/.

318 Available from https://www.cnbc.com/2019/04/03/california-wages-war-against-illegal-marijuana-farms-retailers.html.

The Journal of Toxicological Sciences published a study of marijuana concentrates available in the California medical marijuana market.[319] They found that:

> Fifty seven (57) concentrate samples were screened for cannabinoid content and the presence of residual solvents or pesticides. Considerable residual solvent and pesticide contamination were found in these concentrates. Over 80% of the concentrate samples were contaminated in some form.

A study by a news organization in California showed that there were pesticides in 93% of samples of marijuana from 15 marijuana dispensaries. "It's really like injecting that pesticide right into your bloodstream," said former USC Chemistry professor Dr. Jeff Raber.[320]

In an article reported by Anresco Laboratories, a laboratory that conducts testing of marijuana, they noted that their testing showed that much of the marijuana sold in California's 1,000-plus dispensaries every year is dirty. Some 80 percent of the products were tainted with mold, pesticides, and harmful solvents. "We've seen pesticide levels 1,000 times higher in concentrates than what we might normally find in foods," says Anresco's Kyle Borland. Cannabis grown without any pesticides can be dangerous if its water or the soil or its fertilizer is dirty. Heavy metals such as arsenic, lead, cadmium, and mercury occur naturally in water and soil and in high enough concentrations, cancer-causing compounds can build up over time. Anresco gave marijuana a failing grade for heavy metals.[321]

Unpermitted rat poisons used by illegal marijuana growers in California endanger owls and other wildlife. 70% of northern spotted owls and 40% of barred owls tested positive for rodenticides in northwest California in a study conducted by the University of California, Davis and the California Academy

---

319 Jeffrey C. Raber, Sytze Elzinga and Charles Kaplan (2105) Understanding dabs: contamination concerns of cannabis concentrates and cannabinoid transfer during the act of dabbing, The Journal of Toxicological Sciences (J. Toxicol. Sc.) 797 Vol.40, No.6, 797-803, 2015. Available from: https://www.jstage.jst.go.jp/article/jts/40/6/40_797/_pdf.

320 Available at: http://www.nbclosangeles.com/news/local/I-Team-Marijuana-Pot-Pesticide-California-414536763.html.

321 Anresco Laboratories report Available at: https://cannabis.anresco.com/news/whats-the-matter-with-california-cannabis/.

What's the Matter with California Cannabis? Available at: https://modernluxury.com/san-francisco/story/whats-the-matter-california-cannabis.

For information on marijuana and heavy metals see: https://www.mintpressnews.com/how-hemp-can-can-clean-up-radiation-from-fukushima-nuclear-disaster.

of Sciences. Northern spotted owls are threatened species under the federal and state endangered species laws.[322]

University of California at Davis physician researchers did a study of marijuana used as a medicine.

> We found numerous Gram-negative bacilli and fungal pathogens contaminating medical marijuana. These pathogens potentially pose a grave risk to our patients, particularly the immunosuppressed.[323]

News stories report that many marijuana products are failing safety tests in California. Nearly 20% of all the marijuana products tested in California for potency and purity have failed. California started testing on July 1, 2018. In the first two months, nearly 11,000 samples were checked and almost 2,000 failed. Testing has been especially tough on infused cookies and candies: about one-third have failed. Testing also found unacceptable levels of pesticides, solvents and bacteria, including E. coli and salmonella.[324]

A news story reports that poisonous marijuana was found in some Los Angeles-area stores. State regulations failed to stop sales of marijuana products that are loaded with banned toxic chemicals that could make people sick. Although the state put regulations into effect that banned a long list of toxic pesticides from marijuana sold by retail businesses, lab tests found those pesticides continue to tum up in some products, in amounts that could make a user sick. When they're smoked or vaped they go directly into the bloodstream and may cause respiratory disease and cancer. Lab tests showed that products contained numerous banned pesticides, including myclobutanil, a pesticide that the manufacturer said become poisonous hydrogen cyanide when it's heated up, which is what happens when smoking or vaping the marijuana.[325]

---

[322] Gabriel, M. W., L. V. Diller, J.P. Dumbacher, G. M. Wengert, J.M. Higley, R.H. Poppenga, and S. Mendia. 2018. Exposure to rodenticides in Northern Spotted and Barred Owls on remote forest lands in northwestern California: evidence of food web contamination. Avian Conservation and Ecology 13(1):2. Available at: https://doi.org/10.5751/ACE-01134-130102.

[323] Thompson GR, et al., A microbiome assessment of medical marijuana, Clinical Microbiology and Infection (2016), Available at: https://www.clinicalmicrobiologyand infection.com/article/S1198-743X(1 6)30605-X/fulltext.

[324] Available at: https://onenewsnow.com/business/2018/09/17/ca-testing-finds-major-problems-with-marijuana.
First tests are in, and 1 in 5 marijuana samples in California isn't making grade, Orange County Register. available at: https://www.ocregister.com/2018/07/26/first-tests-are-in-and-one-in-five-marijuana-samples-in- ca-isnt-making-grade/.

[325] Available at: https://www.nbcsandiego.com/investigations/national-investigations/ Marijuana-Poison-Pot-Investigation-506356011.html.

News stories reported that a cancer patient in California may have been killed by a fungus in his "medical" marijuana[326] and a California woman caught meningitis from smoking medical marijuana contaminated with lethal fungus.[327]

A news story reported that a marijuana testing lab in California has admitted to falsifying hundreds of marijuana pesticide testing records that were submitted to the state. The fake data involved 22 out of the 66 pesticides for which marijuana is typically tested.[328]

Colorado

Colorado has had "medical" marijuana for about 19 years (2000) and the below is the best they can do.

The Smithsonian reported that "medical" marijuana in Colorado is often laced with pesticides, heavy metals and fungus.[329]

In a series of Public Health and Safety Advisories after inspections of marijuana companies, the Colorado Department of Agriculture (CDA) warned the public that they found potentially unsafe pesticide residues on medical marijuana plant material and marijuana products produced by many marijuana companies. CDA confirmed the presence of off-label pesticides in the product samples tested. The pesticides they confirmed included:

- Avermectin
- Etoxazole
- Imidacloprid
- Myclobutanil
- Propiconazole[330]

---

326 Available at: http://www.cbsnews.com/news/contaminated-medical-marijuana-pot- believed-to-have-killed-cancer-patient/.

327 Available at: http://www.dailymail.co.uk/health/article-5327367/California-woman-caught-meningitis-CANNABIS.html.

328 Available at: https://www.kcra.com/article/sacramento-marijuana-testing-lab-admits-to-falsifying-pesticide-results/25402844.

329 Brian Handwerk (2015), Modem Marijuana Is Often Laced With Heavy Metals and Fungus SMITHSONIAN.COM MARCH 23, 2015, Available at: http://www.smithsonianmag.com/science-nature/modem-marijuana-more-potent-often-laced-heavy-metals-and-fungus -180954696/.

330 Available at: https://www.colorado.gov/pacific/revenue/search-results?search_api_views_fulltext=MARIJUANA+PUBLIC+HEALTH+AND+SAFETY+ADVI SORY.

A lawsuit Complaint in a Colorado lawsuit alleged that a marijuana dispensary sprayed a dangerous fungicide on its marijuana plants. When heated, the fungicide ultimately breaks down to hydrogen cyanide, a well known poison. The marijuana was then sold to medical and recreational marijuana users without adequately apprising them of that fact.[331]

A 2016 presentation by the Denver Department of Environmental Health showed the following concerns:[332]

- Marijuana is inserted in food products. Marijuana businesses outside of Denver receive no food safety inspections. Marijuana products are not regulated as food by the State Department of Health.
- Marijuana plant-derived oils may have Clostridium botulinum (C. botulinum) spores. There are concerns about micro-environment supporting C. botulinum growth and toxin formation.
- In one case a marijuana ingredient was extracted in old domestic laundry machine.
- There is a concern that unapproved equipment is used.
- The marijuana industry lacks consumer safety expertise and Good Manufacturing Practices (GMP).
- There is a concern about hydrocarbon toxicity from improper ventilation during concentrate production. There has been reduced oxygen and increased CO_2 in grows.
- Cross contamination between grows is a concern.
- There has been heavy metal absorption.
- There is a concern about off-label pesticide residues.
- Hash oil shelf-stability raises a botulism concern with ingestion.
- Unsafe equipment for food/smoking production is a concern.
- In August 2015 the Denver Post commissioned tests and found high levels of contamination in concentrates.

---

[331] Flores v. Livwell, District Court, Denver County Colorado, Date Filed: October 5, 2015, Filing Id: AEAAF1497E99C, Case Number: 201 5CV33528.

[332] Presenter: Danica Lee, Denver Department of Environmental Health, Denver the Mile High City, Consumer Protection & Legal Marijuana in Denver, November 16, 2016, Available at: http://www.bphc.org/boardofhealth/board-meeting-materials/Documents/Denver%20 Danica%20Lee%2011%2016%2016%20.pdf.

The spores mentioned produce a very powerful neurotoxin that causes botulism. Botulism attacks the body's nerves and causes weakness of the muscles that may spread to the neck, arms, torso, and legs. Botulism also can lead to difficulty breathing and even death. Available at: https://www.cdc.gov/botulism/index.html.

- There were no studies on health impact of mixing pesticides, concentrating, burning, and inhaling marijuana.
- Detectable residues can persist in products for many months.
- There were residues persisting in mature plants.
- Even if there are low residues this is still a concern, especially for concentrates.
- The cleaning of ventilation systems, grow rooms, and plant containers is needed.
- They were still seeing spiked residues indicating recent use in some investigations.
- Despitc these corrections they c;ontinue to use marijuana as a medicine for children and those who are severely immunocompromised.

In 2018, the Governor of Colorado issued an executive order along with a health and safety advisory warning people not to use marijuana cultivated by a company because they allegedly used off-label pesticides called pyriproxyfen while cultivating marijuana. Affected products include marijuana flower, trim, concentrates, and infused products.[333]

In 2012, researchers from National Jewish Health entered 30 illegal grow operations in Colorado to evaluate them for potential hazards including mold, pesticides and fertilizers. They concluded that "airborne levels of mold spores that we found inside these structures may subject the occupants, emergency personnel and other individuals to significant health hazards, especially allergies, asthma, hypersensitivity pneumonitis and other respiratory diseases."[334]

According a State of Colorado study, workers in marijuana production facilities can be exposed to a number of health hazards:

1. Biological hazards can arise from directly working with plants. Biological agents can include bacteria and fungi that have the ability to adversely affect human health in a variety of ways.

---

[333] Kirk Mitchell, Health warning issued on marijuana cultivated by Colorado Wellness Centers, kmitchell@denverpost.com,The Denver Post, November 21, 2018, available from: https://www.denverpost.com/2018/11/21/colorado-wellness-centers-marijuana-health-waming/

[334] Available at: https://www.denverpost.com/2017/07/31/marijuana-leaving-colorado-homes-mold.

2. Mold-Marijuana production requires increased levels of humidity, which have been found to be as high as 70 percent. This increased humidity in the presence of organic material promotes the growth of mold.
3. Case reports in the medical literature have described episodes of allergic reactions, hypersensitivity, and anaphylaxis to marijuana. Skin contact through personal handling of plant material or occupational exposure has been associated with hives, itchy skin, and swollen or puffy eyes.
4. Chemical hazards pose a wide range of safety and health hazards such as exposure to:
   Carbon dioxide (CO_2)
   Carbon monoxide (CO)
   Volatile organic compounds
5. Chemicals that pose health hazards include:
   Pesticides - Pesticide poisoning - effect varies depending on the nature of the pesticide; nervous system effects, skin or eye irritation, endocrine disruption, and cancer
   Insecticides Fungicides
   Disinfectants/cleaning chemicals[335]

Massachusetts

Massachusetts has had "medical" marijuana for about 11 years (2008) and they continue to permit contaminated marijuana to be dispensed. At one medical marijuana dispensary, according to a news story, there was a claim of the presence of mold as well as hydrogen peroxide used to clean affected cannabis. Said one source: "When I worked in cultivation everyone was getting red rashes.... No ventilation in the room and certainly no one forcing us to wear a mask for safety."[336]

The Massachusetts Department of Public Health inspections of medical marijuana facilities were made public through a public records request. A news story reported that the inspections found many violations of state laws

[335] Available at: https://www.colorado.gov/pacific/cdphe/marijuana-occupational-safety-and-health.
[336] Available at: https://digboston.com/is-there-moldy-cannabis-in-mass.

with most reports showing multiple violations including contaminants in marijuana flower and pre-rolledjoints.[337]

In a 2018 news report, the pesticide bifenthrin was found in "medical" marijuana in a "regulated" dispensary in Massachusetts.[338]

A TV Station in Massachusetts investigated the purity of medical marijuana working with a patient to independently test samples bought off the shelves. They found marijuana that not only should never have been sold, but uncovered gaping holes in the state regulations that are designed to keep medical marijuana safe and contaminant-free.[339]

A 2018 news report stated that Massachusetts health officials shut down a medical marijuana dispensary and quarantined their product over concerns about pesticide use.[340]

According to another news report, compliance officers in Massachusetts made an unannounced inspection of a marijuana provider and "identified operations that violate the medical use of marijuana regulations and were determined to pose an immediate or serious threat to the public health, safety, and welfare."[341]

Michigan

Michigan has had "medical" marijuana for about 11 years (2008) and they are permitting untested marijuana to be sold.

In 2019, the Michigan Department of Licensing and Regulatory Affairs issued a health and safety advisory due to the release of non-laboratory tested marijuana products supplied to provisioning centers by Choice Labs, LLC. Since marijuana patients may be immunocompromised these steps were taken.[342]

---

337 Available at: http://www.masslive.com/politics/index.ssf/2018/0l/from_gummy_bears_to_open_doors.html.

338 Available at: http://www.masslive.com/politics/index.ssf/2018/02/public_health_department_suspe.html.

339 Available at: http://www.wcvb.com/article/5-investigates-what-s-in-your-weed/19581415.

340 Available at: https://www.wcvb.com/article/health-officials-shut-down-medical-marijuana-dispensary-over-pesticide-concems/25590852.

341 Available at: https://www.masslive.com/news/2019/02/mass-wellspring-medical-marijuana-dispensary-in-acton-temporarily-shut-down.html.

342 Available at: https://www.clickondetroit.com/michigan-marijuana/michigan-issues-recall-of-marijuana-products.

A February 26, 2019 news article noted that in Michigan, medical marijuana is again being recalled from a licensed provisioning center after it failed to meet state testing standards. This is the eighth recall of medical marijuana in a span of two months. Marijuana grown by medical caregivers was still being sold untested to medical patients at provisioning centers medical marijuana tainted with substances from chemical residue, arsenic, cadmium, E. coli, and mold. Testing labs have asked officials to change their minds in the name of patient safety.[343]

A February 1, 2019 news article from Michigan noted that medical marijuana failed to meet state standards when tested - and some of the strains were contaminated with the heavy metals cadmium and arsenic, according to the Bureau of Marijuana Regulation. A business coalition claims selling untested marijuana poses a serious safety risk to patients. Michigan's most vulnerable patients are buying purported medical marijuana products that could legitimately harm them.[344]

Oregon

Oregon has been at this since 1998 - about 21 years. They have done poorly. In January 2019, the Oregon Secretary of State published an audit of Oregon's framework for regulating marijuana. The auditors concluded that regulators failed to meet even basic promises. Just 3% of recreational marijuana retailers had been inspected and only about a third of growers. The state's medical marijuana program, long a source of black market diversion both in the state and nationally, has "structural weaknesses" that "greatly increase the risk of diversion." The "tracking of Oregon's marijuana supply and inspections is lacking" and "data errors in the state tracking system hamper the agency's ability to use the information to identify potential black market leakage." While all recreational marijuana in Oregon must be tested for pesticides and solvents, the state does not require testing of most medical marijuana, putting these vulnerable users at risk. The state still does not have a mechanism to verify test results and has not assured consistent practices among licensed labs to confirm products are reasonably safe. Limited authority, inadequate

---

343 Available at: https://www.mlive.com/news/2019/02/medical-marijuana-recalled-in-detroit-after-failing-state-testing.html?utm_medium=social&utm_source=facebook&utm_campaign=jacksoncitpat_sf%C3%A5.

344 Available at: https://www.mlive.com/news/2019/02/marijuana-containing-arsenic-cadmium-recalled-from-michigan-medical-shop.html.

staffing, and inefficient processes reduce the program's ability to ensure labs consistently operate under accreditation standards.[345]

Utah

Utah passed a limited "medical" marijuana law in 2014. The Centers for Disease Control and Prevention found that synthetic products falsely labeled as cannabidiol, or CBD, sickened as many as 52 people in Utah from October 2017 through January 2018.[346]

On December 8, 2017, the Utah Poison Control Center (UPCC) notified the Utah Department of Health (UDOH) of reports of emergency department visits associated with reported exposure to products labeled as CBD (cannabidiol), a nonpsychoactive compound derived from Cannabis sativa, the marijuana plant. Patients experienced adverse reactions, including altered mental status, seizures, confusion, loss of consciousness, and hallucinations. These reactions prompted concern for potential adulteration with a synthetic cannabinoid. Sale of CBD is currently illegal in Utah, although CBD is readily available online and in shops. This investigation highlights the hazards of consuming unregulated products labeled as CBD.[347]

Washington State

Washington has had "medical" marijuana for nearly two decades (1998). The Huffington Post reports that marijuana pesticide contamination is widespread and in some cases pesticide residue levels are 1,600 times greater than the legal desirable amount.[348]

A news report stated that a complaint submitted to regulators at the Washington State Liquor and Cannabis Board (WSLCB) by a group of industry members accuses Peak Analytics, the state's largest cannabis testing

---

[345] Oregon Secretary of State audit: Framework for Regulating Marijuana Should Be Strengthened to Better Mitigate Diversion Risk and Improve Laboratory Testing. Available at: https://sos.oregon.gov/audits/Documents/2019-04.pdf.

[346] Available at: https://www.cbsnews.com/news/52-people-sickened-by-fake-cbd-oil-in-utah/.

[347] Notes from the Field: Acute Poisonings from a Synthetic Cannabinoid Sold as Cannabidiol-Utah, 2017-2018 MMWR Weekly May 25, 2018/67(20);587-588. Available at: https://www.cdc.gov/mmwr/volumes/67/wr/mm6720a5.htm?s_cid=mm6720a5 _w.

[348] Available at: http://www.huffingtonpost.com/2013/05/24/marijuana-pesticides-contamination n 3328122.html.

lab, of consistent and large-scale inaccuracies. This made marijuana batches appear cleaner and more potent than they actually are.[349]

Conclusion

Microbiological and chemical contaminants pose a potential threat to marijuana users. Bacteria and fungi can cause opportunistic infections in immunocompromized individuals and even dead organisms may trigger allergies and asthma. Marijuana bioaccumulates heavy metals in its tissues, so avidly that hemp crops have been used for bioremediation of radiation. Heavy metals can cause a myriad of human diseases, so their presence in crops destined for human use must be minimized. The use of illegal pesticides is a rising crisis, and a breakdown in ethics and public health. The states cannot be trusted to manage this.[350]

About the author

David G. Evans, Esq., is Senior Counsel for the Cannabis Industry Victims Educating Litigators (CIVEL) who educate lawyers on how to make the marijuana industry accountable to their many victims. Mr. Evans was a plaintiffs litigator in personal injury and employment law cases. Attorneys who desire more information can contact Mr. Evans at seniorcounsel@civel.org. The CIVEL website is: www.civel.org.

Before opening up his law practice in 1992, he was a Research Scientist in the Data Analysis and Epidemiology Services Unit, Division of Alcoholism and Drug Abuse, New Jersey Department of Health. He analyzed legal and regulatory requirements regarding: drug and alcohol abuse, research and data collection, courts, criminal justice, domestic violence, drug-free workplaces, juveniles, confidentiality, treatment, drug testing, AIDS, drug use forecasting, and discrimination.

---

[349] Available at: https://www.leafly.com/news/industry/lea:fly-investigation-washingtons-top-cannabis-lab-inflating-the-numbers.

[350] John M. McPartland, Kevin J. McKeman,Cannabis sativa L. - Botany and Biotechnology pp 457-474 Contaminants of Concern in Cannabis: Microbes, Heavy Metals and Pesticides. Available at: https://link.springer.com/chapter/10.1007%2F978-3-319-54564-6_22.
See also: https://www.mintpressnews.com/how-hemp-can-can-clean-up-radiation-from-fukushima-nuclear-disaster.

Disclaimer of Legal or Medical Advice

This should not be considered legal or medical advice. This is for informational purposes only. Use of and access to these materials does not in itself create an attorney - client, or any professional relationship, between David G. Evans and CIVEL and the user or reader. Mr. Evans or CIVEL cannot vouch for any study cited herein since they did not do the study. The readers should consult the study and make their own interpretation as to its accuracy. Please also be advised that case law and statutory and regulatory laws cited herein may have been amended or changed by the time you read this.

The author acknowledges the research assistance of Anne Hassel, MPT

All website cited here were last accessed on June 30, 2019

* * *

Dear Legislator, 7/17/2019

MVA is dedicated to supporting victims harmed by the marijuana industry and the normalization and promotion of the marijuana culture. We inform the public, government officials and legislators of the personal damage that marijuana causes.

PROTECTING THE MARIJUANA INDUSTRY BY PASSING THE STATES Act (S. 1028 by Warren/Gardner and H.R. 2093 by Blumenauer/ Joyce) WILL CAUSE MORE DRUGGED DRIVING VICTIMS.

Marijuana significantly impairs driving ability including time and distance estimation and reaction times and motor coordination.

1. The National Highway Traffic Safety Administration lists marijuana as the most prevalent drug in fatally injured drivers with 28% testing positive for marijuana.
   NHTSA, Use of Controlled Substances and Highway Safety; A Report to Congress (U.S. Dept. of Transportation, Washington, D.C., 1988)
2. The crash risk for a driver drunk on alcohol is higher than a driver on marijuana, but to suggest it is safe to drive after using marijuana is irresponsible. An even greater danger is the combination of alcohol and marijuana that has severe psychomotor effects that impair driving ability.

.http://cesar.umd.edu/cesar/cesarfax/vol19/19-49.pdf

3. What about our kids? Vehicle crashes are the leading cause of death among those aged 16-25. https://www.cdc.gov/mmwr/preview/mmwrhtml/mm6448a1.htm?s_cid=mm6448a1_w.
4. Weekend nighttime driving under the influence of marijuana among young drivers has increased by 48%. Ibid.
5. About 13% of high school seniors said they drove after using marijuana while only 10% drove after having five or more drinks. Ibid.
6. Another study showed about 28,000 seniors each year admitted to being in at least one motor vehicle accident after using marijuana. https://archives.drugabuse.gov/news-events/news-releases/drug-impaired-driving-by-youth-remains-seriousproblem.
7. The marijuana industry is backing legalization. Do we want more dangerous drivers on our roads so they can make money from selling marijuana?
"Unsafe Driving by High School Seniors: National Trends from 1976 to 2001 in Tickets and Accidents After Use of Alcohol, Marijuana and Other Illegal Drugs." Journal of Studies on Alcohol. May 2003.

By: David G. Evans, Esq. I managed the New Jersey Intoxicated Driving Program that included drugged drivers.

Thank you for your consideration,
Sally Schindel, Marijuana Victims Alliance
MVA Marijuana Victims Alliance
MVAA.info MVAAliance@gmail.com

A Marijuana Related Fatal Crash

It's criminal to legalize THC marijuana, a powerful and addictive drug, that is killing our youth in so many ways. The death of my innocent 22-year-old daughter is another tragic example.

My daughter Jennifer Corinne Hrobuchak was vibrant, intelligent, and driven to be a productive and meaningful member of our society. She was tall, had the most beautiful hair and the brightest smile, with green eyes to match. Jen played lacrosse well and earned a college scholarship to a small school in Northern Ohio where she blossomed into an incredible woman.

She graduated with honors in May of 2012 with a degree in Intelligence and Analysis Research. She now spoke Spanish and Arabic fluently and could translate both languages, which in the world of today is critical in her field. My heart swelled with pride as she accepted her diploma and glided across the stage. Her goal was to work for the FBI or another intelligence organization. Her work as an intern for HIDTA (High Intensity Drug Trafficking of Ohio) earned her a plaque stating she made outstanding contributions to the program.

After a cruise with a friend to celebrate her years of hard work, she began a new job. Not more than a couple of weeks into training, one of the store managers she oversaw called her at about 12:30 a.m. to say there was an alarm going off in her store. She asked Jennifer to meet her at the store, and my daughter, being the responsible person she was, got up, got dressed, and made her way to the location in her new Camry, given to her as one of the perks.

As she crossed an intersection not far from her home, a man came racing through the intersection at 82mph, speeding through the red light. He slammed into the side of my daughter's car, sending it over the embankment and straight into the front wall of a Lube Stop building, collapsing it on Jennifer's car.

Jennifer passed away at the scene from the severe injuries she sustained. The 26-year-old man who caused her death was not injured. He was high on "medical marijuana" given to him in his home state of Michigan. He was just passing through our state and decided he would break every law and kill my daughter.

After he took a plea and his charges were severely reduced to a felony 3, he spent a total of only 15 months in prison. This man had several previous intoxicated driving charges and run-ins with the law. He admitted he was smoking marijuana before the crash, and there was marijuana in the car. His life goes on with a slap on the wrist and our life is devastated forever. He obtained this marijuana legally which is another slap in the face for our family.

Every day of my life is difficult now. I see all of my daughter's friends getting married and starting their families. These events were taken away from Jennifer and our family. The pain I live with is so intense that, as I write this account, tears of sadness and pain run down my cheeks. The world has lost a beautiful woman and one who would have made a difference.

My mission is to tell the account of what took her incredible life away so that others become aware of the dangers on our roads. It's criminal to legalize this powerful and addictive drug that is killing our youth in so many ways. We need to wake up to what this is really about and become aware of how we are just pawns in the game plan of the marijuana

By Jennifer's Mom, Corrine Gasper, Ohio

Corinne.lamarca@gmail.com

Dear Legislator, 7/17/2019

MVA is dedicated to supporting victims harmed by the marijuana industry and the normalization and promotion of the marijuana culture. We inform the public, government officials and legislators of the personal damage that marijuana causes.

The STATES Act (S. 1028 by Warren/Gardner and H.R. 2093 by Blumenauer/Joyce) WILL CAUSE MORE MENTAL ILLNESS INCLUDING PSYCHIATRIC DISORDERS AND SUICIDES.

Marijuana use can cause impairment of memory, attention, motor skills, reaction time, and the integration of complex information and impaired cognition and other neurological damage.[351]

The American Psychiatric Association reports that current evidence supports, at a minimum, a strong association of marijuana use with the onset of psychiatric disorders. "Adolescents are particularly vulnerable to harm, given the effects of cannabis on neurological development."[352]

The National Institute on Drug Abuse (NIDA) research shows that marijuana use is linked with depression, anxiety, and suicidal thoughts among teens.[353]

In 2017, the National Academy of Sciences (NAS) landmark report written by top scientists concluded after a review of over 10,000 peer-

---

[351] Abbie Crites-Leoni, Medicinal Use of Marijuana: Is the Debate a Smoke Screen for Movement Toward Legalization? 19 J. Legal Med. 273, 280 (1998) (citing Schwartz, et al., Short-Term Memory Impairment in Cannabis-Dependent Adolescents, 143 Am. J. Dis. Child. 1214 (1989)).

[352] American Psychiatric Association, 2013 "Position Statement on Marijuana as Medicine," paragraph 1 found at: https://www.psychiatry.org/home/policy-finder

[353] https://www.drugabuse.gov/publications/drugfacts/marijuana August 2017.

reviewed academic articles, that marijuana use is connected to mental health issues such as psychosis, social anxiety, and thoughts of suicide and learning, memory, and attention loss (possibly permanent in some cases).[354]

A new study shows that young people with marijuana dependence have altered brain function that may be the source of emotional disturbances and increased psychosis risk that are associated with marijuana abuse. The alterations were most pronounced in people who started using marijuana at a young age. The findings reveal potential negative long-term effects of heavy cannabis use on brain function and behavior.[355]

* * *

My son is a marijuana victim. Marijuana killed his soul and ruined his brain. His suicide note makes that very clear.

Andy Zorn was a happy, resourceful kid with big dreams. He realized some of them, working and saving and planning his future. He served in the U.S. Army as a paratrooper with 82nd Airborne. He earned an AA degree at community college after his discharge in 2004.

But Andy had experimented with marijuana and alcohol at age 14. Perhaps that is when a foundation was laid for his not being tolerant of the substance as an adult. By age 25 he was exhibiting signs of psychosis and fearing suicide.

The six years that followed were a nightmare of calls to suicide help lines resulting in involuntary stays in county behavioral health hospitals, court ordered mental health treatment, loss of his right to own a weapon due to the danger he was to himself. He lost his ability to hold a job, continue in school, to keep his home.

The Veterans Administration had also treated him and of course suspected PTSD but Andy never agreed with that. He had no symptoms of PTSD, mainly just severe depression and the diagnosed Severe Cannabis Use Disorder.

Andy was arrested in Arizona for marijuana possession, one of the best things that happened to him in those years because it afforded him the incentive to be clean and sober in a court diversion program that opened a window in his addicted mind and allowed him a shot at recovery and re-entry

---

[354] Health Effects of Cannabis and Cannabinoids: Current State of Evidence and Recommendations for Research. See: http://nationalacademies.org/hmd/~/media/Files/Report%20Files/2017/Cannabis-Health-Effects/Cannabis-chapter-highlights.pdf.

[355] https://www.news-medical.net/news/20180116/Study-reveals-negative-long-term-effects-of-heavy-cannabis-use-on-brain-function-and-behavior.aspx.

into a productive life. He reconnected with family and friends he had isolated from in his addiction.

Sadly though, when the drug testing stopped, the marijuana addiction took him right back. Andy easily obtained an Arizona medical marijuana card, claiming pain in a leg that had once been broken. That afforded him access to a regular supply of potent product that owned his mind.

I spoke with the marijuana dispensary manager about Andy's death and his severe addiction. I did that with the hope she would help the next person like Andy recognize the harms and risks of the product. But she said she would not because it is not addictive, and Andy must have been using another substance. Andy was not. His toxicology report proves that.

As long as this marijuana industry is allowed to operate in this reckless way, there will be more marijuana victims. I offer Andy's Story with the dream that his words in his suicide note will resonate with someone who cares enough to help save the next victims. Marijuana killed his soul plus ruined his brain.

Please help stop this insane rush to build this industry marketing a harmful and risky substance, promoting its use, misleading young people into believing it is harmless. We victims are being left in its wake.

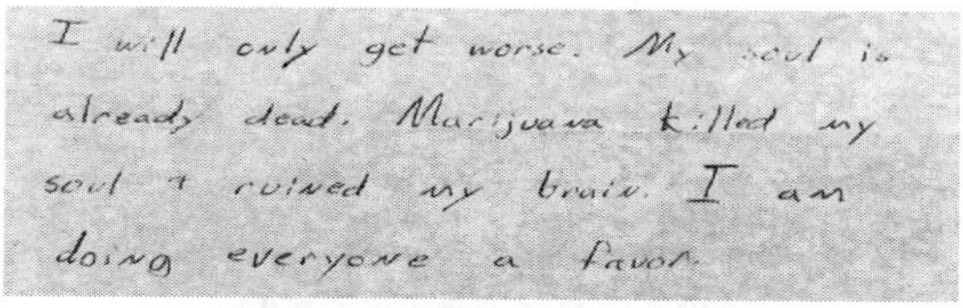
I will only get worse. My soul is already dead. Marijuana killed my soul + ruined my brain. I am doing everyone a favor.

Andy served our country. But marijuana took his freedom.

Thank you for your consideration, Sally Schindel, Andy's Mom, Arizona

MVA Marijuana Victims Alliance
MVAA.info MVAAlliance@gmail.com

Americans Against Legalizing Marijuana

Re: STATES' RIGHTS AND MARIJUANA **7/16/19**

Dear Legislator,

Americans Against Legalizing Marijuana oppose the distribution of high-potency kid-friendly marijuana products that cause addiction and mental illness. Marijuana advocates promote the myth that marijuana regulation is a "states' rights" issue. This is not true. The Supreme Court ruled twice that federal law preempts state marijuana laws and that this is a federal matter. United States v. Oakland Cannabis Buyers' Cooperative, 532 US 483 (2001); Gonzales v. Raich, 545 U.S.1 (2005). It is indisputable that state marijuana laws do not supersede federal laws that criminalize the possession of marijuana. United States v. Hicks, 722 F.Supp.2d 829 (E.D. Mich. 2010). Justice Gorsuch has held that federal marijuana laws were within Congress's constitutional authority to regulate interstate commerce and the federal laws did not violate the 10th Amendment (states' rights). United States of America v. Rutherford. 472 Fed.Appx. 863 (CA 10 2012).

The states are doing a terrible job of regulating marijuana. See the attached paper that was submitted to the FDA: **"The Failures of the States to Regulate Marijuana. Studies Show That Marijuana Products Have High Levels of Contaminants Including Pesticides, Fungus, Heavy Metals and Solvents"**

MARIJUANA EXPOSURES AMONG CHILDREN INCREASE BY UP TO OVER 600%

The rate of marijuana exposures among children under the age of six increased by 610% in the "medical" marijuana states according to a study in Clinical Pediatrics. The data comes from the National Poison Data System. 75% percent of the children ingested edible marijuana products such as marijuana-infused candy. Clinical effects include drowsiness or lethargy, ataxia [failure of muscle coordination], agitation or irritability, confusion and coma, respiratory depression, and single or multiple seizures.
http://journals.sagepub.com/doi/full/10.1177/0009922815589912

LEGALIZING MARIJUANA WILL CAUSE MORE OPIATE USE

Legalizing marijuana will cause more marijuana use. Marijuana use is associated with an increased risk for substance use disorders. In 2017, the National Academy of Sciences landmark report written by top scientists after a review of over 10,000 peer-reviewed academic articles concluded that marijuana use is connected to progression to and dependence on other drugs, including heroin. [1] New research suggests that marijuana users may be more likely to misuse prescription opioids and develop prescription opioid use disorder. The investigators analyzed data from more than 43,000 American adults. The respondents who reported past-year marijuana use had 2.2 times higher odds than nonusers of meeting diagnostic criteria for prescription opioid use disorder and they also had 2.6 times greater odds of initiating prescription opioid misuse. [2]

References regarding opiates

[1] Health Effects of Cannabis and Cannabinoids: Current State of Evidence and Recommendations for Research. See:
http://nationalacademies.org/hmd/~/media/Files/Report%20Files/2017/Cannabis-Health-Effects/Cannabis-chapter-highlights.pdf
[2] https://www.drugabuse.gov/news-events/news-releases/2017/09/marijuana-use-associated-increased-risk-prescription-opioid-misuse-use-disorders

Thank you,

Carla D Lowe, President AALM

Human Rights Watch and American Civil Liberties Union (ACLU):
Every 25 Seconds - The Human Toll of Criminalizing Drug Use in the United States for the record before the Subcommittee on Crime, Terrorism, and Homeland Security

https://www.hrw.org/sites/default/files/report_pdf/usdrug1016_web_0.pdf

EVERY
25 SECONDS
The Human Toll of Criminalizing Drug Use
in the United States
HUMAN
RIGHTS
WATCH
ACLU
AMERICAN CIVIL LIBERTIES UNION

Chapter 3

Funding Limits on Federal Prosecutions of State-Legal Medical Marijuana*

Joanna R. Lampe

Federal law generally prohibits the production, distribution, and possession of marijuana for both medical and recreational purposes. Nonetheless, in recent years, many states have repealed state law criminal prohibitions on some marijuana-related activities, and medical and recreational cannabis businesses now operate openly in some parts of the United States.

In response to the growing disparity between state and federal law, Congress has enacted appropriations legislation prohibiting the Department of Justice (DOJ) from expending appropriated funds to prevent states from implementing their own medical marijuana laws. Federal courts have interpreted the appropriations rider to prohibit DOJ from bringing criminal drug prosecutions against certain private individuals and entities involved in the state-legal medical marijuana industry, but they have differed as to the scope of conduct the rider shields from prosecution.

This Legal Sidebar first outlines the legal status of marijuana under federal and state law. It then discusses the medical marijuana appropriations rider and analyzes how federal courts have interpreted the provision. The Sidebar closes with key considerations for Congress related to the appropriations rider and the disparity between federal and state marijuana policy more generally.

---

* This is an edited, reformatted and augmented version of Congressional Research Service Publication No. LSB10694, dated February 4, 2022.

In: The Legal Issues Surrounding Marijuana
Editor: Sade W. Sato
ISBN: 979-8-89113-427-0

Federal and State Marijuana Regulation

In recent years, a significant divide has developed between federal and state marijuana law. On the federal side, the Controlled Substances Act (CSA) imposes stringent regulations on the cannabis plant and many of its derivatives. Unless an exception applies, the CSA classifies cannabis and its derivatives as “marihuana.” (The statute uses an archaic spelling; this Sidebar uses the more common spelling, “marijuana.”) Congress classified marijuana as a Schedule I controlled substance when it enacted the CSA, reflecting a legislative determination that the substance has a high potential for abuse, no currently accepted medical use, and “a lack of accepted safety for use ... under medical supervision.” Because Congress has made that determination, Schedule I substances may not be dispensed by prescription in compliance with federal law. In contrast, controlled substances in Schedules II through V have accepted medical uses and pose progressively lower risks of abuse and dependence. Unlike substances in Schedule I, those substances may be dispensed by prescription for medical purposes.

It is legal to produce, distribute, and possess Schedule I controlled substances in the context of federally approved scientific studies, subject to CSA regulatory requirements designed to prevent abuse and diversion. However, activities involving Schedule I substances not authorized under the CSA are federal crimes that may give rise to large fines and significant prison sentences.

The CSA definition of *marijuana* excludes “hemp,” legally defined to mean the cannabis plant or any part of that plant with a delta-9 tetrahydrocannabinol (THC) concentration of no more than 0.3%. Hemp, which includes low-THC varietals of cannabis and low-THC cannabis derivatives such as the non- psychoactive cannabinoid cannabidiol (CBD), is not a controlled substance subject to the CSA (though it may be regulated under other federal laws).

In addition to the federal CSA, each state has its own controlled substance laws. State controlled substance laws often roughly mirror federal law, and many states have adopted similar versions of a model statute called the Uniform Controlled Substances Act. However, there is not a complete overlap between drugs subject to federal and state control. States sometimes opt to impose controls that are either more or less strict than those of the CSA. One area where federal and state controlled substance laws diverge in a number of ways is marijuana regulation.

While every state once broadly prohibited the production, distribution, and possession of marijuana, in the past few decades many states have repealed or limited such prohibitions. As of February 2022, all but two states have changed their laws to permit the use of cannabis for medical purposes. State medical cannabis laws vary in scope; some states authorize medical use only of low-THC products that may fall outside the CSA's definition of *marijuana.* In addition, 19 states, two territories, and the District of Columbia have amended their laws to remove state prohibitions on recreational marijuana use by adults age 21 or older. (One such amendment has been struck down in state court.)

Notwithstanding the recent changes to state laws, any activity involving marijuana that is not authorized under the CSA remains a federal crime anywhere in the United States, including in states that have purported to legalize medical or recreational marijuana. Under the Constitution's Supremacy Clause, federal law takes precedence over conflicting state laws, and the Supreme Court has held that state laws authorizing medical marijuana use do not affect the CSA's restrictions. Thus, when states "legalize" a federally controlled substance such as marijuana, the substance becomes legal under state law only.

Funding Limitations on Medical Marijuana Prosecutions

In each fiscal year since FY2015, Congress has included provisions in appropriations acts that prohibit DOJ from using appropriated funds to prevent certain states and territories and the District of Columbia from "implementing their own laws that authorize the use, distribution, possession, or cultivation of medical marijuana." The FY2021 provision lists 52 jurisdictions, including every U.S. jurisdiction that had legalized medical cannabis use at the time it was enacted.

On its face, the appropriations rider bars DOJ from taking legal action against the states directly in order to prevent them from promulgating or enforcing medical marijuana laws. In addition, federal courts have interpreted the rider to prohibit certain federal prosecutions of private individuals or organizations that produce, distribute, or possess marijuana in accordance with state medical marijuana laws. In those cases, criminal defendants have invoked the rider before trial, seeking the dismissal of their indictments or injunctions barring prosecution. By contrast, courts have generally declined to apply the rider outside the context of initial criminal prosecutions. For instance, the Ninth Circuit has held that the provision does not "impact[ ] the ability of a federal district court to restrict the use of medical marijuana as a condition of probation."

In the 2016 case *United States v. McIntosh*, the U.S. Court of Appeals for the Ninth Circuit considered the circumstances in which the appropriations rider bars CSA prosecution of marijuana-related activities. The court held that the rider

> prohibits the federal government only from preventing the implementation of those specific rules of state law that authorize the use, distribution, possession, or cultivation of medical marijuana. DOJ does not prevent the implementation of [such rules] when it prosecutes individuals who engage in conduct unauthorized under state medical marijuana laws. Individuals who do not strictly comply with all state-law conditions regarding the use, distribution, possession, and cultivation of medical marijuana have engaged in conduct that is unauthorized, and prosecuting such individuals does not violate [the rider].

Relying on *McIntosh*, the Ninth Circuit has issued several decisions allowing federal prosecution of individuals who did not "strictly comply" with state medical marijuana laws, notwithstanding the appropriations rider, and several district courts have followed that reasoning. As one example, in *United States v. Evans*, the Ninth Circuit upheld the prosecution of two individuals involved in the production of medical marijuana who smoked marijuana as they processed plants for sale. Although state law permitted medical marijuana use by "qualifying patients," the court concluded that the defendants failed to show they were qualifying patients, and thus they could be prosecuted because their personal marijuana use did not strictly comply with state medical marijuana law.

In the 2022 case *United States v. Bilodeau*, the U.S. Court of Appeals for the First Circuit also considered the scope of the appropriations rider. The defendants in *Bilodeau* were registered with the State of Maine to produce medical marijuana, but DOJ alleged that they distributed large quantities of marijuana to individuals who were not qualifying patients under Maine law, including recipients in other states. Following indictment for criminal CSA violations, the defendants sought to invoke the appropriations rider to bar their prosecutions. They argued that the rider "must be read to preclude the DOJ, under most circumstances, from prosecuting persons who possess state licenses to partake in medical marijuana activity." DOJ instead urged the court to apply the Ninth Circuit's standard, allowing prosecution unless the defendants could show that they acted in strict compliance with state medical marijuana laws.

The First Circuit declined to adopt either of the proposed tests. As an initial matter, the court agreed with the Ninth Circuit that the rider means "DOJ may not spend funds to bring prosecutions if doing so prevents a state from giving practical effect to its medical marijuana laws." However, the panel declined to adopt the Ninth Circuit's holding that the rider bars prosecution only in cases where defendants strictly complied with state law. The court noted that the text of the rider does not explicitly require strict compliance with state law and that, given the complexity of state marijuana regulations, "the potential for technical noncompliance [with state law] is real enough that no person through any reasonable effort could always assure strict compliance." Thus, the First Circuit concluded that requiring strict compliance with state law would likely chill state-legal medical marijuana activities and prevent the states from giving effect to their medical marijuana laws. On the other hand, the court also rejected the defendants' more expansive reading of the rider, reasoning that "Congress surely did not intend for the rider to provide a safe harbor to all caregivers with facially valid documents without regard for blatantly illegitimate activity."

Ultimately, while the First Circuit held that the rider bars CSA prosecution in at least some cases where the defendant has committed minor technical violations of state medical marijuana laws, it declined to "fully define [the] precise boundaries" of its alternative standard. On the record before it, the court concluded that "the defendants' cultivation, possession, and distribution of marijuana aimed at supplying persons whom no defendant ever thought were qualifying patients under Maine law" and that a CSA conviction in those circumstances would not "prevent Maine's medical marijuana laws from having their intended practical effect."

Considerations for Congress

It remains to be seen whether and how the difference in reasoning between the Ninth Circuit and the First Circuit will make a practical difference in federal marijuana prosecutions. In theory, the First Circuit's analysis could make it easier for defendants to invoke the appropriations rider to bar federal prosecutions, because they could do so even if they had not been in strict compliance with state law. In practice, however, resource limitations and enforcement priorities have historically meant that federal marijuana prosecutions target individuals and organizations that clearly have not complied with state law. Thus, one of the First Circuit judges who considered *Bilodeau* agreed with the panel's interpretation of the rider but wrote a concurrence noting that, in practice, the First Circuit's standard might not be "materially different from the one that the Ninth Circuit applied."

While the medical marijuana appropriations rider restricts DOJ's ability to bring some marijuana prosecutions, its effect is limited in several ways. First, marijuana-related activities that fall outside the scope of the appropriations rider remain subject to prosecution under the CSA. By its terms, the rider applies only to state laws related to *medical* marijuana; it does not bar prosecution of any activities related to recreational marijuana, even if those activities are permitted under state law. Second, as the Ninth Circuit has explained, even where the rider does apply, it "does not provide immunity from prosecution for federal marijuana offenses"—it simply restricts DOJ's ability to expend funds to enforce federal law for as long as it remains in effect. If Congress instead opted to repeal the rider or allow it to lapse, DOJ would be able to prosecute future CSA violations as well as past violations that occurred while the rider was in effect, subject to the applicable statute of limitations. Third, participants in the cannabis industry may face numerous collateral consequences arising from the federal prohibition of marijuana in areas including bankruptcy, taxation, and immigration. Many of those legal consequences attach regardless of whether a person is charged with or convicted of a CSA offense, meaning the rider would not affect them.

Congress has the authority to enact legislation to clarify or alter the scope of the appropriations rider, repeal the rider, or decline to include it in future appropriations laws. For instance, Congress could amend the rider to specify whether strict compliance with state medical marijuana law is required in order to bar prosecution under the CSA or provide a different standard that DOJ and the courts should apply. Congress could also expand the scope of the rider to bar the expenditure of funds on prosecutions related to recreational marijuana or other controlled substances.

Beyond the appropriations context, Congress could also consider other changes to federal marijuana law that would affect its interaction with state law. Such changes could take the form of more stringent marijuana regulation—for instance, through repeal of the appropriations rider or increased DOJ funding to prosecute CSA violations. In contrast, most recent proposals before Congress generally seek to relax federal restrictions on marijuana or mitigate the disparity between federal and state marijuana regulation.

Some proposals would remove marijuana from regulation under the CSA entirely or move it to a less restrictive schedule so that it could be dispensed by prescription for medical purposes. Other proposed legislation would leave marijuana in Schedule I but limit enforcement of federal marijuana law in states that elect to legalize marijuana. Additional proposals would seek to address specific legal consequences of marijuana's Schedule I status by, for example, enabling marijuana businesses to access banking services, facilitating federally approved clinical research involving marijuana and other Schedule I substances, or removing collateral consequences for individuals in areas such as immigration and gun ownership.

For further information on proposed reforms and legal issues related to marijuana's status under the CSA, see CRS Report R45948, *The Controlled Substances Act (CSA): A Legal Overview for the 117th Congress*, by Joanna R. Lampe.

Chapter 4

Does the President Have the Power to Legalize Marijuana?*

Joanna R. Lampe

The legal status of marijuana has been a topic of recurring interest in recent years, as states, federal legislators, and federal executive agencies consider how to regulate cannabis and its derivatives. What role can the President play in determining the legal status of a controlled substance such as marijuana?

That question came to the forefront during the 2020 Democratic presidential primary, with multiple candidates supporting legalization of marijuana and several pledging to legalize the substance nationwide if elected, either indirectly through administrative proceedings or directly by executive order. More recently, some commentators have called on President Biden to end criminal penalties for marijuana possession and use or grant clemency to federal marijuana offenders. Although the President cannot directly remove marijuana from control under federal controlled substances law, he might order executive agencies to consider either altering the scheduling of marijuana or changing their enforcement approach.

This Sidebar outlines the laws that apply to controlled substances like marijuana, then analyzes several approaches a president might take to change controlled substances law as written or as enforced. The Sidebar closes with a discussion of key considerations for Congress related to presidential power over controlled substances regulation.

---

* This is an edited, reformatted and augmented version of Congressional Research Service Publication No. LSB10655, updated November 4, 2021.

In: The Legal Issues Surrounding Marijuana
Editor: Sade W. Sato
ISBN: 979-8-89113-427-0

Controlled Substances Law

Federal Law: The Controlled Substances Act

Under federal law, unless a statutory exemption applies, most cannabis and cannabis derivatives are classified as marijuana, a Schedule I controlled substance under the Controlled Substances Act (CSA). (The CSA generally uses an alternative spelling, "marihuana," but this Sidebar uses the more common spelling.) The CSA imposes a comprehensive regulatory framework on certain drugs and other substances—whether medical or recreational, legally or illicitly distributed—that pose a significant risk of abuse and dependence. The framework broadly aims to protect public health from those risks while ensuring that patients have access to pharmaceutical controlled substances for medical purposes. To advance those related goals, the CSA (1) requires entities engaged in legitimate activities involving controlled substances to register with the government and take steps to prevent diversion and misuse and (2) imposes criminal penalties for unauthorized activities involving controlled substances.

Substances become subject to the CSA through placement in one of five lists, known as Schedules I through V. A lower schedule number carries greater restrictions, so controlled substances in Schedule I are subject to the most stringent controls. Schedule I controlled substances have no currently accepted medical use, and it is illegal to produce, dispense, and possess such substances except in the context of federally approved scientific studies. By contrast, substances in Schedules II through V have accepted medical uses and may be dispensed by prescription for medical purposes.

As discussed further below, a substance can be placed in a CSA schedule, moved to a different schedule, or removed from control under the CSA either by legislation or through an administrative rulemaking process overseen by the Drug Enforcement Administration (DEA) and based on criteria set out in the CSA. The CSA also directs the Attorney General (who has delegated CSA scheduling authority to DEA) to schedule substances as required to comply with the United States' treaty obligations. Congress placed marijuana in Schedule I in 1970 when it enacted the CSA. Since that time, DEA has denied multiple petitions from stakeholders seeking to move marijuana to a less restrictive schedule or remove the substance from control under the CSA. In 2018, Congress amended the CSA to provide that hemp—defined to include cannabis products containing no more than 0.3 percent of the psychoactive cannabinoid delta-9 tetrahydrocannabinol (THC)—is not a controlled substance subject to the CSA. (Hemp products may, however, be subject to regulation under other provisions of federal law.)

State Laws

In addition to the federal CSA, each state has its own controlled substances laws. As a general matter, state controlled substances laws often mirror federal law and are relatively uniform across jurisdictions because almost all states have adopted a version of the Uniform Controlled Substances Act. However, there is not a complete overlap between drugs subject to federal and state control.

Marijuana regulation is one area where the gap between federal and state controlled substance laws is particularly salient. In sharp contrast to the stringent federal control of marijuana, in recent decades nearly all the states have changed their laws to permit the use of marijuana (or other cannabis products) for medical purposes. In addition, 18 states and the District of Columbia have passed laws removing certain state criminal prohibitions on recreational marijuana use by adults.

Notably, however, states cannot actually legalize marijuana, because the states cannot change federal law and the Constitution's Supremacy Clause dictates that federal law takes precedence over conflicting state laws. As long as marijuana is a Schedule I controlled substance under the CSA, all unauthorized activities involving marijuana are federal crimes anywhere in the United States, including in states that have purported to legalize medical or recreational marijuana.

Presidential Power to Legalize or Decriminalize Marijuana

Discussion of whether the President can legalize or decriminalize marijuana raises the question of what it means to "legalize" or "decriminalize" a Schedule I controlled substance. "Legalization" of marijuana could mean moving the substance from Schedule I to another schedule of the CSA so that it would be legal to produce, distribute, and possess marijuana for medical purposes, subject to the CSA's registration requirements; or it could mean removing marijuana from control under the CSA altogether.

"Decriminalization" generally refers to maintaining some form of prohibition of marijuana but enforcing the ban only through non-criminal sanctions, such as civil monetary penalties.

Descheduling or Rescheduling Under the CSA

Either Congress or the executive branch has the authority to change the status of marijuana under the CSA. Congress can change the status of a controlled substance through legislation: Congress includedmarijuana in Schedule I by legislation when it enacted the CSA, and has more recently passed legislation to impose controls on other substances, including synthetic cannabinoids and fentanyl analogues. In the alternative, the CSA empowers DEA to make scheduling decisions through the notice-and-comment rulemaking process, in consultation with the Department of Health and Human Services (HHS) (HHS has delegated its factfinding role in this process to the Food and Drug Administration (FDA)). The CSA provision directing DEA to schedule controlled substances as "required by United States obligations under international treaties" may limit the agency's authority to relax controls of marijuana; another CRSreport discusses considerations for Congress related to marijuana's status under international drug controltreaties.

If the President sought to act in the area of controlled substances regulation, he would likely do so byexecutive order. However, the Supreme Court has held that the President has the power to issue an executive order only if authorized by "an act of Congress or . . . the Constitution itself." The CSA does not provide a direct role for the President in the classification of controlled substances, nor does Article II of the Constitution grant the President power in this area (federal controlled substances law is an exercise of Congress's power to regulate interstate commerce). Thus, it does not appear that the President could directly deschedule or reschedule marijuana by executive order.

Although the President may not unilaterally deschedule or reschedule a controlled substance, he does possess a large degree of indirect influence over scheduling decisions. The President could pursue theappointment of agency officials who favor descheduling, or use executive orders to direct DEA, HHS, and FDA to consider administrative descheduling of marijuana. The notice-and-comment rulemaking process would take time, and would be subject to judicial review if challenged, but could be done consistently with the CSA's procedural requirements. In the alternative, the President could work with Congress to pursue descheduling through an amendment to the CSA.

Presidential Pardons and Prosecutorial Discretion

Just as the CSA does not grant the President the authority to unilaterally change the classification of a controlled substance, it also creates no presidential power to alter the general penalties applicable to controlled substances offenses. While the President cannot change the law as written, he has substantial control over how the law is enforced. For instance, the Constitution grants the President the power "to grant Reprieves and Pardons for Offences against the United States." That clemency power extends to all federal offenses, "except in Cases of Impeachment." The President may grant a pardon at any time after an offense is committed: before the pardon recipient is charged with a crime, after a charge but prior to conviction, or following conviction. The power is not limited to pardons for individual offenders: the President may also issue a general amnesty to a class of people. It therefore appears that the President could provide clemency for some or all past federal marijuana-related offenses without making any changes to the CSA. However, such an exercise of the clemency power might not address all possible collateral legal consequences of marijuana-related activities, because some of those consequences do not depend on a person being charged with or convicted of a CSA violation. Clemency also would not prevent prosecution of future offenses if the same President or a future administration ended the policy of amnesty. Furthermore, the presidential clemency power extends only to federal offenses; it does not affect offenses under state law.

In addition to, or instead of, granting clemency, the President could direct the Department of Justice (DOJ) to exercise its discretion not to prosecute some or all marijuana-related offenses. Although DOJ generally enjoys significant independence, particularly with respect to its handling of specific cases, the President has the authority to direct DOJ as part of his constitutional duty to "take Care that the Laws be faithfully executed." DOJ is primarily responsible for prosecuting criminal violations of the CSA and possesses significant prosecutorial discretion in doing so. Under the Obama administration, DOJ issued several guidance memoranda outlining enforcement priorities related to marijuana. Although that guidance expressly reserved DOJ's full authority to enforce the CSA, it suggested that prosecutors should not prioritize enforcement against low-risk activities, including individual use of medical marijuana.

Under the Trump Administration, DOJ rescinded the Obama-era guidance in 2018, but retains broad discretion to decide what federal offenses to prosecute. Like the pardon power, DOJ prosecutorial discretion would limit prosecution only for federal offenses, and would provide no guarantee against future changes to DOJ's enforcement policy.

State Law

If the President worked with DEA or Congress to remove marijuana from Schedule I of the CSA, it might raise the question of how the change in federal law would interact with state laws that criminalize some orall marijuana-related activities. Under the United States' federalist system of government, the President has no direct power to change state law or compel the states to adopt federal policies. Pursuant to the Supremacy Clause, Congress *can* preempt state law through federal statutes like the CSA. However, the CSA provides that it does not preempt state laws "unless there is a positive conflict between [the CSA] and that State law so that the two cannot consistently stand together." If marijuana were rescheduled or descheduled at the federal level, it would be possible for people to comply with both the CSA and more stringent state laws—for example, by abstaining from using marijuana. Thus, that change to federal lawstanding alone would not alter the status of marijuana under state law.

Considerations for Congress

If Congress wishes to remove or scale back federal legal restrictions on marijuana beyond what the executive branch chooses to pursue, it has significant authority to do so. While the CSA does not grant thePresident the power to change the status of a controlled substance or the punishments for controlled substance offenses, Congress unquestionably holds the power to amend the CSA to reschedule or deschedule a controlled substance or change applicable penalties. If the legislature decides to relax federalregulation of marijuana, bills currently pending before Congress would move marijuana to a less restrictive schedule or remove the substance from control entirely.

(Amending the CSA would not changethe status of cannabis under other federal laws, including the Federal Food Drug & Cosmetic Act.) In the alternative, Congress could choose to limit the enforcement of federal marijuana law without altering the substance's classification under the CSA. For example, an appropriations rider enacted every year since FY2014 prohibits DOJ from using taxpayer funds to prevent the states from "implementing their own laws that authorize the use, distribution, possession, or cultivation of medical marijuana."

In addition, while Congress cannot directly change state laws, it may be able to override state laws via preemption or enact measures designed to encourage the states to change their own laws. With respect to the first option, when legislating pursuant to an enumerated power, Congress can expressly preempt state laws and could likely amend the CSA to override state marijuana controls. As an analogous precedent, the2018 farm bill carved out non-psychoactive hemp from the CSA's regulation of marijuana and prohibited the states from banning the interstate transport of hemp. As for the second option, Congress can use its spending power to encourage the states to adopt certain policies by conditioning federal funds on the enactment of desired legislation.

If, in the alternative, Congress seeks to maintain existing controls, it would have some authority to do soeven if the executive branch decided to reduce legal restrictions on marijuana or limit enforcement of marijuana laws. The CSA is a statutory regime, and Congress has the ultimate authority over what substances are subject to federal control. Thus, if DEA chose to move marijuana to a less restrictive CSAschedule or remove it from control entirely, Congress could potentially overturn DEA's determination orenact legislation directly placing marijuana in Congress's preferred schedule. However, if the executive branch elected to issue pardons or grant amnesty for marijuana offenses, or to exercise prosecutorial discretion to decline to prosecute such offenses, Congress's options would be more limited.

Congress could restrict funding to DOJ if it disagreed with the agency's enforcement strategy, but the legislature cannot directly force DOJ to pursue certain cases. As for the pardon power, the main checks onexecutive clemency are political, and there is no way for Congress to rescind a pardon once it has issued.

Index

D

E

F

N

O

P

Q

R

S

T